The Colony of British Guyana and Its Labouring Population: Containing a Short Account of the Colony, and Brief Descriptions of the Black Creole, Portuguese, East Indian, and Chinese Coolies ... Collected ... from Sundry Articles Published ... at Different

H V. P. Bronkhurst

AN INDIAN COOLIE FAMILY.

THE COLONY

OF

BRITISH GUYANA

AND ITS LABOURING POPULATION:

CONTAINING

A SHORT ACCOUNT OF THE COLONY, AND BRIEF DESCRIPTIONS OF THE BLACK CREOLE, PORTUGUESE, EAST INDIAN, AND CHINESE COOLIES, THEIR MANNERS, CUSTOMS, RELIGIOUS NOTIONS, AND OTHER INTERESTING PARTICULARS AND AMUSING INCIDENTS CONCERNING THEM.

COLLECTED FROM DIFFERENT SOURCES, AS NEWSPAPERS, ETC., AND FROM SUNDRY ARTICLES PUBLISHED IN THE ENGLISH AND COLONIAL NEWSPAPERS AT DIFFERENT TIMES,

AND ARRANGED BY

REV. H. V. P. BRONKHURST,

WESLEYAN MISSIONARY;

Author of "A Pocket Compendium of Christian Theology;" "The Origin of the Guyanian Indians ascertained;" "Where shall I spend Eternity," &c.

"No one knows all things, and no one but knows something."—*Hindu Proverb.*

"Men's works have faults since Adam first offended,
And some [perhaps] in this are thus to be amended."

LONDON:
PUBLISHED FOR THE AUTHOR,
T. WOOLMER, 2, CASTLE STREET, CITY ROAD, E.C
AND 66, PATERNOSTER ROW, E.C.
1883.

TO THE REVEREND

THE GENERAL SECRETARIES, AND THE OFFICERS OF THE

WESLEYAN METHODIST MISSIONARY SOCIETY;

THE RETURNED MISSIONARIES FROM BRITISH GUYANA

NOW IN ENGLAND;

THE METHODIST FRIENDS IN ENGLAND WHO TAKE A DEEP INTEREST

IN THE COLONIAL MISSION WORK;

AND TO MY CREOLE FRIENDS AND FELLOW COLONISTS IN

BRITISH GUYANA,

THIS VOLUME

IS RESPECTFULLY DEDICATED BY THEIR OBEDIENT SERVANT,

THE AUTHOR.

PREFACE.

In placing this humble and unpretending volume, treating on "The Colony of British Guyana and its Labouring Population," before my numerous English and West Indian or Guyanian friends, I have briefly to state that many years ago a clerical friend in England, who had laboured as Missionary in the Colony, requested me to write some accounts about British Guyana and its people, &c., for the information of the English Methodist people, who have always taken a very deep interest in the Colonial Mission work; the articles or sketches thus written by me at different times and published in the columns of *The Watchman and Wesleyan Advertiser* having been received with welcome feelings by my Methodist friends there. I was in a similar manner requested by some of my friends in the Colony to write occasionally in the local journals some accounts about the Indian and Chinese Coolie population, &c., which I did in *The Royàl Gazette, The Creole, The Colonist*, and other newspapers, as opportunity offered. Most of the readers who had perused the articles knew not whence they emanated, for they were anonymous communications. Now, all these different articles, sketches, and letters written since 1861 are collected together, revised, enlarged, and put in a readable book form, with a host of other hints and information touching the Colony and its people, culled from the different Colonial publications and newspapers, so as to make this volume (of nearly 500 pages) interesting and amusing. One interesting fact, however, I may mention here (I do not think it is out of place), and that is, the sugar crop of last year (1882) has been the largest ever known in the history of the Colony: one hundred and forty thousand hogsheads of sugar, with rum in proportion, were made during the year. This at once shows that the Colony is in a very flourishing condition, and soon the planters hope to be able to make two hundred thousand hogsheads of sugar.

A few minor changes have taken place in the Colony since the last chapter was written, and the MS. sent to England, and I have therefore been unable to consult my book, so as to make the necessary alterations or improvements. Among the changes, I may refer to the education question, which was finally settled last year. On the educational scheme His Excellency Sir H. T. Irving, K.C.M.G., Governor, remarked:—"Under the head of Education a substantial reduction has been made on the expenditure of last year. In accordance with the pledge given in my previous address that steps would be taken to correct the disproportion of expenditure to results, an ordinance has been passed to abolish the former Board of Education, and to vest in the Governor and the Court of Policy the power to make rules for the grant of Government aid to the primary schools. This power has been exercised; and rules have been promulgated by which the aid to the schools being made to depend on the number of children taught and the quality of the teaching, the disproportion of cost to result, which had attracted your attention, will be corrected. The rules have been so framed that if all the schools were efficient, and yielded complete results, the earnings of the schools would be about the same as at present; and any reduction, therefore, in those earnings will be the measure of the existing want of efficiency of the schools. Under the present system, the payments to the schools, in shape of salaries and result grants, are equivalent to about $8 a head on the number in average attendance: under the new system the schools will receive $4 a head as a fixed minimum allowance, and will earn a proportion, or the whole, of the remaining $4, according to their success in producing results."

The *Berbice Gazette* has made some sensible remarks on this vexed question. "In nearly every country," (the editor remarks) "the duty of educating the young is assumed by the State, manifestly so in England, but here, judging from the remarks of His Excellency the Governor, it is looked upon as the duty of managers, or, in other words, Ministers of religion. This implies a strife between rival denominations, and two or three or more schools in a place where one school would be sufficient to meet all the wants of the population, and the consequence is, a large number of inefficient schools. We don't at all contend for a high education, but we wish to see it good and useful, and towards such an education no one in the community would grudge to contribute.

"We are no more in favour of compulsory attendance at school than His Excellency the Governor, but perhaps we know more about the people than he does, and, from what we do know, we are of opinion that compulsion is necessary. Immediately after emancipation it was not so; *then* the parents sent them to school willingly, but their circumstances are very different now. It is not perhaps so much unwillingness on the part of parents to have their children educated, as, at least on the part of a good many, their inability to provide them with proper clothing, books, &c., and for the sake of what the children may be able to earn. The subject of elementary education we must look upon as a most important one for the future welfare of the country. His Excellency the Governor has placed before us his views on the subject: either, 'I will give managers of schools so much money to carry them on;' or if they cannot agree to that, the Government will carry on the schools itself; and now it is for managers to decide."

Possibly the reader may meet with some typographical errors in this volume, and I trust he will be considerate and indulgent in his criticisms, as I have not been able to superintend the publication of it.

My best thanks are tendered to my friends who have assisted me with their information (on different subjects contained in this volume), advice, &c., &c.

H. V. P. BRONKHURST.

GEORGETOWN, DEMERARA,

March, 1883.

CONTENTS.

INTRODUCTORY CHAPTER.

SOME INTERESTING NOTES ABOUT ANCIENT INDIA, OR THE LAND WHENCE THE GREATEST NUMBER OF OUR IMMIGRANTS COME, AND SOME OTHER FACTS ABOUT OUR CREOLE PEOPLE, ETC.

1. The great central Peninsula of Southern Asia, or Continental India, called also the East Indies (by way of distinction from the West Indian Islands—which extend from the mouth of the Gulf of Mexico and the Strait of Florida, in a curving chain, to the coast of South America, terminating near the Venezuelan shores—so called from a mistaken notion that these islands lay in the route to the East Indies), which is one of the most fertile regions of the globe, stretching from Cape Comorin in the South to the Himalaya mountains in the North, is the noblest trust ever committed to the British nation. The distance between these two places is nearly 1,900 miles, and about 1,800 miles from the Indus river to the opposite extremity of Assam. The area is certainly no less than 1,000,000 square miles, though estimated much higher by some authorities, equal to nearly one-third of the united surface of European countries. The length of the coast line is rudely calculated at 3,280 miles, of which 1,830 belong to the Western side, and 1,450 to the Eastern. This vast territory is occupied by one-sixth of the human race, speaking different languages and dialects, and practising and observing different customs and religions, and all on the most intimate terms with the English nation and Government. Though most of the inhabitants of India have dark skins (colour or complexion), varying from a clear olive brown to an ebony black, dark eyes, and long flowing black hair, they are yet as docile and intelligent a people as any on the face of the earth, and readily mix with and accept the

British rule sooner than any other people. The country whence the greatest number of our immigrants come to British Guyana and the West Indian Islands, is in some places low, flat, and dry; in others mountainous and wet. There are many sandy, treeless plains, *maidans*, and many fine dark forests—*jangals*. India is a fine country, but, unfortunately, wave after wave of invasion, intestine wars, devastating famines, crushing despotism, bribery and oppression in multiplied forms, and, above all, the blighting influence of an abominable superstition, have combined to neutralize its advantages, to depress, in every respect, the state of its population.

2. The sad acknowledgment must, however, be made, that the responsibility of such a charge is felt by only a few of those to whom it has been delegated. Except when famine is decimating large districts, or their beleaguered countrymen are carrying on a contest against fearful odds, the great majority of the British nation never give India a thought. Still there are a few who take a lively interest in the welfare of that vast country and people of different tongues. The same sad acknowledgment must be made of this our very prosperous Colony—British Guyana, which, on account of the large importation of its labourers, is closely allied to British India.

3. The large Peninsula of India has for centuries been known by the name of INDIA, or HINDUSTAN, which term requires some explanation before we proceed to notice or speak of the people (who come thence to British Guyana and the West Indian Islands), their peculiarities, their languages, customs, religions, &c., on which the reader will find abundance of information in this book.

4. What we now call INDIA, or HINDUSTAN, was anciently the country or kingdom of Bharata, the son of Dashyanta, whence Bharata, or Barata-Varsha, its ancient name. It was called also ARYA-VARTA (literally *the abode of the Aryans*). This name or term was limited in its application to that part or portion of the vast territory between the Himalaya and Vindhya mountains, stretching northwards and westwards into Europe. The Aryans (literally *noble, venerable, respectable*—Arâdhya, *venerable*), once a domi-

nant race, were Sanskrit-speaking people, who waged war with the "descendants of various Scythian hordes who, at a remote period, entered India by way of Beluchistan and the Indus, called by the Sanskrit writers *Mlechchhas, Nishadas, Dasyas, Pariahs*, &c., *i.e.*, barbarians, outcasts. The more powerful and civilized of these aboriginal tribes appear to have retired before the Aryans into Southern India, and there to have retained their independence, and with their independence the individuality and essential structure of their vernacular dialects" or languages.

5. Among the many races which have sprung from Hindustan, that mixed body of *Pariahs*, which was rejected according to Hindu law, at a period of almost fabulous remoteness, claims attentive consideration, and up to the present time very little has appeared in English on the subject. The class of *Mlechchhas, Nishadas, Dasyas*, called *Pariahs* or *Tchandalas*, are only mentioned once in the *Institutes of Manu*, and then with great contempt, as being the lowest of the low. They form an interesting study for the thoughtful, inasmuch as they (being the gypsies and wandering races) appear to have been the inventors of the brick for building purposes, as is attested by the most ancient Hindu historians—Vina-Snati and Veda-Vyasa. In the first instance this class was composed of individuals who had lost caste, and who, therefore, were rejected from their original localities, and forced to seek refuge in the forests—where, as numbers increased, they resumed their former caste positions among themselves — having their Brahmans (priests), Kshatryas (warriors), Vaysias (merchants), and Sudras (agriculturists). The Brahman Vamana, the conqueror of Prithu, a man of active intelligence, advised the Artaxchatria Aristanata, whose throne had been firmly established by the victories, to readmit the Tchandalas (Pariahs) according to caste, and restore them their rights; and had this advice been followed, the sanguinary servile wars which desolated ancient Hindustan would have been avoided. According to Brahmanical chronology, some eight thousand years before our era, the Artaxchatria or great King Pratichta issued an edict or Karana against them, by which they

were forbidden to practise the religion of Brahman, and not permitted the perusal of the *Vedas*. Despite the many obstructions and disadvantages, in two thousand years, more or less, they had grown in vast numbers, so as to form one-third of the population of the whole country. This aroused the fears of Artaxchatria Agastya, and the rigorous persecution which ensued threw them back into their former wretched condition in a few months. The Hill tribes (*Paharees*) of the Himalaya, having for the second time invaded the plains of Hindustan, and destroyed Asgartha, the city of the Sun, Agastya, after narrowly escaping destruction himself, managed to defeat them, and used the occasion for the spoliation of the Tchandalas, who were accused of aiding the mountaineers. By a Karana, he confiscated the entire possessions of the Tchandalas, and ordered that they should be compelled to make bricks and pottery for the benefit of the Vaysias, to whom they were furthermore assigned as slaves or serfs. When the Prince died, the Tchandalas, or Pariahs, had been reduced to less than half of their original number. Under his successors, however, the rigour of this persecution was slightly relaxed, and about B.C. 4000 they had become a nomadic race once more, with flocks and herds, living in the most primitive manner. Between 3000 and 4000 B.C. they emigrated, according to Hindu authorities, towards the West in crowds, entering the countries of Scindh and Arya, in the direction of the Euphrates and Tigris, towards Babylon and Chaldea, the chief of these expeditions being under Artaxa-Phasicol. It was thus, therefore, that the primitive wanderers emerged from the Holy Land of Palestine, the country of the chief of the tribes. All this may be read in the *Avadana-Sastra*, and, however exaggerated, is nevertheless authentic history. From these exiled Pariahs or Tchandalas sprung the Greeks, PHŒNICIANS (whence the British people are supposed by some to have originated), Cymri, Romans, Danes, Normans, and other races. The various Scythian hordes who, at a remote period, entered India, and waged war with the Aryans, to whom I have made reference in the preceding paragraph, were probably the Tchandalas I have here described. These Tchandalas, composed of different tribes, were the Tur-Aryans or Turaniyans (Dravidians) of the Scythio-Shemitic family, now occupying Southern India, whose ancestors, like all the tribes composing the Aryan family, save and except the Sanskrit-speaking nation, immigrated into Europe, and settled themselves in the several countries to which they gave their names. The Anglo-Saxons are said by some writers to have sprung from these Scythio-Shemitic-Turanians.

6. The word INDIA or HINDU, though occasionally found in Sanskrit writing, is not thereby proved to be a Sanskrit term. There is no such word as that known in the now dead classic Sanskrit. The very Brahman Pundits and European scholars who possess the greatest knowledge of Sanskrit have repudiated the notion or the assertion of the name INDIA or HINDU being of Sanskrit origin. The lamented learned scholar, Sir William Jones, in a note to his translation of a Royal Grant of land in Carnata, given in Vol. III. of the *Asiatic Researches*, Art. 3, observes :— "The word *Hindu* is applied likewise in a verse of CALIDAOS to the original inhabitants of this country (India); but the *Pundits* insist that it is not *Sanskrit*. Since the first letter of it appears to be radical, it cannot be derived from INDU, or the moon ; but since a sibilant is often changed into an aspirate, it has been thought a variation of *Sindhu*, or Indus. To that etymology, however, we may object that the last consonant also must be changed ; and that *Sindhu* is the name of a river, and not of a people." The word *Hind*, or *Hindu*, in the Sanskrit language is therefore of foreign importation.

7. In the *Sekander Nameh* of Nizami (the history of Alexander the Great in Persian by Nizami, who died in A.D. 1180) there is an enigmatical verse (probably also containing a date which cannot now be ascertained) which an intelligent Brahman, BAPU MEHTA, well acquainted with the Persian language, quoted as a proof of the word HIND being of Persian origin, and not Sanskrit :—

"Be Hindustan, piri az Khur fatad—
Pedar merdei ra be Chin gao Zad"— *i.e.*

"In *Hindustan* an old man fell from an ass ;
In *China* a cow was born to one whose father was dead."

This is indeed a strange and remarkable verse, in which the word *Hind*, or *Hindustan*, occurs, but it does not to my mind establish the fact of its being a Persian word or name. It may be a Persianized, but not a real Persian, word. In the *Sharaf Nama* (a Persian dictionary) *Hind* is described as a people, and as a large country, having one side bordered by China, and the other by Sind.

8. Alexander the Great (Sekander), the conqueror of Persia, after the defeat and death of Darius, passed on towards India between B.C. 330-323, crossed the Hydaspes (Indus) at Attock, and encountered and defeated Porus at Gujrat on the banks of the Jhilam. Alexander took 9,000 prisoners, slew 12,000 men, among whom were the chief officers of Porus and his own sons, and captured eighty out of between three and four hundred elephants which Porus and his officers had assembled to prevent his (Alexander's) landing. It is supposed by some that no public event of any interest could be recorded before Alexander's entry into India, and his encounter with Porus, whom he afterwards restored to his royal dignity, besides enlarging his territory. There are historic traditions, however, current, giving sufficient information as to the existence of BACCHUS, who was the first conqueror of India; of SESOSTRIS; of SEMIRAMIS, who lost two-thirds of her army in India; of DARIUS, the son of Hystaspes, who sent Scylax down the Indus, &c. From all these traditionary statements we gather the fact that the country was known by the name of HIND, or INDIA, long before Alexander or Sekander the Great thought of crossing the Indus. Though the name INDIA is so seldom mentioned, yet the people and productions of this vast country were known to the Jews generally, and to Solomon, about B.C. 1015.

9. INDIA is for the first time mentioned by that name in the Book of Esther as forming a limit of the territories of Ahasuerus in the East, as Ethiopia was in the West, and this in the year B.C. 521. The Hebrew form HODDU, which is an abbreviation of HONADU, is identical with *Hindu* or *Sindhu*, as well as with one of the ancient names of the country, *Hapta-Hendu*, as it appears in the Vendidad. The Hebrew name HODDU, for *India* or *Hindia*, is the same

as HOD, signifying *glory, excellence, beauty*, and is equal to *the land of Hod*, or *the land of Glory;* and in this sense the Hebrew name HONADU exactly corresponds to a pure Tamil root, *Indr*, or *Odu* from *Olhi* (excellency, glory, beauty, strength), and the name sometimes given in ancient Hindu writings for India, PUNYABHUMI, or DHARMABHUMI, the land of virtue, of excellence, of glory, of strength and beauty; and JAMBU or NAVLAM-DWIP, the Island or Peninsula of the Tree of Life, being one of the Seven *Puranic* divisions of the globe. The word INDU or HIND, I am convinced, is a pure Tamil term and means *dark*, so also does the Tamil word SENDH, or SINDH, which means *red;* hence INDU, HINDU, or SINDHU, *dark, red people*, and the place of their abode HINDUSTAN or HINDU-STALAM (*the abode of dark, red people*).

10. Whatever may be the origin or derivation of the word INDIA or HINDU, it is certain that it is not Sanskrit nor Persian. The names of nations and places are to be sought for in their own languages rather than in that of foreigners, and therefore I am inclined to think that the word INDIA, being a pure Tamil term, found its way into the Hebrew vocabulary and thence into the Persian language, and in course of time it was adopted by the *Muhammedans* and applied to the country which we now call INDIA or HINDUSTAN; and the term becoming generally known to signify the place, and the people occupying the territory, was universally accepted by the people themselves.

11. It is from this vast territory or empire that the greatest bulk of our labourers, called COOLIES, come to work on the different sugar plantations, and the owners of the estates, and planters as a whole, are entirely dependent upon them. They are indeed a blessing and not a curse to the Colony. It is, however, a painful fact for me to observe here that in the breasts of the *rude, ignorant*, and *uneducated*, or the *young* and *thoughtless*, or *inexperienced*—the *Kamine* and not the *Chale Admi*—exists a strong prejudice against not only the Aborigines, Portuguese, and Creole races, but against the Coolies, who come from India, because of their colour and complexion. They are looked down upon as barbarians, as uncivilized

or semi-civilized beings, as persons unworthy of a moment's consideration, only fit for the cane-field, to toil in from sunrise to sunset. These statements may possibly be denied, but facts are stubborn things, and actions speak louder than words. Some unacquainted with history have gone so far as to assert that the Coolies, or labourers, from India, are beyond the capability of being civilized. The same feeling that prevailed in British India is still exhibited in this Colony and elsewhere in the West Indian Islands where Coolies are imported. Without any apology whatever I place before my reader a communication which appeared in the *Bombay Times* of February 14, 1857, bearing on this subject, a careful perusal of which will no doubt enlighten my reader, and set him a-thinking:—

"A HINDU OF SMALL CRANIUM *vs.* A BRITON OF LARGE CRANIUM.

(*a*) "In the *Bombay Times* of the 26th November last appeared a communicated article, headed 'The Limited Capability of the Hindus as a Nation for Civilization,' which has been brought to my notice. On going over this effusion from the large brain of an Anglo-Saxon, I was no less amused than chagrined, because this specimen of pedantry involves theories which, in these enlightened days, can only be brooked and received by men the circumference of whose crania, or rather of the substance contained in them, must fall considerably short of that which the writer of that article has been pleased to assign to those of the Hindus. I wish the writer had kept his favourite theory, which he seems to have derived from the particular school of phrenology to which he belongs, to himself, or allowed it to linger in some corner of Europe, or to smoulder away in the study-room of his great authority, the late Dr. Samuel Morton, of Philadelphia; but by his endeavour to propagate it in a new soil, as uncongenial to it as rocks to wheat, he cuts a very uncouth figure indeed. He may, no doubt, succeed in getting more or less admirers, and even followers, from among his own countrymen in this land, whose shallowness of mind may be ready to greet any doctrines invented by malice and propagated through jealousy—doctrines which are calculated to degrade the character of the natives of India in the eyes of Europe; but such endeavours on his part to procure followers would have been better confined to his tea-table talk, when there is nothing else for such idle philosophers to amuse their comrades with, except by talking nonsense, or attempting to excite their admiration by displaying before them the results of their deep study of the manners and customs of the *Niggers* around them. One of such philosophers might even go one step further, and tell his countrymen that he had just measured the dimensions of the skull of his *Mussal* Balloo, which had long been, from its great prominence, an eyesore to him, but (thank God) that he had found after all that it was two inches less than his own, which people had noticed to be too small for a European head. So far it may be tolerable. But then if he were to attempt at his desk to establish a theory on this experiment that the Hindu is an inferior race to the European, as indicated by the small crania of the former compared to those of the latter, and, in his over anxiety to save the public mind from wasting itself on things which he considers to be impracticable, to propound his theory for the edification and guidance of those who are engaged in the task of public instruction, he would surely render himself more than ridiculous in the eyes of those whose comprehensive mind looks upon the whole human race as one family, living under the influence of different local circumstances.

(*b*) "I admit that the capability for civilization is different in different nations, or, as the writer of the article in question has been pleased to call them, different races, if by the term 'race' he do not mean to show that they are as wide of each other as the mastiff from the lap-dog, though, from the spirit of his writing, such appears to be his favourite opinion; but with this qualification, that this capability for civilization is totally under the influence of the physical, moral, and political circumstances under which these different nations are placed, and is susceptible of variation according to the change which political revolutions, physical catastrophes, the state of moral and physical education, and numerous other causes, are calculated to effect in those circumstances. It can hardly be imagined that the characteristics of the different nations are fixed, and can never be influenced by inward circumstances beyond a certain point, and that if their progress in civilization stopped at a certain stage, as in the case of the Hindus and other Asiatic nations, it was because that inherent stimulating principle, which they once possessed, and which had pushed them onward up to that point, was exhausted, as the writer of the article in your paper supposes. His idea is, that each race of the great human family possesses a given amount of internal impulse which pushes them on, but stops them at different stages in their progress of civilization; and this theory he endeavours to reconcile with passages from the Christian Scriptures, forgetting that by so doing he not only militates against the fundamental truth which guides the progress of the whole human race in this world, as can be shown from numerous instances from universal history, but is insensibly led to blaspheme against the attributes of God as displayed in His works. As there is time for everything, as there is time for 'Japhet to dwell in the tents of Shem,' and perhaps longer; though there are no sufficient data as yet furnished by history, nor have any shining acts of virtue appeared on the part of Japhet, which can warrant even this concession; yet to suppose the progeny of one brother to be doomed to eternal degradation, and that of the other to be so blessed as to rise to a height which has no terminating point, is an idea which can only enter into a brain whose functions are in anything but equilibrium, however large it may be. Besides, by thus separating the Hindus, Persians, and similar nations of Asia, from the fraternity of the blessed sons of Japhet, in whose circle he includes the Anglo-Saxon race, to which he seems to belong, and making a motley of all the nations of Eastern Asia, including the Chinese and other tribes, ascribing their common origin to the cursed seed of Shem, the writer of the article in your paper has betrayed no uncommon degree of ignorance of the science of Ethnology, whose charms could not possibly have escaped his wide observation. The study of comparative philology, to which many learned men, even in his own country, have lately directed their attention, and which is one of the most unfailing criteria whereby to test the truth developed in this new science, has thrown such a flood of light on this point, that all the brilliancy of the talents of this writer in your paper will not be able to outshine it. It has now been clearly established that the Hindus, Persians, and other tribes of Western Asia, as also all the Indo-Germanic tribes of Europe, of which branch the Anglo-Saxons form but a twig, belong to one common Aryan stock of the great human family. Such being the fact, I am at a loss to imagine on what authority the writer in your paper shovels the Hindus and other kindred tribes all at once into the cursed stock of Shem, and, selecting his own twig, because it appears in its full foliage and flourishes in the present century, ingrafts it into the blessed branch of Japhet. Was there not a time when Mahomed, Jengis Khan and Timoor Lang, of the cursed stock, threw the whole of Asia and Europe into a panic, when there was not a single big head to be found in the whole of the latter continent, now abounding to an overflow in such commodity, to impede the overwhelming progress of the barbarians, who were devastating it for centuries? Moses, Abraham, Solomon, David, and, at last, Jesus Christ, whose morals and religion, according to a host of Christian divines, are held to be the sole cause of the present rise of the European nations in the scale of civilization, were but Asiatic Jews, to whom the writer in your paper would not, perhaps, be easily persuaded to concede that dimension of the heads which his craniometry ascribes to those of his own nation, and particularly of the Anglo-Saxons. Even the degraded Hindus, whose civilization he strives so prominently to show as deserving a place in the category of impossibilities, have produced poets, philosophers, and mathematicians, such as Vyas, Gautam, Kalidas, Bhawanbhut, Aryabhat, Bhasker Acharya, and a host of others, whose original lofty genius is now universally allowed by those who have deeply studied them to be by no means inferior to that of Shakespeare, Locke, and Newton, making due allowance, however, for the remote age in which they flourished. If he would but turn over the pages of the ancient history of India, whenever they are available, or look to the remotest scenery now obscured by the mist of antiquity, he would be able to discern a spot somewhere towards the North-West, from which he would trace out the current of the progress of conquest of the Aryas (ancient Hindus), flowing south-east from beyond the Hindu Koosh, forming in its passage in that direction the whole continent of India into a vast lake, and terminating down as far as Java and Borneo, spreading throughout these immense territories new ideas and new religions; and yet all these changes occurred at a time when even the first tabernacle of the Anglo-Saxons had not been formed, and were wrought by the ancestors of those whom the writer in your paper now describes as incapable of further development, only because the twig from which he happens to protrude appears now in its fresh and flourishing foliage, as compared to that old and withered branch. He may be correct in one sense of the law of vegetable physiology, but then to assert that the same law which causes one branch of the tree to wither, will not produce the same effect on the other, is a paradox which no physiologist has yet had the courage to advance. How could the particular school of phrenology to which the writer in your journal seems to belong account for all those grand and extraordinary changes wrought by the Asiatics in times gone by? changes which could be viewed in no other light than that of a prelude to the act in which it has pleased Providence to appoint the long neglected Britons to take a prominent part since the last century—changes which were no more than original patterns given, on which the modern Europeans have made but improvements. If the Europeans have invented printing, steam engines, railroads, and electric telegraphs, their great boasts in these days, perhaps *vox et prœterea nihil*—it was the Asiatics who invented and taught their masters the very letters which they now print, the first principles of mathematics, astronomy, chemistry, and mechanics, which contributed so largely to the development of these modern inventions; it was the Asiatics who made them acquainted with even such things as cotton and silk, with which they now clothe themselves so profusely, and which they have now turned so ungrateful as to leave the poor descendants of the people, who showed them those useful articles, to pick up the last rags of, not sufficient even to cover their nakedness. The writer in your paper most unmercifully stigmatizes the poor Hindus as incapable of further civilization and improvement, and exults in the glory of his own nation, ignorantly ascribing this change, which commenced but (comparatively speaking) yesterday, to the natural superiority of the latter over the former, when he is fully cognizant of the secret springs invented by the brains of his own nation, which are calculated so effectually to work the rapid downfall, not only of the Hindus, but of all the nations of Asia, with the wilful intent and purpose never to allow them to raise up their heads again. The grinding policy of the British Government in India is the great machine containing all these secret springs, though covered outwardly with all the shows, pretensions, and anxieties for the improvement of the condition of the people whom they secretly and inwardly detest and abhor. Even under cover of these pretensions to the improvement of the country by means of roads and canals, railways and electric telegraphs, their real motive is not kept concealed, nor can it be kept so from reflecting and intelligent minds, inasmuch as all these means of improvement are calculated to prove ultimately—nay, some statesmen candidly and openly declare the real intent and purpose to which they ought to be made subservient—to be so many powerful appliances in their hands for effectually promoting their own self-aggrandisement, for the extension of their own manufactures and commerce, and for the consolidation of their own power. It cannot be denied that the natives may and do derive benefits from all these means for the improvement of the country, but indeed they can have no more share in the matter than what the servants have after the trays have been removed from off the sumptuous dinner table of a well-pampered gourmand. Even the universities, colleges, and schools, the undeniable types of a pure and disinterested sympathy towards the ignorant and benighted natives,—colleges and schools for whose planning and organization more than a quarter of a century has already been spent, in mere tapes and foolscaps, and lacs of Indian sterlings have already been pocketed by the blessed sons of Great Britain, who have engaged themselves in the laudable cause of the enlightenment of the native mind, and yet the plan is represented by their own brothers at this moment to be as imperfect and in as infant a state as it was in the year 1823, when the Honourable Mountstuart Elphinstone first took up the question of native education on this side of India.—Even the colleges and schools, I repeat, appear to have been turned to no other purpose than that of doling out their best *alumni* to the collectors, the secretaries, and other high functionaries in the shape of translators and letter-writers, summaries and report drafters, magisterial proceeding writers,&c., tasks which had all along been performed by these functionaries themselves, but are now prepared for their signature by their subordinates, receiving allowances which compared to theirs are a mere trifle—with the great relief and the credit of having performed the work so well into the bargain; while the poor native, who does all this, is left degraded and unnoticed in a corner to bemoan his fate, and is, moreover, as a consolation to his poor heart, caricatured abroad, as a being possessing a small cranium, indicative of his natural inferiority to the race which tyrannizes over him ! ! ! I ask the writer in the *Bombay Times* in his sober senses to tell me whether there is one-thousandth part of the field left open to the native in these days which was open to him before the ascendency of the British power in India ? Are not all the avenues to his promotion, or to the development of his mental energies, purposely and intentionally shut up; and shut up almost hermetically, to be never opened to him again? Is not he placed in the lowest grade of the service of the State in all its departments, never to rise a single step, whatever may be his abilities, his knowledge, his experience, and his age, beyond a certain low degree, whilst European boys, fresh from Haileybury or Addiscombe, inexperienced and half educated, prone as yet to many boyish tricks, are put over their grey heads, to begin their Indian career in a line which terminates with a membership of the Council of India!!! Notwithstanding all these salient instances of the grinding policy of the British nation to keep the natives down, these helpless creatures are taxed in the bargain for not equalling their masters, and the fact is unjustly and perversely attributed to their natural incapacity for civilization. But the sober, reflecting, and disinterested portion even of the European community, of whom, thanks to God, there is no lack in India, cannot for a moment be induced, from such ratiocination as is set forth by the writer in your paper, to conceive that a country which could produce, at times comparatively modern, such conquerors and statesmen as Zenghis, Timoor, Baber, Akbar, Shivajee, Bajeerow, Nana Pharnavis, Mahadjee Sindhia, and a host of others—a country which could produce poets, legislators, statesmen, divines, philosophers, astronomers, and mathematicians, equal, or perhaps superior, to those of any other civilized country on earth—a country which could produce men in those rude days, whose minds could conceive the idea and execute the plan of such noble, stupendous, and elegant works as the excavations at Ellora, Elephanta, and several other places in India; the various hill forts, of great magnitude, in places high and difficult of access in the Deckan; the beautiful temples and pagodas—such as Trimal Naikh's Tank and Palace, the Choultry (a splendid granite hall, 333 feet by 82, on 128 stone pillars); the Tyanana Swamy *Pagoda*, 300 feet high; the great fourteen-story *Pagoda* of Tanjore, built in the eleventh century; the massive granite *Pagoda*, 1,000 feet by 660 feet, at Rameswaram, on the Coromandel Coast—scattered throughout the length and breadth of India; and last, the elegant and magnificent arches near Delhi, the Taj Mahal at Agra, the great canal of Joanpoor, and numerous other works of civil and military architecture—I say, if a country could produce men to do all these genuine works, unaided, and in times which modern Europeans are pleased to call barbarous, can it not as well produce in these days of civilization, with the refined and systematic training of our modern universities and colleges, men like Wellesley, Munro, Elphinstone, Napier, and Outram, if the same scope and the same advantages were given or afforded to them? But the fact is, that the European mind is so strongly and perversely prejudiced against the natives, that this legitimate and reasonable proposition is often scouted, ridiculed, and denounced, as a cobweb spun by the small brain of an ignorant Hindu.

(*c*) "The effusion of such a writer as the one in your journal, taxing the natives at one sweep as an inferior race, because they do not equal the Europeans, reminds me of the story of a tyrannical father, who gave only three annas to one of his sons to try his fortune, whilst to the others, his favourites, he gave three lacs of rupees each, as the capital stock with which to trade. In the course of ten years he called them all together, and asked them what they had done with the moneys which had been entrusted to them. Those who had three lacs given to them, showed in their account books the increase of their stock to thirty lacs, while the unfortunate young man who had received three annas only, produced three hundred rupees in ready cash. The inconsiderate and tyrannical father, being enraged at the production of this paltry sum, took a whip into his hands and commenced chastising the young man, who, whilst undergoing the operation, asked the old gentleman to ascertain the quotients of the sums originally given and the amount presented by himself and his brothers, and then he would be satisfied that his gain far exceeded that of his brothers. This lesson alone is sufficient to restore the large but disordered brain of the writer in your paper to its healthy functions.

(*d*) "The writer in question will not be able to deny that the policy pursued by the Anglo-Saxons in the East is such as is famously calculated to degrade not only the Hindus but all the Asiatics, in the scale of civilization and enlightenment, far beneath the point which the latter attained when they were left to themselves, and when they had free scope for the exercise of their mental faculties and energies. The knowledge and experience which the Anglo-Saxons have derived from the history of past ages have fully taught them that their hold in the East can never be maintained but by degrading the natives and representing them to the British inhabitants of their mother country as a race incapable of further civilization, lest the people's voice in Europe should enlist a sympathy in favour of the Indians.

(*e*) "Such grand conceptions and schemes for the degradation of so vast a continent as India could not have emanated from men of small brains, and the Anglo-Saxons, from the characteristic prominence of their foreheads, is certainly the only race befitted by Providence to achieve such an important and creditable task; but with my little brain, I should like to take the liberty to give a bit of advice to the writer in your paper, that before he could permit himself to look upon the prominence of the *crania* of his race with complacency, it would be as well for him to pry a little internally, and see if they have a corresponding heart to make them as perfect a race of human beings on earth as could be wished in the sight of God and man.

(*f*) "I may, however, inform my reader here, for his benefit, that the civilization of the Anglo-Saxons, and indeed the whole European nation, and of all races, has been conditioned on contact. It is the remark of a great German historian, Niebuhr, perhaps the greatest historian of modern times: 'There is not in history the record of a single indigenous civilization; there is nowhere, in any reliable document, the report of any people lifting themselves up out of barbarism. The historic civilizations are all exotic. The torches that blaze along the line of centuries were kindled each by the one behind.'"

There is nothing for me to retract from the above general statements.

12. The following general facts concerning the black and coloured people of British Guyana and the West Indian Islands may not be uninteresting to my reader. The late Rev. W. C. Dowding, M.A., who had lived many years in the West Indies, speaking of the black population in general, observed: "They are now in the fullest career of improvement, and after knowledge of them, as parishioners, both young and old, in the school, in the family, and at the sick bedside, it is impossible not to call them a most promising people; intelligent, orderly, and, for the most part, religious. It is not necessary for our purpose that we should make out a case, and I have no wish to hide either their foibles or their faults. It would be strange, indeed, if they had not both; but let it be remembered that *within the last twenty years* these people were saleable like the brutes that perish; suffered (almost

encouraged) to live as the brutes; and it needs must be considered a most significant fact, that they have risen to the requirements of their condition so rapidly, and taken possession of their freedom with so little effort. Whilst in these regions many are still thinking of the Negro as an animal who wears a monkey face, and says 'Massa,' with just wit enough to be cunning, and just English enough to lie, there is a race growing up in these Western Islands, seemly in their bearing, and very often handsome (civilization and improvement fast *Creolizing* their features, and effacing the uncomeliness of the African type); their peasants as intelligent and intelligible as our own; their advanced classes already a powerful *bourgeoisie*, of whose future position we have an instalment in this, that even now (and I pray it be carefully marked) it has its merchants, its barristers, its clergymen, its magistrates, its Members of Assembly, and (even) its Members of Council." This requires no further comment from me.

13. I may mention here the names of several Negroes who raised themselves to very high positions in life. Eustace, a Negro of the Island of St. Domingo, was an eminent philanthropist: he devoted all his means to providing for the sick and needy, nursing and sheltering orphans, and apprenticing destitute youths. He lived and laboured only to make others happy. In 1832, the National Institute of France awarded him the sum of one thousand dollars. Job Ben Solomon, Antony William Amo (of the Universities of Halle and Wittenberg), Doctors of Philosophy; Ignatius Sancho, and Francis Williams, ranked high as scholars; Annibal was a Lieutenant-General in the Russian army; Lislet Geoffroy was an officer of artillery in the Isle of France. Other prominent characters, both in the Colony of British Guyana and out of it, could also be mentioned, but it is not necessary. This magnificent Colony is in the hands of the descendants of these worthies I have just mentioned, and it is entirely in their power, and within their reach, to raise themselves in a similar way to very high positions in life.

14. I am happy to notice, however, that the majority of the Coolies who come to this Colony keep up a constant

correspondence with their friends and relatives left behind in India. The following facts I extract from the Honourable Immigration Agent-General's *Annual Report* for the year 1882:—

"38. A considerable correspondence is kept up with the mother country, both by the ordinary postal service, and through this department in connection with the agent at Calcutta. Some of the letters sent through the former medium of communication contain money and bills, and at times fail of reaching their destination, owing possibly to incorrect addresses; these find their way back to the Colony, and the owners are advertised for, a list being also kept at the Immigration Office. During the past year, 591 letters were sent through this department, post free, to the agent in Calcutta for delivery, and 187 remittances, aggregating £478 11s. 8d., in sums varying from 10s. to £25.

"This system adds not a little to the duties of the Agent in India, and is doubtless less satisfactory to the Indian authorities than the plan pursued in the neighbouring Colony of Trinidad, where the remittances are made through the Receiver-General direct to the Comptroller-General of India, who is placed in funds by the Agent when advised, and the several amounts paid through the Treasury Officers in the Mufasal.

"39. The following returns give a fair idea of the stake of the Indian Immigrant community in the Colony. They own 13,074 cattle, and large flocks of goats, 174 carts, and 28 cabs.

"The following Table shows the purchase and sale of real property by Indian immigrants:—

Number of Purchasers.	Number of Deeds.	Value.	Highest.	Lowest.
70	65	$12,152	$850	$35

"The Registrar-General has been good enough to supply the above figures, and other valuable tabulated information.

"The Portuguese, who have long monopolized the shop-keeping, have discovered keen competitors among the Indian and Chinese immigrants, who now own 1,174 shops. I am indebted to the Chief Commissary, Mr. Turner, for the subjoined information which he has been good enough to extract with much trouble:—

Portuguese Shops for the sale of Rum, Wine, and Malt Liquors, Opium and Gange, Dry Goods, Meat, Cooked Food, and Drugs			... ...	1,644
Chinese	ditto	ditto	ditto	634
East Indians	ditto	ditto	ditto	540

"40. Government Savings Banks have already been established in the three counties at George Town, New Amsterdam and Suddie, and were the number considerably increased, and offices opened at each police-station and branch post-office, as recommended by the Postmaster-General, a large portion of the immigrants' earnings, which is now squandered in drink and narcotics, would find its way into these institutions."

15. These facts here stated fully prove that the Colony of British Guyana is well adapted to meet the requirements and desires of the Indian, Chinese, Portuguese, and others, and that they can get on and prosper better in this "land of mud" than in their own native countries or homes. The only regret is, the condition of the Colony, and the facilities of making money by money or wealth hunters, are not sufficiently made known to the different classes of people in India and elsewhere. Possibly this book may fall into the hands of my numerous friends, clergy as well as laity, in India, and I would sincerely and earnestly request them to inform the thousands of the labouring classes there that British Guyana (Damra or Demeraila, as the Coolies are pleased to call it) is "Nau-Nâdu," Achchâ Dês (good country), free from famine, where labourers can always find work, and never suffer hunger. A person who has eaten lobba and drunk Creek water will never leave Demerara for ever, is a well-known saying in the Colony, and the truth of this is more or less confirmed every day. There are many Indian Coolies who have left the Colony for their home, and yet it is a fact that a very large number of them come back to labour on the sugar estates. What I on many occasions publicly gave utterance to, in conversation with several of my planter friends, but which they did not approve of, has been warmly taken up and recommended by Major Pitcher in his communication to H. A. Firth, Esq., Emigration Agent for British Guyana in Calcutta. The following I extract from Major

Pitcher's Report, published in the *Royal Gazette* of Saturday, January 13, 1883:—

"The Colonial authorities, by grants of land and bounties, tempt time-experienced men to stay. In my humble opinion it would be a wiser policy if, for a few years to come, another plan were given a trial, and that is to encourage all good men entitled to a free passage to return to their homes, undertaking with such as might be worth retaining to give them on re-emigrating such advantages in the way of curtailment of indenture and grants of land as the Colony could afford. The grant or terms might be proportionately increased for every Coolie whom the returning emigrant might succeed in inducing to accompany him. Under such a system, continued for say ten years, a more popular knowlege of emigration would spread through the recruiting field, and in this idea I am supported by the practical opinion of the emigrant I have above referred to. Anthony Trollope wrote:—'It is natural enough that men should hesitate to trust themselves to a future of which they know nothing. It required that some few should come out and prosper and *return with signs of prosperity.*'

"Through a returned French emigrant I am informed that drinking and gambling prevail amongst the Coolies resident in the French Colonies to a deplorable extent, and that the reason for so few returning from Guadaloupe and Martinique when their five years' term expires, is due to cash bounties being offered in lieu of passage, which bounties are speedily gambled away. My information may be wrong, but I fail from the correspondence to discover that Government has any better. Coolies do certainly not return from the French Colonies in such numbers as might fairly be expected.

"Amongst returned emigrants there seem to be some popular notions on the subject. Trinidad (Chini Ta'l) has the preference, then Demerara (Damra or Demeraila). All speak well of Jamaica. Little is known yet of either Figi or Natal. Mauritius (More righteous and Mirch) is admitted to have advantages in the shortness of the journey, the cheapness of the return passage, and (for the lazy) in the payments of monthly wages in the place of a daily task, or rather piece-work; but industrious people prefer the latter. Rightly or wrongly, Mauritius has acquired a doubtful reputation in some of the lower districts, and at Gorakhpur I was told by a recruiter that Coolies would sometimes say that they were ready to go to any Colony but Mauritius. We know from the latest report that this feeling is most unjust to Mauritius of the present day, and any discredit attaching to it must be a reflection of the old days of 'Vagrant hunts,' or of its French neighbour Bourbon (Birboon).

"Over the French Colonies heads are shaken. French masters are credited with beating their Coolies, and with indifference to the Coolies' morality in the direction of drinking and gambling. No one appears ever to have met or heard of any Coolie who had been to Cayenne. Of Surinam it is said that the Coolies are not so well housed and looked after as they are in Demerara, and that they do not earn so much money, but that the Dutch are kind masters. Such little as has been heard of Natal is good.

"I hardly think that colonial planters can be aware of the inordinate value attached by Asiatics to 'chits,' or testimonials. If they were, they would be careful to give every man of good conduct, on leaving, a testimonial as to character. Better still, if the colonial authorities would give to the well-conducted certificates of good conduct when leaving, and the more highly emblazoned the better. Such testimonials would be flourished by the emigrant on return, to the envy of his village neighbours, who, with reference to any outward signs of wealth, might remark that 'perhaps he stole it,' but would look on the 'chit' or certificate with real respect. A returned emigrant exhibited to me the other day, with a face full of honest pride, a receipt in English for the price of a cow which he had bought from some planter for forty dollars."

* * * * * *

"One Din Muhammad returned from Demerara eighteen months ago, after an absence of fifteen years; took his wife out with him, and brought her back. Had money, but his wife's illness and death, six months ago, cost him a great deal. Was now going to try his luck in Natal, though he would rather go to Demerara, if only the season were open.

"Spoke with intense scorn of Hindustan, as being unfit to live in after Demerara. No short-commons there, no famine. I drew him out by suggesting that it was very cold, that they could not get fish, and so on, which elicited from him lavish praise of everything and every one connected with Demerara as compared with Hindustan. With him was his son, a boy of five or six, and particularly bright and intelligent. The child had returned from Demerara speaking English, but could now only say a few words, which, however, he seemed very pleased to have an opportunity of using."

16. I must not extend this Introductory Chapter any further, as the reader will find ample information given in the book on all subjects necessary for him to know about the country and people. I may, however, state here that a new derivation of the origin of the name "Demerara" has been suggested to me by an educated Coolie in the Colony, who returned to British Guyana very recently. He said Demerara is derived from the *Victoria Regia* lily (referred to in the first chapter), and means *Tâmarei-ûru* =TAMARARA (a corrupted form), or DEMERARA, the Land or Country of the White Lotus or Lily, on which sits Siva, wearing a tiger-skin garment. This plant was formerly venerated by the Egyptians as much as it is now by the Hindus. It is a sacred flower among the Coolies of British Guyana, and hence DAMARURU, the country in which this large plant is found.

17. In conclusion, whatever may be the prosperous condition of the Colony, there is no denying the fact that the want of efficient labourers is keenly felt, from time to time, on the different sugar estates in the Colony, and anything that is done to alleviate this want is certain to meet with the approval of the planter community. It is one thing to procure labourers from all parts of the world; it is quite another thing to retain them. Demerara has to redeem her character to a certain extent amongst the neighbouring islands, where it is asserted that the Colony is a "City of refuge" for the scum of the West Indies. The Colony does not require city loafers and wharf loungers, but it does urgently stand in need of steady and industrious labourers, and these can only be retained by offering them special inducements to remain and settle down in the Colony. The Barbadian agriculturist as a rule may be considered, in contrast with the Coolie, a skilled labourer, and when he really settles down on an estate, it is generally found that his services are extremely valuable; but let the same man remain in George Town, and he

becomes a perfect nuisance to his neighbours, and to all who come in contact with him. After the most careful inquiry we find that the great majority of cases brought before the notice of the police magistrates, from day to day, for the use of indecent language, for assaults, &c., are against Barbadians; consequently it is to be regretted that means cannot be devised to secure their transport to, and selection on, estates immediately after their arrival. Whatever steps may be taken to secure the extension of Barbadian immigration, we are of opinion that the following items should be borne in mind, that something should be obtained from the labourer in the shape of indenture, that he will remain a certain time in the Colony; that he will proceed to an estate immediately upon his arrival; and that the payment of his return fare be made dependent upon the report made by the manager of the estate upon which he has resided.

N.B. The reader will find elsewhere in this book some remarks on West Indian Creole labourers.

CHAPTER I.

A BRIEF DESCRIPTION OF THE COLONY OF BRITISH GUYANA IN GENERAL.

1. AMERICA, or the New World, was discovered in the year 1492 by Christopher Columbus, a native of Genoa. It is distinguished from all the other great divisions of the globe by the size and grandeur of its mountains, lakes, and rivers. It is divided by the Gulf of Mexico and the Caribbean Sea into two vast peninsulas—one of which is called North, and the other South America, and united by the Isthmus of Panama or Darien. And British Guyana is situated in the north part of the South American Continent, and is supposed by some to have been discovered by Vasco Nunes and Diego de Ordas. As early as A.D. 1580, according to Schomburgk, some inhabitants of Zealand, one of the Provinces of Holland, effected a settlement near the river Pomeroon, and subsequently on the banks of the Essequibo.

2. *Guayana*, *Guianna*, or *Guiana* (called by some of the earliest French visitors to this Colony in 1693 "*Caribane*," the origin possibly of the name Courobana, which has puzzled some of our antiquaries, as applied to the East Coast of Demerara), was so named from a tribe of Indians called "Guayannols." It lies between 8 deg. 40 min. north lat., and 3 deg. 30 min. south lat., and between the 50th and 68th deg. of long. west of Greenwich. In the Dutch language the word *Guiana* signifies the wild coast; and, indeed, before the people from different parts of the world began to settle here, it was a wild country, with extensive savannahs or plains (wet and dry), and a dense mass of unrivalled foliage, comprising palms, mangroves (*Rhizophora Mang.*), Courida bushes (*Avicennia Nitida*), ferns, and other plants and useful trees, where the prowling beast, the dreaded reptile, the wild bird, and the noxious insect roamed at large.

3. British Guyana, the *now* most important colony of Great Britain in the West Indies, was once an asylum for the redundant population of Barbadoes and other islands in the Caribbean Sea. It was taken possession of by the English in the war between England and France, when Holland was overrun by the French and incorporated in the French empire. The colony is called "the British Guyana," to distinguish it from the Venezuelan or Spanish, the Dutch, the French, and the Brazilian or Portuguese Guyanas. It extends from Venezuela to the river Corentyne, which last is the line of division between British and Dutch Guyana. It comprises the three provinces or counties of Demerara, Essequebo (or Essequibo), and Berbice. Formerly Berbice was under a separate Government, but in 1831 it was united to Demerara and Essequibo under one Government, having for their capital Georgetown. When the Dutch had possession of the Colony, they called their capital Stabroek, which has since been changed to Georgetown by the English. The present public market, a handsome iron building of large dimensions, erected in 1881 by an American, a Mr. Matt. Mackay, in the city still goes by the name of Stabroek market. At the time of the Dutch the fort and public buildings were higher up the river than they are now, at Diamond Point, and the suburb of Kingston, between the town and the sea, was built up by the British Garrison, being the coolest and healthiest quarter, and was called so after the capital of Jamaica. The barracks in the immediate neighbourhood of Kingston Wesleyan Chapel and the sea-wall are called "the Evelary Barracks."

4. Although this "magnificent province," or colony, has been in the possession of the English nation since 1803, very little notice seems to have been paid to it in the mother country. A noble lord, who twice filled the office of Secretary of State for the Colonies, spoke of it in Parliament as one of the West India Islands. A similar mistake was made only a few years ago in the *Cotton Supply Reporter*, published at Manchester, the great manufacturing emporium of the North of England. Many people, even ministers and clergymen, in England speak of British Guyana—part of the

American Continent—as one of the West India Islands, and those missionaries who are appointed from year to year by the Wesleyan Methodist Conference to labour in this Colony sometimes look upon their appointments with dread, and believe that they are going to a country where they will soon, very soon, be cut down. They seem to think that British Guyana—Demerara—is Africa, "the white man's grave." Dire visions of fever and ague, and ghosts of the victims of "pestilential swamps," haunt their imagination, and they banish the thoughts of such an inhospitable, unhealthy country from their memories. The English are not the only nation who speak of the Colony as one of the islands; there are some in the very Colony itself who make a similar mistake. The very children who attend our public and private schools have often spoken of the country as an island.

5. British Guyana contains about 100,000 square miles of land, nearly the whole of which is productive, but the greater part in the highest degree fertile. Its whole length, from east to west, is 280 miles, and its breadth, from north to south, from 300 to 450 miles. Its population, according to the decennial census taken on April 3, 1881, is estimated at 252,186, of which 69,554 are immigrants from India and China. A few years ago there were 7,656 aborigines, and I believe this number is included in the above. In fact, it is almost an impossibility to find out the exact number of the aborigines, the lords of the soil, on account of their roving and unsettled habits. The following Table may not be uninteresting to my reader:—

BIRTH PLACES OF THE PEOPLE.

British Guyana	149,639
India	65,161
China	4,393
Madeira and Azores	6,879
West India Islands	18,318
Europe	1,617
North America	205
Africa	5,077
Other places	897
Grand Total	252,186

Included under the head "Born in British Guyana," chiefly under the age of sixteen years, are :—

Males.	Females.	
7,718	7,055	born of parents from India.
454	387	" " " China.
2,558	24,897	" " " Madeira.
10,725	32,339	

Of the 252,186 inhabitants of the Colony, there are :—

In Georgetown	47,175
In the County of Demerara, exclusive of Georgetown...	112,268
In the County of Essequibo	45,582
In the Town of New Amsterdam	8,124
In the County of Berbice, exclusive of New Amsterdam	39,037

Total. 1881.	Total. 1871.	Increase. 1881.
252,186	193,491	58,695

6. British Guyana is a well-watered garden. It is watered by four larger and six smaller rivers, but improperly called creeks; the larger rolling vast bodies of water into the ocean, and capable of being navigated fifty, seventy, one hundred, and one hundred and fifty miles from their estuaries, thus opening all parts of the rich and magnificent land to the enterprise, industry, and commerce of man. The course of these rivers is from south to north, and their origin is difficult to trace in the wild and mountainous interior. We require a second enterprising and plodding Schomburgk or Livingstone to travel many hundreds of miles away in the interior to find out their origin. The whole of this rich land is formed by the vast quantity of mud which has been brought down from time to time by these rivers: hence British Guyana is sometimes sarcastically called, "The Mud Plain," "The Mud Country," "The Land of Mud," and its natives, or those born in the land, are playfully called "Mud-heads," but it is a very wrong and unjust expression to be used to the people of the soil. The Demerara (called *Lemdrare* by Raleigh and his followers; *Rio de Mirara* by the Spaniards; and *Innewary*, or *Demerary*, by the Dutch), or *The Wonderful River*, is of a dirty yellow, and is one mile and three-quarters wide at its mouth.

Borselen, an island about twenty miles up this river, was once the head-quarters of the Dutch, and the capital of this settlement. About thirty miles from our present town up this river we meet with sandhills from 100 to 150 feet high, and nearly perpendicular—a fine place for marooning or picnicking. From these hills white sand is procured in abundance. The Essequibo — called by the Indians *Araunauma*, by Hakluyt *Devoritia* or *Dessekeber*—named after one of the officers of Diego Columbus, D. Juan Essequibel, is the largest river in British Guyana. It is next in size to the Orinoco, and hence called by the Indians "the younger brother of the Orinoco." At the mouth of the Essequibo, and further up, are situated several islands, about 365 in number, some of which are from twelve to fifteen miles long. The principal islands, which are inhabited, and which have sugar estates on them, are Waakenaam (signifying "in want of a name") or Margaritta, Leguan (from El Guano), Tiger or Arowabische, Hog, and Troolie. And the Berbice is the third large river which waters this magnificent province. At its mouth it is upwards of two miles wide. It was in the upper part of this river that the remarkable *Victoria Regia* lily, whose flower is larger than a man's head, and the leaves five feet across, was discovered in 1836, by Sir Robert Schomburgk. At the mouth of this river is situated the Crab Island. The six smaller rivers of British Guyana are the Pomeroon, Boerasiri, Mahaica, Mahaicony, Abaris, and Canje. The Corentyne, which is another large river, commences about twenty-five miles from the source of the Essequibo, in the Acarai mountains. The Cayie, the Barima, the Morocco, and the Warrima, are also large creeks which water the land. All the rivers and creeks in the Colony abound in huge alligators or caymans, water pythons, or camudi-snakes (*Annaconda*), fish, &c., &c. The cataracts and rapids met with in the course of the rivers are exceedingly interesting, numerous, and beautiful. Some of them are large, and others small. The great "Fall of the River Demerara" is about sixty feet high, and is situated about three hundred miles from the embouchure of the river. But the greatest fall or cataract (far greater than the once celebrated and unrivalled

Niagara) in the world now, is the one which was recently discovered by Mr. C. B. Brown. It is called the Keituric Fall, on the river Potaro, a tributary of the river Essequibo.

7. British Guyana is a rich country; but scarcely anything has been yet done to develope its resources. Here the production of sugar almost exclusively engages the attention of the people of every class. It has been the staple of the Colony, and, despite the European beet-root, I believe and trust it will long continue to be so. But why should this interfere with the development of the other resources of the Colony? It is true that a fostering care must be bestowed upon the planting interest, and every possible assistance be given to procure the essential labour at the lowest possible rate; but could not that be done simultaneously with encouraging other productions? I believe that it could. At present we are entirely dependent upon foreign markets for our food and raiment; and yet we allow the extensive lands of our "magnificent province"—the "paradise of the labouring man"—to lie waste, to lie uncultivated. I am of opinion, that if the Colony of British Guyana is ever to be developed at all, it must be by other hands than those of Europeans, though British pluck and perseverance may supply the capital and devise the means. On the Coolie or the Chinese must the future of the Colony depend, except in the matter of sugar production, and every one knows that sugar planters regard with justifiable jealousy any attempt to give the Coolies land of their own to cultivate, knowing that it is so much taken away from sugar cultivation, and that the expense of introduction will have been lost. Perhaps the planting interest cannot reasonably be expected to push forward any scheme not connected with sugar, but I think they forget that as the population increases there will be a labour supply becoming available in the Colony itself, and that gradually the necessity of our introducing Coolies at such enormous expense, only for the sake of a few years' work, will be obviated. There is too much Conservatism amongst the class which rules the roast in Demerara, and until a broader view is taken, I am afraid that Demerara will only be valu-

able for its sugar belt. This exclusive sugar-growing business has been most injurious to, and I believe the bane of, the Colony, and, indeed, of the West Indies. I, for one, would heartily bid Godspeed to any enterprise which tends to divert native labour and capital from this exclusive sugar cultivation.

8. In the interior of the Colony we have vast savannahs capable of pasturing thousands of cattle, sheep, and horses; immense primeval forests, where the sound of the woodman's axe has never yet been heard, extending some hundreds of miles, with the finest of woods, which are wholly unknown in the European markets. Green-heart, purple-heart, mora, bullet-tree, wallaba, crab-tree, and other woods, are all valuable, and are used for house-frames, stellings, planking of vessels, &c., and furniture. From the seeds and bark of the green-heart and mora, a valuable medicine called birbirine is prepared, and used in cases of fevers and dysentery. Also, when the Indians are unable to procure food, they grate the seeds of the green-heart and mora, and mixing the starch thus obtained with decayed wallaba-wood, they eat it. These trees vary in height from 120 to 150 feet. The pine-apple, which is seldom to be seen in Europe, except upon the tables of the wealthy, is cultivated without much trouble and labour. The different varieties of the orange tribe; the shaddock, a large orange-like fruit, as big as a child's head; and the grape fruit, something between the orange and the shaddock, all thrive in this region of perpetual spring and summer. The mango in its manifold varieties, the best of which are equal in delicacy to the ripe peach; the sapodilla, full of a rich pulp and syrup, not surpassed in deliciousness by a full ripe pear; the sugar-apple, the sour-sop, the guava, and a variety of plums and other luscious fruits grow in the Colony, not only for the sustenance, but also for the enjoyment and happiness of man. The cocoanut-tree is one of the palm species, and one of the most beautiful trees that grow. In the course of some years it runs up to a height of forty or fifty feet, sending forth all the time a profusion of large, drooping leaves, like a beautiful plume of feathers. From its fifth or sixth year it puts forth fruit; and when established, like the tree of life, spoken of in

the Apocalypse, it blooms every month, exhibiting its fruit in every stage of growth, from the flowery blossom to the full ripe fruit. When the fruit has reached a certain growth, it contains in a large nut, that weighs eight or ten pounds, about a pint of delicious milk or water, which forms a cool delightful beverage. If the nut is left to ripen on the tree, this milk gradually hardens, first into a clear white jelly, and then to a hard kernel, from which is extracted a valuable oil. The hard shell of the nut can be formed into cups susceptible of a high degree of polish; while the thick fibrous covering by which it is enclosed, furnishes valuable material for mats and stuffing for chairs and sofas in lieu of horsehair. Speaking of the cocoanut-tree, a Hindu sage in the *Múdurei* says, "Be not anxious for an immediate reward for anything good you may have done; for the fine and strong good-grown cocoanut-tree returns from its top the water it drank by the roots. That benefit which has been shown to a good man will, doubtless, be in some way returned." We have also vast tracts of land capable of producing the finest cotton, wheat, and rice in the world, which thousands of persons who would not, or could not, work upon sugar estates, could gladly cultivate on their own small patches. A few years ago the rice grown in this Colony was introduced into the London market, and it was pronounced the best, and topped Carolina, which was then at the head of the list. A rice-growing company was formed in the City, but because a few of the merchants and planters were opposed to the scheme, it died a sudden death after nine days' wonder or talk. Valuable as sugar is, it is worse than impolitic to hang all our fortunes on one staple; and this grain only requires to be once fairly started to supplement adequately our saccharine friend. The United States were settled over a century before they made a bale of cotton, and now cotton grows in the States in abundance. This Colony is flat, rich, easily flooded, water is abundant, and the seasons are admirably adapted for the culture of cotton. A few of the planters and proprietors tried the growth of cotton, but they soon got tired of it. Sugar! sugar! was their cry. We have in British Guyana stores incalculable of balatta (a substance resembling indiarubber, obtained from the milk of the bullet-tree) and other commercial gums. We have also ranges of mountains with mines of gold, and various specimens of crystals, jasper, and other precious stones, &c. Thousands of square miles of land of incalculable richness surround the Colony, and yet only a small portion of it is under cultivation. Sugar is the chief and almost the only thing that is cultivated here. This seems to be regarded as "the one thing needful," and is the subject of daily (week days and Sundays alike) conversation among the planters. They think of sugar going to bed, and think of sugar when they rise in the morning. All the politics in the Colony have a tendency to this "all-important" and "all-absorbing" subject. Hence, I believe, Mr. A. Trollope, in a playful manner, and yet with a good deal of sly raillery, remarked, "The form of [British Guyana] government is a mild despotism tempered by sugar." Truly, as he has said, British Guyana flows with sugar and rum. Two planters found themselves one Sunday morning in a church in Essequibo, when the following conversation took place between them during the reading of the Church service, which reached the ears of the congregation :—

"Intermingling with the pious ejaculations of the priest and the responses of the people were overheard,—'Man, I had a splendid week's work; 160 hogsheads; the like of it has never been heard of.' *O ye whales, and all that move in the waters.* 'What was the weight of your bags, and how many to a hogshead?' *O all ye beasts and cattle.* 'Seven bags to the hogshead, and each bag 200 lbs. weight.' *O ye children of men.* 'And is that what you're bragging about? Why, I allow nine bags to the hogshead, and every one 240 lbs.' Here the first speaker became quite devout and turned to his prayer book, as if it were the only thing in the world he cared about."—Extracted from the *Royal Gazette* of Nov. 27, 1880.

British Guyana is a wealthy colony, it is true, but it requires means at command to attract shepherds, miners, agriculturists, cultivators of sugar, and all others who have a willing mind and strong arm to engage in any branch of industry.

9. The interior of the Colony teems with living beings, beasts, reptiles, insects, and birds, both *injurious* and *useful* to man. Among the beasts of prey and those *injurious* to man, we may mention the jaguar or tiger, puma, tiger-cat, alligator, salempenter, crab-dog, yawarrie, cougar or deer-tiger. The playful and lively monkey and sakuwinki, water-haas, peccary, deer, lobba, agouti, and iguana, are among the *useful*. It is a common belief among people here that if a stranger eat the lobba flesh and drink the creek or bush water, he will never die out of this country. Among the reptiles may be mentioned the water python or camudi, which lurks by the river banks, a species of the East Indian or American boa-constrictor; the rattlesnake, which gives timely warning; the kono-kosi or bush-master, the terror of man and beast; and the labairi, speckled with a dirty brown. We have heard of another most venomous snake called the parrot-snake, to be found in the interior, but we have never seen it. Among the principal insects of British Guyana we find ants, beetles, bêterouge, butterflies, centipedes, wood-slaves, chigoes (or jiggars), cockroaches, marabanters (Jack Spaniards or wasps), mosquitoes, and sandflies, which are very troublesome little things, scorpions, spiders, and tarantulas. And among birds, which we have in endless variety, we may mention the parrots and macaws of all colours, green, blue, yellow, and scarlet; paroquets, which fly overhead in screaming flocks; the cassique or mocking bird, which imitates almost every sound it hears; and the cock of the rock, which lives in lonely places, as the caves of the rocks. It is crowned with a fine double crest, the wing and tail plumes are brown and white, and the other parts of its body are of a deep orange tint. The campanella, or bell-bird, is one of the most beautiful-looking birds, whose voice, like the tone of a high-sounding bell, is heard in the interior at the distance of three or four miles when silence reigns. Like the cock of the rock it is a bird very difficult to be caught. Wild ducks, pigeons, herons, cranes, currie-curries, gauldings, and spoonbills, are birds which are used for food. There is in this Colony a strange-looking black bird called the "Who you" or "Jumbie" bird,

with a long tail. Like the owl, it never stirs in daytime. But at night it will leave its roosting-place, and hop about on the ground crying, "Who you?" The words are so distinctly uttered, that the voice of the bird has been mistaken for a human voice. Some time in August, 1877, whilst returning home at night from Victoria Wesleyan Chapel, on the east sea-coast, the groom told me that several years ago (when slavery was in existence) an African working on a plantation, finding that some accident had happened to the engine at work, was running fast to his master's house to report the circumstance. On the road he was asked, "Who you?" and he, believing it was a human voice proceeding from the bush, stopped to answer the question. A little farther on he was similarly accosted, and stopped to explain the reason why he was running. When he found that it was only a black bird that asked him "Who you?" he was so frightened that he ran home to his house without going to his master, and fancied that the "Jumbie" in the form of a black bird was following him all the way, and died from fright.

10. The mountains of British Guyana are not to be seen on the sea-coast, but far away in the interior. The Ouangowai (or Mountains of the Sun), the Sierra-Acarai, Kaiawako, Carawaimi, Caruma, Mocajahi, Kai-Irita, or Kai-Iwa (or Mountains of the Moon), Tinijaru, Sierra-Yauina, Canuca or Canocow, Twasinki, Pacaraima, and others, are to be found far away from the coasts. These mountains vary in height from 3,000 to 5,000 feet above the table land, or 7,500 feet above the level of the sea. The most important of these mountains is the Peak of Roraima—red rock—which ascends 7,520 feet above the sea. This is a most remarkable mountain. The Indians in their dances and war-songs sing of "Roraima, the red-rocked, wrapped in clouds, the ever-fertile source of streams." In consequence of the darkness which frequently prevails when thick clouds hover about its summit, it is likewise called the Night Mountain; and then the Indians sing, "Of Roraima, the red-rocked, I sing, where with day-break the night still prevails." A quotation from a work entitled *Roraima and British Guiana,* by Mr. J. W.

Buddam Whetham, will best describe this wonderful mountain :—

"At the foot of the mountain the hilly ground lay in patches of yellow stony savannah, and dark strips of woodland rising in elevation as they approached its base. Then came a forest-clad ravine whose further side sloped stately up to a distance of about 3,000 feet, and springing directly out of this sea of green rose a perpendicular wall of red rock, 1,500 feet in height. Hardly a shrub broke the sheer descent of the shining cliff; scarcely a line of verdure marked where clinging grasses had gained a footing on its smooth face. The south-eastern corner was slightly rounded, and its tower-like appearance increased its general resemblance to a Titanic fortification, a few miles in length, rising from a forest glacis. The glancing rays of the sun struck the red sandstone layers which shone like glass and stood out in bold and bright relief above their green base. A fly could hardly have rested on the slippery slabs. . . . The level summit line was backed by forest trees, which to us appeared like bushes, and from their feet, like skeins of floss silk swaying in the wind, three waterfalls descended and were lost in the woods below. But towards the northern end of the mountain, a magnificent cascade, whose lips seemed to be below the summit, sprang in a broad silvery arch right down into the green depths, barely touching the rocky walls in its descent."

In the interior of Guyana is found another rock called *Ataraipu*, or the Devil's Rock, which forms a kind of natural pyramid. This rock is the greatest geological wonder of Guyana. The whole height of this pyramid rock is about 900 feet above the river Guidaru (which in the Indian tongue signifies a kind of war club, and is a tributary of the Essequibo), and 1,300 feet above the sea. Fanciful hieroglyphics and picture-writing on the rocks of granite, quartz-porphyry, gneiss, and jasperous sandstone, are also to be seen in many places in the interior of British Guyana. This part of the rocky region reminds one of the Sinaitic Valley, which it was our privilege to visit in the year 1857. "The figures represented are of the most varied and singular description; rude outlines of birds, animals, men and women, and other natural objects; but it is not a little curious that among the sculpturings should be found some clumsy sketches of large vessels with masts (evidently of modern date), on some granite rocks at the Ilha de Pedra, on the river Negro. In many places the hieroglyphics appear to represent writing, and the characters have, in many instances, been traced to bear resemblance to Hebrew and other dialects; whether this is merely a coincidence, or whether there actually exists a connection between the languages of the East and West, is a problem for the learned to solve." How, when, and by whom, these fanciful hieroglyphics and representations were made on these rocks, has yet to be ascertained. Perhaps by erecting a staging against the face of the rock, or when the river was much above its usual height, these inscriptions might have been made or cut out with a pointed iron tool. The figures were evidently cut with great care, and at much labour, by a former race of men, Indians, for some great purpose, probably a religious one, as some of the figures give indications of worship.*

11. The nature of the climate of British Guyana is hot, but cooled by the trade wind, and not liable to great changes of temperature. On account of the occasional occurrence of yellow fever, which epidemic is a fatal foe to "new comers" and seamen, this Colony has been looked upon in the same light as some parts of Western Africa, as "the white man's grave." On account of a few deaths which have occasionally occurred here, the character and good name of this Colony have been at stake in England. I have heard from our young missionaries, sent out by the Methodist Conference, and have also myself heard, before I came to the Colony in 1860, what exaggerated or untruthful accounts have often been given of the unhealthfulness of British Guyana. I believe there are many in England who would almost shudder at the thought of being obliged to pass a short time here. One missionary was told by some of his friends and relations that no sooner would he land in Demerara, than he would get sick and die right off. It would be really laughable, if the matter were not so exceed-

* See this subject fully treated in my *Guyanian Indians*, Sect. VI., pp. 35-41.

ingly serious, to contemplate the horror with which this much-vaunted El Dorado of Sir Walter Raleigh is regarded by the English people. There are Europeans who have been living here for many years, who bear testimony in their own persons to the immunity from disease that may be enjoyed in this Colony. Here one may live in good health if he only wishes. It would seem as if here, more than anywhere else, Providence had placed the life and death of each man in his own hands. It is true that the preservation of health may necessitate some self-denial; but certainly no greater sacrifice than the importance of the object to be gained deserves. Educated men from England coming to settle here soon learn the importance of paying proper attention to health; but sailors and soldiers are not easily taught to seek what is for their advantage, and they are constantly overstepping the bounds of prudence, and hence they sicken and die. This is a very healthy country for those who are suffering in England from consumption. Here they can live much longer than they can in England, and probably they may get quite rid of the disease. In future let the missionaries, and others appointed to labour in this Colony, be plainly told, on their appointment, that for those who take care of themselves Demerara has not more dangers than other parts of the world. "There never was a land so ill spoken of, and never one that deserved it so little."

12. Speaking about the nature of the British Guyana climate, Dr. Hancock, who resided in the country for twenty-five years, bore this testimony:—

"Guyana is most favourably situated of any part of the world, perhaps, with respect to the winds and sea breezes. It lies in the main tract of the equinoctial current, whilst hurricanes, so terrific and destructive amongst the West Indian Islands, are unknown here, and the equinoctial gales are extremely steady and uniform. . . . . In the interior parts of Guyana the purity of the air is such that in the dry season the stars appear like brilliants in the deep azure sky at night, and we not unfrequently perceive planets in the daytime. At the same time the splendour of the moon and the zodiacal light contribute to make the nights most pleasing, and to throw a charm on every object. The testimony of the wood-cutters constantly assures us that the wooded parts and inland forests are never found to be unhealthy to either Europeans or others. These are facts which I can vouch for, and, to show that they are not contrary to reason, let it be considered that it is not the absolute degree of temperature that determines the salubrity of any climate; but, as every one knows, it is the great and sudden changes from heat to cold, and from cold to heat, which chiefly render any country unhealthy. Now, there is probably no country on the globe where the temperature is more uniform than in Guyana."

Again, Sir R. Schomburgk, a more recent authority, states that

"The salubrity of the interior is proverbial, and there are many instances of longevity among the settlers on the banks of the rivers Demerara, Berbice, and Essequibo. The natural drainage is here so perfect, that all impurities are swept off by the torrents of rain, and the purity of the air is so great, that the planets Venus and Jupiter may be seen in the daytime. While descending the Upper Essequibo in December, 1838, we saw, one afternoon at three o'clock, the sun, the moon, and the planet Venus."

The year is divided into two wet and two dry seasons. The long wet season commences about the middle of April, and, with westerly winds prevailing, lasts until August. The dry season then begins and continues until November. December and January constitute the short wet season, and February and March the short dry season. The sea breezes prevail with scarcely any intermission throughout the dry season. The temperature seldom falls below 75 deg. Fahr., or rises above 90 deg. Fahr. The mean annual temperature of Georgetown is 81 deg. Fahr.; and the average rainfall is 100 inches. In his annual report to the Government for 1878, the Health Officer states:—

"The port of Georgetown ought to be placed at the head of the list of seaports with regard to healthiness. The number of seamen who entered the port of Georgetown during 1878 was 10,982; of these 455 were admitted into the seamen's hospital, out of whom only four died—one from accident, living only a few hours after admission; three of chronic dysentery of long standing, a disease in no way connected with the climate. It is a remarkable fact that not a single death took place from illness contracted in the Colony."

In a climate like Demerara, where malaria is one of the principal ills against which the inhabitants have to contend, the following paragraph will not be without interest:—

"The monks of the Abbey of Tre Fontane, in the malarious Roman Campagna, where a few years ago no one could sleep at night without contracting disease, have made their property habitable and healthy by means of plantations of the eucalyptus. Trees four years old are twenty-six feet high and twenty-eight inches in circumference, while those eight years old are fifty feet high and nearly three feet in circumference. The eucalyptus owes its fever-dispelling properties principally to the enormous quantity of water which it can absorb from the soil—twice the weight of its leaves in twelve hours—and to its property of secreting an aromatic essential oil, by which its oxidation produces peroxide of hydrogen—one of the most powerful disinfecting agents. The monks also find it good to drink a tea made from the leaves of the tree."

13. In the towns, villages, and hamlets of British Guyana we have living people from nearly all parts of the globe. Here are Europeans, comprising the English, Scotch, Irish, French, Dutch, and Portuguese from Madeira; Coolies from India and China, speaking their own languages, and the many dialects, and observing nearly all the customs of their countries; a few Maltese from Malta; Arabs from Morocco and Fez in Algiers, North of Africa; Negroes, originally from Africa; Creoles from the West India Islands, as Barbadoes, St. Eustatius, Martinique, Antigua, &c.; together with a large and respectable class of black and coloured persons born in the country, and generally designated Creoles. On the banks of the rivers and creeks, both within and beyond the boundaries of the Colony, there are a few (perhaps mustering about 7,000 or 8,000) wandering tribes of Indians, the lords of the soil.

14. In point of fertility, British Guyana has no competitor. Its soil is alluvial, and no doubt this will account for the fertility which pervades it. Its staple products are sugar, rum, and timber. As observed above, this magnificent province is rich in minerals, especially gold, so much

so that a gold company was formed and incorporated by ordinance some years ago. In consequence of a dispute about the boundary line between this Colony and that of Venezuela, the company had to stop. It is to be hoped that the company will resume its operations, seeing that its success is calculated to further the interests of the Colony, and to establish its importance.

15. The geological productions of Guyana are second to none; its natural history also is profuse in all its departments, and affords ample field for naturalists, as well as for the education of persevering students who would be informed in this useful branch—this branch which teaches us so much about Him who has so liberally and richly provided for British Guyana.

16. Altogether the Colony is taking great strides in all departments of civilization—commerce extending on all sides; institutions being multiplied for the education of youth, and especially for the diffusion of that knowledge which is greater than all other. Already it has the blessings of railway and steam communication, thus rendering traffic easy to all;* it has its Atlantic telegraph, thereby bringing into subjection, to some extent, time. There are five principal newspapers published in the Colony, the *Royal Gazette*, the *Colonist*, the *Berbice Gazette*, the *Argosy*, and the *Demerara Daily Chronicle* (since Nov., 1881). The *Royal Gazette* is a tri-weekly paper, the *Argosy* a weekly issue, and the *Colonist* and *Demerara Daily Chronicle* daily (Sundays excepted, though the latter paper is pre-dated) publications. The *Official Gazette* is issued by the Government on Wednesdays and Saturdays. Several years ago there were some other papers published in the Colony, but they have long ceased to exist; their names—the *British Guyana Times*, the *Creole*, the *Liberator*, the *Marabunta*, the *Watchman*, the *Monthly Messenger*, the *Working Man*, the

* The Demerara Railway Company have a line reaching as far as Mahaica, a distance of about thirty miles from Georgetown, along the east sea-coast. The contemplated or proposed extension of it as far as Berbice, after several discussions in the Court of Policy and Combined Court (the local parliament), has not as yet been carried out.

Demerara Times, and the *Weekly Penny*. There is also a weekly paper published in Georgetown in the Portuguese language for the benefit of the Portuguese residents or colonists. Our museum, though not very large and extensive, as some of the museums are in England, yet is quite large enough at present for this rising Colony. The different annual exhibitions held in the Colony fully prove that British Guyana is a rising colony. California, Australia, and India have all risen, and so will British Guyana. California was once almost a waste; but thousands of persons rushed to it from all parts of the world, and now it is one of the largest cereal-producing countries on the face of the earth. People went to Australia in search of gold, and thousands are now making fortunes, or at least handsome competencies, as shepherds and agriculturists. And people flocked to India, and are now amassing wealth from sources that twenty years ago were never dreamt of even in that highly-favoured land. The much-dreaded Africa now holds forth inducements to mankind at large to come to her, and obtain from her hands the tempting diamonds. She will rise to eminence yet, and so will this Colony. A brilliant future is in store for British Guyana: it is destined to be prominent among the colonies, the El Dorado, or *The Gilded*, of Sir Walter Raleigh, the land of glories and enchantments, the fairy land of the *Arabian Nights' Entertainments*, the happy home of the immigrant, and the pride of its sons.

17. All that I have said so far is the bright side of the picture. I have now one more picture to show, which is of a dark or gloomy aspect or kind. People in the Colony are wont to pride themselves upon their prosperity, and are apt to say that in no colony and in no country is money more easily made than here, and poverty less known. There may be truth in this assertion as to the art or secret of making money or a fortune, and retiring from the busy scene of life in some comfortable corner in England, but what is the state of the people? This fact is altogether lost sight of by the money-makers or wealth-seekers. Vice and misery, crime and want are apparent and sadly conspicuous around us. Look at the streets of the city of Georgetown, where vice daily flaunts

itself more unblushingly than in the worst of English seaport towns; examine the hovels where human beings are huddled together like swine, and purity of life is forgotten or never known; dive into the alleys, lanes, yards, and the byeways, and observe the young children growing up in ignorance and vice, forgetful alike of the laws of God and man. Another great and sore evil in the Colony is the preponderance of illegitimate* offspring, which gives local political economists the greatest concern, and which they hitherto have been unable to deal with. The great majority of the illegitimate births are amongst the black population, and the utter indifference shown by the average black woman to her child is nothing short of appalling. The children are systematically neglected, and often are subjected to shocking physical cruelty. One cannot but be struck with awe to witness the deplorable situation in which juveniles are placed from time to time by being dragged before the magistrates for petty larcenies, &c., &c. These ragged and uneducated boys and girls, and men and women too, prowl about the city to the annoyance of the inhabitants, getting more and more debased in their morals, and ultimately terminating in incurable criminals, fit subjects only for a prison. In some parts of the Colony, where the number of missionaries is limited, and where the missionaries are not able to reach the people to instruct them, there is evidently a gradual retrogression to the habits of savage life, seen and remarked on by the public officers who visit the districts on duty.

18. Ten years ago a certain gentleman residing in the county of Berbice, speaking of the Creoles of the Berbice

* The expression "illegitimate children" in British Guyana is, by some curious official arrangement, unjustly or illegally applied to the children of Indian Coolie parents, although they are regularly married according to their idea of the ceremony. Unless the Indian or Chinese Coolies are married by a magistrate of the district, or the head of the Immigration Department in Georgetown, or his deputy in the different districts of the Colony, their children or offspring are not considered lawful, or born in wedlock, though the parents of the children might be married by a Christian minister, or according to the custom of their country by one of the Pujaries, or heathen priests.

River, called the "Dark District," wrote as follows in the *Creole* :—

"The Creoles of the Berbice River, or their parents, belonged to Dutch settlers. They still speak the Dutch language. If you talk to them on any matter of common life, you must have an interpreter, or you must repeat in several forms what you wish to tell them, before they understand you. Will Sunday preaching in English reach these people? Preaching in a language understood by the hearers is a powerful instrument for good; but who ever before dreamt of preaching in an unknown tongue, as a means of civilization? We blame the Roman Catholic Church for praying in an unknown tongue, though in their books the people have a translation of the prayers. But to these people both prayers and sermons are in an unknown tongue. We know that this was strongly felt by an L. M. clergyman in this very district [the dark river district of Berbice]. We heard him utter the sentence in as simple language as possible. A leader repeated it in talkee-talkee Dutch. The congregation then repeated it after the leader to show that they caught the idea. This was a tedious process, but the hearers carried something home with them to think of afterwards. When the British Government took over the Cape of Good Hope, the Dutch Reformed Church was kept up, but the parishes as they became vacant were filled with Scotch ministers and Scotch schoolmasters. The salaries began on their appointment in Scotland. But they had to spend a year in Holland to learn the Dutch language. British Guyana, with the exception of the small space between the Devil's Creek and the Courantines, was a Dutch Colony, and Surinam an English one. During the French war they changed hands, and at the peace of 1814 each party retained what they possessed. Demerara and Essequibo in 1826, and Berbice in 1836, were divided into parishes, and English and Scotch ministers appointed to them. Their preaching, however well suited to their own countrymen, seldom reached the understanding of the Creoles. Both ministers and schoolmasters, particularly those located on the river districts, ought to have had some such special training, similar to that provided by the Cape of Good Hope, to prepare them for their work. But they had none, and this is one cause of the state of the Berbice River now [namely, the gradual retrogression to the habits of savage life witnessed by the public officers who visit the district on duty]. Another cause is to be found in the gradual removal of the means of civilization—viz., depriving the inhabitants on both sides of the river of easy access to each other, and of intercourse with the estates and the town, the centres then, as now, of civilization, by shutting up the roads [the roads have since been opened], the gradual removal of both the resident clergy, with State-paid and voluntary Roman Catholic, English, Scotch, and London missionaries. One of each once 'laboured' in this district; now there is not one."

What a fine opening for missionary operations in Berbice! Even in much enlightened British Guyana there are still many dark places which are full of the habitations of cruelty, wretchedness, and misery; especially in the distant villages, wood-cutting establishments, &c., in the river districts of the three counties, is this the case. On the estates, too, within easy distance from towns, there are dark places of cruelty. The cry from every direction falls on the ears of the Christian missionary, "Come over and help us!" "No man careth for my soul!" Is it not our solemn duty to instruct and do them good?

CHAPTER II.

A PEEP INTO THE PAST, WHEN GUYANA WAS FIRST MADE KNOWN TO THE EUROPEANS, AND WHAT FORTUNE THEY SUCCESSIVELY HAVE HAD.

1. Our knowledge of Guyana as a British Colony, strictly speaking, commences from the time it was taken possession of by the English, in the war between England and France, when Holland was overrun by the French, and incorporated in the French empire. But Guyana as a vast, extensive Colony—now divided into Venezuelan Guyana, British Guyana, Dutch Guyana, or Surinaam, French Guyana, more commonly known as Cayenne, and Brazilian Guyana—was known to the European nations at a much earlier period. If all the printed and manuscript documents in the Government Secretary's office could be searched and properly arranged, we should have a most interesting volume of the history of the Colony we now occupy. From the Sloane Collection of MSS., exceedingly rare and very curious, published in the *Royal Gazette* of July 24, 1879, I extract the following particulars, which will greatly interest my reader, and give him a correct idea of the different settlements or colonies formed in Guyana. The anonymous writer says:—

2. "The first Christian that ever attempted to set footing on Guiana, to the southward of Oranoque, was Pedro de Acosta, a Spaniard, with two small corvils, 300 men, anno 1530, settled in Parema, was drove thence by the Indians the same year, many slain, and their goods and chattles became a booty to the Careebs.

3. "The second colony was settled at Cayan by Gasper de Sotelle, being 126 families, from Spain, anno 1568, but were expelled by the Careebs and Paracoates, anno 1573.

4. "The third settlement was by three ships from France, at

Wiapoca, anno 1607, and being 400 men, began to plant tobacco, and to think themselves secure, and too frankly to converse with the natives; they were all cut off, anno 1609, except a few mariners.

5. "The fourth colony was of 160 families from France, landed at Cayan, and fortified themselves, anno 1613. The Paracoates began to offer them friendship; they were in a few months many destroyed, and the rest forced to quit the place and return to France.

6. "The fifth colony consisted of 280 Zealanders, with two small ships, landed their men at Cayan, anno 1615, but could not bring the natives to a trade; were often gauled by the Indians, and were at length forced to quit their post. Returned to Zealand the same year.

7. "The sixth colony was undertaken by one Captain Gromweagle, a Dutchman, that had served the Spaniard in Oranoque, but understanding a company of merchants of Zealand had before undertaken a voyage to Guiana, and attempted a settlement there, he deserted the Spanish service, and tendered himself to his own country, which was accepted, and he dispatched from Zealand, anno 1616, with two ships and a galliot, and was the first man that took firm footing on Guiana by the good likeing of the natives, whose humours the gentleman perfectly understood. He erected a forte on a small island thirty leagues up the river Dissekeeb, which looked into two great branches of that famous river. All his time the Colony flourished; he managed a great trade with the Spaniards by the Indians with great secrecy; he was a great friend of all new colonies of Christians of what nation soever, and Barbados oweth its first assistance, both for food and trade, to this man's special kindness, anno 1627, at which time they were in a miserable condition; he dyed, anno 1664, and in the 83rd year of his age, a wealthy man, having been Governor of that Colonie forty-eight years.* In this

* "In the year 1624, a ship of Sir William Curteen, a merchant of London, in her voyage from Brazils, put into the road since called Austin, and after a short stay sailed from thence, visiting all the bays on the west and southern parts of the island, and finding the land to promise much of the nature of Brazils, and adorned with curious prospects, rather than mountains, and stored with wild hogs, judged it worth especial notice: particularly one Thomas Powell, then in the same ship, who after his arrival in England presented his observations to the then Earl of Pembroke, a great

Colonie the authour had the good fortune to meet with some ingenious observations of the former Governor, of what had

---

lover of plantations. Thereupon, the Earl, by permission of King James, prepared a ship with a hundred and sixty passengers, who left England the 26th of January, anno 1625, and arrived in Barbados, May the 2nd, at which time Powell entered upon and took possession of the island in His Majesty's name, for the use of the said Earl of Pembroke. After which the said Captain Thomas Powell remained Governor in the island, and having understood the Dutch had a plantation in the River Dissekeeb on the main of Guiana, whose Governor, one Gromweagle, he was particularly known to, despatched his son Thomas Powell, to desire Captain Gromweagle to send him such things as were proper to plant for food and for trade. The gentleman willing to gratify an old friend (for Powell and Gromweagle had been comrades in the King of Spain's service in the West Indies) persuaded a family of Arawacoes, consisting of forty persons, to attend Powell to Barbados, to learn the English to plant, and to carry with them cassava, yams, Indian corn, and other pulses, plantains, bananas, oranges, lemons, limes, the pine-apple, melons, &c., and, for to produce a trade, they carried over tobacco, cotton, and annatta, a rich dye (a commodity the English never yet know how to manage). To all which Barbados was naturally a stranger. The Indians fell to planting soon after their arrival at Barbados, and all things grew well, and came to great perfection, agreeing with the soil and clime, and they soon had all things necessary for life.

"Anno 1628, Captain Hawley was sent in the ship *Carlisle*, to visit and supervise the Earl of Carlisle's affairs in those parts, who invited Captain Powell and his secretary aboard, and there clapt them into irons, and they were despatched for England, and Captain Hawley left one Wheatley, and soon after him one Woolverston. The Indians, not liking these several changes, pressed their contract, made between them and Mr. Powell at Dissekeeb, which Captain Gromweagle had undertaken should be performed, viz., that at the expiration of two years, if they did not like the country, or should, upon any other occasion, desire to go back to Dissekeeb, they should be transported with their reward, which was to be fifty pounds sterling in axes, bills, hoes, knives, looking-glasses, and beades; but instead of performing the agreement with the poor Indians the then Governor and Council made slaves of them, separating the husbands and wives of some, parents and children of others, one from another. Anno 1631, one of them getting on board a Dutch ship, got passage for Dissekeeb, which proved of all consequence to Captain Gromweagle, who had like to have lost his Colonie for that cause only, and was forced to marry a woman of the Careebee nation, to balance the power of the Arawacoes, and afterwards was at the charge of great presents, to make up the business between the Dutch and the Arawacoes nation. It hath been observed that a curse attended some of those persons concerned in that horrid breach of faith."

been transacted in Guiana in his time, to whom the world is obliged for many particulars of this story.

8. "The seventh was a small factory at Berbishees, about the year 1624, is now a strong garrison, and belongs to two merchants of Flushing, Mynheer Van Ree, and Mynheer Van Pear, a place that abounds with excellent horses and cattle, and is a good factory for annatta, dye, and drugs.

9. "Sir Walter Raleigh's first voyage, 1598, and his last unfortunate voyage, 1618, and the business of Mr. Harcourt at Wiapoca, and being written with their own pen, I shall say nothing of them, only that if Sir Walter Raleigh had lived, he would have left matter for a grateful story; he left so good and so great a name behind him with the native Indians in those parts, that the English have often been obliged to remember with honor.

10. "The eighth colony was a ship and a barque from France, which landed their people at Meriwina, anno 1625. The next vessel that came could hear no news of their colony, and were, without all doubt, destroyed by the natives.

11. "The ninth colony was three ships from Rochell, anno 1626, with 534 men, some women and children; they settled at Suramaco, lived three years in peace, but sickness falling amongst them, and the Indians being troublesome, (those few that were left) deserted the colony and went to St. Christopher.

12. "The tenth colony was two ships and a small vessel from France, anno 1639, with 370 men settled at Suramaco, and the year after came to them from France many families. They lived peaceably until the year 1642, at which time they had great supplies of men, ammunition, and provisions from France, grew careless, spread themselves to Surinam and Curanteen, had difference with the Indians, and were all cut off in one day.

13. "The eleventh colony was one Mr. Marshall with 300 families of English employed by the Earl of Warwick, &c., who settled Suranam, Suramaca, and Curanteen, anno 1643, lived peaceably until the year 1645, at which time they espoused the quarrel of the French and were cut off by the natives.

14. "The twelfth colony was of Dutch settled by the Zealanders in the rivers Borowma, Wacopon, and Moroca, having been drawn of from Tobago, anno 1650, and the year following a great colony of Dutch and Jews drawn off from

Brazil, by the Portuguese settled there, and being experienced planters, that soon grew a flourishing colony.

15. "The thirteenth colony was of French at Suramaco and at Cayan, where the greatest part were cut off by the Careebs and Sacpoyes, anno 1642.

16. "The fourteenth colony was at Surinam, anno 1650; about 300 people of the English nation from the Island of Barbados under the command of one Lieut.-Colonel Anthony Rowse, a gentleman of great gallantry and prudence, and of long experience in the West Indies; his making a firm peace with the Indians soon after his landing, and reviving the name of Sir Walter Raleigh, gave the English firm footing in those parts, and it soon became a hopeful colony.

17. "These people had the accommodation of a ship from Francis Lord Willoughby of Parham (then at the Barbados), and the loan of a parcel of Indian trade; the Lord Willoughby settled a plantation amongst them at Suranam, another at Comonina, upon which he disburst at least 26,000 pounds.

18. "Anno 1654, Lieutenant-Col. Rowse having established this Colony left it in a flourishing condition, and in perfect peace with the Indians, and one Major William Byam was chosen Governor, a judicious gentleman, and in that condition it stood, daily increasing until the year 1660, at which time his Majesty being happily restored to his just rights, Francis Lord Willoughby (amongst other pretences in the West Indies) laid claims to Suranam by virtue of a compact with the first settlers, and in consideration of his great disbursements in those parts, and although there was no difference on that point between the inhabitants and his Lordship, it passed in favour of his Lordship and Lawrence Hide, Esq., second son to the Earl of Clarendon, as lord proprietors of that province, under the appellation of Willoughby Land. But Major Byam was continued Deputy-Governor to the proprietors, and was commissionated Lieutenant-General of Guiana.

19. "Anno 1665, the Lord Willoughby sailed from Barbados to Suranam, and upon his lordship's arrival a contagious sickness began at the town called Tararica, and spread itself all over the Colony, swept away many people, and during his stay at Surinam he had like to have been murdered by one Mr. Allen, who was of opinion his lordship coveted his estates. Mr. Allen was charged with blasphemy before his Lordship arrived in those parts, but cleared of the fact, yet (in his

Lordship's sense) held strange opinions, as that there could be no subject held lord proprietors, because it both clipt the wings of monarchy, and infringed the liberty of the subject. Mr. Allen cut off two of the Lord Willoughby's fingers, and wounded him in the head, expecting at the same stroke to have slain him, and afterward poisoned himself; several people this year left Suranam, strange jealousies having possessed them, which broke out into great discontents which his Lordship endeavoured to satisfy them in, by a kind message sent to the Colony by one Captain John Parker, which proved effectual.

20. "The same year, in the month of October, the author having been commissionated Commander-in-chief of a small fleet and a regiment of soldiers, for the attack of the Island Tobago, and several other settlements in the hands of the Netherlanders in Guiana, as Moroco, Wacopou, Bowroome, and Dissekeeb, and having touched at Tobago, in less than six months had the good fortune to be in possession of those countries, and left them garrisoned for his majesty of Great Britain, and sailed thence for Barbados, where meeting with the news of the eruption of war between the two crowns of England and France, endeavoured to persuade Francis Lord Willoughby to reduce those several small garrisons into one stronghold, and offered that was the way to make good our posts in those parts, having to do with two potent enemies, but his Lordship, that was his majesty's captain-general in those parts, was of another opinion, and before he embarked on the unfortunate voyage for the reducing of St. Christopher's, in which design he perished by a hurricane, the wages he had prescribed for supplies to the forementioned garrisons proved ineffectual; and they were lost the year following to the Dutch after they had endured great misery in a long siege by the French.

21. "In the month of March, 1665, Lieutenant-General Byam, in pursuance of an order from Francis Lord Willoughby, commissionated one Captain Peter Wrath (a Kentish gentleman) with a party of men and vessels, to attack the Dutch colony of Aprowaco, which was prosecuted with success. In August following, Captain William Powell, from Suranam, took the French colony of Sinamare, sacked the place, and brought them away prisoners. This year the English could boast of the possession of all that part of Guiana abutting on the Atlantic Ocean, from Cayan on the south-east, to Oronoque on the north-west (except a small colony in the river

Berbishees), which is not less than six hundred English miles.

22. "In February, 1666, one Captain Abraham Crynseus arrived at Suranam, with a fleet of seven sail from Zealand, where the colony for want of supplies, and being discontented, and having been greatly afflicted with sharp sickness, and despairing of any relief, surrendered themselves to the High Puissant States of Zealand, upon the articles heretofore inserted in Wm. Byam's narrative of Guiana.

23. "Anno 1667. In the month of April, Captain Crynseus sailed from Suranam, for the taking in of the Island Tobago, leaving Captain Ram, commander of his land force and Governor for the Lords of Zealand, in Suranam.

24. "In August next, Henry Willoughby, Esq., Commander-in-Chief, accompanied with Sir John Harman, their land force one regiment of foot, their fleet consisted of nine sail, departed from Barbados, for the attack of the Island Cayan, under the command of Monsieur de Leisler, Governor there for the French King. In September following they arrived there; and the place soon became a subject of their mercy, they sacked the place, carried away some of the people prisoners, but left the greater part, seized of the island, but little to defend themselves with against the natives, as the French have complained since.

25. "From thence in October they sailed to Suranam, a river and country seventy leagues north-west from Cayan, laid close siege to the fort by sea and land, and after a sharp encounter (both sides sustaining losses) Captain Ram, Governor for the State of Holland, was forced to surrender to the said Henry Willoughby, Esq., who in a few days left the Colony, carrying Captain Ram and his soldiers prisoners to Barbados, and leaving the foot and Colony under the command of one Colonel Barry.

26. "In January, Henry Willoughby returned from Barbados to Suranam, and there destroyed some plantations, and removed a great part of the Colony to the Island of St. Jago, or Antigua, put Colonel Barry by his government, and commissionated in his stead one Serjeant-major James Banister, an inhabitant of the place.

27. "Between the first re-taking of this Colony from the States of Zealand, and this month of January, the Lord of Zealand had despatched to Suranam divers ships to ascertain their interest, but were denied possession, at which the State

agents made many protestations, and sent home to Zealand many complaints which occasioned the Lords Ambassadors of the Netherlands, then in England, to make their addresses to His Majesty for reparation, which, after due proof of the fact, His Majesty consented to; and likewise despatched a second order for the delivery of the said province, to which order William Lord Willoughby yielded obedience, and Captain Abraham Creynseus, in the right of his masters, the Lords of Zealand, was put in full possession of all the province, called Willoughby Land, the 30th April, 1668.

28. "Thus having given an account of all such of the English, Spanish, French or Dutch nations, as have planted or attempted to plant colonies on Guiana, from the year 1530 to the year 1668, I shall now only mention those brave Spaniards, that from the first discoveries of the West Indies, to the year 1647, some with great force, others with few followers, have attempted the discovery of the many provinces in the main of Guiana; as well up the great river Amazons as from the Atlantic Ocean, and from the Orinoque, most of which perished in their designs, and have left little behind them, saving the remembrance of their brave undertakings; I find them mentioned in several authors of divers nations, and many are carefully collected by Mr. Hakluyt, viz.:—(1) Diego Deordas, (2) Juan Cortez, (3) Jasper de Sylva, (4) Juan Gosales, (5) Phillip Duverore, (6) Pedro d'Lympas, (7) Jeronimo d'Ortel, (8) Ximenes, (9) Pedro d'Orsua, (10) Father Jala, (11) Hernandez Diserpa, (12) Diego d'Vorgas, (13) Cacerez, (14) Alonzo d'Herera, (15) Antonio Sedenno, (16) Augustine Delgado, (17) Diego d'Lozada, (18) Riveso, (19) Ped. d'Orsua, jun., (20) Montiseno, (21) Philip d'Fonta, (22) Juan d'Palma.

"NUMBERS AND THE HABITATIONS OF THE NATIVES.

29. "The most numerous nation of Indians in Guiana are the Careebs, and these are inhabited in Aricare about six thousand Careeb families. In Wiapoca, Macorea, and Abrewaco, eleven thousand Careeb families.

30. "In the river Marrawina, about eight hundred Careeb families. And up the same river, and towards the head of Sinnamar lives about 1,400 Paricoates, the great masters of poison in America; they pretend to poison fountains, are a people very formal, marry ever with their own nation, have little commerce but for their poison, which they sell to other

nations. The Careebs have some judgment in the art of poisoning their arrows, and are great masters in the cure, but short of these people.

31. "In Suranam, Commowina, Suramaco, Copenham, and Curranteen are about 5,000 Careeb families, and there lives in Suramaco and the upper parts of Suranam, about 1,400 Turroomaes, and up Curranteen about 1,200 Sapoyes.

32. "From the west side of Curranteen to Wina, there live about eight thousand families of Arawacoes, the best humoured Indians of America, being both very just and generous-minded people; and in little villages by the sea-side lives about four hundred families of Warooes; in Maroca and Wina, and in the islands of Oranoque river, and near the mouth of that river, lives about five thousand families of Warooes, the only shipwrights of those parts (for all the great Periagoos are made by them, they make their vessels, their cordage, sails, hammocks, bread, and drink, all of one tree; they likewise make great Periagoos of another wood called white wood, they differ from all other Indians in life and manners, have nothing for delight, whilst all other Indians are great lovers of fine gardens, drinking, dancing, and divers other pleasures), are a people bloody and treacherous, and not to be conversed with, and, therefore, I advise all people that sail into those parts to discourse with the Warooes nation with their arms in their hands.

33. "From Wina to the utmost part of Awarabish, on the west side of Oranoque, and the rivers Oranoque, Poraema, and Amacora, are about twenty thousand Careeb families. The Occowyes, Shawhorens, and Semicorals, are great powerful nations, that live in the uplands of Guiana, either under the line or in south latitude, and there hath none so conversant with them as to make a judgment of them as to their numbers.

34. "But it is most certain they are settled in a most fertile country, and cover a vast tract of land, beginning at the mountains of the sun on the west and north, and extending themselves to Rio-Negroe, five hundred miles south and east, a famous river that enters itself into the great Amazon. They have a constant war with some nations on the islands in the Amazons, and are often beaten by the wily Carcets, who often, when they are engaged abroad, visit their towns to their no small prejudice. And thus much of the natives."

CHAPTER III.

A PASSING GLIMPSE AT THE ANCESTORS OF THE MODERN COLONISTS IN OLDEN TIMES, SEVENTY-FIVE YEARS AGO, OR IN 1806.

1. There are very, very few persons indeed, nowadays, who know anything at all about the burning questions, the occupations, the amusements of the brave old Colonists—ancestors of modern Colonists—rough-and-ready, hard-drinking old gentlemen, who, over their claret and Madeira, read with eager interest the latest despatches containing the exploits of the British fleet, which at that date was surrounding itself with a halo of glory. To them, and others, whether in British Guyana, or England, or Holland, the reproduction of the following extracts from newspapers, published in the early days of the Colony, may not be uninteresting.

2. The Colony was under the charge of a military governor, owing to the death of Governor Beaujon, whose widow was advertising that claims against her late husband should be sent to her house in Cumingsburg. In the course of the year the new man arrived, and we read that—

"It appears that a very elegant entertainment was given to Governor Bentinck at the Freemasons' Tavern, by the merchants and planters of this Colony, resident in London, previous to His Excellency's leaving that capital."

3. The Governor of these Colonies did not always have an easy time of it, for the Colonists were not afraid to air their grievances, and carry them to the foot of the throne. In the neighbouring Colony of Berbice, in his address to the Court of Policy and Criminal Justice, we find His Excellency Governor Van Imbyze Van Batenburg dealing with a memorial to Viscount Castlereagh, from the planters and other inhabi-

tants of Berbice, in which the Governor is charged with unconstitutional proceedings, with chicanery, with countenancing extortion by public officers, &c., &c., and this is the language which he employed in referring to one of the petitioners:—

"Whilst I was in London I had very little connection with that man (Baillie); his ridiculous pride and pretensions made me not very desirous of seeing him often. The only reason that I can give for his joining Mr. Blair in the diatribe is his natural propensity to slander and crime; of which the clearest proof was brought before the public in a late prosecution entered against him in London, for the publication of a libel, wherein he is called by the Solicitor-General a malignant, malevolent, black-blooded libeller."

4. Not much mealy-mouthedness about Governor Batenburg, who it is evident used language to express his thoughts, not to conceal them. A lordly establishment this fine old gentleman must have kept up, judging from a list of his effects, which, later in the year, I see advertised for sale. It is amusing to compare the modest equipages of modern governors with the following catalogue:—

"An excellent coach, chariot, curricle, phaeton, cataran, chaise, landau, with suitable harness, and eight excellent carriage and riding horses. Also, a quantity of old Madeira, claret, &c., and two pipes, three hogsheads, and four quarter-casks London particular Madeira."

5. The freedom and force of the personal invective used by Governor Batenburg characterize the bulk of the controversies of the age. What does my reader think of the following "spirited" correspondence, which is by no means peculiar to these two writers?—

"*To Mr. George Handasyde.*

"Sir,—I find clearly that you are a nasty, dirty fellow, a liar as well as a drunken blackguard. I sincerely wish I had never concerned with such a poltroon as you are; your news to Mr. Perkins to-day I have just heard of.

"I am, Sir,

"J. M. HENRY."

Reply.

"Sir,—In answer to your damn'd nasty, lousy note, I announce with all the appellations you give me to yourself. I sincerely wish I had never seen such a person of your description.

"GEO. HANDASYDE."

Answer.

"You dirty puppy, let me not hear from you again, until it is to settle our accounts (you lying dog).

"J. M. HENRY."

6. Some men nowadays *think* in language similar to the above, and occasionally express it in their verbal communications with each other, but the style may be considered as totally lost to newspaper correspondence. The freedom of expression, however, which was permitted (and practised) by Governors and others in personal controversies, was denied the press in dealing with matters in any way concerning Government. The editor of the papers already referred to ventured on the following apparently offensive paragraph:—

"Van Braam, Esq., formerly captain in the Dutch navy, is appointed grave-digger to this Colony. From the number of applicants which, we understand, there were for this situation it would seem that the 'loaves and fishes' are no less an object of desire here than in Europe."

Nothing much in this, my reader will say, but this is what followed its publication:—

"I am directed by the Governor to inform you that His Excellency has seen with much displeasure some illiberal and ill-natured reflections and paragraphs which have lately appeared in your weekly papers. As they can have no other tendency than by exciting irritation and animosity amongst the inhabitants to disturb the tranquillity of the Colony, His Excellency expects you will conduct your publication with more propriety in future, and thereby prevent the necessity of a more severe correction. You are required to publish this Reprimand in your next paper.

"C. T. TINNE,

"Govt. Secretary.

"*King's House, Stabroek.*"

Of course the editor had to exercise a discreet silence, for it would have been awkward to have had the handle of the press removed. As it was, with the handle in working order, it was a work of no ordinary labour to get the paper published at four o'clock on Saturday afternoon, and occasionally there was a few minutes' delay. The publisher was more particular to a minute than certain newspaper publishers are nowadays, and he was very scrupulous, too, about his own rights and privileges on certain occasions. He gives notice that during Easter Eve he will not deliver papers after six o'clock. Concerning the postal arrangements we learn that—

"A new regulation has been made at the Post-office respecting the conveyance of letters, &c., to and from Berbice. The post will in future depart every Sunday and Thursday morning, and return every Tuesday and Saturday evening."

7. There was evidently no post along the East Coast, for the enterprising publisher announces the establishment of an "express boy," who will start at five o'clock in the afternoon, reach Mahaica at eight o'clock on Sunday morning, and Mahaicony at twelve the same day.

The editor was ever on the look out for the arrival of the English news, and occasionally he gets impatient, as witness—

"What is become of the Mail? God in heaven only knows; it has not yet arrived here."

The Mail, however, always came in sooner or later, and then the paper teemed with news of battle, of brave deeds, of brave men. Take a few paragraphs and compare them with the modern "extracts from our English files to hand by the Mail":—

"By the welcome arrival of both the January Mails on Wednesday last (March 12th), we have been put in possession of much important news. From Barbados we have also learned the destruction of the French Squadron in the West Indies by Admiral Duckworth—an event which was before considered as certain—and the capture of the Cape of Good Hope by General Baird and Sir Home Popham.

"Immense preparations are making in London for the funeral of Lord Nelson. His Royal Highness the Prince of Wales is to be the chief mourner, if the court etiquette will permit it, and the members of both Houses of Parliament are to attend.

"The inhabitants of Barbados have entered into a subscription with great zeal, for the erection of a statue in bronze to the memory of Lord Nelson in some conspicuous part of Bridgetown. Lord Seaforth has given £100.

"The Marquis Cornwallis it appears died in India soon after his arrival there. Thus in the short space of a few months has Britain been robbed of three of her choicest ornaments, a *Nelson*, a *Pitt*, a *Cornwallis*."

8. Of Lord Nelson it was impossible for the press to speak too highly. The news of his death had cast a gloom over the British empire, and every one was striving more than his neighbour to pay tribute, in prose or verse, to the memory of the illustrious hero. The editor was not behind his contemporaries, as may be supposed, he was too loyal for that. He favours his readers with a sketch of Lord Nelson's life, from which we take the following extract:—

"The life of Sir Horatio Nelson was providentially saved by Lieutenant Nisbet, his son-in-law, on this disastrous night. The Admiral received his wound soon after the detachment had landed, and while they were pressing on with the usual ardour of British seamen. The shock caused him to fall to the ground, while, for some minutes, he was left to himself, until Lieutenant Nisbet, missing him, had the presence of mind to return: when, after some search in the dark, he at length found his brave father-in-law, weltering in his blood on the ground, with his arm shattered and himself apparently lifeless. Lieutenant Nisbet immediately applied his neck-handkerchief as a torniquet to the Admiral's arm, carried him on his back to the beach, and, with the assistance of some sailors, conveyed him into one of the boats, and put off to the *Theseus*, with a tremendous though ill-directed fire from the enemy's battery.

At ten o'clock the same night the Admiral's arm was amputated on board, immediately after which he began his official letter, and finished it at eleven.

"By some mistake in taking up the arteries when the painful operation of amputating the arm was performed, the Rear-Admiral afterwards suffered so much that he was obliged to go to England for advice."

9. Returning to the news brought by the Mail, which I must explain always touched at Barbados, that being the main rendezvous in the West Indies for mercantile fleets, I read as follows:—

"We are concerned to learn that the ship *George*, which sailed from this port for London on the 18th of March, was taken on the 1st April close under St. Lucia by a schooner of one gun and twenty-nine men, and carried into Martinique. The *George* mounted eighteen guns, and is stated in the account which has reached to have had thirty-two men, who, when landed at Martinique, were hooted at with much indignation for their non-resistance to so insignificant a force.

"The *Fly*, schooner of Berbice, was taken by a French privateer, but afterwards retaken by a British man-of-war, and carried to Barbados, much damaged.

"Mr. Boulton, the scientific and venerable proprietor of Soho, Birmingham, whose public exertions have so uniformly been distinguished by a patriotism the best directed, has solicited the permission of Government that he might be allowed to strike a medal, at his own expense, in commemoration of the brilliant victory off Cape Trafalgar, and to present one to every seaman who served that day on board the English fleet. The permission was immediately granted.

"The trial of Colonel Picton, late Governor of Trinidad, for an arbitrary stretch of power with respect to Louisa Cameron, one of His Majesty's subjects in that island, came on in the court of King's Bench, on the 24th of February, when, after a long hearing, the Governor was found guilty."

The offence for which the Governor of Trinidad was placed on trial was the cruel and revolting treatment of a girl of thirteen years, who had been caught stealing. Dealing with her after a fashion which used to obtain in the army towards soldiers given to peculation, the girl was strung up by the wrists with nothing for her feet to rest on but a spike of wood.

The counsel for the prosecution said the practice in the army was called picketing, but since it had been adapted to women it ought to be called after the brave adapter—Pictoning.

10. Compared with the political and the military and naval news, mercantile affairs received very meagre attention, and only occasionally were they deemed worthy of notice except in a general way. The report from the London market is condensed into a couple of lines, stating that the average price of muscovado in June was 39s. per cwt. The following paragraph, containing what the editor describes as "interesting mercantile information," owes its importance chiefly to its political significance :—

"Government have this day come to the resolution of allowing, in all our West India Islands, a bounty of two shillings sterling per quintal upon fish of every description which may be imported in good condition from the British settlements in North America and Newfoundland; the same to be paid in the Islands upon delivery. The bounty to commence the first June next, and to continue for twelve months."

11. During these troublous times when the air was busy with the sound of cannon and the clash of cutlass, it was not to be supposed that the Colony was spending the time in drowsy peace unaffected by the general turmoil. The fighting was at the door. Privateers came prying into the harbour, and often sailed away with valuable vessels and cargoes. His Majesty kept war vessels cruising along the coasts, but they could not be everywhere at once, and occasionally in their endeavours to seize the enemy they made awkward mistakes, such as this :—

"Captain Cameron, of Her Majesty's ship *Nimrod*, fell in with the *William*, bound for Berbice, a few days ago, which (not knowing what she was) he chased for five hours, during which the *William* threw her letters overboard, and both ships ran aground before the mistake was discovered."

12. The shipping in the harbour in those days seems to have been equally as numerous as it is now; and, regularly, every month a large convoy of square-rigs cleared for various

ports of the United Kingdom, under charge of a man-of-war, which protected the fleet until it reached the main rendezvous in one of the West India Islands, where vessels from the West Indies generally assembled, and started on the home passage together, under the charge of two or three of His Majesty's fierce war dogs. In connection with local shipping we read that—

"A beacon is about to be erected on the East Coast of this Colony, the expenses of which are to be defrayed by a duty of six stivers per ton on every merchant vessel arriving here after the 1st of December next. And further, every such merchant vessel which shall be of more than 100 tons burthen, and coming from the mother country, must bring five tons of gravel ballast for each fifty tons of their burthen; in default of which they are to pay, beside the above-mentioned rate, a sum of five guilders for every ton of such ballast which they may be deficient in."

13. So far as I can gather, Essequibo by this time had no shipping of its own, and was fast losing its individuality in its rapidly developing neighbour. Its inhabitants were not averse to the amalgamation, judging from the following:—

"A petition has been presented to His Excellency the Lieutenant-Governor, signed by all but two of the inhabitants from Conazeeke Creek, Essequebo, to the District, praying to be taken under the jurisdiction of Demerary, which we understand has been granted."

14. In those days, as in our own, there were dissensions in high militia places, as we learn from the following memorandum:—

"Major Arthur Blair, Commandant of the Demerara Cavalry, having declared to His Excellency the Governor that he would not, in all points, obey the order of the Lieutenant-Colonel Commandant of all Colonial Corps, although this was specified in the commission given him by the Governor, His Excellency cannot permit so palpable a disobedience of orders, and therefore feels himself under the necessity of superseding Major A. Blair in his rank and command of the Demerara Cavalry.

"The Governor regrets exceeding that such a measure,

however unavoidable, should be required for the good of the service."

Major Blair seems to have been a general favourite with his officers and men, and immediately on the publication of the above notice, there was a meeting of the Corps held at "New Union Coffee House," to discuss the matter of his supercession, at which the gentlemen present resolved to send in their resignations rather than serve without their major, and, at the same time, they subscribed one hundred guineas to buy him a sword.

15. The striking characteristic in these people of the old days was their earnestness in doing whatever they undertook to do. They served in the Militia, not as we do nowadays for amusement or idle occupation, but expecting and eager for active duty. They were as earnest, too, in their modes of enjoyment. A fête or gala day was duly prepared for, and its hours used to the best advantage. Let us instance:—

"Wednesday last being the anniversary of His Majesty's birth, was observed here with all possible demonstrations of respect. The Militia, under the command of Major Macrae, marched to the Fort, notwithstanding the unfavourable state of the ground from so much previous rain, and fired three vollies in a manner that did them credit.

"A. Fleischman, Esq., attorney at law, embraced the opportunity of offering his acknowledgments to those friends who so kindly attended and assisted him during his illness, by giving a grand dinner, ball, and supper. Nearly eighty persons, of both sexes, attended. Mr. Fleischman, who has been fourteen years in this Colony, was further honoured with the company of the Hon. A. Meertens and his Lady."

Where shall we find A. Fleischman's representative in the present day, either in the legal or in any other circle?

16. The patriotism of these old heroes was particularly observable in their mode of observing the days of their patron saints:—

"On Monday last, being the anniversary of St. Patrick, a very numerous party assembled to celebrate the day at the house of J. Jackson, Esq., who very handsomely volunteered his long room for the occasion."

17. The company sat down to "an excellent dinner" at six in the evening, and "they did not think of departing till five o'clock next morning." It was a long *sederunt* that, but when we read the annexed lists of loyal and patriotic toasts which were drunk on the occasion, it must be admitted that, with the time required for speechifying and drinking, the wonder is the company got through it so early :—

"*Toasts.*—'The King,' 'The Queen and Royal Family,' 'The Duke of York and the Army,' 'Lord Barham and the Navy,' 'General Montgomerie and Prosperity to the Colonies,' 'The Day,' 'The 23rd April and Sons of St. George,' 'The 30th November and Sons of St. Andrew,' 'The United Kingdom and Success to its Arms,' 'The Commanders on the Station,' 'The Governors of Demerary and Berbice,' 'The Memory of Lord Nelson,' 'The Memory of Mr. Pitt,' 'Admiral Lord Collingwood,' 'General Sir John Moore,' 'Sir John Thomas Duckworth,' 'Lord Cathcart,' 'General Baird and Success to his Expedition,' 'Sir Richard Strachan,' 'The Marquis Cornwallis.'"

18. The "entertainments" to which the Colonists treated themselves and each other were "elegant" in more than expression. They knew how to live, and ate and drank of the best. The editor in one of his papers remarks :—

"So many vessels have lately arrived from London that the luxuries of Europe are at present very plentiful in this Colony. Almost every comfort and convenience of life may now be obtained with nearly as much facility as in that great metropolis itself."

19. And here, in connection with the introduction of luxuries into the domestic life of West Indians, I may lay a bit of information before my reader which is worth perusing. Few people know that as far back as 1806, ice formed an article of import into these latitudes :—

"*From the Martinique Gazette.*—The Boston newspaper of the 10th February contains this paragraph :—'No joke—A vessel has cleared at the Custom House for Martinique with a cargo of *ice!* We hope this will not prove to the speculators a slippery speculation.' The brig *Favorite*, Captain Person, in fact, sailed the 15th of February from Boston, and fortunately arrived here (St. Pierre) on Wednesday night, the 5th of March, and is now disposing of her cargo to great advantage in the harbour.

"It will be a remarkable epoch in the history of luxury and enterprise that on Thursday, the 6th of March, 1806, *ice creams* were eaten at Martinique, probably for the first time since the formation of the world; and this, too, in a volcanic island lying fourteen degrees North of the Equator; and that for three days ice creams have been eaten at St. Pierre the same as at Paris.

"Messrs. Tudor and Savage, on the 26th of December last, obtained an exclusive privilege for the importation and sale of ice for ten years."

20. Amongst the "locals" and advertisements in this old book, I find some that, almost as they stand, would be appropriate at the present day. Here is one which I insert for the benefit of whom it may concern, without charge:—

"All those who are friends to the Demerary Hotel are expected to come forward to settle their accounts, and those that do not comply must abide by the consequences."

Hotel accommodation was rather limited in Georgetown in those days, for every private house almost had accommodation for "man and beast;" but the private boarding house existed, as we conclude from this notice:—

"The widow of A. C. Warnecke has the honour to inform the public that it is her intention to DINE GENTLEMEN on a liberal plan for a monthly subscription, as soon as she can obtain the names of six respectable persons."

21. One of the "locals" refers to a discovery which may interest the members of the Demerara Rifle Association. Referring to a new rifle the editor says:—

"The novelty consists chiefly in the piece being loaded at the breach instead of the muzzle. An elegant rifle, on this new and ingenious construction, has already found its way to this country, and may be seen among the large and valuable assortment of military accoutrements, &c., &c., now on sale at Mr. T. Marsh's store."

22. We read of a racing match between an English mare, backed by ten bags of cotton, against a Virginia horse, backed by twenty-five bags of coffee; the distance, from the Block House to the Kitty, and the horses "to be rode by their respective owners." Cotton won, on which the editor remarks that it is a truism in planting circles that cotton *must* win.

23. There was a grand lottery this year (1806), conducted on more satisfactory terms than the big affair of 1878, in connection with the Romish Church in Georgetown, for we read that it was drawn—

"In the presence of a sworn clerk in the Secretary's Office of the Colony of Berbice, where the GOLD REPEATER representing the 'Miracle of Moses' was drawn with No. 805."

24. Of municipal affairs we read that the dams and drainage of the town were not what they ought to have been, and much inconvenience and discomfort ensued in consequence:—

"On Monday and Tuesday last, this town was again quite overflowed, to the great inconvenience and prejudice of the inhabitants. On Tuesday afternoon the inundation was particularly great; some gentlemen came in a boat close up to the American Coffee House, but one fat gentleman who was not fortunate enough to have so safe a conveyance, but trusted to the negroes, was, by a mistake of the latter, completely soused in the muddy flood."

25. The town had a Fire Brigade, but it was of very little use, and was not much depended upon. A fire occurred near America Street one night in an old negro woman's hut, while she was absent in the country, and, by the aid of some gentlemen in the city, it was put out chiefly by the application of mud. Next day, when the old woman returned, she raved and stormed herself into fits, because her house was so awfully messed; on which the editor remarks that perhaps it would have been more satisfactory to her feelings to have let it burn. An incident of the same fire is duly recorded:—

"In the confusion which the alarm caused some whimsical circumstances occurred. Among the rest, one gentleman who was loudly vociferating for his trousers had his shirt brought him instead, in which, with his legs through the armholes, he sallied forth to do his part in the extinguishing business."

26. Mr. Henry Bolingbroke, who wrote an account of Guyana a few years after it was taken possession of by the English in or about the year 1796, and dedicated his work to Mr. Wyndham, Under-Secretary of State for the Colonies, anticipated the progress of British Guyana, which is becoming the most important Colony of Great Britain in the West Indies, and an asylum for the redundant population of Barbadoes, and other islands in the Caribbean Sea. He points out how the settlements of the Dutch on the Demerara, Berbice, Corentyne, and Essequibo rivers were benefited by intercourse with Barbadoes. He looked upon the acquisition of Cayenne and the purchase of the Portuguese territory to the north of the Amazons by the English, as a matter that could easily be arranged, and the whole slip of land between the Amazons and Orinoque be made a British Colony, which absorbing all the capital, enterprise, and labour of the islands held by the English in the Caribbean Sea would soon develope into a great Continental British possession, which would amply compensate for the loss of the North American Provinces, which had recently established their independence. He also compares it with the countries lying along the mouth of the Plate river, and the acquisition of Buenos Ayres, which was achieved by the English during the war, and he considered Guyana a more advantageous possession than any of them. His speculations with regard to the future of Guyana and its relations with Barbadoes are of more interest to the reader, as they are, to a certain extent, in the course of being realized. Georgetown, or rather Stabroek, as it was called in his time, contained only some 1,500 white inhabitants, 2,000 free coloured, and 5,000 blacks. The fort and public buildings were higher up the river than they are now, at Diamond Point, and the suburb of Kingston between the town and the sea was built up by the British garrison, being the coolest and

healthiest quarter, and was called so after the capital of Jamaica. He describes the English adventurers, chiefly merchants and planters from Barbadoes, as more enterprising than the Dutch, and their occupation of the Colony during the war, and the demand it created for British goods, and the increase of commerce with the islands, as greatly conducive to its advancement, and says that the planters of Barbadoes had as much capital embarked in Guyana as they had in use in their own little island, which is only valuable from its being to windward of all the other islands, and having a good bay, which affords secure anchorage for the navy on the station:—

27. "The Colonies in Guyana, independently of supplies they have received from Africa, are daily getting more negroes from the West India Islands, some of which being nearly worn out from long cultivation, the proprietors of estates there find it very difficult and expensive to make them produce what they used to do. Circumstanced as they are, working on a withered soil, they are certainly justified in abandoning that land for better in Guyana, where there is such an extensive choice. The natural consequence we are to expect from such a procedure in the course of time, is the total abandonment of the barren islands, for the more fertile soil of the continent. The islands I allude to, are Curasso, Eustatia, Saba, St. Martins, Tortola, Tobago, Grenada, and St. Vincent, which will be either partially or wholly forsaken in a few years. When I was at Tortola, in 1805, there was neither a garrison to defend it, nor a governor to govern it; therefore it is visibly enough seen that the then ministry did not think the revenue or value of it would warrant the expense of maintaining a regular establishment there. Barbadoes is declining fast in its revenue and productions, but its situation being to windward of all the other islands, and having a good bay, makes it a most desirable place to be retained by our Government. It is now the head-quarters for the Commander-in-chief, and Carlisle Bay affords a secure anchorage for the navy on the station. But the planters of Barbadoes have as much capital employed in the Colonies on the continent, as they have actually in Barbadoes; this certainly is a strange assertion to make, but it is no less true, and will always be the case while Guyana presents such a boundless tract of country to cultivate; indeed, I have no

hesitation in saying that Demerary owes its present situation and importance to Barbadoes. The planters from that island first emigrated, with their negroes, and their rapid successes were an inducement for other islands to follow the example. The English planters having so much capital employed there, with other circumstances, was the inducement for the British to take it in 1796, which fully completed what had been so ably begun: the English merchants, struck with the advantages offered them by the capture of the Colonies, spared no pains to form establishments and extend cultivation, which eventually raised them to the rank they now hold." (P. 177.)

28. It is no wonder, then, that we have such large numbers of black, coloured, and white Barbadians continually coming over to Demerara for a living. And these black Barbadians are fifty years ahead of the black Creole Demerarians in intelligence, habits, &c. No Demerara Creole can floor a Barbadian.

CHAPTER IV.

A DESCRIPTION OF THE CITY OF GEORGETOWN, THE CAPITAL OF THE COLONY.

1. The following pathetic lines were found in an old escritoire, which formerly, and not so long ago, belonged to a distinguished and learned member of the Civil Service. The concluding verses of the ode were very superior to the others; at least the cockroaches thought so, for they ate the others and left this:—

ODE TO DEMERARA.

VERSE I.

"Demerara, land of trenches,
Giving out most awful stenches;
Land of every biting beast
Making human flesh its feast;
Land of swizzles, land of gin,
Land of every kind of sin!
Why have I been doomed to roam
Far, so far, away from home?"

2. A traveller visiting this country must not think of seeing high lands and lofty mountains, covered to their summits with perpetual verdure. The land is quite low and flat, and, therefore, he need not expect to behold it looming in the distance. "The first indication of land is characterized by a long irregular outline of thick bush, on approaching which groups of elevated trees, chiefly palms, with occasionally an isolated silk-cotton (*Bombax Ceiba*), or the tall chimneys of the sugar plantations, with the smoke curling upwards, begin rapidly to be recognized, and indicate to the experienced trader the very spot he has made. . . . Once in sight of land the scene rapidly changes in appearance, from a long, low outline of bush to the different objects which characterize the attractive

scenery of the tropics. . . . Before the river Demerara is fairly entered, the course steered is towards the lightship, situated about twelve miles from Georgetown. This beacon is a floating vessel at the entrance of the difficult navigation of the river. In fine weather, and during the daytime, it may readily be seen with the naked eye, and at night a bright fixed light indicates to the navigator the anxious object of his search." After nearing the lightship, the lighthouse and Fort Frederick are soon recognized, and in little more than an hour the traveller, as by magic, is ushered through a crowd of large ships, steamers, and small vessels, into a large town, with its motley inhabitants collected from all parts of the world, speaking their own languages or tongues wherein they were born. The new comer fancies himself in the land of confusion or Babel of languages and dialects. The harbour is the mouth of the river itself; and several wooden *stellings*, or jetties, project from the shore, on which the passengers and goods are landed. All the houses and places of worship are built of wood grown in this Colony. In the centre of the city of Georgetown stands an elegant structure called the "Guyana Public Buildings," built of brick, and stuccoed with Roman cement, in imitation of freestone. Very lately a few good brick buildings have been erected in Georgetown. The streets and roads in town, and its vicinity, have been formed of the ballast of vessels trading to the Colony, each ship being required to leave a certain quantity. Broken rock stones (brought over from Massareeni, H.M. Penal Settlement, on the river Massareeni, a tributary of the Essequibo) are used to macadamize the streets of the city. The extent of Georgetown, the capital of the Colony, is from Plantation *La Pénitence*, the extreme boundary of the town on the south, to the Fort, situate at the entrance of the river, a distance of a mile and a quarter to a mile and a half.

3. Those who knew Georgetown as it was twenty years ago, and are able to compare it with the city of to-day, have abundance of material for many a pleasant retrospect. Between the metropolis of to-day and that of the date to which I refer, there is a difference so wide and marked that if a Colonist

who had known the one were to return now to the site of his former haunts, he would have some difficulty in discovering any of the old landmarks, and might doubt if this were really the city in which he once lived. The change, I am proud to say, is one of improvement, and, despite the perpetual cry of dull times and small profits, the march of progress is still going on, giving promise of changes as distinct in another score of years as those we can now contemplate. It is not easy to say whether the commercial or the residential quarter of the city has undergone the greatest improvement.

4. Water Street, in which is transacted the whole mercantile business of the town, in fact, the whole business of the Colony (Berbice and Essequibo included), at the time of which I write, was a narrow tortuous street, in some parts resembling the "auld brig o' Ayr," where "twa wheelbarrows tremble when they meet," ill-favoured, ill-lighted, and full of close, musty smells, from which it was so impossible to escape that the resident had, *nolens volens*, to get used to them. It was a busy place, however; and, looking back, it seems that the crowd of passengers in business hours was greater and more continuous than it is now; but this may have been more apparent than real from the narrowness of the thoroughfare throwing the passers-by closer together. The merchants of those days were a hard-working, industrious lot. Every morning at sharp six o'clock every store was opened for business, and the heads of the various establishments were there to see that all connected with them were at their posts. Think of this, ye luxurious successors, who creep into Water Street at seven o'clock, grumbling that the hour of opening the business of the day is absurdly early! Men who are now enjoying enviable positions in the West Indian commercial circle in London were amongst those who every morning as the clock struck six saw their businesses, wholesale and retail, set a-going, and who, allowing themselves small time for breakfast, lunch, or club, toiled till late in the afternoon, when they retired to their houses, which, as a rule, were over their stores. There were few recreative institutions in those days for the enjoyment of athletic exercises or æsthetic indulgences, and but for

the compulsory and salutary exercise in the militia service, the majority of Water Street men would have had little to divert them from Monday to Saturday. The mess-house over the store was a recognized institution in every establishment of any size, and there can be no question that it was a valuable one, engendering a fine *esprit de corps*, and providing the *employés* with the comforts of a home. It served its purpose excellently well, but its day is over, and it is now all but a thing of the past. Its decadence commenced when the custom was introduced of employing Creole lads as clerks in the stores, for naturally these lads preferred to live with their own people. Twenty years ago Creole clerks were very few, and in a walk along the street one could almost have counted on the ten fingers the number of them employed in the various stores, English or Portuguese. Nowadays they are to be found in every place of business in town, and their numbers are increasing so rapidly that the question of where they are all to find employment is becoming a serious one. But not only in the matter of salesmen have the stores undergone a change,—their whole appearance and style have completely altered, together with the class of goods, and, I may say, the class of customers also. Some of our commercial houses will compare with what are considered high-class shops in any English town, and it is a generally acknowledged fact that the enterprise of our local merchants keeps Colonists more alive to the fashions and inventions of the day, than are the citizens of many places situated within easy distance of the great centres of European life.

5. It was a fortunate calamity, if such an expression be permissible, that befell the city that Sunday afternoon, April 3, 1864, when the cry of FIRE, the clanging of bells, bugle calls, and the shrieks of houseless men and women, awoke the quiet of the Sabbath into a scene of the wildest confusion and terror, such as, perhaps, had never been witnessed, and, I sincerely hope, never will be again experienced in the Colony. By this dreadful fire, or conflagration, in Water Street, some one hundred and thirty clerks had been thrown out of employment; but to the honour and credit of

the merchants in whose employ they were, be it said, that they took immediate steps to prevent the clerks being thrown upon any plan of relief from the outsiders. The loss sustained by the merchants and others, including properties and goods, amounted to about *three millions* of dollars. Just three months after (July 4, 1864) there was another terrible conflagration, when the greater part of Water Street was reduced to ashes, with immense destruction of valuable properties and goods to the amount of 1,500,000 dollars. These two fires furnished the opportunity that was wanted to remodel the street, and make it worthier of the Colony of which it was the heart. Had the old houses, and the old street, been to the fore still, the enterprise I have alluded to could never have developed itself, for the new business could never have been possible in the old stores, any more than the old business could be carried on profitably in the new buildings. Out of the ashes of the old, narrow, twisted highway arose the fine, wide, imposing Water Street of to-day, and I can point to it as one of the grandest commercial quarters, not only in the West Indies, but in countries of more pretension. In the residential portions of the city the changes that have been effected are quite on a par with the improvements in the places of trade. The old custom of merchants living over the stores has become obsolete, and their houses are now to be found ornamenting Main Street, and some of the more remote streets of the city. Perhaps nowhere more than in Main Street is the improvement in street architecture observable. At the date of which I am writing, small cottages, some of them in a tumble-down state, "Portuguese" shops and buildings in every stage of decay, were to be seen, with here and there a really good house, forming a striking contrast to its neighbours. To-day, there is an almost unbroken line of fine residences from one end of Main Street to the other, on both sides, and it is not too much to say, that a finer avenue is hardly to be met with out of the large capitals of the world. The less pretentious portions of the city have not been forgotten, while the more fashionable streets have been undergoing ornamentation and improvement. The former practice of lighting up our streets with oil has been done away with by the introduction of gas since December 31, 1872. The town is well supplied with large iron water tanks, as the citizens chiefly depend upon rain for this indispensable article, and in dry seasons water is supplied from these tanks at a very reasonable price. Every householder is expected to have a vat in his yard to supply himself and his tenants with water—rain-water. In addition to all these almost every street in the city has what the Creoles call "a stand-pipe," or pump, whence water is obtained by the poor people, and others, for drinking and culinary purposes, &c. The public Water Works in Camp Street are in such a state of perfection, that the whole city could be supplied with water in a very few seconds, and our properties are not now liable so easily to be destroyed by fire as formerly. The Fire Brigade is always in good working trim, and ready at any moment to turn out to give assistance.

6. At one time to walk through certain streets after a heavy shower of rain was like stalking over rough pasture land, but now there is scarcely a lane within the municipal boundaries that is not macadamized, or covered over with burnt earth. Wherever one goes in his city rambles, from east to west, or north to south, he comes upon some healthy sign of accumulating wealth and improving taste in the street buildings, whether these are for household or congregational purposes. The church of St. Philip, the magnificent Roman Catholic Cathedral,* the Wesleyan Trinity and Bedford Chapels (in Werk-en-Rust, and Camp Street) and buildings, the Hand-in-Hand block, the large hotels, the British Guyana

* The oldest church or place of worship in the Colony, now greatly needing repairs, is on Fort Island, in the Essequibo, which is justly venerated by the descendants of Dutchmen for their fathers' sakes. It was opened for Divine service in 1771, and is consequently 110 years old. Mr. Adam, one of the oldest inhabitants of Fort Island, said that he had seen the fifth roof put on it. It is gratifying, however, to see that it is not merely regarded as the idol of sentiment, but is occasionally used practically for religious and social purposes. Rev. W. Harper, of the Church of Scotland, sometimes visits the people on Fort Island and holds Divine service in this old church, which is altogether pewless. The people either have to stand or carry their benches with them.

Bank, the new and handsome Law Courts, the new "McKay Markets," with a high tower and clock; the large, strong, and substantial Almshouse, more fitted to be the Governor's residence than a paupers' home, and many other places that will occur to the local reader, all give the most unqualified proof of the great advance we have made both socially and commercially during the two preceding decades. We may quarrel and grumble as we please, and say to each other in our mutual misery that business is wretched, and the Colony is going to the dogs, but we must not be taken at our word. There is the evidence of our increased wealth and improved position to be seen by all, in the private residences and public and sectarian institutions we have been able to build for ourselves. Of late, much has been done to beautify the city of Georgetown, and when the works at present in course of construction, and in contemplation, are finished, it will be worthy to be the capital of the "Magnificent Province." When the buildings which compose the present ice house are removed, and a sightly edifice is erected in their place, and the ground, where the temporary market stood, cleared and put in order, the *coup d'œil* from the steamer stelling will be an imposing one, and probably unequalled in the West Indies. It has been frequently remarked that the presence of handsome buildings and elegant surroundings of any description has an elevating and refining effect on the manners of the populace, and in this we believe there is a certain amount of truth. Whatever may be urged against those who have administered the Government of late years, it cannot be denied that the efforts of the authorities to improve and beautify the city have been unremitting. It is also true that private individuals have in many cases been equally energetic; and the consequence is that our capital excites the admiration of strangers visiting it. I trust that the spirit of improvement may not subside; for there exist no better means of educating the people than accustoming them to the sight of beautiful things. We have every reason to regard our city with honest pride and lively satisfaction; and in bringing this brief retrospect to a close, I would express the hope that twenty years hence those of us who are still in the fight may be able to look back and draw a comparison between the present and the past, as favourable to the former as is that we of to-day have to record between what we now have and what twenty years ago we had.

7. Almost the whole of the plantations in the Colony are represented by these Water Street mercantile houses, or individual partners of them, and the patronage which they exercise in the appointment of managers and other officers of estates is very great. They are a powerful body, and their combined action, even against the Executive Government, should they be antagonistic to it, is, in most cases, irresistible. It is but justice, however, to them to say that, as a rule, they act with moderation, and never oppose themselves to the Government merely for the sake of opposition. On the contrary, they will generally be found acting in concert with the local Government, unless when that Government is controlled by the baneful influence and instructions which often emanate from the ignorance of the Colonial Office officials.

8. Besides the houses I have just referred to, there are a great many dry goods stores—that is, shops for the sale of cloth and finery of all kinds in that line. Some of these, I am informed, are owned by men of means and capital, but many of them are of mushroom growth, and disappear, after a brief existence, between the jaws of that voracious individual, called the Administrator-General, or are wound up under trust, to be succeeded by others of a similar description, notwithstanding the warnings thus given to those who support them and give them credit.

9. Among the merchants of Water Street I must not neglect noticing the poor and frugal and industrious Portuguese—although destitute of education and intellectual training—who has, in many cases, raised himself far above his original position, and has, in some instances, taken his place beside the wealthy English merchant. Several of them in Water Street are much respected and trusted, and have accumulated considerable wealth. I need only mention one, Mr. Manoel Fernandez, who died some years ago at Madeira, his native

island, where he had gone for the benefit of his health. This man was altogether uneducated. He could neither read nor write, but his mercantile transactions became so large that it was necessary for him to be able to sign his name, and this he was able to accomplish. And that name was given for thousands and tens of thousands of dollars, and was readily taken by every one having dealings with him. Quiet, almost to taciturnity, he had little to say, yet he kept his eyes about him; and, with native shrewdness, and a large amount of good sense and foresight, he availed himself of every opportunity of making successful commercial speculations, the result being that he died leaving a large amount of property and money. There are others of the same class who have been successful, although probably few to the same extent.

10. With the exception of some vegetables, such as plantains, yams, cassava, sweet potatoes, &c., the Colony is almost entirely dependent upon the United States for its food supplies. These are flour, salt pork, salt beef, cheese, butter, salt fish, which is largely consumed, and a number of other articles. In short, it may be said the only product of the Colony is sugar, with its necessary complement of molasses and rum. Its wide savannahs ought to afford pasture for numerous herds of cattle, but, strange to say, this is not the case. The supply cannot keep pace with the demand, and large numbers of cattle are imported from Oronoco, of very inferior quality, partly arising from their deterioration during their sea voyage. Occasionally a cargo of cattle from Porto Rico arrives in the Colony. These are generally much superior to the Oronoco cattle. Sheep do not thrive in the Colony, principally owing to the swampy nature of the soil and the rank grass on which they have to feed, which is not suitable for them. The consequence is that the mutton principally consumed in the Colony is imported from the United States. There are Creole sheep, and when looked after and attended to, as they sometimes are on sugar estates, and when fed on the refuse of the sugar manufacture, their mutton is superior in flavour to almost any other mutton; but it is rarely that you

can buy such mutton in the market, it is reserved for managers and their friends.

A gentleman thoroughly conversant with cattle farming, recently writing in the Demerara *Argosy*, observes:—

"Mr. Thomas Porter, when residing at 'Paradise,' imported several fine specimens of the Zebu, both bulls and cows, and he also succeeded in raising splendid crosses. His oxen at four years used to sell for $80 to $100 and over per head. There are still good specimens of cattle to be seen on the pasture of 'Enmore,' but they show the marked ill effects of in-and-in breeding, and I question if four-year-old oxen can now be fed to be worth more than $50 to $60. Others have added to the stock of East Indian cattle, but nothing has been done in the way of refreshing the breed of cows such as the original stock represented, and to this I consider is due the falling off in the breed of cattle. In my native county and in the northern counties along the Moray Firth, where the breed of cattle has been improved to an extent beyond belief, the secret was the selection of breeding stock; fabulous prices were paid for both bulls and cows, and in no case were bulls allowed to interfere with their own progeny. The result has been that farmers turn out two-year-old oxen worth three times the price that three-year-olds sold for forty years ago. To resuscitate and improve the breed of cattle in British Guyana, the example set by the northern farmers ought to be followed; the best cows now to be found in the Colony ought to be selected as breeding stock, and all inferior animals should be fed off for the butchers. The indiscriminate way in which bulls of any and all descriptions are allowed to graze about should be prohibited by law in the same way as is provided for stallions, and only bulls of a given size should be allowed to be at large. Fresh stock should be imported in both bulls and cows, with the especial object of improving the size and weight of our herds, and I would suggest the United States or Jamaica as a more likely field to draw a supply from than from England. In both countries the breed of cattle has been brought to almost a level with the mother country, and we know that stock from Jamaica in particular are more easily acclimatized than those from England. The Coolie element as cattle farmers throws some little difficulty in the way of carrying out a general system of improvement; they object to the shedding of blood, hence the wretched droves of small bulls that are thrown on the market. I cannot believe but that this might be overcome, and that all bull calves could be emasculated as they are dropped, same as is done in Europe. The crofters in Scotland with their few cows have become quite as ambitious to put in a good appearance at the local shows as their more opulent neighbours, and none of them ever think of keeping a bull; they send their cows to the best bull in the district, and I have little doubt the Demerary Coolie would soon find out that it would be to his interest to do the same."

11. The assembly rooms, where balls and parties on a large scale are given, is an unseemly building outside, but admirably adapted inside for the purposes for which it was erected. The balls are held in the upper flat, and wide and spacious galleries run along each side of it, where the non-dancing part of the company can promenade and flirt to their hearts' content. These galleries are open to the breeze, which renders the room delightfully cool and pleasant. My friends in England will be surprised to learn that such a ball-room is more cool and pleasant than the close and confined rooms at home, and much more agreeable. There are no offensive smells from gas or a confined atmosphere. The bottom flat is occupied by the Georgetown Club. This Club is admirably conducted and is somewhat aristocratic in its pretensions, and exclusive. There is also another Club in Georgetown called the "British Guyana" Club, which is not quite so aristocratic. Four others of recent date have been formed in the city. Nothing can exceed the kindness of the members of these Clubs to strangers. It is enough that you are a stranger in a strange land to command their hospitality; for the hospitality of the Demerarians is proverbial, and you must be on your guard against it, otherwise their swizzles, so pleasant and delightful to the taste, with which you are plied, may be too much for you. It is sufficient if you are acquainted with one member of the Club. Your friend takes you there, places your name in a visitors' book, and introduces you all round to those present. Then begins your difficulty and your trial. Every one thinks he has a claim upon you to drink with him; and every one asks you. You wish to be civil, and you do your utmost

to be civil and polite; but if you have a regard for your head and your sobriety, you feel yourself, at times, compelled to decline the proffered drink; and you are right. At the Georgetown and British Guyana Clubs you can have excellent lunches and dinners, but a stranger, although admitted to the Clubs, can order nothing—that must be done for him by a member, and he will never be at a loss on that score; and besides, he will never have to pay.

Report says that not very long ago a State-paid clergyman found himself one Sunday afternoon in the house of a planter friend of his, where he met some other friends. Soon a discussion upon religious topics was begun, and it became very animated and somewhat scientific, one of the parties to the controversy being a local scientist of some mark, when it became necessary to clinch an argument by a reference to a standard authority. The servant was called and told to go upstairs and fetch the *Evidences of Christianity;* she would find it lying on the shelf. The girl went and came back immediately carrying a double flask of gin! "The servant was evidently a reader of missionary literature, and had, with Mr. Russell, come to believe that gin and true religion are closely allied, the presence of the former being inseparable from the latter and one of its least mistakable evidences."

12. The following description of Georgetown, taken from Mr. J. W. Bodham-Whetham's book on *Roraima*, will be read with interest:—

"Georgetown is a handsome, well-built town, with broad streets, avenues, excellent stores, and shops of all descriptions, and with a lively, well-to-do air that is invigorating as the heat is depressing. In the streets, besides the white race, you meet sharp-featured Madrassees, Hindus of various castes, Parsees, Nubians, half-breeds. Stepping timidly along may also be seen two or three 'bucks,' as the natives from the interior are called, dressed—if dressed at all—in a motley suit of old clothes, and only anxious to sell or exchange their parrots and hammocks, and then return to their wilds. From a merchant's store filled with European goods you step into a little shop redolent of the East, and stocked with bangles and silver ornaments worked by their Cingalese proprietor. There stands a Portuguese Jew, ready to fleece the first 'buck' whom he can entice into his cheap general store, and here sits stolid John Chinaman, with his pigtail wreathed round his head, keeping guard over his home-made cigars.

"The Government building is a large, fine-looking structure; the numerous churches are graceful and picturesque, and everywhere there is a home look about the town, without pretension, that is very attractive. The reading-room is cool and very comfortable, the library well managed, and the museum in the same building is likely to become a very valuable acquisition to the colony.

"Opposite the 'Kineteur' hotel is the Club, which is the pleasantest resort in the town, as it receives the full benefit of the trade wind, which on certain occasions, by-the-by, wafts other zephyrs than those fresh from the beautiful hibiscus hedge in front, and is much frequented by its members. Stretching far away from this Club towards the sea-wall is Main Street, and there and in the neighbouring parallel one the principal houses of Georgetown are situated. Main Street is broad and picturesque; a series of wide trenches* with green sloping banks divides it, and on each side runs a fine road. The residences which line it are all detached, and of various styles of architecture, from a three-storied edifice with towers and cupola to a low, wide-spreading structure with but one floor above the basement. But all are built for coolness as well as comfort, and their wide, shady verandahs are the favourite resorts of the family. Many of the gardens are brilliant masses of colour, resembling a rich oil-painting, rather than a delicate water-colour like those of European lands."

Our new Governor, Sir Henry Turner Irving (who arrived in the Colony, May 4, 1882), expressed his pleasant surprise at the appearance of Georgetown, which in every way surpassed any other city in the English West Indies.

* As there is no natural fall of water, these open trenches, which are seen everywhere in the country as well as town, are necessary to carry off surface water to prevent flooding in the wet seasons. By sluice gates the town trenches can be flooded when required.

CHAPTER V.

THE AFRICAN SLAVE TRADE AND THE CONDITION OF THE PEOPLE.

1. WHEN slavery—"that greatest curse that can afflict the social system"—"that plundered more than four millions of men and women of all the rights of humanity, and doomed their offspring through perpetual generations to the same hopeless bondage and oppression"—existed in the Colony of Guyana during parts of the eighteenth and nineteenth centuries, cargoes of valuable slaves were, *nolens volens,* caught and shipped from the Coast of Africa and brought to the shores of Guyana in ill-ventilated vessels. The masters or owners of slaves were gods, and their law, their word, supreme. They were quite indifferent about sacred things, and gave themselves up to the sinful pleasures of the world. Those days were indeed days of darkness, dissipation, and oppression of the worst type that ever saw the sun. The planters' reign was a "reign of terror," and they had to work with their sword on their thigh :—

"On Friday fortnight upwards of twenty Spaniards landed in Capoey Creek, on the Arabian coast; but on the burghers immediately assembling and making a great noise they thought proper to re-embark without effecting anything."

In addition to the naval force to protect its interests at sea, the Colony possessed a large and powerful militia to join with the regulars to protect the land from invasion, and to preserve internal order, which latter at times was not such an easy matter. Occasionally their duty was diversified with a job like this, which they looked upon as a bit of fun :—

"The purpose for which the militia were ordered out last Sunday morning was to assist in the apprehension of runaway and Bush Negroes; a number of whom there was every reason to suppose made a practice of coming into town on a Sunday, The object was to surround the market place with the militia, and guard the avenues with regulars while the Dienaars did their duty inside. . . . Every male Negro who could not produce a satisfactory pass was presently taken and placed under a guard till owned by his master."

"The lives of the Bushas, or masters, were not safe from the Bush Negroes." If these Negroes were cruel, their masters were worse, and more degraded, and perfectly inhuman. Just about this period (A.D. 1794) the well-known Quaker philanthropist, Stephen Grellet, in his youthful days, left his native land (England) on a visit to British Guyana, probably to settle down and make the Colony his future home. During his stay in the Colony and intercourse with the planters—the reigning monarchs of the time—and others, he paid particular attention to their manners and customs, and ways of living. He soon got tired of the Colony, and returned to his own native country. Stephen Grellet is long since dead, but he has left his testimony behind as to the moral condition of the people in the Colony in his day. His words are:—

"It [British Guyana] is a place of much dissipation. I do not recollect during the whole time I was there, that I saw anything in any one that indicated a feeling of religious sensibility. There was no place of worship: no priest of any kind, except one who had been there a few years, and was a dissolute drunken man. It was of the Lord's mercy that I and the whole land were not destroyed like Sodom and Gomorrah."

Strong language this, but not too strong when the actual real state of the country and the condition of the inhabitants are taken into consideration.

2. Hartsink, an old Dutch writer, gives a list of the various classes or tribes of slaves that were introduced into the Colony for the purpose of continuous, hard, payless toil on the sugar and coffee estates. There were the *Andras* or *Dongos* from Inda and Ardra, towns near the western sea coast of Africa. The men and women of this class or tribe had gashes upon

their cheeks, and the higher orders amongst them were marked only about the foreheads, like the *Kroomen*. The *Naquo* slaves had streaks or curves upon their bodies, representing the various animals. The *Mallais*, an excellent people, and accustomed to hard labour, and who brought high prices in the slave market, were tattooed, differing very little from the *Tibou* and *Guiambo* Negroes. The *Aquiras*, who were active and faithful to their owners, had marks upon their back and breast resembling lizards and snakes. The *Tibouians* had long gashes upon the cheeks, breast, and stomach; they were of the worst kind, good for nothing except light housework. The *Forus* were known by deep scratches upon their temples; they were a bad people, lazy, thievish, and addicted to filthy habits. The *Guiambans* resembled very much the Tibouians and Forus in character and marks. The *Tidans* and *Jaquins* had upon their cheeks several spots or points, and were true to their masters when kindly treated. The *Ayois* Negroes were known by long gashes stretching from ear to ear. These, no doubt, were the soldiers of Africa; and were the terror of all the rest of the Negroes. They held their lives of no account when their passions were roused, and pursued their objects with an ardour it was difficult to restrain. They were a martial and enterprising race, and well inclined to work, which they performed better than any of the other nations. The "runaway" or "Bush Negroes" we so often hear spoken of in the Colony, and who gave serious alarm to the white inhabitants of the land, on account of their numbers increasing rapidly, probably might have belonged to this class or tribe—the Ayois.

"They made predatory excursions in the neighbourhoods they infested, and carried off provisions or whatever else they could lay their hands upon; and such were the sentiments of revenge they entertained against the white men, that whenever they happened to surprise any of them, they seized them, hurried them away to the woods, and put them to the most miserable deaths. The mangled bodies of their victims, afterwards discovered, afforded revolting evidence of the most barbarous treatment. Rivalling the ferocity of the animals with whom they herded, they maintained, however, a kind of discipline amongst themselves, electing a chief, whom they strictly obeyed, and always acting in concert under his orders. Rendered desperate by their situation, those lawless savages became the terror of the country."

The *Annamaboe* Negroes (sometimes called *Fantynes*) were known by certain points or spots burnt in with gunpowder upon the forehead. They were a well-conducted tribe, and best suited of all for constant work on sugar, coffee, and cocoa plantations. The *Akinsche* and *Ashantees* belonged to this tribe. The *Acra* Negroes were brave, strong, and good slaves: "The *Abo* and *Papa* tribes were little meddled with; the last were said to have a kind of poison placed under their nails, with which they threatened to kill any one, if exasperated; hence, perhaps, the disinclination that was shown to interfere with them." The *Cormantyne* Negroes had no characteristic marks, but were known by their fine smooth black skin. They were unforgiving in their temper and revenge. The *Loango* or *Goango* (no doubt the present *Kroomen*) were a vicious race, and practised cannibalism and obeahism. Their teeth were so exquisitely sharpened that they could easily bite off a finger, and all the other Negroes hated and feared them. There were also imported into the Colony of British Guyana the Negroes from *Goree*, who had upon the temples three gashes about three fingers broad; Negroes from *Sierra Leone*, with four gashes upon the forehead; Negroes from *Cabo Monto*, with a gash upon each cheek, extending from the head to the chin; and Negroes from *Cape La Hoe*, on the Gold Coast, who were marked over the whole body with figures of birds and animals, and wore round the neck a string of red sea shells, which was regarded as a kind of armlet or chain. Perhaps the portions from the old volume of the *Essequibo and Demerary Gazette*, published in 1806—seventy-five years ago—(extracts from which were reprinted in the *Royal Gazette* of 1878, see chapter iii.), which strike a reader of modern days with the greatest force, and jar most against his feelings, are the advertisements and paragraphs dealing with the slaves. To us living in these days of legal, if not social, equality, the following sentences occasion a peculiar surprise:—

"Masters should not allow their boys to *ride* the horses to water; they must know that Negroes are not fit to be trusted. It is more safe, more proper, for the slaves to lead them, and at the same time it has a more decent appearance.

"Yesterday evening, a negro was discovered hanging on a tree in the middle walk of Vlissengen. The poor devil had rigged himself out for his exit in, no doubt, his best clothes. . . . The owner of this infatuated wretch is at present unknown.

"We have heard that it is customary in some Colonies to cut off the head of any negro making away with himself, and fix it on a post. This mode appears to us to be very eligible. . . . The idea of returning to their native country without a head would fully check the foolish delusion."

How strange, too, to read the following advertisements!—

"For sale, a very clever boat captain. He is sold for no fault whatever, and only to enable his owner to discharge a debt.

"For sale, a young, healthy and clever housemaid, who can work well with her needle, and is an excellent washer. She is sold for no fault whatever, and is warranted healthy.

"By permission of his Excellency the Governor, the Subscribers will expose for sale, at Beurdeaux's Logie, on Saturday next, the 23rd instant, under license,

230 PRIME WINDWARD COAST SLAVES,

in high health, imported in the ship *Thomas*, from the Windward coast."

Occasionally, it would appear, a Colonist coveted his neighbour's maid-servant, and used improper means to make her his own. If the following does not implicate Joseph Beete, senior, Esq., and expose his trafficking with Lamon, who seems to have been a well-known character, then we read it awrong:—

"Notice: The Subscriber will give Four Joes Reward to any person who will apprehend and lodge in the barracks a Negro woman belonging to him, named Lamon, a Creole of Barbados, with her boy-child Charles. She is too well known in this Colony to require any further description, and is supposed to be harboured on the West Coast of the River, at or about Plantation Best, belonging to Joseph Beete, senior, Esq., where she has a husband. She has been frequently on that plantation, and from the repeated offers by the proprietor to purchase her below her value, the subscriber has reason to suppose she is encouraged."

The oddest notice, however, to modern minds, amongst these sayings and doings of the past, is the following account of a triple execution:—

"This morning at twelve o'clock, were executed pursuant to the sentence of the High Court of Justice, three Negroes, named Tom, Sandy, and Billy, for breaking open the store of Mr. Emmerson, and stealing divers articles therefrom some time since.

"During the time of the above sentence being carried into execution, one Neyburg, a white man, was placed in the platform under the gallows, with a large board affixed to his breast, on which was written, 'Buyer of stolen goods,' he having purchased the articles from the above Negroes."

There are many persons in the Colony and England who, perhaps, had never read or heard the names of the different tribes of Africans introduced into the labour market of Guyana, and the treatment they received at the hands of their masters, and therefore I have taken the trouble to describe them for their information. The learned works from which I have gleaned these facts have been out of print, and cannot now be obtained, and hence this description will be all the more interesting to my reader.

3. Such, in brief, is the description to be gleaned from the old Dutch writers and others, of the qualities and value of the several tribes of African Negroes brought as slaves to Guyana, to till the land and enrich their masters and owners of estates or plantations. England still owes a great debt to Africa's sons for the great injustice done to them. It is a debt that can never be paid back for centuries to come. "It would be quite impossible nowadays to trace out the descendants of any of these tribes I have just described. They have all mingled into one large human family, the *Black Creole*, and

have relinquished, it is to be hoped for ever, most of the characteristic marks, both physical and moral, by which their progenitors were distinguished."

4. The nature and working of the cursed and abominable system of slavery in the West Indies is so well known to every one in the Colony, that it becomes quite unnecessary on my part to repeat the awful and saddening story. The cruelty of the lash, which was often steeped in brine, or pickle and pepper, is something very dreadful to think of. Twenty-five was the number of lashes laid on the bare back of the slave, when a dry leaf or piece of the boll was found in the cotton, or a branch was broken in the field, &c.; fifty for all offences of the next grade; a hundred for standing idle in the field; from a hundred and fifty to two hundred for quarrelling with fellow slaves; and five hundred, laid on with the greatest possible severity, for any attempt to escape or run away from an estate or plantation. The estate overseers and gang drivers,—in one word, "taskmasters"—made the slaves to serve or work with rigour, and they made their lives bitter with hard bondage in all manner of service in the field; all their service wherein they made them serve was with rigour. I have been informed by a gentleman, a native of the Colony, that up to the day before the slaves were actually emancipated or proclaimed free, the lash was freely used by the drivers on a certain plantation near to Georgetown, and that, on the morning of the emancipation, several freed slaves walked up to the house of the "Boss"—manager or overseer—and asked if they were not going to be whipped that morning for obtaining their freedom. Horrible indeed are the tales I have heard from time to time about the cruelty and blood-thirstiness of the employers towards their slaves in the Colony. The descendants of the old slave population have been very much kept down by the powerful, opulent race, the Europeans, and very many privileges which they should enjoy have been kept from them. Instead of regarding that—

"All men are equal in their birth,
Heirs of the earth and skies;
All men are equal when that earth
Fades from their dying eyes;"

colorophobia, one of the baneful effects of that unhallowed system of human slavery, has been fostered by the British nation, and this, now and then, manifests itself in larger or smaller measure, especially when the social and moral, though not, perhaps, so much as the religious, status of the Creole—coloured and black—people of the Colony is considered. This it is that keeps the people down from rising higher in a moral and social point of view. There is no denying the fact that the British nation, or their offspring in the Colony, have not done their duty to the descendants of a people and race who were once their slaves, in raising them, by giving a ready helping hand; they have done, probably, everything to keep them down. The very ministers of the Gospel—those holy men who should be free from all prejudices—have done the same. Their actions speak louder than words. The coloured man had, and in too many instances still has, to contend not only with the ordinary difficulties of life, but with the prejudices of caste, making his humble progress in the world more rough and painful than that of the man boasting of a fairer skin. Years ago, the consolation used to be that *Time* would soften and tone down all bitter feelings; but years have passed, and the same feelings remain. A long period of dominance on the one side and of servitude on the other has engendered sentiments of unfriendliness and distrust that neither side can easily remove, and which will, doubtless—as I have before remarked—long continue. It must not be supposed that coloured people regard the whites with feelings of antipathy—*au contraire.* They regard them as the principal progenitors of their race and civilization; but cannot ignore the fact that they are not entirely separated from the African race, except by refinement and culture, and this connection white residents in these Colonies continually refer to in no measured terms of reproach. The Indians of America, the Maoris of New Zealand, have been often cited as superior races to those of African descent; but if the saying that the fittest will survive be accepted as an axiom, there is reason to reverse that opinion; for, judging from the progress of the coloured race in numbers, position, and education in America and the West Indies, they will be flourishing and prosperous long after the Red Men of the far West have disappeared from the face of the earth; and at the present day there is no likelihood of the future realization of Macaulay's prophecy if applied to the aboriginal New Zealander. Every one of the slaves was known by some classical name, as Pompey, Cato, Socrates, Cæsar, Hannibal, Jupiter, Juvenal, Venus, Juno, Demosthenes, &c., or by other names of places or countries, as London, Edinburgh, Scotland, France, Paris, Liverpool, &c., or by names such as these—Tuesday, Friday, Sambo, Quashy, Cuffie, &c., which names are still retained. The slaves received their names at the hands of their masters, and were often "branded" the same as a cow, or horse, or mule, instead of being baptized by any Christian minister.

5. During the time that slavery existed in the Colony such a thing as marriage was altogether unknown and unheard of; nay, even prohibited; and yet children were born, and grew up to the inheritance of slavery. "Unrestrained by the presence of refined and virtuous women, and enjoying a perfect impunity of power over all surrounding associations, the Colonists surrendered themselves to a life of unbridled depravity. Having no scandal of public opinion to encounter, and being wholly liberated from all religious and social obligations, they formed intimate relations with the humblest of their slaves, beginning, perhaps, with some vague sense of personal responsibility, but gradually breaking down all the barriers of honour and decency, until the whole country presented a scene of demoralization that would scarcely be credited in the present age. The only chastity, as a religious duty, taught the women was, that they must have a child once a year to enrich the planter, who was the master. The authority of the master was omnipotent, and it was employed without remorse in promoting the indulgence of the worst passions. The result was, that the majority of the planters of the West adopted the customs and privileges of the despots of the East. A seraglio was established on almost every property; and the harem of a planter, if it did not emulate the luxury and pomp of the Turk, transcended its prototype in coarseness and sen-

suality. The slave . . . . was still his menial; her children became his property, were still accounted slaves, and were often compelled to the labour of the field without being allowed to derive any advantage from their European descent. This, however, was not the general rule. The mother and her offspring were frequently made free by purchase, and the children brought up to some trade or business." Such offsprings of temporary unions were called "coloured people," and the same appellation is still applied to all persons, however fair, of African and European descent. The children of mixed blood were called by various names, as, for instance, the children of the "Negro" and "half-caste" were called "Samboes;" the children of a Negress by a white man or a white woman by a Negro, "half-castes;" the issue between a "half-caste" and white, "Tercerones," or "Quadroons," or "Quaterons," being persons quarter-blooded; the children of a white person and a quadroon, "Mustees" or "Mestees;" and the children of a "Mustiphinie" by a white father, or *vice versa*, "Quinterons." As a Mustee or Mustiphinie has but one sixteenth of Negro blood, and a Quinteron is only one thirty-second from being white, all distinctions finally vanish, this being the last gradation, with no visible difference in colour or features between them and the whites. The conduct of the European residents towards this class of citizens has, it cannot be denied, been in too many cases *illiberal and highly wrong*, especially as they, and two or more generations, in most instances, are wholly without crime in respect of their birth. Lord Macaulay, I think, mentions in his *History of England*, that a similar class prejudicial feeling existed between the Mercian and Northumberland tribes. But that has passed away; and so the class feeling in British Guyana is gradually dying out. There is no excuse for this dislike, especially while among them are many persons than whom the community can desire no better members. They are enterprising, a few of them wealthy, and every way worthy of confidence and respect.*

* Mr. P. B. Shillaber, who visited the Colony of British Guyana between forty and fifty years ago, and during his stay in the

"The great drawback," says an old Scotch planter in the Colony, "to the usefulness of the Creole, however, is his way of putting off things, and an absence of dash and through-put, but there are not wanting Creoles who are as active, conscientious, and intelligent as the best European I have ever met. It amuses me to listen to the supercilious talk of some white people about the comparative merits of themselves and others, for I have lived long enough in the country to know how shallow and hypocritical is the so-called prejudice; to see men begging favours of the same persons they used to disparage, and glad enough to take the humblest situation under them. I could give a dissertation on 'prejudice,' with illustrations from real life, that would rather subdue the silly gabble of some of my very superior high-bred fellow-Colo-

Colony worked as a compositor in the *Royal Gazette* office, writing from Chelsea, Mass., June 1, 1881, to the *Argosy* newspaper, and referring to the colour prejudice in the Colony, says: "I soon learned to disregard the colour line, though with prejudice very strong when I went there. I was grievously shocked, my first day at Dr. Struthers's Scotch Church, to see a substantial and respectable old Scotchman come in, with a wife as black as the ace of spades, and a half dozen cream-coloured children, and take a pew as if he belonged there. A few nights after I was at Mr. Lugar's and was shown to a seat in an empty pew, but afterwards five ladies came in, whom my modesty prevented my regarding closely, but I soon found that they were deeply coloured. The delicate attentions they paid the 'stranger within their gates,' finding the place for him in the Services, proffering their ornate fans, &c., in the most ladylike manner, won him enough to make the entire change easy afterwards.

"There was another walk which I religiously took every Sunday afternoon, to the barracks, professedly to see the soldiers parade and hear the band music, but really to see the most beautiful woman my eyes had ever rested on, and I have seen no one since that could fill the bill. I worshipped her at a distance, however; her time and attention being engrossed by the officers of every rank, who hung round her carriage like bees around a flower, and Col. Bunbury, of the 69th, who weighed fully 300 pounds, as he climbed upon her carriage-wheel, in his bob-tailed coat, presented features of devotion, behind, that made the injudicious laugh, especially those who were crowded out. She was a planter's wife, with lots of money, possessing angelic beauty, and culture the best to be obtained in Europe, and still she was not happy. Her blood had a tinge of colour, and her character, it was said, had a darker stain upon it, though I would never believe it."

nists, who, strange to say, left affluence and aristocratic connections at home to come to Demerara to accept, and gladly enough, a situation of a few pounds a year with their board." The Toronto, Canada, *Globe* has the following:—

"'Brother Smith, what does this mean?' 'What does what mean?' 'Bringing a nigger to this church.' 'But he is intelligent and well educated.' 'Who cares for that? He is a nigger.' 'But he is a friend of mine.' 'What of that? Must you therefore insult the whole congregation?' 'But he is a Christian, and belongs to the same denomination.' 'What do I care for that? Let him go and worship with his fellow-niggers.' 'But he is worth five million dollars,' said the merchant. 'Worth what?' 'Five million dollars.' 'Worth five million dollars! Brother Smith, introduce me.'"

The children born by marriages between the coloured and the white are healthy and strong. Indeed, nature appears to desire marriages between different families and nations, because such crossings of the various races improve and invigorate the species. Medical science fully teaches this to be a fact. Humboldt and others have observed that the offspring of Europeans and Ethiopians are peculiarly robust and active. From numerous observations of a similar nature, he argues that the best mode of eradicating hereditary diseases, madness, consumption, epilepsy, &c., &c., in their early tendency, is by the commixture of the species in intermarriage, which often prevents the transmission of disease to the next generation.

One remarkable feature noticeable, however, is that whilst the blacks and their children, who are also blacks, are woolly-headed, their children by Europeans, Chinese, and Indian Coolies have long, straight hair, and fine features. A short time ago, a lad entered a druggist's shop in town, and called for "a half-bit's worth of scented, purified, perfumed, cold-drawn castor oil for the hair." *Druggist.*—"For whose hair, my bright youth?" *Boy.*—"Me own, an' who else you tink? You ent know I have to tend school to-morrow, and I want to smell nice." *Druggist.*—"But (pointing to the boy's head) you don't call that hair, do you? I would call it wool." *Boy.*—

"I know dat jest as well as you; but if you want to know,—the lambs of God carries wool, but the beasts of the field carries hair, so which best? I'll give you a 'early 'tendance' ticket if you answer me now."

At this stage the druggist was called to attend to some one else, so the question remains unanswered.

Here is another little bit of street conversation: "Yes, I tell she, I aint shame o' me nation, I is black, yes, but black too much bettah dan dem composition people; and she see me daughter, and me daughter moh fairer than she self; and she tell me daughter, 'Girl, your hair is really lang,' and me daughter say, 'Yes, me hair is lang, and I can comb it too, I am not like "among you" neegah wha alarm de whole street when you go for comb you hair.'" The rest of the conversation turned upon church matters, and developed into a religious drawl.

6. The utter or total abolition of slavery in the West Indies has materially changed the condition of the once enslaved people, and placed the posterity of those persons in an entirely new relation. There are many in the Colony who were once slaves, but who, since their emancipation, have risen, by the blessing of God, beyond and above the mere day labourers. (See *The Origin of the Guyanian Indians*, p. 46 [3].) Several of the native labourers and tradesmen are doing well, and are better off than many people of the same class in England and elsewhere. Yet in the Colony we have thousands of idle drones, and worthless fellows who *will not* work, and who are consequently useless to themselves and a pest to their neighbours. In support of my statement I extract the following from a letter which appeared a short time ago in the columns of the *Colonist*, dated April 21st, 1881:—

"The Kroomen are a hard-working race, and a more willing and quiet race of people cannot be found; but we have to look into the future as well. We will see at a glance that however hard-working and industrious the Kroomen as a race may be, their offspring by no means take after them in that particular, for where will a more lazy, lawless, careless, and worthless lot of wretches be found than amongst the black labouring Creole population of British Guyana? Seeing a Creole gang of women and girls, from the ages of from 13 to 20, mustered on an estate, from the different neighbouring villages, for the purpose of applying artificial manure in the fields, or for carrying megass in the buildings when sugar-making is going on, or of men for the digging of trenches, which work occasionally occurs on an estate, and sometimes other descriptions of work requiring the exclusive use of the shovel, a stranger at first sight would be inclined to the belief that that estate, at least, was well supplied with strong and robust Creole labourers. But that is just where the stranger would make a mistake, for after the completion of the particular work on which they were there and then engaged he might run the cultivated parts of the country through and he wouldn't find them, at least not any of the men. Although these people will engage to carry megass in the buildings and apply manure in the cane-fields, yet they scorn the idea of going into the fields and doing ordinary work, such as weeding grass and threshing canes; in fact, they think it quite beneath their dignity to do it. While they are young they think of no such thing as working hard, their only thoughts are on getting men to work for them, and many of them do succeed in securing a mate, but does he work? As long as the man is young and in the prime of health things go on well with them, the man supporting her and himself too, and perhaps a few children, on what he works for during about two months of the year, and steals during the remaining ten, but when ill health and old age begin to approach, then the woman feels that she must work or starve; and it is of just such a class that the Creole gangs of weeders are composed. From their excessive poverty at this stage, when they do begin to work, they are in such a hurry to make up for lost time that they are utterly incapable of performing their task with anything like neatness; and in their anxiety they turn out the most wretched work that could be found in any cane-field in the world. Owing to their improvidence, thriftlessness and laziness in youth, when they have arrived at this advanced stage of degeneration, in the case of any of their children being boys, they are utterly unable, from the want of means, to apprentice them to a trade requiring any length of time for its acquisition; and these boys, having a decided objection to work until they are driven to it by nothing short of starvation, will, on the arrival of that time, catch at anything which offers and requires the smallest outlay of capital for implements and the least amount of physical and mental exertion. Thus it is we get our mule-boys, for all the implements they have to provide amount to a piece of rope wherewith to flog the mules, and this they steal. But these boys, unlike the men and women, after the cessation of their work or the finish of sugar-making on the estate, are actually to be found in the day-time. But where? Not in the cane-field, unless they are there for unlawful purposes, but around the trenches and in the savannahs catching fish; and it would seem that they have very strong propensities for loitering about the plantation farms. So continues the chapter of their lives from boyhood to manhood, fatherhood, gaolhood, and boyhood again. I believe I could fill a mighty big volume on the worthlessness of the Negro Creoles of British Guyana, but I close my remarks now on the blacks—at least for the present."

7. I deeply regret to state that among a large class of native black and coloured Creole agriculturists a condition the reverse of prosperous exists. I allude to the cattle and provision farmers, many of whom, through the enforcement of the law relating to making up roads, allow their property to be sold at execution, on account of their having failed to comply with the conditions imposed by Ordinances. These lands so sold are generally bought by Portuguese and others, who turn them to better account, doing justice to themselves and to the Colony which they have made their home. Squatting is a word that stinks in the nostrils of political economists, and unfortunately British Guyana (in common with the West Indies generally) has acquired an unenviable notoriety as being a country affording every facility to those who love to lead a life of indolence under the shade of their own banana-tree. Our tropical climate is said to be enervating, and to have the effect of destroying in most constitutions the activity and energy which are popularly supposed to be innate to the natives of more temperate latitudes. Persons born in the Colony are by many imagined to be lackadaisical creatures, as limp physically as they are morally; but this impression is a mistaken one. For I can point with pride to many of our prominent

citizens, and say, "They are Creoles." But it is certain that many natives of this, as well as other tropical climates, do entertain a very decided objection to anything approaching hard work, and they most certainly have a very high regard for their own comfort and dignity. In fact, I am sorry to see that many sit down quietly and allow their affairs to go to ruin, when a little timely exertion or a little hard work, which they foolishly consider degrading, would have the effect of saving them. [See Chapter IX.]

CHAPTER VI.

THE INTRODUCTION OF FOREIGN LABOURERS INTO BRITISH GUYANA.

1. IMMIGRATION or Colonization may be considered from two points of view: as the substitution of the existing labour, or as the introduction of a more advanced, instructed, and industrious race to people the Colony, and by contact to improve the conditions of the natives or people of the country. Soon after emancipation or the abolition of slavery, the landowners or large capitalists in the Colony saw that they must at once turn their attention to foreign labourers to cultivate their lands, hitherto worked by forced labour, or abandon their several valuable properties in British Guyana and return to Europe. Not only was this the experience of Guyana planters or proprietors of sugar estates, but the very islands —Trinidad, Guadaloupe, &c.—felt that they needed foreign labourers. The earliest or the very first attempt to supply the labour market of the West Indies with Asiatics may be seen from the following statement, which I extract from the *Essequibo and Demerary Gazette* of 1806, already referred to:—

"The East India Company are said to have taken up the *Fortitude*, Captain Hughes, a vessel of 500 tons, for the purpose of carrying 450 Chinese settlers and a cargo of piece goods to Trinidad."

Later on we read that some two hundred Chinese were introduced, and possibly some of our readers intimate with the history of Trinidad may be able to say what became of these people, and if any of their descendants are to be found in the island at the present day.

The old resident proprietors of the plantations did not want the European-British or German immigrant—who readily leaves his country, established habits, and family ties, with the hope of becoming a proprietor, of finding a new fatherland for himself and his children—to come to the "magnificent province" of British Guyana to work as a field labourer on the sugar estates in the same manner as the Negroes—slaves—were forced to work, or other natives of the sunny climes were expected to work, and to put himself at the disposition and power of the proprietors. Even supposing the British and German emigrants, who readily leave their homes for distant lands, had turned their steps toward British Guyana, as field labourers, they would have been almost useless. They never could have endured the hardships, the trials, &c., as labourers in the open fields, exposed to the sun, nor would they have withstood the malaria of the coast districts. A very different class of immigrants or field labourers was required for the plantations of Guyana. Though the European immigrants do not come to our agrarian establishments as the substitute of our servile element, yet some who come to the Colony bring with them, notwithstanding, a certain value. They and their descendants have created an important population and given value to lands which before were worthless.

2. "Give me my heart's desire in Coolies" (said Anthony Trollope) "and I will make you a million hogsheads of sugar without stirring from the Colony." Indian and Chinese Coolies were the only class of people or immigrants that could suit as agricultural labourers and as settlers, and meet the requirements of the wealthy owners of sugar plantations in the Colony. Though the importation or introduction of these labourers from the distant East is very expensive on account of the means of communication, yet these Coolies or labourers alone have been the salvation of the Colony, and to them we are indebted for its present prosperous condition. What we now want is *free labour*,—the introduction of *free settlers* into the Colony. The fear on the part of the planters has been that the labourers would be drawn away from the sugar estates. "Of course it is very desirable that a large amount having been expended on the introduction of immigrants, [Coolies,] and much expense incurred during the period of their acclimatization, the planters should have the benefit of their labour

when they are well seasoned and in prime working condition. *But this is no part of the bargain.* They serve the time for which they are indentured, and after that they are free to go where they choose. It is a well-known fact that they often shift from one estate to another before the period of their indentureship expires; they commute for the remainder of their term of service frequently. No one complains of this, because it is a recognized practice. Then why should it be a grievance if they go to settle up the rivers [or anywhere else in the Colony]? Will the estates be denuded of labourers by their departure? By no means." As I shall have occasion to refer to this subject again, I shall stop here.

3. The Portuguese from Madeira were the first immigrant labourers, who arrived in British Guyana in the years 1843 and 1844. They are unmistakably a hard-working people, and by their industry and thriftiness have raised themselves to affluence. "*Quem trabalha tem alfaïa,*" "He that works has furniture," is their daily motto. Many, yea, nearly all of them, have become within these few years rich merchants, shop keepers, tavern keepers, proprietors of cattle farms, plantain estates, &c. Yet they are looked upon as enemies, more than rivals, despised and taunted with the appellation of "*white nigger*" by the Negro population of the Colony. The fact that the Madeirans, in a strange land, and among a people speaking a strange language, have managed to get so large a share of the retail trade of the Colony into their hands certainly indicates that they are peculiarly adapted or fitted for this kind of employment, and hence the hundreds of Portuguese retail shops in the country. But how did they become possessed of these shops, the well-kept plantain farms, and cattle farms, and other handsome and large residences in the city of Georgetown, and the extensive stores in Water Street, and the well-stocked liquor shops in almost every corner of the streets of the city? By the sweat of their brow, by genuine hard work, perseverance, energy of mind, thrift, and an unswerving determination to rise from the position of common labourers. Thousands of our Creole labourers get their wages weekly or monthly, and spend their money from day to day as their

wants require to be supplied. They live, to use a familiar expression, from hand to mouth, and in this respect are like some thousands of our fellow men in England and other countries. But the Portuguese work, save, and start afresh in business,—in opening shops in different places, which are not only a great convenience, but an absolute necessity. And therefore "it is absurd and childish to blame the Portuguese for their success in trading, and those natives of the Colony who wish to share in that success will act more wisely if they try and *find out what commercial qualities* in the Portuguese have enabled them to achieve their success, in spite of the disadvantages inseparable from their position as foreigners. And then on finding out what has led to the prosperity of the Portuguese, let them *try and imitate them*, wherever they are worthy of imitation. The retail trade of the Colony is open to all inclined to embark in it. Anybody is free to try it, and we should be glad to see a goodly number of Creoles fairly competing with Madeirans in this now extensive and important branch of our colonial traffic. The Portuguese may *now* be more expert in this sort of thing than the Creoles, but the latter, if they choose to go at it with a will, might in due time become equally clever and successful at buying and selling. At any rate it is only by a fair competition of this sort, in which the Portuguese are met on their own ground, so to speak, that the natives of the Colony can attain to the position the Portuguese now occupy. Certainly it will not be done by *talking* nonsense on the subject, or by *mere talking at all;* much less by anything like illegal and unchristian acts of violence, which can only bring punishment and disgrace upon those who are foolish and wicked enough to perpetrate them." The Portuguese have certainly not only made British Guyana a SECOND HOME, a SECOND MADEIRA, but they have also by dint of perseverance made a name for themselves, and now realize the truthfulness of their favourite proverb, "*Cobra boa fama, e deita-te a dormir:*" When your name is up, you may lie in bed till noon.

4. Not many years ago there was a retail shop opened by a Creole, a Mr. J. O——, at the corner of Smyth and D'Urban

Streets, and another shop a little higher up in D'Urban Street, kept by a Mr. W——. These two shops, owned by two respectable black men, were an eyesore to the people in the neighbourhood, and were scarcely or never patronized by their fellow Creoles. And when these two shops in turn were visited by the black people, it was with the intention of ruining the owners. Articles from the shops were certainly taken, but never paid for, and the poor men had consequently to close their shops.* In some instances, no sooner a small retail shop is opened than the owner fancies himself a great merchant, and lives, or rather tries to live, like the rest of the well-established merchants, and hence he is not able to meet his creditors, who trust him with goods, &c. He lives beyond his income, and dishonestly spends the money which does not belong to him, and hence he cannot succeed in business, and be able to compete with his fellow-townsman, the Portuguese retail shopkeeper. He necessarily fails in business, and the short-lived shop is closed for ever. Among the Creole black

* Twenty-six years ago a gentleman happened to be in a Portuguese shop, when he overheard the following conversation :–

Black Man.—" Wha make awe' blackman no keep shop ? Because awe no able foo make money like them Portogee fella."

Portuguese Shopman.—" I'll tell you why ; when Portuguese makes nine dollars, he spends six and puts by three ; but when black man makes nine dollars, he spends eighteen."

Black Man (laughing).—" How you make da out ? Hi ! hi ! hi ! Yaw ! yaw ! yaw ! "

Portuguese Shopman.—" Why, this way : when black man makes nine dollars, he spends it, and gets into debt for nine more ; and the latter nine dollars he never pays."

Black Man (losing his temper) " No, buddy ! me ! Take you money, an gie me two bottle a rum. Mine ! tranga one, yay."

The above is almost word for word what he heard ; and as he was then in a house of business in Georgetown, the substance of this conversation was quite correct. One of these black shop-owners, having an account of $200, would pay in $100, and run up new accounts of $150 or $200, which, with the old balance, would be a debt of $250 or $300. The upshot was, of course, these black shop-owners failed ; and in looking over their books, if they kept any at all, the amount of book debts irrecoverable was awful ; and especially with the shop-owners' relations, who, as a matter of fact, kept a running account on the Dr. but never any on the Cr. side of the books.—*Extracted from the " Colonist " of November* 25, 1881.

people there is no placing confidence in each other, there is no assisting each other, and there is no co-operation, which traits of character we see exhibited by the Portuguese, East Indian, and Chinese immigrants. The Portuguese are "a wide-awake" set of people in the Colony. Their only object seems to be to make money by all fair or unjust means. They give themselves—men and women alike—little or no rest in this pursuit. What a marked difference exists between them and the unambitious Coolies, and what a difference, too, between them and the Creole African! For instance, we place a Portuguese and black together on a sugar estate, and furnish them with the same description of work; we take them both at the same age, of course, say eighteen years. At the expiration of twelve years we look them up, but where do we find them? Look amongst the plantain farmers, shopkeepers, or house and land proprietors for the Portuguese; for the other, look amongst the occupants of the common gaol or Massareeni. This is the general run of the black labouring Creole population, though there are exceptions, and they are very few indeed. Mr. Pharaoh Chase (a Wesleyan), and Mr. James, of Golden Grove Village on the East Sea Coast, have established village sugar factories on a small scale, to enable them to manufacture their own sugar. Another sugar mill has also been erected on the east bank of the River Demerara, at Rome Village, by Mr. William Parkinson, a Wesleyan Local Preacher and Class-leader. These are honourable exceptions to the general rule.

5. The Coolies * were the next in order to be imported from the East Indies to labour or toil in the open cane-fields, exposed to the hot sun; but as I shall have occasion to speak of them more particularly in following sections, I shall make no remarks at present.

6. Seventy years ago, H. Bolingbroke (author of *A Voyage to the Demerary*) wrote: "The Chinese Colonists would form the most valuable accession to our present stock of labourers which could be introduced. . . . Guyana is adapted to be

* For the derivation of the word "Coolies" see *Guyanian Indians*, page 48.

the China of the West, and may be instructed by the nation, who ought especially to be its model." The Chinese, who are an ubiquitous race, find themselves, like the English people, in almost every part of the known world. Australia, Java, California, Singapore, &c., &c., are all inhabited by them. They were introduced into the Colony of British Guyana for the first time in the year 1853. Although they "appear a sturdy, lively, merry-hearted race," yet "they are low in the scale of moral advancement. They are ignorant, degraded people, and filthy in their habits, but will improve under good example and tuition. Their characters are reported to be fierce, cowardly, and vindictive by those who have brought them" (see Dr. Dalton's *History of British Guyana, in loco*). Although they are valuable as "settlers" in the Colony, the experience of nearly all the planters concerning them has been that they are "not suited for all sorts of work on a sugar estate; but the work which they will condescend to do, they excel in, whatever it may be. As long as they undertake to do it, they do it well; but I think" (says a writer in the *Colonist*) "that the principal cause of their abhorring and refusing to do some descriptions of work on an estate lies in the fact that there are so few of them on any estate, and being the general favourites of the manager, they are upheld in their caprices, and, like the only child, they are spoiled. I am of opinion, however, that if there were many of them, the particular work which they take a fancy to would not be sufficient for them all the year round, and I am inclined to believe that they would then do that which they could get to do. They are of an ambitious turn of mind; and having a great love for commerce, they would work hard so as to try and accumulate funds by which they might be enabled to become—as a great many of them have done already—makers of, and dealers in, charcoal, and eventually to become respectable shopkeepers, and even merchants." We have in the Colony Chinese carpenters, cabinet-makers, builders of houses, &c. The two places of worship in the County of Demerara, one in Georgetown, in connection with the Episcopal Church of England, and the other at Peter's Hall, in connection with the Plymouth

Brethren, of which Mr. Lowe is the minister, were I believe planned and built by the Chinese carpenters. The shops or stores of Messrs. Wo Lee and Co., and others in Lombard Street, are well fitted up and stocked with Chinese commodities, all new and rare, and largely patronized by ladies and gentlemen. The clerks, too, employed by these Chinese gentlemen merchants, are civil and obliging. The Chinese merchant is generally a fat, round-faced man, with an important and business-like look. He wears the same style of clothing as the meanest Coolies, but of finer materials, and is always clean and neat; and his long tail, tipped with red silk, hangs down to his heels. He is always good-natured; and he will show you everything he has, and does not seem to mind if you buy nothing; but if you buy a few things of him, he will speak to you afterwards every time you pass his shop, asking you to walk in and sit down, or take a cup of tea, without milk and sugar, of course, which seems to be the Chinaman's principal drink, morning, noon, and evening. The Portuguese and Chinese are the only people in the Colony—in the city especially—who keep barbers' shops, and the latter have plenty to do, shaving heads and cleaning ears; for which latter operation they have a great array of little tweezers, pricks, and brushes. Not many months ago, there was a rumour to the effect that the Chinese merchants in Demerara and Berbice intended forming a company, and then chartering a steamer, not only to import Chinese articles, but to bring out Chinese as "free settlers" to the Colony. I sincerely hope that though Chinese immigration, like the East Indian immigration, may be a costly one, steps will yet be taken once more to import Chinese Coolies into our midst; I have never yet seen any successful private attempt at immigration or colonization. All such promoters have been compelled after all to petition the local Governments for help. It is only within the last year or two that agitation on the subject of Chinese immigration can be said to have ceased. When two vessels arrived with a complement of labourers in 1853, the planters were not long in finding out the superior qualities of the new arrivals. Diplomatic difficulties interfered with the inauguration of a system under Government supervision until 1859; and in 1866 the Convention between the Chinese Government and the French and British representatives at Pekin brought about its sudden suspension. One of the stipulations in this Treaty was, that the immigrants should be entitled to back passage on the expiration of their indenture; and as the introduction of each individual had cost the revenue something like £24, it was found that the Colony could not bear the imposition of such a heavy obligation. Ultimately it was arranged that instead of back passage each immigrant should be entitled to $50 at the end of five years' servitude; but Chinese immigration has never regained a permanent footing, the last arrival being a ship from Canton with 388 of all classes and conditions. Investigation made in 1875, with a view of reopening agencies, showed that 2,000 emigrants were leaving Amoy per month, and that during the seven years preceding 153,000 had left Swatow, while in the same period 260,000—or something like the entire population of British Guyana—left Hong Kong to seek a home elsewhere.

7. In 1864 Mr. O-Tye-Kim (a gentleman of Chinese extraction) from Singapore, connected with the Plymouth Brethren, came to the Colony with a view to preach the Gospel to his countrymen. Many still perhaps in the City of Georgetown will remember the faithful and stirring address he delivered in the "Old Colony House" in High Street, now pulled down to make room for a very handsome building in course of erection to be called "The Law Courts." Mr. O-Tye-Kim was a very useful man, and an earnest preacher of the Gospel, and did much good among his countrymen! He afterwards rejoined the Episcopal Church of England, and received the assistance he required from the Bishop of the Diocese (the Right Reverend W. P. Austin, D.D.). Early in February, 1865, he petitioned the Governor (Francis Hincks, Esquire) and the Honourable Court of Policy to grant him a tract of land on the Camoonie Creek, which falls into the Demerara River immediately below Plantation *Glasgow*, and vote him the loan of 1,500 dollars, to enable him to form a settlement of free Christian Chinese. Though the petition was at first opposed

by several men of the Honourable Court, Governor Hincks, "who perhaps had at first given his countenance to it, or whatever else may have been the motive power," was determined to carry out Mr. O-Tye-Kim's scheme. When the subject was again introduced in the Court, "the obstructive members succumbed," and the prayer of Mr. O-Tye-Kim's petition was granted. This infant or newly formed Chinese settlement up the Demerara River was in the latter part of February, 1865, visited by the Governor, and Admiral HOPE who was on a visit to the Colony, and on the suggestion of the Magistrate of the city it was named "Hopetown." It became a flourishing settlement under the energetic and plucky manager, O-Tye-Kim. He performed in person the different duties of preacher, surveyor, storekeeper, and general manager. It was, however, a great blow to the new settlers when unexpectedly he disappeared from the Colony.

8. When in the year 1861 the Rev. Dr. Lobschild, a Prussian Missionary, paid a visit to the Colony "with the object of inquiring into the condition of the Chinese in the land of their adoption, and of making suggestions to the authorities where he saw that something might be done for their amelioration, Dr. Lobschild was so much struck with the desirability of British Guyana for Chinese settlers that he advocated the establishment of village communities, up the rivers, in favourable localities." The Chinese, though they love their native land, and strongly desire at their death to be buried there, are yet a people who make themselves as happy and comfortable in foreign lands as in their own country. In this and other respects they are very unlike the East Indian Coolies. There is greater likelihood of the Chinese immigrant Coolies permanently settling in the Colony than the East Indian Coolies. It was a great mistake at the very outset for the interested parties—the proprietors of estates and other planters in the Colony—to arrange with the Indian Government to give the imported Coolies a return or free passage back to their native land. It is this return passage that is in the way of our Indian Coolies settling in the Colony. The Chinese never had such privileges allowed them, and hence we have

nearly all who have come to the Colony. A few, of course, have left at their own expense, and some others have died; still we have a large number of them in the City and other parts of the Colony. Chinese settlements will be far more preferable and advantageous than the Indian Coolie settlements. At least, I have been told so by those who have had a great deal to do with them.

9. It is very unfortunate to the Colony that we have no more Chinese Coolies imported from the "Celestial Empire." Referring to this subject, the editor of the *Royal Gazette*, in his publication of January 1st, 1870, observed:—

"With regard to Chinese immigration, the more one reflects on the difficulties thrown in our way in procuring people, the more room is there for surprise when it is found that Chinese emigrate in large numbers to other countries. In California alone there are one hundred thousand, and they are said to be extremely industrious, tidy, saving, and civil; there are in San Francisco some three or four hundred Chinese stores, and the large body of people are engaged in all kinds of trades and callings down to those of cook and washer. It may be that the great majority, if not all, of these people are voluntary immigrants, paying their own passage, or having it paid for them by friends or persons on whose aid they can rely; but we find also that Chinese are imported into Peru, Cuba, and other places under contracts of service, and in no instance has it been stated, so far as we are aware, that there was attached to the emigration any condition or stipulation with regard to a return passage, such as the Chinese Government would now insist upon in respect to the people emigrating to this Colony. When the Pacific Railway was in course of construction, a Dutchman supplied the Company with not three or four or ten hundred Chinamen, but *thirty thousand*, and, from all that appears to the contrary, they must have been procured under a labour-contract of some kind. It is stated further that the same enterprising gentleman has started a scheme for supplying planters in the Southern States of America with 100,000 labourers annually. If the truth were known, it would, we feel confident, be found that the emigration of the 30,000 was without any stipulation about a back passage, and that should Mr. Schaap succeed in his gigantic scheme of emigration, it will also be free of any such condition. It has occurred to us, although possibly there may be no foundation for the supposition, that too much delicacy and consideration is exhibited by our Government in dealing with that of China, and that something like timidity on our part encourages them in being much more exacting than would be the case if we showed a bolder front. There has been recently some fresh communication between the two Governments on the subject of emigration, and there is reason to hope that more favourable terms have been or are likely to be obtained, but the result has not yet been made public."

We are now in A.D. 1882, and yet there is no sign or likelihood of the "Celestials" finding their way to the "land of mud," to the land flowing with sugar, rum, and molasses.

10. The Government of the "Celestial Empire" very justly put an end to further exportations of labourers to the island of Cuba, because the Cuban Government, or rather the "Companies" who imported Chinese Coolies, not only violated the terms of contract entered into, but treated the Coolies most tyrannically and most brutally. Peru did the same. But why there should be any hesitancy, on the part of the Chinese Government or other local authorities, to permit the Celestials to emigrate to British Guyana, is a question that cannot be satisfactorily answered. In British Guyana the Chinese and all other nations enjoy equal privileges and are free subjects. The Coolies, of course, so long as they are under indentureship to an estate, are expected to remain there and do the work expected of them; but then they are not shut up in the barracks or ranges in the evening and on Sundays; even though indentured, they are allowed full liberty to visit their friends in any part of the Colony, and in sickness every possible kind attention is paid to them. The following extracts from well-authenticated documents will give my reader some idea of the ill-treatment and tyranny which the Chinese Coolies have from time to time received and experienced from the planters, masters of the estates, both in Peru and Cuba, and at the same time give him some further idea of what a slave's life must have been years ago when British Guyana was a slave-holding and slave-importing Colony.

Times, indeed, have wonderfully changed. The extracts referred to are as follow.

A correspondent, dating from Lima recently, says:—

"All classes have suffered from the war, but the Chinese, whose lot has always been a hard one, have more reason to complain than any one else. Slavery in the South was a pleasure in the majority of instances as compared with the sufferings of the unfortunate Coolies on the sugar plantations of Peru. Have the public abroad any idea of the life of a Coolie on the majority of the plantations? He is aroused before daylight, and turns out with his fellow prisoners to answer the muster-roll. Should he be lax in attending, two or three blows are sure to fall to his lot. He is driven to the field or sugar-house, as the case may be, and immediately set to work. During the forenoon he is allowed half an hour to cook his half pound of rice, his occasional piece of meat or fish, and perhaps a scrap of vegetables. This apology for a meal over he returns to his labour, which is vigilantly superintended by a task-master. At dusk he is driven back to his pen, where he eats what serves as his second meal, and then to bed. A pound of rice per day is the contract stipulation as a rule, and even this quantity is not fairly distributed. The boundaries of the estates are carefully watched to prevent men leaving them, and at night time they are all locked up together in the 'galpones,' as their prisons are termed. The lash is unsparingly used as the punishment for the smallest peccadillo, and it is most cruelly applied by the half-blooded Spanish Negroes, who evidently enjoy their brutal task. Evasion is the most heinous crime in the code of a plantation, ranking far higher than murder. It is always severely punished, and the offender, if carried back alive, which sometimes he is not, is kept constantly 'on the chain.' This term is employed to describe a man who has a ring of iron welded round one of his ankles, to which is attached a long chain with a weight at the end. Frequently, instead of this weight, the chain terminates in a similar welded ring round the leg of another unfortunate. Another plan is also becoming general, and a straight bar, terminating in two rings, is welded on to the victim's legs, compelling him to move somewhat like a pair of living compasses. Sometimes an iron band is welded round the body, with a chain running from it to a ring round the ankle. In all cases constant and extreme suffering is entailed. The iron rings produce sores on the legs, and the poor wretches then stuff rags or other soft substances in to alleviate the pain they suffer from the wounds and the stinging of the insects which swarm in the cane-fields. The tales of their sufferings, if fully told, would attract sympathy the world over.

"When passing through a plantation, I have had the bars of a moveable gate taken down by a man who could not rise from the ground, and who, on my questioning him, answered that he had been so severely injured shortly before that he had lost the use of the lower part of his body, and that, as the doctor had said he had only a few days to live, he had been carried to this gateway to see that the bars were kept constantly in position to prevent cattle straying through them. Death was in the man's face while I spoke to him, yet from the manner in which he spoke one could see he took this inhuman treatment as a matter of course, and that long subjection had taught him to believe that such a sentiment as human sympathy has no existence. Another man I once saw have a penknife driven repeatedly into his back between the blade bones while his elbows were so tightly drawn together behind that his chest bones appeared to be bursting through his skin. Only the other day ten men who had been kidnapped in Lima and carried to a plantation in the North attempted to effect their escape. They were recaptured, carried back, treated most inhumanly on the journey, and then laid on the ground and flogged until their bodies bore little semblance to humanity; then, last and most degrading and disgusting cruelty of all, the overseers drove their heavy rowelled spurs into the bleeding bodies, until to the gashes of the lash were added the spur-galls which in civilized countries the law considers cruelty and punishes as such when inflicted on animals."

Extract from the Report of Consul Roosevelet, of Matanzas:

"The quarters of the Negroes and Chinese in Cuba are usually a large stone house, forming a long parallelogram, with one entrance. The interior is divided into two divisions, and the rooms are situated on the four sides of a large yard. The rooms open into this yard, and rarely have windows. One division is for the males, and one for the females; but as there is free communication between them there is practically no separation of the sexes. The rooms adjoining the entrance are usually large and well lighted, with a balcony or porch in front. These are occupied by the 'mayoral' or driver, who is the controller and immediate governor of the labourers; said driver assigns their tasks, administers correction, &c., under instructions from the administrator. One day in the week is given for rest and recreation, but not necessarily on Sunday. The owners of adjoining estates manage among themselves so that labourers of two plantations never are idle on the same day. They object to free intermingling, in order to prevent the intrigues, combinations, &c., which at one time frequently culminated in insurrections.

"The recreations of the Negroes are few and simple. They dance, sleep, and sun themselves; beyond this they have no amusement. They are called to labour at five o'clock in the morning, and have two intermissions during the day for meals; at six o'clock in the evening they are back in the barracks locked up for the night—a life of unceasing toil, unalleviated by any domestic joys, without contact with the outer world: no interest, ties, or thoughts beyond the confines of the plantation, they plod on from childhood to death, and finally are buried in some neglected spot to become the bogeys and ghosts of superstitious fancies. Their lot of late has, however, been much ameliorated. The lash is practically abolished, and the interest of the owners compels them to be more lenient and less exacting. The total extinction of the slave trade has taken away the only sources of supply of labour, and though humanity be silent, selfishness produces a more careful preservation of the only labour existing. In former years a slave could readily treble his cost in five years, and as there was a constant entry of Negroes, the planter could readily replenish his force. It was cheaper to work the slave to the verge of death than to preserve him carefully at a producing age. This is all past now, and sad as may seem to be the condition of the Negro, it is immeasurably better than some twenty years ago."

CHAPTER VII.

OUR CHINESE COOLIE IMMIGRANTS, AND THE ABORIGINAL INDIANS.

1. THE Chinese are a race of people who "have those habits of body which can bear the exertions of industry between the tropics; and they have those habits of artificial society which fit them for a variety of labours to which rude savages cannot be brought to attend. Above all, they have a rational foresight, and may be entrusted with the care of their own maintenance, without danger of that heinous improvidence—that careless alternation of intemperance and sloth—which besets the African Negro who is his own master." They are persevering and enterprising in all they do or attempt. They readily transport themselves from their country to distant foreign lands to seek their fortune. Give them but a fair prospect of gain, and there is no part of the world to which they will not travel. Like their rivals and fellow-Colonists, the Portuguese, they "are pre-eminently a people devoted to money-making. The great object of their idolatry, practically, is Mammon. They may strew flowers, burn pieces of gilt paper, and bow themselves before their gods many and lords many; but to Mammon they give their thoughts, their affections, and their labours." They are not—like the great majority of our East Indian Coolies, whose only garment is a long strip of calico wound round the body—addicted to hoarding; but spend their money when they have earned it, being very fond of good living, and thus circulate the money in the Colony, and keep the trade going. The habits of the Chinese in this respect remind me of a class of Mysorians in Southern India called "*Khaliauts*," who are very unlike the ordinary Coolies

that we obtain from India. They work, and mean work; they have an *esprit de corps;* they are chosen men, well formed, strong, and vigorous, and by proper management can be worked almost as well as English workmen or labourers. What they earn they spend in eating and clothing, and they are great consumers of flesh, and hence their strength for manual labour. They are not a people to hoard up the money as our Coolies do in the Colony, but spend readily what they have earned by the sweat of their brow. These Khaliauts would form a very valuable accession to our present stock of labourers, if they could only be obtained and introduced from the Mysore territory.

2. Our Chinese Coolies or labourers—like their monosyllabic language, which no foreigner can understand, or easily learn or acquire—are a peculiar people, and their habits, customs, &c., are also peculiar. Yet they are an interesting people, and make good labourers. Men and women among them dress alike: they wear a loose jacket and pair of trousers of blue cotton. The men wreathe their pigtails round their head, and wear hats of their own making. They may be called *Topiwalla* or *Topikarar* in this respect. As a rule, our Chinese Coolies are a notorious set of fowl-stealers. They are guilty of bare-faced larcenies, wholesale perjury, &c. Their gambling and opium-smoking propensities, and the establishments or dens connected with them, which, unfortunately, are frequently visited by the black people and others, are too well known to need any description here. The Joss houses in which their unholy rites are celebrated, in which, alas, the black Creoles—to their shame be it said—take a part, are a blight, a stain and a disgrace to the Christian land in which they live. Though, in a moral point of view, the bodily presence of the Chinese is not advantageous, yet they are unmistakably good labourers.

3. China,—which is eleven times the size of the British Isles, with twelve times the number of people,—whence our "Celestials" have come to British Guyana, seems to be referred to in Isaiah xlix. 12, where we have the expression, "These shall come from the land of Sinim." Dr.

W. Smith, in the third volume of his *Dictionary of the Bible*, p. 1328, referring to this country, remarks :—

"There is no *à priori* improbability in the name of the Sinæ being known to the inhabitants of Western Asia in the age of Isaiah; for though it is not mentioned by the Greek geographers until the age of Ptolemy, it is certain that an inland commercial route connected the extreme east with the west at a very early period, and that a traffic was maintained on the frontier of China between the Sinæ and the Scythians, in the manner still followed by the Chinese and the Russians at *Kiachta*. If there was any name for these Chinese traders who travelled westward, it would probably be that of the Sinæ, whose town Thinæ* (another form of the Sinæ) was one of the great emporiums in the western part of China, and is represented by the modern *Thsin* or *Tin* in the province of *Schensi*. The Sinæ attained an independent position in Western China as early as the eighth century B.C., and in the third century B.C. established their sway under the dynasty of *Tsin* over the whole of the empire. The Rabbinical name for China, *Tsin*, as well as 'China' itself, was derived from this dynasty."

The name of the country in its plural Hebrew form means "*bushes*," "*woods*," &c., and hence *erets sinim*, the land of bushes, the land of woods, &c., where several of the Jews—the descendants of the *ten* lost tribes—are supposed to be found.

4. It is this passage in Isaiah (xlix. 12) which has led many persons to suppose that the lost *ten* tribes of Israel had found a home in China—"the Celestial Empire." It is a well-known fact that the Jews are a Shemitic race, and Dr. Hales (quoted by Dr. A. Clarke in his Commentary) has given the Chinese—at least those occupying the eastern part of China—a Shemitic origin. The Rev. Joseph Wolf, in his Journals, written between the years 1831 and 1834, according

* The *Periplus* says, "Beyond the Khreuse lies a city called Thina, not on the coast but inland, from which both raw and manufactured silk are brought by land, then down the Ganges, and from thence by sea to Malabar." Ceylon (Sielediba or Taprobane), "one of the most ancient of emporiums for silk" brought or introduced there, appears to have been known to the Chinese at a very early period.

to Rev. Dr. W. H. Poole, affirms as an undeniable fact that the lost tribes of Israel are all found in China. And if the theory advanced by others *be true*, viz., that the Continent of America was peopled from China in very early times, the lost tribes of Israel must be found among the Aboriginal Indians whom we daily meet with. Mrs. Dixon and other writers positively assert that the Indians of America are the *ten* tribes who were lost. It is a well-known fact also that wherever the Jews are dispersed or in whatever country they may be found they have preserved much of their own peculiar physiognomy, and certain of their religious and ceremonial rites which we see wanting in the Chinese immigrants and the Aboriginal Indians we meet with. There are, however, some in the Colony and elsewhere who go in heartily for the theory that the British people—the Anglo-Saxons—and they alone, are the Israelites of the lost ten tribes of the house of Israel: they will be better able to deal with the subject than I am. At the same time it is my firm belief and candid conviction that America—probably the north part—received a colony of the ubiquitous Chinese, but *from what part* it is impossible now for any one to say; but I do deny the assertion, too often made, and the supposition, that all the American Indians belong to the Chinese stock. The traits of resemblance, however striking, in physiognomy, complexion, &c., between the "Celestials" (Chinese) and (to coin another word of similar formation) the "Terrestrials" (the Indians) are, to use the expression of the Rev. J. Talboys Wheeler, on this very subject of identity between these two nations, "the mere effect of chance."

5. Other writers (equally learned as Hales, Wolf, &c.) have ascribed a very different origin to the Chinese, which Professor Max Müller has endorsed. The Chinese, according to later writers, do not belong to the Shemitic but to the *Yellow Race*, called the *Mongol Race*, of the Turanian type. All the members of this race, however, do not exhibit these distinct features. Some of their characteristics would seem to identify them with the Caucasian Group. Speaking of the formation of the skull of the Chinese and the Aboriginal

Indians of America, Humboldt says: "The skulls of the American tribes display the same broad and pyramidal form as the heads of the Turanian nations. Travellers have been struck with the general resemblance which certainly subsists between these two departments of mankind. What we have been stating as to the exterior form of the indigenous Americans confirms the accounts of other travellers, as to a striking analogy between the Mongol and the American. This analogy is particularly evident in the colour of the skin and hair, in the defective beard, high cheek bones, and in the direction of the eyes. We cannot refuse to admit that the human species does not contain races resembling one another more than the Americans, Mongols, Mantchoux, and Malay." This is a weighty statement, certainly; and it would appear from it that the Aboriginal Indians are the offshoots or descendants of the Mongolian Chinese who now live in our midst as our fellow Colonists. That there is a striking similarity between the two I admit, especially in the features and beardlessness, though several Chinese and Indians have beards and hair on their face; only they will not let them grow.

6. "The colour of the skin," according to Humboldt and some others, is certainly a very convenient characteristic to fix upon in order to identify the various races, but it cannot always be depended upon, since the shades of colour merge into one another. Though the American Indians may be of light-coloured skin, yet it is a well-ascertained fact that these very Indians (Red Indians, as they have been frequently but incorrectly called) often have dark brown or almost black skins like many Coolies from the East Indies. The white or Caucasian race are often very darkly tinted. Arabs are often of a brown colour, which nearly approaches black, and so are a large majority of the natives of Hindustan, and yet they belong to the Caucasian or Shemitic type or race. The Abyssinians, although very brown, are not black. Among the members of the white in northern latitudes, especially women, the skin has often a yellowish tint. About the hair, the skull, &c., referred to by the learned Humboldt, Dr. Luthardt (in his *Fundamental Truths of Christianity*) observes:—

"The differences of these varieties of the one human race are but of an external kind. They relate only to the hair, the colour of the skin, and the form of the skull; and these are mere externals, which circumstances might alter, and which they can be proved to have done. *What a difference there is, for example, in outward appearance between the modern and the ancient fair-haired Germans! The modern Magyars, too, are as different as possible from their ancestors the ancient Huns, who have been depicted to us as so frightful, that we may well suppose the present Magyars to have no resemblance to them.* [The italics are mine.] It is only in some remote parts of Hungary that one meets with the ugliness which was peculiar to the Huns. It is besides a fact that civilization alters even the bodily structure. Intellectual improvement produces corporeal improvement, as, on the other hand, man may degenerate even in his bodily structure [as, alas, is evinced by the Aboriginal Indians]. Nor has climate less effect upon man than upon the domestic animals. With all this is connected the fact that no characteristic of any single race, is either essential to that race or exclusively its own, but that the transitions are fleeting, and contrasts only reached by means of intermediate degrees. Neither a definite form of skull and pelvis, nor the colour of the hair and eyes, nor any other specific characteristic, belongs exclusively to any single race; in which, in one and the same nation, the greatest difference as often exists. The German male skull differs from the female in magnitude (100·79 in horizontal circumference, and 100 90 in the size of the cavity and weight of the brain), and still more in its typical distinction, in a far greater degree than the skulls of different races do from each other."

Just as the modern population of Rome do not *absolutely* reproduce the features of the ancient Latin races, and just as the modern descendants of the old inhabitants of Germany have undergone many modifications, which would render it difficult at the present day to find in the greater portion of that country general characteristics based upon the structure of the head, hair, &c., so I believe the Aborigines of America, in like manner, have considerably undergone many modifications in their features, structure of the head, &c., so as apparently to lose all traces of their identity with the natives of Hindustan. "The defective beard" or beardlessness among the Mongolian Chinese and the Aboriginal Indians is remarkable indeed, but why hair does not grow on their faces I cannot tell. Perhaps the climate and manner of living have something to do with it. The Malays occupying the Indian Archipelago, who are closely connected with the Indo-Chinese, have no beard or hair at all growing on their faces, and their breasts and limbs also are destitute of hair; but the Javanese (among whom the Brahmanical religion flourished from an epoch of unknown antiquity till about the year 1478, when that of Muhamad superseded it, and who possess a civilization, a history, and antiquities of their own, of great interest), belonging to the same family, have a glossy black moustache. The Slavonian family, in their features recalling the Caucasian type, have also a defective beard. The Cingalese—who are not a Mongolian race—have in like manner very little or no hair at all on their faces. Hundreds of the black people seen in the city of Georgetown, and the Colony in general, have scarcely any hair at all on their faces. Even in Europe there are many who are smooth-faced, with scarcely any hair on their faces or chins. The broad and pyramidal form of structure of the heads of several of the Indian tribes is simply perhaps owing to the artificial and cruel means employed when they are infants to flatten and elongate the head, a fact which has been proved by some travellers.

7. To what I have stated in the above paragraphs I may further add, that there are anthropologists who have spent a great deal of their time in trying to discover the real origin of the Indians of America, but up to the present their studies have led to no satisfactory result. They will not, however, bring their minds to believe that the Indians of America as a whole nation have any connection or relationship whatever with the yellow or Mongolian race, the Chinese. From all I have said on the subject, the reader will perceive that learned men, men of science, are divided in their opinions. However, it is my firm conviction (and I may be wrong in it) that all the Aboriginal Indians inhabiting the Guyanas have had very little or nothing whatever to do with the Chinese, who belong to the Turanian or Mongolian race. I believe that they are the descendants of the Hindus and Malays, or Indo-Malayan race

from the Indian Archipelago, to the south and south-east of Hindustan and Ceylon. The likeness or resemblance in features between the Chinese and Indians is striking indeed at first sight, but on close or careful examination a difference is discernible. I have myself frequently seen on the different sugar estates in the Colony, and in the City of Georgetown also, Coolies come from some parts of Northern Hindustan, with features resembling the Chinese, and who could very easily pass for Chinese, but who have no Chinese blood running in their veins. Should these Chinese-looking Hindu Coolies of Northern India contract marriages with the "Bokeens," I am positive their offspring or children would resemble very much the "Bok" children, and show a kind of family likeness between the two nations.

8. The following description of the Indo-Malayans exactly corresponds with the character and description of the Aborigines of the Guyanas:—"The colour of all these varied tribes [of the Indo-Malay] is of light reddish brown, with more or less of an olive tinge, not varying in any important degree over an extent of country as large as all Southern Europe. The hair is equally constant, being invariably black and straight, and of a rather coarse texture, so that any lighter tint, or any wave or curl in it, is almost certain proof of the admixture of some foreign blood. The face is nearly destitute of beard, and the breast and limbs are free from hair. The stature is tolerably equal, and is always considerably below that of the average European; the body is robust, the breast well developed, the feet small, thick, and short, the hands small and rather delicate. The face is a little broad and inclined to be flat; the forehead is rather rounded, the brows low, the eyes black, and very slightly oblique; the nose is rather small, not prominent, but straight and well shaped, the apex a little rounded, the nostrils broad and slightly exposed; the cheek-bones are rather prominent, the mouth large, the lips broad and well cut, but not protruding, the chin round and well formed. . . . On the whole the Malays are certainly not handsome. In youth, however, they are often very good-looking, and many of the boys and girls up to twelve or fifteen years

of age are very pleasing, and some have countenances which are in their way almost perfect. I am inclined to think they lose much of their good looks by bad habits and irregular living. . . . Their lives are often passed in alternate starvation and feasting, idleness and excessive labour, and this naturally produces premature old age and harshness oftentimes. In character the Malay is impassive. He exhibits reserve, diffidence, and even bashfulness, which is in some degree attractive, and leads the observer to think that the ferocious and bloodthirsty character imputed to the race must be grossly exaggerated. He is not demonstrative. His feelings of surprise, admiration, or fear, are never openly manifested, and are probably not strongly felt. He is slow and deliberate in speech, and circuitous in introducing the subject he has come expressly to discuss. These are the main features of his moral nature, and exhibit themselves in every action of his life. Children and women are timid, and scream and run at the unexpected sight of a European. In the company of men they are silent, and are generally quiet and obedient. When alone, the Malay is taciturn; he neither talks nor sings to himself. When several are paddling a canoe, they occasionally chant a monotonous and plaintive song. He is cautious of giving offence to his equals. He does not quarrel easily about money matters, dislikes asking too frequently even for payment of his just debts, and will often give them up altogether rather than quarrel with his debtor. Practical joking is utterly repugnant to his disposition, for he is particularly sensitive to breaches of etiquette, or any interference with the personal liberty of himself or another. As an example, I may mention that I have often found it very difficult to get one Malay servant to waken another. He will call as loud as he can, but will hardly touch, much less shake his comrade. I have frequently had to waken a hard sleeper myself when on a land or sea journey. . . . The Malays are almost invariably kind and gentle, hardly ever interfering at all with their children's pursuits and amusements, and giving them perfect liberty at whatever age they wish to claim it. But these very peaceful relations between parents and children are no doubt in a great measure due to the listless and apathetic character of the race, which never leads the younger members into serious opposition to the elders." The writer (A. R. Wallace) from whose writings I have given this extract has unconsciously been describing the manners, habits, &c., of the Aborigines of the South American Continent, and this description cannot be applied to the Mongolian Chinese in any sense or shape whatever. As I have already stated in this chapter and elsewhere, I believe "that whatever may be the difference of opinions among the learned, and whatever physiological and craniological differences may exist between the American Indians and the Asiatics, there is not the slightest doubt that the Continent of America—North and South—was peopled from Asia in general, and Hindustan and the Indian or Indo-Malayan Archipelago in particular," and not altogether from the Celestial Empire. The Malayan race as a whole (says the above writer) undoubtedly very closely resembles the East Asian populations, from Siam to Mandchouria. I was much struck with this when in the Island of Bali I saw Chinese traders who had adopted the costume of that country, and who could then hardly be distinguished from Malays; and, on the other hand, I have seen natives of Java who, as far as physiognomy was concerned, would pass very well for Chinese.

In my *Guyanian Indians* (section ii.) I have pointed out that the Hindu merchants in very ancient times sailed westward, &c., and that the ancient Hindus were an enterprising people, always on the move, migrating or voyaging to distant countries. Marine insurances are mentioned in the Laws or Institutes of Manu (the Moses of India), and Professor Wilson was of opinion there was commerce by sea between India and China at a very early date, the navigators being Hindus. The earliest intimation we have of an overland trade is found in Pliny's account of the embassy from Ceylon to Rome. Just as the Hindus found their way to other distant countries from their home, so there is no doubt they found their way also to the American Continent; hence their descendants the Aboriginal Indians.

9. Francis Newman has fully proved the Shemitic character of the Berber dialects, which are spoken in many varieties all over the northern coast of Africa, from Egypt to the Atlantic Ocean, wherever they have not been supplanted by the language of the conquering Arabs. In ancient times the Shemitic family of the Peninsula of Arabia sent one Colony into Africa, where the ancient Shemitic language has maintained itself up to the present day. This is the Ethiopic or Abyssinian language, commonly called by the people the *Gees* language. With the language other practices, and customs, and ideas, &c., have found their way. In like manner the Malays have for several centuries been influenced by Hindus from the southern portion of India, Chinese, and Arabic immigration. The Rev. John Trapp (one of the earliest English commentators on the Bible) says: "Joktan, the grandson of Eber (great grandson of Shem), with his sons, were seated in the East Indies, but, having fallen from Eber's faith to heathenism, they are written in the dust: there is little mention made of them in the Scriptures." Wherever we see a striking similarity of things in general, in manners, customs, practices, habits, &c., there evidently the Shemitic element has been at work. The Indians of Guyana in all these matters are more like the natives of Hindustan than the Chinese we have in our midst. If the reader is of an inquiring mind, I would advise him to study the different races in the Colony by whom we are surrounded, and he will find that there exists a greater similarity between the Indians and Hindu Coolies in hundreds of instances, than between the Indians and the Chinese.*

10. I think I have, considering my limited space, said enough on this dry and yet not uninteresting subject. It matters very little to what race the Chinese Coolies or immigrants belong. They come to the Colony of British Guyana from the Celestial Empire, where fans, parasols, pipes, snuff-boxes, purses, and other curiously worked nicknacks are

* On this subject read my *Origin of the Guyanian Indians Ascertained, &c.*

made. They are indeed an ingenious people. They have their defects or faults, like any other nation in the world. "Gambling, which paralyses labour," says M. de Bourboulon, "is one of the prevalent causes of their pauperism, but there is another and more disastrous—dissipation. The thin varnish of decency and restraint with which Chinese society [in China] is covered conceals a widespread corruption. Public morality is only a mask worn above a deep depravity surpassing all that is told in ancient history, and all that is known of the dissipated habits of the Persians and Hindus of our own day." In British Guyana between the black Creoles and Chinese there has existed a strong, bitter, prejudicial feeling towards each other, and so far as I have been able to ascertain there is no likelihood of a Chinaman ever marrying a black woman, or a black man ever marrying a Chinese woman. A similar feeling exists among the East Indian Coolies also towards the black race. Of course I do not refer to isolated cases of such marriages which have taken place in the Colony, nor do I refer to the illicit intercourse between the Chinese, East Indian immigrants, and black women: but I speak of the immigrants as a whole. Whatever may be the faults of the Chinese, and however depraved and superstitious, they are undoubtedly an industrious race, and from them many a good lesson may be learnt by the labouring Creole population, and others, too, who lay claim to respectability.

11. The language spoken by these people is very unlike the Indian and the other languages spoken in the Colony. The language is made up of monosyllabic words, and is not alphabetical like the English or many other European or Indian languages. The language itself is the alphabet, and consists of tens of thousands of what for convenience' sake may be termed letters, and each such letter is a word, an idea, or the name of a thing. Right spelling in the Chinese language does not consist in the right selection and order of letters (so to speak) in the word, but in the right sequence of the strokes and dots (which are the only substitute for an alphabet) in the word. A knowledge of three or four thousand of such letters or words is sufficient for the reading of most books in that

language, and to be able to read fluently the Chinese Bible or the Confucian Books, a knowledge of some 5,000 or 6,000 of them is necessary; some composed of fifteen or twenty strokes and dots, some again so nearly alike that it wants a practised eye to distinguish them. The pronunciation of the characters is difficult to foreigners, from the fact that certain tones of voice, and, in many cases, certain aspirated or guttural modulations, are necessary to be carefully observed. The characters now in common use among the Chinese are called the *Li* and *Kiai*, which were invented some 2,000 years ago by two officers in the court of Ts'in Sze-hwang, the first absolute Emperor of China. A different one again, of a stiffer style, called Sung character, invented about 1,000 years ago, is used sometimes in printing. The printed or written language is intelligible to educated Chinese in all parts of the Empire, just as the numerals 1, 2, 3, 4, 5, 6, 7, 8, 9, 0, are understood over all Europe; while the spoken language has many dialects, often differing widely from each other, so that men living in different prefectures of the same province are oftentimes unable to understand each other, unless they have made their dialects a particular study, just as the numerals above referred to are pronounced differently in different European countries. Many of the Chinese characters or words, when pronounced according to the book or classical style, are different from the pronunciation given by the people in conversation: *e.g.*, the character for "voice," according to the classical style, is called *s-i-n-g*, but it becomes *s-i-a-n-g* in the dialect of the people. Dr. A. Clarke, Samuel Shuckford, and some others have supposed the *Chinese* to be the first original language, referred to in *Genesis* xi. 1. The *Hebrew*,—the *lingua sancta*, called also the *Jews' language*,—in which the Scriptures of the Old Testament were written, is supposed to be so by some others. But recent philological researches have rendered it all but certain that the Hebrew or the Chinese was not the original language. The Sanskrit is supposed by many very able scholars to possess that honour. Whatever may be the opinions of learned men about the primitive or first language spoken in the world, China seems to be the only country or land in which primary instruction is most widely spread. Schools are found even in the smallest hamlets, whose rustics deprive themselves of some of their gains in order to pay a schoolmaster. It is very seldom or rarely you meet with an entirely uneducated Chinese even in British Guyana. They are emphatically an educated race of people.

12. In almost every respect the Chinese are superior to East Indians, either as field-labourers or free Colonists. In 1875 several influential merchants of Georgetown submitted a petition to the Combined Court, praying that efforts might be directed towards the resumption of emigration from China, and setting forth the fact that, in contradistinction to East Indians, the Chinese were excellent disbursers as well as earners of money. They are more prolific as a race than any other nationality in British Guyana. If the Settlement on the Camoonie Creek can be accepted as a test of national industry, there cannot be a doubt that the introduction of free immigrants, leaving them to the freedom of their own will so long as they do not seek to leave the Colony, would soon pay for itself. Whatever view may be taken, it is certain that internal competition from the tea districts of India itself, coupled with plentiful harvests and increasing national prosperity, will soon force the question of labour supply upon the earnest attention of the Legislature; and it is to be hoped that some satisfactory solution will be effected.

CHAPTER VIII.

OUR INDIAN COOLIE IMMIGRANTS.

1. INDIA, as a country where field or agricultural Coolies in abundance could be easily procured, being long known to the planters and proprietors of the different sugar estates in the Colony, they, as a matter of actual necessity and compulsion, were driven to direct their attention to that country for labourers. The apprenticeship system of the slaves in the Colony, previous to their unconditional freedom or emancipation, served its purpose for a time, according to the desire and notion of the planters, but after their actual liberation from bondage they showed signs of reluctance and unwillingness to do the same kind of work, and in the same manner, they were accustomed to on the different estates. That they ought to labour for their living they were perfectly aware, but the kind and mode of labour which they preferred the planters did not seem to relish. And because the black Creoles did not in every case pursue agriculture on estates belonging to others, and because also in many instances the liberated slaves did not toil in the way and to that extent the planters desired, it became indispensable to meet the requirements for labourers in some other way, and from some other quarter. Hence the call, the effort, and the appliances for East Indian labourers or Coolies; and hence also the thousands who are imported into the Colony from year to year. The black labourer had been offered employment on the different estates, upon his own terms, which he readily accepted, but the planter soon found to his loss that no dependence could be placed in him (the labourer), because he would not work steadily. Was it then strange that the planter should anxiously turn his attention elsewhere for labourers, so that not only he, but the merchant,

the professional man, the tradesman, ay, even the labourer, might in the end derive advantage from an increase in the population, and from the success attending the planting and working the sugar estate? No one understood this scheme better than the shrewd and intelligent Negro. Of what use to him would have been his emancipation and civilization if it consigned him to a nomad and vagrant life; if the channels of industry, commerce, and education thrown open to him were to be again unavoidably closed; if, with the withdrawal of capital and the extinction of agricultural and commercial employment, the European race had been compelled to leave these shores, the genius of British enterprise retiring disheartened from an anticipated field of active employment? But immigration offered to fulfil every want, and India especially *was to be*, and indeed *has been*, the salvation of sugar-growing British Guyana. Not very long ago the Honourable Wm. Russell, referring to Indian immigration, said that "it was a matter of almost life and death importance to the Colony. If they (the planters) were shut out from India, they might as well make arrangements to abandon the plantations." However true this may be, no country or Colony can be considered prosperous that entirely depends for its prosperity upon a flow of foreign labour which may be stopped at any time. Though the costly immigration from India may be all that could be desired by those who are deeply and immediately interested in its continuance, yet it is only a permanent, settled or fixed resident agricultural population that could render the future development of British Guyana certain.

2. There is in the Colony, I confess, too much sham or spurious voluntaryism talked about by Christian ministers and other benevolent persons: voluntary labour; voluntary road making and draining; voluntary sanitary works; voluntary support of Christian ministers: all of which, alas, have proved wretched failures. It is not voluntaryism we want, and it is utterly useless to depend upon the people. We want in the Colony universal compulsory education; compulsory labour; compulsory sanativeness; compulsory cleansing of miasmatic villages, filthy houses, filthy clothes, filthy bodies, filthy tongues;

and the correction of brutal manners. We want a strong, heavy-handed compulsion to make us prepare the way so that our children—if not we ourselves—shall take an honourable position among the human inhabitants of the earth. To see a race of people retrograding farther and farther from the ever forward marching ranks of civilization, and destined, in consequence of the backward course they are taking, to be wiped out of the ranks of existence, merely for the want of the strong and severe helping hand of the Government under whom they are gasping their last breath of morals and life, is not only sorrowful—it is outrageous. Of course there is no pretence herein made to a knowledge of the *modus operandi* by which they are to be reclaimed. But it does seem that a general system of apprenticeship, the same as the Indian and Chinese apprenticeship or indentureship, should be inaugurated; that all black Creole children beyond a certain age, not regularly at school, should be apprenticed for three, five, or seven years to the estates, to coasting vessels, to stores and wharves and the shipping, as porters, and also to trades. There should be also provision made for the compulsory attendance of the apprentices at night schools for technical instruction, and prizes for merit be offered. In this way the rising generation would mark a new era in Creole life, restrict the enlarging boundaries of pauperism, and in time enable the proprietors of sugar estates and others to look no longer to distant countries for labourers. It is sad, however, to think that British Guyana should be compelled to depend upon a flow of foreign labourers, and that, too, for so many years, since emancipation.

3. The whole of the mountain regions extending from the Circars in the north-western direction of Calcutta, and over the higher branches of the Maghanadi (Great River) to the table-land of Omercuntuck, and west of it to the sources of the Tapti and Whurdha, are localities in India where "Hill Coolies"—Dunjas or Boonas—are found in abundance. Other districts also, as I shall presently show, abounded with such labourers as the Colony required for its extensive plantations. An Emigration Agent, with necessary instructions and power, was appointed to send out as many Coolies as were

required from year to year. About the year 1838, the experiment of importing a ship load of these labourers was tried, and about 400 of them from Calcutta found immediate employment on arriving in the Colony. "This appeared to answer very well, and, in consequence of the success of the undertaking, it became a question for the future how to introduce these people in greater numbers into the Colony. When, therefore, the several Immigration Ordinances allowed of such an attempt as a public measure, agents were appointed in India to provide the necessary supply of Coolies, and ships were engaged to bring them from the far distant Peninsula of India to the fertile lands of British Guyana. The bounty payable on each adult Coolie was sixty dollars per head, or about twelve pounds, which, in the event of a vessel bringing 300 or 400, along with a cargo of rice and other East India products, made it a very profitable speculation for ship owners." But when the Coolies did come in large numbers, fully expecting of course to make their fortune in the distant West by estate labour, after a fair trial, the planters and proprietors discovered that they were not the kind of labourers they required. Most of them were not "*Hill Coolies*" as they were represented, nor were they *Paharrees*—a hardy class—who dwell in the hills of Rajamahal, nor *Katties* and *Khols* who occupy the Peninsula of Gujurat—all famous as a labouring class of people—but old and helpless, infants and greybeards, blind and lame: in short, the offscourings of the streets of Calcutta and Madras were sent out to till the soil of the rich country that could afford to squander away its money. The Coolies whom we now get from India are no better. In numerous instances we have not only had men unfit for labour from bodily infirmity, but we have also had men who were idiots, and men who were perfectly blind, and who must have been blind when they left the shores of India. All such incapables on their arrival became the inmates of some hospital or the almshouse, and are therefore a dead burden on the planters and the Colony.

4. Most Colonists are aware that immigrants from India are divided into three classes. Children under ten years of age

are classified as "infants"; those between ten and fifteen years of age as "minors"; and all above fifteen years of age as "adults." On their arrival in Demerara, the Coolies are distributed among the planters, by the advice and direction of his Excellency the Governor—to each planter according to his application, his means of providing for them, and his willingness and ability to pay the cost of immigration by yearly instalments. They are sent to no estate till a Government officer shall have reported that there is suitable accommodation provided for them. There must be a hospital for them on the estate, and a doctor engaged at an annual salary to attend them. The rate of their wages is stipulated, and their hours of work. The term of apprenticeship or contract on an estate is for five years, and in former years they had the privilege of leaving the estate to which they were bound or indentured at the end of the first three, transferring their services to any other master, which was not very pleasant; but now they are obliged to serve their full term on the estate to which they are sent by the Agent General, as per advice of the Governor; and at the termination of ten years' residence in the Colony they are entitled to a return passage to India, not the males or husbands only, but their very wives and minors or infants, if they have any, in the same ship with themselves. Very recently, an anonymous contributor signing himself, "Argus," writing in the *Argosy* of August 12, 1882, in a jocular manner, of a supposed convention or meeting of the Coolies in the Colony, says:—

"So much has been said from time to time, and more of recent years than formerly, about the extreme desirability of retaining time-expired Coolies in the Colony, that I should hesitate to take up any of your space with more words on the subject; but it may possibly interest you to hear that the Coolies are taking steps amongst themselves to deal with a kindred evil, the nature of which will be ascertained from the following notes:—'A meeting of Coolie citizens was held this week, RAMCHOWDER in the chair, the object of the meeting being to arrive at some means of checking the tendency of planters and merchants, pension-ripe officials and others, from leaving the Colony and retiring to England, just at the time when they are becoming of real service to the Colony. The chairman said the subject was one of the greatest importance to the community, and he hoped his fellow-citizens would view it in its full importance and exert themselves together towards checking the evil. Much had been said about us poor Coolies leaving the Colony when our contract is out; and the newspapers had made the most of the number of rupees each ship had carried away; while the dry goods merchants complained that instead of the cash earned in the Colony being circulated in the Colony, it was hoarded by the Coolies to be carried and spent elsewhere. But when one merchant left the Colony he took away with him, or he sent on before him, which was the same thing, as much money as all the Coolies in every 'return' ship during one or even two or more years took with them. This was very deplorable, for it beggared the Colony, and it was time steps were taken to keep these men from running away. Unfortunately we had no means of depriving them of their power to accumulate capital, but we must try and reduce their power of saving so that they shall not have the same temptation to run back to their country. We must try and make this land as like their own home as possible. We must introduce lords and titled gentry (they can be had cheap now in England, especially in the bankruptcy courts) for our successful citizens to associate with, for it is noticeable that the retired Colonist has a great liking to get associated with titled folks. We must also introduce titled ladies; for the wives of retired Colonists like to be able to speak familiarly of Lady Crackware and Countess Splinterboom. Of course we could not do too much at once, but a beginning must be made, for every year the evil of this exodus is becoming more rampant. All felt the sinister consequences. The shopkeepers felt it, so did tradesmen, domestics, poor people, social institutions, everything and everybody. The money made in the Colony ought to be spent in the Colony, and if we Coolies are to be prevailed upon to stay here, we must have support in our efforts to keep time-expired merchants and officials here beside us.' The meeting supported Mr. Ramchowder's sentiments, and a deputation was appointed to wait upon the Governor to ask him to give the matter his serious consideration."

Although the Chinese Coolies come within the above regulations, they are denied a return passage at the expiration of ten years' residence. The Coolies are wide awake to their own interests; they labour hard and earn money in abundance.

5. We have in the Colony Coolies from all parts of India, from Madras, Bangalore, Hyderabad, Masulipatam, Mysore, Pondicherry, Cuddalore, Tinnevelly, Trichinopoly, Tanjore, Vellore, Madura, Malayalim, Ceylon, Bombay, Juggernat, Calcutta, Benares, Allahabad, Lucknow, Cawnpoor, Delhi, Nepaul, Lahore, Cabul, and many other places. To be more graphic, we have in the Colony the agricultural race, called Gajurs, from the north-west frontier of India, the Punjab, or Country of the Five Waters; the Dunjas and the Bheels from the north-eastern part of Gujurat, or rather from the jungles and hilly district of Malwa; the Kulies and Khols who inhabit the Peninsula of Gujurat; the Khatties from the Peninsula which has taken the name of Khattywar; the Hindus, who are in general tall, well-proportioned, and of a martial disposition; the Bengalies (very few indeed), from Bengal; the Khands and Sauris from Orissa, which receives its name from Oriyos or Odros, a branch of the Hindu immigration; the Ghonds from Gondwana, which lies to the north and east of Orissa, and which stretches from Cuttock throughout the Berar and the Saugor territory; the Parsees from the presidency of Bombay; the Gentus, or Telingans, from Southern India; the Canarese, the Mussulmans, the Malabars, and a host of others, according to their different castes and ranks, have found their way to British Guyana as labourers to work on the sugar estates. All who were within reach have been taken and sent to Demerara; and labourers are now no longer to be obtained in the vicinity of large towns or populous cities, the demand of labour for local purposes and other Colonies being such that immigrants have now to be procured from the interior of the country, two or three months' journey from the port of embarkation, in districts far removed from the reach of the local employer, and, as a consequence, the expenses of procuring labour for our Colony become greater. The Coolies who have been imported of late have been brought from the interior and high land, many days' journey from Calcutta. Every new batch of these people brought to

Demerara comes from a greater distance than the preceding one. And now again there is some difficulty experienced by the Emigration Agent in Calcutta. Labourers are not readily and easily to be had as before, for India has to supply other labour markets as well. There have been occasions, of course, when it was found impossible to secure the number of recruits to meet the indent or make up the complement for vessels chartered; but, taking one season with another, the labourers requisitioned from the East have been found sufficient for the requirements of sugar planters in Demerara. In September of 1876, for instance, Mr. Firth wrote to the Governor, in reply to a letter rebuking him for his failure to meet the indent for the season. In the course of this exculpatory epistle Mr. Firth affirms that the most strenuous efforts had been made, new depôts having been opened in outlying districts to which recruiters had never before penetrated, the corps of recruiters largely augmented, and the *per caput* fee largely augmented. Acknowledging the utter hopelessness of meeting the views of the Government by forwarding immigrants in sufficient number, Mr. Firth appealed to Mr. C. Eales, who was acting in the like capacity on behalf of Mauritius, for some forecast of recruiting prospects. Responding to Mr. Firth's appeal, Mr. Eales pointed to the tea plantations of Assam and Cachar, coupled with the abundance and cheapness of food grains in India, as the causes operating against emigration. That agricultural Coolies were very scarce some years ago far nearer home than the West Indies is demonstrated by an extract from the letter of Mr. Eales to Mr. Firth, in which one of the largest landed proprietors in Assam and Cachar is represented as saying:—"During my late visit to Cachar I had an opportunity of hearing and seeing a great deal about tea management. Many questions require solution; but none press so urgently on us as the *labour* force question. So many new estates and extensions have been opened out within the last two years that the supply of labour has not equalled the demand; and by force of necessity managers have been compelled to resort to all sorts of ways to keep their promises to their principals and fulfil their engagements. This struggle for existence has become so terrible that if something be not done at once to stay the hands of competitors there can only be one issue to tea enterprise, and that is *utter collapse.*" In his anxiety to justify his present position, and give assurance of his unabated zeal, it is but natural that Mr. Firth should forget or ignore the tribulation of former years, one secret of which Mr. Eales professed to supply in the foregoing extract. To the difficulties which abundant harvests in the East Indies always impose on recruiters is now added, however, an epidemic of fever, which has at once reduced the number of eligibles and incapacitated some of the sub-agents and their allies. It would seem, therefore, that while there is an anxious competition for Coolie labour both at home and abroad, there is a counterbalancing motive at work in the low price of grains, now nearly fifty per cent. below the usual average price. It has been so often repeated as to have become almost a truism that so long as East Indians can enjoy the comforts of life at home in comparative inertness, indifferent success will attend all efforts at inducing them to emigrate, and this is the burden of Mr. Firth's vindication. In actual practice it has been found that the only opportunity of colonies competing for Coolie labour is the extremity of those whose services they seek to impress. Even now a sudden rise in the price of grain, or unfavourable prospects for next harvest, would doubtless restore the balance and render Mr. Firth's labours light. It cannot be denied, however, that there is an utterly incongruous element in a system which places foreign on almost equal terms with British Colonies in obtaining labour from a country under British Sovereignty. If it illustrates anything, it is another phase of that one-sided free trade of which such bitter complaint has often been made. In times of Indian famine it might be highly desirable that British and foreign Emigration Agents should be at liberty to vie with each other in transporting famishing wretches to a land of plenty; but in periods like the present the British Colonies ought in all fairness to have the field to themselves.

6. We have from time to time received large batches of Coolies from India; and at present, according to the report for

1880 of Mr. C. B. King, Acting Immigration Agent General, we have an immigrant population—Indians and others—of 68,241; an excess of 3,427 on the number given in December, 1879; and according to the half-yearly return of immigrants for the half-year ended June 30, 1881, we have in the Colony 15,923 males and 6,735 females under indenture; and 29,846 males and 16,548 females of all races not under indenture; making a total of 45,769 males, and 23,283 females—or 69,052 of both sexes indentured and unindentured. From the report for 1880 it appears that the proportion of men to women was 100 to 49·07, and of males to females of all ages 100 to 49·07, being almost identical with 1879, but five per cent. more women to men than in 1878. This disproportion of the sexes has often been decried as a crushing handicap on the immigration system; and to it are attributable, besides a host of other evils, the frequent cases of wife-murder through infidelity and the desertion of one man for another. There is no disguising the fact that it is in effect directly provocative of much immorality of different kinds; besides enhancing the difficulties of obtaining recruits in India and stimulating discontent amongst many male immigrants already in the Colony. The plight was bad enough in all conscience of the amatory rustic described in Burns's poem on "Halloween," "who wedlock's joys since Mar's year did desire"—presumably meaning that from time immemorial he had been vainly in search of a suitable partner. But in contrast to Demerara there are brides in Scotland enough and to spare; so that the inference is that "Uncle John" was either extremely fastidious or that his own personal attractions were not of a nature to entrance the female heart. But with only 49 women to 100 men, it is evident that 51 Asiatic immigrants, however anxious for connubial bliss, may wait as wistfully as Mother Hubbard's dog for the bone which was never forthcoming. Only the most eligible can obtain spouses, and the natural result is that those who are left out in the cold will take the earliest opportunity of migrating to a country where matrimonial anticipations are easier of realization. A planter, writing to the *Colonist* of June 14, 1881, on the subject of the disproportion of the sexes, says:—

"The unfortunate state of the Colony as regards the stationary, if not retrogressive, number of its population, demands the full attention of the Government. In the leading article of your impression of the 11th you show very conclusively the fact, but you say nothing as to the reason. I maintain that the reason is not difficult to find; it is due to the insane and suicidal system of introducing such an overwhelming majority of men. The Government has a great control over the immigration of Asiatics, and could insist on a larger proportion of women or a smaller proportion of men, if it is really true that women are not to be had. In the essays on Immigration lately written, Messrs. Kirke, Bellairs, and Maxwell all say very much the same, which is, that the stream of immigrants to replace the number lost by death must be perennial so long as so few women are imported or introduced. If an equal number of the sexes came, they would very likely form families, and settle down and have no longer any wish to leave the country of their adoption. I for my part would be most happy, if possible, to receive two or three large allotments of nothing but women; for just look at the population of this estate as per last census:—Coolies—men, 405; women, 192: total adults, 597. Black and Coloured—men, 155; women, 91: total adults, 246. Chinese—men, 61; women, 17: total adults, 78. Portuguese—men, 16; women, 16: total adults, 32. Men, 637; women, 316: total, 953. This is over two men to each woman, so that the reproductive population is, at most, out of 953, only 632. The consequence is that the number of children is only:—Coolie boys, 141; Black, 34; Chinese, 9; Portuguese, 16: total boys, 200. Coolie girls, 110; Black, 38; Chinese, 11; Portuguese, 15: total girls, 174. Total, 374. 316 women have only 374 children. If other parts of the Colony have a similar population, is it surprising that our "natural increase" is a nonentity? What else can be expected in a community where the disparity of the sexes is so great? Government is almost powerless to regulate the immigration from Europe and Barbadoes; but with regard to the Chinese and Coolies it can and it ought to insist on a becoming number of women, and a becoming number is one woman to one man, and even then the result of previous error must be felt. Your readers can easily imagine the question from the point of view of morality, religion, and crime. I simply wish to draw attention to the fact as the reason why British Guyana has to continue the ruinously expensive and most difficult and complicated system of continual external supply of labourers."

7. The large import of Coolies from India several years ago was principally owing to the famines or droughts with which the country was visited. On one occasion, 1860, more than thirteen millions of people, or nearly the population of Spain, were affected by severe drought. Of these, four and a half millions suffered cruelly, and half a million perished. Four millions of acres were thrown out of cultivation, and the peasantry lost in cattle and produce nearly five millions sterling. The State remitted £400,000 of revenue, and spent £250,000 on public works. Besides the untold aid given by private parties on the spot, India contributed about £45,000, and England £120,000. This country, too, rendered its timely aid to the perishing thousands. "Crowds of women and children, presenting the most miserable and emaciated appearance, were seen spreading over the jungles, sifting the earth for the 'Gokhroo' thorns, or picking the few berries left on the 'Ber' bushes. Grain of the most unwholesome description, which had been buried for years, and which the medical officers pronounced to be almost poisonous, was exposed for sale in the bazaars. Many poor creatures were found dead by the road-side, and deaths from starvation were of constant occurrence. Families fled from their houses in search of food, and villages and districts were rapidly becoming depopulated." The rains following the droughts were unusually heavy, causing extensive inundations. The invalids at Churna lost their all; portions of Lower Bengal were submerged and the crops destroyed. Pestilence ensued in Hughli district when the waters subsided. Its effects are thus described by a contributor to the *Paridarshak* (and quoted in the *Indian Reformer*): "The funeral fires are constantly blazing like the conflagration of a forest. In the streets and huts is always heard the doleful sound of Haribol! Haribol! When the destitute and helpless die, they are thrown into the river." Such, and even still worse, were the distressing accounts contained in the East India daily papers. Famine

and pestilence combined raged throughout the whole length and breadth of that land of beauty, and made havoc of its inhabitants, entering into every house and family, and causing some thousands of these poor wretches to seek another country. The year 1877 was another dreadful year in Southern India, when many millions of people, occupying vast tracts of country, had been deprived of all ordinary means of support, and, notwithstanding the unwearied effort and lavish expenditure of Government, and the bounty of England, the suffering and mortality had been fearful. Not only England, but her very Colonies readily and cheerfully rendered their assistance in relieving the poor famine-stricken sufferers. The friends of the different Missionary Societies also had given large sums of money to be expended by their own missionaries in aid of poor Christians and in support and training of orphans. All these visitations — famines, pestilences — and other circumstances too, have from time to time induced many to leave India for British Guyana, and other Colonies, in search of work.

8. Though we have a large immigrant population, our great want has been "agricultural labourers" to suit the requirements of the planters, and "settlers" to suit the requirements of the Colony. Hundreds of our Coolie immigrants have never been agricultural labourers at all in their own country. They never held a plough, nor had a hoe in their hands, till they came to the Colony, though during their residence on the estates they have learned to use the hoe and the shovel, &c., and to become useful estate labourers. In Southern India cultivation of land or agriculture may be considered the principal or the only calling of the Tamil nation. All other professions or trades were, and still are, in absolute subjection to the cultivating tribes *Kányátchi-Kârar*, or lords of the soil, who derived their superiority from the rights of the plough. Intercourse with foreign nations, the extension of commerce, and other circumstances, however, have in latter times materially altered the manners of the olden time, and infringed the privileges of the landed proprietors. Notwithstanding this, they are emphatically an agricultural people.

All the Hindus of Southern India may be divided into two principal classes, the *Valang-Keiyár*, the right hand caste, including the whole of the agricultural Tamil people; and *Idang-Keiyár*, the left hand caste, including chiefly the trading and manufacturing Tamil people and others, who endeavour, and generally with success, to evade agriculture. We have had *more* of this kind of people sent out as field labourers to work on the sugar estates in the Colony, and *less* of the real kind, who are the very class of people the planters and others would desire to have as permanent settlers. The veneration in which the Tamil people of the Valang-Keiyâr hold the plough may be judged from the following translation of a couplet by Kamban "*on agriculture:*" "THOSE TRULY LIVE WHO LIVE BY THE PLOUGH: ALL OTHERS DO NOT LIVE, AS THEY ARE IN SERVITUDE AND DEPEND UPON THOSE THEY SERVE,—*is it not so? Is it not thus in the ancient world the precept was written? Is it not wrong, therefore, to compare with these any that are born in the sea-surrounded earth?*" There was a time when a ship brought from the Presidency of Madras, as Coolies, to labour on the sugar estates, barbers, horsekeepers, cooks, household servants, hereditary beggars (*Mallei Vaz-hakki*, as the natives of Madras call them), pedlars, cattle-minders, grass-cutters, policemen (peons), mountebanks, jugglers, dancers, dhobies, &c., which gave great dissatisfaction to the planters and proprietors of estates; but the captain of the ship and the medical officers in charge were not to be blamed, for they were mere paid servants to fulfil a certain engagement. But since that unfortunate event we have had from the Madras Presidency "some of the best labourers in the Colony, and a most industrious set of people." (See *Commission of Inquiry*, p. 75.) Emigrants from the Presidency of Madras have done well and prospered in the Colonics, save and except British Guyana, where they are looked upon as worthless, and everything that is bad. The late Immigration Agent-General (Hon. J. G. Daly), in his letter to the Government, referring to this class of immigrants, said: "The experience of planters in this Colony may be unfavourable to that race, and prejudice may exist in consequence. I am aware of the faults of the Madras labourer; *he is very prone on occasion, but more particularly at times of festivity, to give way to drinking and quarrelling*, and in domestic service he adds the vice of pilfering and stealing, but I have always heard that for endurance and real hard work he is much superior to the Calcutta Coolie." But hard drinking, swearing, pilfering, stealing, and quarrelling propensities, though unfortunately discernible or glaring in the Madras Coolies, are not perhaps so glaring in the Creoles of the Colony, and the lower orders of the English or any European nation. We have but to turn to the pages of *Whitaker's Almanack* for proof. Among the Calcutta Coolies also are to be found a very large number of lazy, worthless vagabonds who, instead of working honestly, eke out a living by begging from place to place, and find themselves in the different gaols in large numbers, and indeed make the gaols their home.

9. Though the Colonial Government has no Emigration Agency established in the Presidency of Madras, yet a large number of Coolies find their way to the Calcutta depôt, and embark for British Guyana. The subject of an Agency in Madras, and the character of the Coolies from that Presidency, have been referred to by the members of the Court of Policy and the planters in general from time to time. In 1872, when there was some difficulty felt in Calcutta by the agent in procuring labourers from the Bengal Presidency, the late Mr. J. Oliver, member of the Court of Policy, said that in one or two discussions they had had in that court a short time ago, it was suggested that as there were many difficulties in the way of obtaining a sufficient number of labourers from Calcutta, and obstacles in the way of getting Chinese immigrants, they should reopen a Madras Agency at the close of the season 1872, in order to obtain, if possible, a full supply of labour from the South of India. Before, however, bringing this matter before the Government in a tangible form, it was thought by the few who had taken the matter into consideration that it would be desirable to obtain the opinion of the planting interest generally on the subject. Their previous experience of Madras immigration had not been of such a nature as was calculated to induce the Executive Government

of the Colony to reopen it without allowing the planters an opportunity of having a full discussion upon the subject, and of expressing their opinion as to the desirableness of such an undertaking; and in order to carry out this principle the president of the Royal Agricultural and Commercial Society was requested to issue a circular to the representative of every estate in the Colony, stating the difficulties in the way of getting an adequate supply of labourers from Calcutta, and asking each of them to give his opinion as to the advisability of reopening a Madras Agency. At the same time they were asked, in case they objected to the proposal, if they would kindly state their reasons, in order that they might see whether their objections might not be overcome; and they were also asked to give a proximate idea of the number of labourers that would be required during the next season from Madras. In reply to this application, out of the 128 estates in the Colony 107 had sent in a favourable response, four had expressed their acquiescence in the project, and the remaining eleven were small properties which could hardly be taken into consideration, so that in reality, out of the 128 estates that were in the Colony, there were only twelve that had not replied favourably to this proposition, and out of that number six were not in the habit of taking immigrants, and the remaining six were scattered about the Colony. Therefore, he thought he might fairly say that the response which had been given to the application which was sent to them might be considered to be unanimous, and that the estates which would apply for the people, if they could obtain them from Madras, would represent more than nine-tenths of the whole export of the Colony. Applications had been received for about 7,200 people, or something like 21,000 for the three seasons now before them. This was a very large application indeed, and if they took the usual number which came in the ships, it would make twenty vessels. Now, the largest number they had ever had from one port was in 1869, when they had eighteen vessels from Calcutta; and when they considered that the total number of ships that ever arrived at this Colony from Madras was only thirty-five, it was not difficult to arrive at the conclusion that the planters did not make very large applications for people from that particular locality. Touching the answers that were sent in by the various planters, he might mention that there were remarks made in them concerning *the very high character of the Madras Coolies in the Colony as efficient labourers and useful agricultural people*; and if that was the case, as there was no question it was, and there were such large applications for these people, there was every reason to suppose that a Madras Agency, if earnestly conducted, could be carried on almost on the same scale as the one at Calcutta. He did not think it necessary, in bringing forward this question, to go into elaborate details of the immigration system generally. When the matter was first brought forward, two parties took different sides and differed in their opinion on the subject; but there could be no doubt that the larger the number of people that could be brought to our shores the greater would be the prosperity of the Colony. . . . . The Governor said, before the matter proceeded any further, he might state that his own views were in favour of the proposition, and that he had already suggested the expediency of establishing an Agency at Madras; therefore he was quite prepared to support the resolution. He did not, in fact, see any difficulty in the way of accomplishing the matter either by this Colony, Trinidad, or any other place. As far as he could ascertain from former correspondence, it appeared to him that immigration from Madras ceased in consequence of the planters not applying for Madras immigrants; but if the circumstances were now changed, as the hon. member said they had, there was no difficulty in the way of getting a supply of labour from that particular locality. Last year the applications that came in for immigrants amounted to about seven thousand; but they could never expect to obtain more than about three thousand, and if they could get a supply from Madras to make up the deficiency, he saw no reason why they should not avail themselves of the opportunity. . . . . There would be no objection on the part of the English Government to allow immigration from Madras: on the contrary, he believed every facility would be afforded for the accomplishment of such an object. If they looked at the French treaty, they would find that much more honourable terms were offered than we gave; and with regard to back passage, according to the Dutch regulations the immigrant at the end of five years was entitled to a return passage from Surinam; whereas here they were only entitled to it after ten years' residence. The only stipulation, in the case of the Dutch Colony, was that if the immigrant did not claim his return passage at the end of five years, he lost all right to it. Therefore it would be seen that there was at least one condition there which was more favourable than ours. Then again with regard to labour. They were bound by the treaty to work six days in seven, whereas in our Ordinance we only required an immigrant to work five days. There our terms were more favourable. Then again, with regard to the hours of labour, under the Dutch system the labourer had to work nine and a half hours, and here he had only to work seven hours in the field and ten in the buildings, and that was a very great difference. . . . . He saw that on a former occasion immigration from Madras was stopped in consequence of the planters ceasing to apply for immigrants. Now, what he would suggest was, that the Government should have power to bring as many immigrants from Madras and Calcutta as could be obtained from those places, and then distribute them to the planters according to their applications. Then those who liked Calcutta immigrants would get them, and those who preferred the people from Madras would be supplied with them.

Mr. McConnell thought that was a very good suggestion indeed.

In 1872 and 1877 we had three or four ship-loads of Coolies from Madras, and the people not readily consenting to come to Demerara, their importation was stopped. Last year, 1881, when the subject of reopening an Agency was discussed in the Court of Policy, the Honourable W. Russell, A. C. McCalman, and others, spoke of the Coolies from Madras in the highest terms. Their only fault is, they take a long time to get accustomed to the Colony, to become useful agricultural labourers.

10. The late Rev. Ralph Stott, Coolie Missionary, speaking of this class or kind of immigrants (the Madrasees) in Natal, says:—"Some have already bought land and built houses, and are following their own trades; others have money, and will commence business as soon as they are at liberty. Several will become fishermen, others market-gardeners, and many pedlars. I am sorry to see some of them now on the Sabbath-day going from estate to estate, with their goods to sell." "It is also very probable that, in a few years, we shall have Indian merchants and shipowners in Natal. The natives of India are wide awake to their own interests; and, now that caste is giving way, and Indians are found as Coolies, east, west, north and south, merchants will follow, especially with Indian produce; nay, many of the labourers themselves will become storekeepers and merchants. This is the case now in Demerara and other places where immigration has been carried on for several years. . . . . The Coolies are not like the Kaffirs, vegetating at their kraals, but a busy, active, enterprising race, taking their share in pushing on the world, right or wrong. Let us, then, set them a good example, and impress upon them right principles, and they will bless us, and be a blessing." Mr. Stott, in my humble opinion, could not have given a better and more faithful description of the state, condition, and character of the Coolie immigrants; and this description of his, *in toto,* applies to the Coolies of Demerara. But while the Coolies are so, yet it has often been a matter of complaint that they leave after amassing some thousands of dollars, when they might permanently remain with us and earn as many more dollars, with both profit to themselves and advantage to the country of their adoption. They leave us, as thousands who have seen them about the streets and public offices can testify, in good and robust health, dressed, according to the fashion of their country, in gaudy garments and glittering with silver anklets and armlets and jewelled nose and ear-rings. Their ornaments alone would, in their native land, be considered a small fortune to people of their class. But the complaint to which I have simply adverted implies that we have not as yet arrived at perfection in our immigration laws.

11. From the hints I have thrown out in the above paragraphs the impartial reader will perceive that the expensive system of immigration, the introduction of Coolies from Madeira, China, East Indies, and other parts of the world, especially the West Indian Islands, is to displace no native labourer, but merely to fill a blank in the civil and social condition of the country. It is a lamentable and ugly fact, however, that we are populating the Colony from India only to depopulate it again at an enormous cost; that we are training up an agricultural population of East Indian free Coolies only to send them away when they have become more useful labourers to us, and accustomed to the country; and that the most certain profits of our industry—in the wages paid for labour—are every now and then sent out of the Colony, never to return in any shape or by any manner of means. "There is no feeling which exists in the heart of man truer and stronger than his love for the land which gave him birth; and especially for the particular locality where he spent the earlier and happier portion of his life. In his declining years, when his locks are whitened by the frosts of many winters, after a long tempest-tossed voyage upon the troubled waters of the sea of life, he loves to sit and think of the long ago. Though the dark waters of the ocean may surge between him and his early home, still memory, with lightning wing, conveys him back to the dear scenes of his childhood. In thought he is young again, roaming on the bank of the rippling stream, as it threads its way through green meadows over the hills and away, without a trouble or care resting upon his young spirit to mar his pleasure. Yes; we have an instinctive and never-dying love for our fatherland; and this sentiment has warmed the bosom of every generation and people since the world was created. In the good Book we have passages abounding in expressions of stirring patriotism. The Jews, when forced to leave the Holy City, Jerusalem, their pride, to which they were attached by their dearest ties, in their exile forgot not its hallowed associations, but prayed that 'the right hand might forget its cunning, and the tongue cleave to the roof of the mouth, if they preferred her not above

their chief joy.' We may take the untutored savage from his home on the boundless prairies of the western lands, and bring him within the bounds, and place him under the laws and usages of civilization, and in his heart that son of the forest longs to dwell again upon the hunting-grounds of his fathers, where he can chase the deer and buffalo free as the air he breathes." The East Indian and Chinese Coolies in like manner love their native land, their home, and whilst abroad they look upon themselves as exiles, and long to return to their native place ere they die. There can be no objection to a man or to a set of people returning to their native land, paying his or their own expenses as the Chinese, Portuguese, and others have to do; but for a whole gang of people, as the Indian Coolies, to return to their native land at the expense of the Colony is, I consider, an unwarrantable iniquity. But the Coolies claim it as their right to be sent back to India, and the nature of the contract or agreement entered into by the employers and employés is such that it must and will remain so, till some new arrangement, if possible, is made with the Indian Government. This one simple fact alone proves that *free labour* is what the Colony of British Guyana requires.

12. One pleasing fact, however, worth noticing here is that many of the Coolies entitled to a free passage back to India, who leave the port of Georgetown after a few months' or years' residence there, long to come back to British Guyana, in some instances paying their own passage. I extract the following from a local paper of December 13th, 1881: "It must be exceedingly gratifying to those interested in the treatment of the immigrants, to find that as many as 133 were re-introduced to British Guyana last year, having been former residents of the Colony. We may take this as some evidence that the legislative enactments which regulate East Indian labour have not failed in their object, and that those of the one hundred and thirty-three souls who had arrived at the years of discretion were well content to try again the conditions of life here. They are described as being steady and industrious labourers—the very class so much wanted on the estates. It is interesting to note the reasons assigned by them as actuating

them in returning here. These reasons are three in the main: first, the freedom from the trammels of caste prejudices which they enjoy here; second, the natural disappointment they feel on their return to India to find that the homes of their relatives and friends know them no more; and, third, the consciousness that to industrious people a good prospect is held out in British Guyana." This is no new fact or statement made by the Acting Immigration Agent General. I know several instances of Coolies living twelve or fourteen years on an estate, going to India for a year or two, paying their passage back, and bringing some friends, and on their arrival going at once to their old estate. Sometimes they return indentured a second time, and ask to be sent to their old estate, a request that is generally granted. If it is slavery, it is strange that they should deliberately choose it, and bring their friends into it. The reader will find reference made to this very subject in the *Guyanian Indians*, sect. viii. p. 57, (3).

18. It has been frequently asserted within the last few years, by those who have given attention to the subject, that the limits of Coolie emigration from India to British Guyana on account of other calls or demands made on the country and other local circumstances, are becoming so circumscribed, so clogged with difficulties, that a total cessation of emigration may be looked forward to at no distant period or day. Others, again, equally interested in the subject and quite as capable of giving an opinion on the matter, confidently assert that British Guyana will never want applicants for emigration to its shores. These assertions may be both true to some extent. However, we do not well to depend too much upon an uncertain opinion. We cannot positively tell whether emigration from India would be continued for any length of time, or how soon our supplies from the India labour market would be stopped or closed. From the tenor of the latest communications from the Emigration Agent in Calcutta, to the Government of British Guyana, one would suppose that there are great difficulties experienced in securing labourers for the Demerara labour market, and the people are not so willing to come to our Colony. [*See paragraph* 4, *above.*] However

desirable it may be to have Coolies from India, and however useful in a certain way they might have been to the Colony, yet they are not such a hardy race of able-bodied men, as the Portuguese, black Creoles, or Chinese, to do the kind of work that is wanted, and to endure the hardships others experience in the same kind of labour or work on sugar estates. What one black man, or Portuguese, or Chinese, will do in a day, it will take three Coolies on an average to do. They, most of them, being vegetarians and rice-eaters, cannot be expected to do hard work, for they are simply unable. This is a fact which no sensible, reasonable man will deny. The most desirable class of immigrants required for the Colony, both as agricultural labourers and as settlers, are not Coolies so much, but an admixture of Portuguese and Chinese, or Portuguese and Africans. The Hindo-Guyanians (or children born of Asiatic or Indian parents), of whom we have a very large number in the Colony (and this number is annually increasing), appear hardier and stronger than their parents, and these can stand the fatigue better, and do harder and more steady work than their parents, and even than the Chinese. These have no particular desire to leave the Colony and accompany their parents when they take their departure for India. All these should be encouraged to remain permanently in the Colony.

14. The expenses connected with immigration, up to the time of passing of Ordinance 7 of 1878, had been borne in the proportion of one-third by the Colony and two-thirds by the planters; but a change in this system was effected by that Ordinance, which provided that the total expenses connected with the introduction of immigrants, including the Emigration Agency of India, and back passages, should be borne by the planters. The cost of the Immigration establishment in the Colony, including the medical department, and a per caput allowance of $10 per head, to be met by the general revenue. The effect of this change pressed unduly on the planters in seasons when a larger number of immigrants than usual was introduced, and with the consent of the Secretary of State for the Colonies a Bill repealing sections 19 and 20 (which provided for the payment of the expenses of immigration) of

Ordinance 7 of 1873 was passed by the Court of Policy in December, 1878, and allowed a return to the old system of one-third of the entire cost being paid by the Colony, and two-thirds by the planters.

The proportion of one-third paid by the Colony in 1880 was $183,073.72. The remaining two-thirds, or $366,147.44, were paid by the planters from the Immigration Fund. The total receipts for 1880 were $604,177.21, which allowed of a balance of $54,956.04 being carried to the credit of the fund.

SUMMARY OF IMMIGRATION EXPENDITURE FOR 1880.

Immigration from India.................	$336,570.01
Back Passages of Indian Immigrants......	111,532.55
The Establishment in the Colony	101,118.61
Total Immigration Expenditure	$549,221.17

The large importation of foreign labourers from India, China, &c., has been, and still is, for the immediate benefit of the planters in the Colony. There was a period when the planting interest—admitted to be the mainstay of the prosperity of the country—was in a most depressed condition. The planters could not keep afloat without exceptional aid and support. They had been subjected by imperial policy to a competition with the foreign sugar producers, for which they were wholly unprepared. Without such exceptional aid they were in danger of sinking, and no one denies that their sustenance was necessary for the very existence of the Colony. But things have entirely changed. The planting interest has gone through the ordeal, and, thanks to the liberal aid it has received for a series of years, it has been resuscitated, and now stands forth a flourishing and prosperous interest. Such being the fact, I leave my reader to form his own conclusions about the justice or injustice, the reasonableness or unreasonableness, of one-third of the entire cost of the introduction of foreign labourers being paid by the Colony, and two-thirds by the planters, who are further exempted from paying duty on their implements and supplies. Though I do not expect my reader to make himself perfectly conversant with all the obscure mysteries of the complex and complicated systems of legislation, judicature, departmental administration, and financial methods of the Colony, yet I am sure he will say (though perfectly orthodox in allegiance and devotion to the sacred sugar cane), as I have heard others say, "Let planters derive their support from their own resources, and not continue to levy such heavy tribute upon the minor industries surrounding them, dependent though they may be upon them."

15. The question may be asked, "Do the Coolies who come to British Guyana for the immediate benefit of the planters always find work suited to them on the several estates throughout the year? Have they never complained of want of work, and the smallness of the wages they get? Do they thoroughly understand what they are coming to do in Demerara when they leave their country?" To pour a grievance, even an imaginary one, into a sympathizing ear is a great luxury, and Coolies do undoubtedly often tell a stranger that they were "fooled" into coming to Demerara. No doubt the recruiters or gomastahs had drawn a picture of the glory of British Guyana, and the easy and rapid way in which money was to be made as soon as they landed in the Colony with something of Oriental extravagance, which the local magistrates in India had brushed away by telling them the plain truth as to what their work and wages would really be. Imaginary grievances the Coolies have in abundance, and they could very easily spare of them to my worthy reader if he would only find time to listen to them. No emigrant ever does know what he is going to, till he finds himself on the spot of his destination. Englishmen and Scotchmen find the backwoods of the Canadian prairies or the woods of the Australian territory not to be a paradise as they dreamed them to be, and often complain very bitterly of the unexpected hardships they have to endure. So the Coolies also do not understand what they are coming to, till they find themselves in British Guyana, and after a few years' sojourn and experience they realize the fact that Demerara is a money-making and money-saving country. They certainly at first find the work hard, and harder than they were accustomed to, but soon they get used to do hard work. The Coolies are able at any time to lay a complaint of bad treat-

ment, insufficient wages, overwork, or any other grievance under which they may believe themselves to be suffering, before a local magistrate or immigration agent; and these complaints are always sifted to the bottom, and, if found true, redress is immediate. In fact so warmly has the head of the Immigration Department been their defender and partisan, that he is nicknamed "the Coolies' papa." In cases of alleged hardship, the Coolies will carry their grievance to head-quarters, and it is by no means an uncommon spectacle to the merchants and store-keepers of Georgetown to see fifty or sixty Coolie labourers appear in Water Street on their way to the Immigration Office. They have come from some estate in the country, armed with their shovels and forks, just as they have struck work, to lay a general complaint against the manager, overseers, and foremen of the estate to which they belong. Usually, the sum and substance of their complaints is that they are not paid sufficiently for their labour, and that they would like some little addition to their wages. The complaints, whatever they be, being carefully taken down in intelligible language, the men are told to return to their work, and that an investigation will take place on the morrow. The next day, the manager of the estate gets an official intimation that such a charge has been made, and that Mr. —— will arrive at a stated time to investigate the case. The agent arrives; the Coolies renew their charge, but with less vehemence and more regard to truth, now that they are in the presence of their masters. The manager refuses to increase their pay, alleging that what has already been promised them is a fair equivalent for their work. A visit is paid to a field where the work in question has been commenced. It not infrequently happens that the immigration agent finds himself unable to come to a decision from his ignorance of planting details; and in such cases four well-known planters are summoned—two chosen by the manager, and two by the Coolies. Both parties then agree to abide by their judgment. With every wish to decide in the immigrants' favour, it is seldom that the immigration agent finds himself able to do so, for the simple reason, that as a rule the work is found to have been fairly valued, and at similar rates to those paid on neighbouring estates at the same time. The regular monthly visit of the immigration agent also affords the Coolies opportunities of bringing complaints, thus saving them the time and trouble a walk to the town or magistrate's residence would entail. The immigrants' time of work is limited by law to seven hours a day in the open air, and ten hours a day under cover in the manufactories; if, however, they like to work a longer time for extra pay, they are open to do so, and most of them gladly avail themselves of this right, by which they secure more wages at the end of the week. The children are free from birth, and when grown up usually develop into the most useful and skilful labourers. As a further inducement to the immigrants to work well, they are entitled to a day's leave provided they labour with tolerable steadiness; and an industrious man or woman never asks in vain for two or three days or even a week's leave, supposing they wish to travel to a distant part of the country. Their children are formed into gangs, and employed at light easy work about the manufactory, or in the fields, receiving from sixpence to tenpence a day, according to their age and ability. The labourers on all estates are under the immediate supervision of several foremen, called "drivers." These men are Coolies themselves, and are specially selected by the manager of an estate as men of superior intelligence and strength, and as having shown themselves thoroughly acquainted with and able to perform the different descriptions of agricultural work they will have to superintend. These men are in receipt of fixed wages, and enjoy many agreeable privileges. It is their duty to stop all disputes, report everything wrong that may come under their notice, and be all day long with their fellow-immigrants in the fields, superintending their work, besides having to accomplish a host of minor duties. To rise to this position is the great ambition of most Coolies, and the hope of one day becoming a driver acts as a very healthy stimulant to induce them to increase their industry.

16. About two years ago (1880) the question was asked in the Court of Policy whether at the present day the predial

work of the sugar estates was enough to keep all the Coolies in the Colony employed, or whether it was true, as the Hon. J. Crosby, Immigration Agent General (now dead) had remarked in his letter, that the Coolies (by their account) could not obtain work at all times, and that when they did obtain it, it was at a rate of wages quite inadequate to support themselves and their families. There was a time, however, when every plantation in the Colony was in a chronic state of starvation for labour and was always glad to get labourers, even when the getting of them required the expenditure of large sums of money as bribes to attract the people from other estates. This state of affairs has disappeared, and as the cultivation throughout the Colony cannot have been reduced to any appreciable extent, as witness the amount of crop for 1879, the planters may with every reason congratulate themselves upon the result which has attended their system of introducing labourers from the East. Unquestionably, it would have been to the direct advantage of the Coolies who were in the Colony during the time of labour scarcity, if the planters had then abandoned immigration or had been unsuccessful in inducing people to come to the Colony, for the easing of the strain on the labour market has enabled the planters not only to reduce their wages to a more reasonable figure, but to become honest and virtuous so far as regards coveting their neighbours' labourers; and we can well imagine that those of the Coolies who remember "the good old days," are loud in their complaints about the money being "too small" this time. But the statistics of estates' pay lists show that though there has been a reduction in wages to a certain extent, there is no real ground for the Coolies' complaints, and that a labourer can make with ease considerably above the sum which the framers of the Immigration Ordinance fixed as a fair day's wage. In alluding in his letter to the outcry of the Coolies that the want of remunerative work was driving them out of the Colony, Mr. Crosby was simply fulfilling a duty he owed to the class whom he is supposed to "protect;" but, with the means within his power of ascertaining the real state of the labour market throughout the Colony, he ought not to have allowed his memorandum to go forth without some note or comment to the effect that the complaint of the Coolies had not received his endorsation. Taken as it stood, his letter, with its memorandum, would lead, and was evidently intended to lead, the reader to understand that Mr. Crosby was of opinion that the Colony was overstocked with labour, and that the Coolie was being driven back to his own country because here he and his family could not get enough to eat. The evidence of Mr. Russell and Mr. Booker, and the reports of the district magistrates addressed to the Executive, were all opposed to Mr. Crosby's view of the question, and local readers would have had no difficulty in arriving at a decision as to which of the opposing views was the correct one; but it is different with readers not in the Colony, who, knowing that the estates' pay lists were practically as open to Mr. Crosby as to the two aforesaid elective members, would naturally be disposed to regard Mr. Crosby's opinion as the more impartial and correct. It may help my reader to arrive at a correct conclusion if I annex here some information furnished by a manager whose attention was drawn to Mr. Crosby's memorandum. On inquiry, he found that twenty-one "time-expired" immigrants on his estate had registered for back passage, and he turned back the pay lists to learn if it could be the smallness of their earnings that was driving the people out of the land. It would have been a tedious job to have taken down each man's earnings during the fifty-two weeks in the previous year, so the manager took the first eight names on the alphabetical list furnished him, and found that the eight labourers had earned in 1879 as follows:—

	Days at work.	Days absent or on leave.	Total amount earned.	Earnings for each day at work.
Bississur	221	91	64 96	29 cents
Bhuttoo	250	62	100 28	40 "
Boobun	248	64	95 08	38 "
Bhurtun	218	94	55 12	25 "
Chumnoo	247	65	85 96	34 "
Doorga	254	58	89 04	35 "
Fukurchamid	280	32	113 88	40 "
Goyaram	196	116	81 76	41 "

The smallest amount per working day recorded above is twenty-five cents, and the manager observed that the man who earned this average was old and infirm and capable of doing only light work. But the average daily wage of the lot is ample, and places it beyond a doubt that whatever might have been the inducement to the twenty-one Coolies to take back passage, it was not to get away from a place of scarce labour and small pay. Notwithstanding all the precaution taken and provision made by the Government as far as labour and wages questions are concerned, there is no denying the fact that the great cause of discontent amongst the Coolies proceeds from labour disputes, and from the belief held by many of them that they are unfairly dealt with by their employers. Whatever truth or falsity there may be in this charge, it can readily be understood how quickly the feeling may produce disturbances. Let us, to estimate rightly the position of the Coolie, place ourselves in his place, and we shall be less surprised at the frequency of these labour disputes. We must remember that these men are in a strange land, amongst people who are alike different to them in language, customs, and ideas. The law may, and does, protect them from injustice and wrong, but this law they know nothing or but little of, it is written in a strange tongue, and to their untutored minds has but a shadowy existence. If they quarrel with their employers upon a question of wages for work done, they can appeal to the law, but they do so with no feeling of confidence, for they have to abide by the decision of officials who are as ignorant of Indian dialects as incompetent to decide by experience upon the merits of the complaint; or if the magistrate refers them to neighbouring planters, their decision is not unnaturally looked upon with doubt.

To say that Coolies coming to Demerara meet with no hardships would not be true. First of all, some of them have been idle vagabonds in India, some of them criminals, who escape the gaol or halter by emigrating; and some of them lads who have run away from home or school. Settled labour anywhere to such a class is a hardship. To the mendicant and the Brahman it is very galling. Some of these people occasionally give employers a great deal of trouble, trying their temper and patience much, and perhaps obliging them in the end to call in the aid of the law, which planters are generally averse to do in dealing with their labourers. The blame here must be laid on the previous habits of the people. Some Coolies are delicate when they come here, and change of climate produces sickness, which increases the percentage of deaths during the first years of residence. Some localities are not so healthy as others, although you will meet with Coolies even in the worst of these localities who have been fifteen and even twenty years on the same estate. There is in the Hindu Coolies, notwithstanding their faults, which are indeed many, something which is worthy of notice: "they have acquired a civilization which shows in them all day long; which draws the European to them and them to the European, whenever the latter is worthy of the name of a civilized man, instinctively, and by the mere interchange of glances; a civilization which must make it easy for the Englishman, if he will but do his duty, not only to make use of these people, but to purify and ennoble them." One of the most gratifying features in our system of introducing Coolie immigrants from India and China is the rapidity with which these heathen men adapt their habits and customs to the higher standard of the boasted civilization of the English people who employ them. The happy change was not so observable in the earlier years of immigration, but latterly it has been very marked. Formerly, it was an unknown occurrence to see a Coolie or a Chinaman in the Insolvency Court; but nowadays they file their petition with all the nerve and independence of a freeborn Briton or an affiliated Portuguese. Mr. Phillips had a Coolie witness under examination in the Court on Saturday, June 24, 1882, and when the learned counsel asked the witness why he made away with his shop by putting it in another man's name, the reply was, "That is notting; White people do um same ting, Coolie man must do um same like a White man." This answer stopped all further inquiry into the morality of the witness's conduct. The same witness claimed past acquaintanceship with the learned counsel, and amused the Court by exclaiming, "Ow, Mass Pillup, you know me; da time you bin da estate, me and you fight buildings house, and me lick you dey." The witness was just a little too much for Mr. Phillips, who, trying to mollify him, remarked :—"You, good lawyer, na?" The witness at once indignantly replied, "Liar! no, me no liar." The Coolies' pronunciation of the word "lawyer" is very peculiar, and leads one to suppose that they regard a lawyer as a man addicted to mendacity. Of course they ought to know better than this.

17. I am glad to remark here that since the publication of my *Guyanian Indians*, in which the subject is referred to, the vexed *Huis t'Dieren Coolie Settlement*—down the Arabian (Essequibo) Coast—question has been disposed of. On this subject the editor of the *Colonist* very judiciously in his issue of December 16, 1881, remarks :—

"As Mr. Kirke remarked to some purpose, the scheme is practically an experiment so far as the Government of the Colony is concerned, though for the settlers themselves it means a comfortable livelihood with the probability of a competency by-and-bye, or comparative ruin, according as fortune or misfortune may hap. The co-operative colonizing of Mr. Thomas Hughes is admitted on all hands to have been a sad failure in the now famous Rugby Colony, though it is at the same time conceded that the execution rather than the conception of the system was at fault. Mr. Hughes chose unsuitable land for his location; and not to speak of college-bred youths fit for anything but the hard work so inseparable from pioneer farming, the earth refused to yield its fruits in remunerative quantity. But a co-operative scheme for the colonizing of Coolies, under the practical wing of the British Guyana Legislature, is widely different from a co-operative scheme for the colonizing of curled dandies under the extravagant theorisms of Mr. Thomas Hughes. The settlers may be considered to resign, concurrently with the transport from the Government of their plot of ground, all reasonable prospect of returning to their native land. They become part and parcel of the soil, for, let joy or sorrow betide, British Guyana must be their home. The experimental scheme commences under happy auspices, though the prospective landholders must have had difficulty in keeping hope alive in their breasts while the preliminaries were being slowly rounded into the most promising form. Several families who contemplated settlement, despairing of their hopes ever being realized, availed themselves of their back passages, the result being the loss of many promising Colonists. It is better, however, to make sure by slow means than to rush headlong into some ill-matured scheme, the consequence of which might be disaster; and it is to be hoped that the success in store for the Huis t'Dieren Settlement will make amends for the loss of those who have gone, and will also encourage the Government to other attempts of the same kind. There is no reason why British Guyana should not become almost a second India. If not rich in metals—though there are those who hold that it is—British Guyana is still rich in internal resources, which, if developed, might offer occupation and livelihood to some millions of inhabitants. According to the Acting Immigration Agent General's half-yearly returns, there are now 69,052 immigrants in the Colony employed in sugar cultivation alone. After acclimatization it is said that the Asiatic thrives even better here than in his native home; and if so, with the natural increase of population the colonizing of every available spot of land within the confines of the country—and at no terribly remote date either—need not be regarded as a figure of speech. The natural conditions are all present, and only those which man himself must supply are yet to be called into existence. It may be that the scheme which has germinated to-day may prove the commencement of a new era for the Colony; for if success should be the upshot the Government will hardly stay its hand, where there are so many broad acres awaiting the hand of the husbandman. There is a great issue for the Colony dependent on the Huis t'Dieren Settlement, and it will be the sincere wish of every one that it may prosper. Of course the trouble is not yet all over, for it is to be anticipated that some of those who contemplated relinquishing their back passage in lieu of land may take exception to something in the newly-passed rules. But the Government have put themselves in the position of saying: 'There is the land; and there is your back passage—take either.' If one will not have the land, another probably will, just as in bargain-making everywhere. And if the experiment suceeds there will be no lack of applicants for exchange; while if it should fail the difficulties in the way of any succeeding attempt will be much enhanced. Now that the preliminaries are fixed, operations will probably be commenced as soon as possible; and it cannot be more than three or four years at the utmost before a fair idea may be formed of how much or how little is to be expected from the system now so nearly inaugurated."

The entire scheme is, in other words, an attempt to establish in the Colony, under the auspices of the authorities, a peasant proprietary. There are some gentlemen, whose long acquaintance with the Colony entitles their views to all respect, and who are not antagonistic to the scheme, but who, nevertheless, doubt the success of the project. They fear the element of cohesion, so necessary to success, will be wanting. This is not an unreasonable view to take of the matter, remembering that each settler is absolutely uncontrolled in the mode of cultivation he may adopt. It may be hoped, however, that the appointment of the Zamindar, under the direction of the Immigration Department, to the general supervision of the settlement will bring about the combination of effort which is requisite to insure the success of the experiment. The important question to the public is: Whether it will be more to the benefit of the Colony to retain the best among the acclimatized Coolies than to be charged with the cost of their homeward passages.

18. The following are the Rules and Conditions for the regulation of grants of land at plantation Huis t'Dieren to Indian immigrants in lieu of back passages to India:—

"1. Each Adult Immigrant who may desire to relinquish all claim to a Back Passage to India may have an allotment of Two Acres of Land for cultivation, and ¼ of an acre suitable for a place of residence.

"2. Children between 10 and 15 years of age, may receive Two Acres of land for cultivation, but no village lot.

"3. Children between the age of 1 and 10 years may receive a grant of ½ an acre of land.

"4. The lands shall be allotted to the applicants in regular and continuous order according to the priority of their applications: Provided that His Excellency the Governor reserves to himself the right to refuse an allotment to any Immigrant whom, on account of physical incapacity or moral obliquity, he may consider unsuited for the settlement.

"5. The Government will fence in a portion of ground for

a grazing ground to be used by the settlers in common in such proportions as the Zemindar may decide.

"6. The Government will deliver to the settlers the front and back dam kokers, main drainage trenches, and public road in thorough order and repair, and will continue to maintain the same, but after the first cost of repair has been paid by the Government the land will be held liable to subsequent expenses under such special or general scheme as may hereafter be determined.

"7. The settlers will have the opportunity of being employed on these works at a reasonable rate of wages.

"8. The Government will be prepared to carry out any scheme of irrigation which may be devised by the settlers, and the cost of which with interest they will agree to repay by a water rate.

"9. The Government will take the necessary proceedings to eject all squatters from *Huis t'Dieren* and *Middlesex.*

"10. Transports of the Land will be given to settlers as soon as possible after the lands are allotted and occupied; provided that at the same time and place each settler shall release the Government of British Guiana from all obligation to furnish him or her with a free passage to India.

"11. The Zemindar, under the direction of the Immigration Agent General, shall exercise a general supervision over the Immigrants, and shall settle any little disputes that may arise between them.

"12. It is proposed to establish a Dispensary on the Estate to be visited at least twice a week by the District Medical Officer; the fee for his advice to be 32 cents for Immigrants applying at the Dispensary, and 48 cents for visits to their houses.

"Settled and approved by the Governor and Court of Policy, this 16th day of December, 1881.

"By Command,

"GEO. MELVILLE,

"Acting Secretary."

Some months after these "Rules and Conditions" were passed by the Honourable Court of Policy, the Honourable Robert W. S. Mitchell, new Immigration Agent General, arrived in the Colony, and, after visiting the abandoned sugar estate of Huis t'Dieren, found the scheme in the aggregate to be unworkable. As a consequence the "Rules and Conditions" have been rescinded *en bloc;* and although the progress of the Settlement may be impeded for the present, much ultimate benefit may be calculated upon. Under the regulations referred to, each adult immigrant whose term of indenture had expired was to receive, in lieu of back passage, two acres of land, and half an acre for village lot—not one-fourth, as was one day stated in the Court of Policy. Children over ten and below fifteen years of age were to receive two acres of land for cultivation, but no village lot, while children between one and ten might receive half an acre of land.

Looking at the two latter provisions, it will be seen at once that they were calculated to encourage what has been so energetically deprecated, viz., the possession of more land by one man than his means enable him to cultivate. To take a not very extreme instance, there might be four children of one couple between ten and fifteen years of age, and between one and ten there might be five. The four children between ten and fifteen would have a collective claim on eight acres, and the five between one and ten on two and a half acres—or ten and a half acres in all, and aggregating fifteen and a half when added to the allotments of the parents. Any one who is at all acquainted with the amount of labour necessary to cultivate the soil in Demerara will at once recognize that with such rules in existence the Settlement would contain the elements of its own destruction. Although yielding its fruits in rich profusion when efficiently tilled, local agriculture requires more vigour than the tickle with a hoe, spoken of by Sydney Smith, as the sole preliminary to a bountiful harvest. Mr. Russell's estimate of a Coolie's cultivating capabilities is two acres, and as, in the hypothetical case above alluded to, the greater part of the family would be non-efficient for several years to come, the inevitable consequence would be the partial cultivation of the entire allotment, or the abandonment to nature of all but a small portion. Under the rules now proposed the allotment to an immigrant and his wife will remain as before; and the condition to the obtaining of three acres more will be the parentage of a family three in number. The Scriptural injunction is thus backed up by the offer of a substantial premium, and it is to be presumed that if the land at Huis t'Dieren is at all worth the having its multiplication and replenishment by the Eastern race will not be of slow progress. A powerful argument in favour of the new regulations proposed by Mr. Mitchell is, that they have already been tried in Trinidad and found to work with fair satisfaction, and it is to be hoped that their introduction in Demerara will result as felicitously for all concerned.

CHAPTER IX.

OUR CREOLE BLACK LABOURERS.

1. The word "Creole," often used in the Colony, does not mean black or coloured, any more than it does white. When Guyana was first colonized as it was by Spain, Creole was taken to mean a native of Spanish America, of European, &c., descent. But after other nations settled in the West Indies, the word has the more easily understood definition of a descendant of a settler or of a Colonist. The meaning of the word was not changed, only, as other countries besides Spain came in, it applied to them as well as to Spain. Thus, the children of two Africans from Gambia are to the present day, as they always have been, called Creoles of Demerara, in the same way that the children of an Englishman and an Englishwoman from London, or a Scotchman and a Scotchwoman from Lanarkshire, are called Creoles, or the issue between a woolly-headed Negress and a red-haired Scotchman. This is the true application and use of the word "Creole;" but in general use it is intended to signify the natives of the Colony of mixed blood, and is a term also in general use for the black labouring population, of whom we have a large population in the Colony. I have already in Chapter VI. pointed out the fact that several from this class have raised themselves to higher positions than being mere ordinary agricultural labourers, &c.

2. The constitution of society in British Guyana, and indeed throughout the West Indies, is very peculiar. The one human race, of one blood only, is cut up or divided into three distinct classes or castes,—the Whites or the Europeans, who are the lords of the soil; the Coloured people, the result of unholy, ungovernable passions of the monsters of iniquity of olden days; and the Blacks, whose parents and grand-parents were

held in hopeless bondage. To these may be added the Indian, Chinese, and Portuguese Coolies or labourers, who have come to the Colony and formed their own societies. The coloured race look down upon the blacks and form no association with them, but the respectable class among them more or less associate with the whites, and the whites, considering themselves to be a highly superior race, look down upon both the coloured and black people with scorn and derision. There was a time in the history of the Colony when "the mean white tyrant master" looked upon a coloured or black man not as a fellow creature, not as a brother man, not as a human being responsible to his Creator for the talent entrusted to him, but as a chattel—property—no better, except in pecuniary value, than his mule or his dog. Happily times are changed: all stand now on an equality with each other in the eye of the law, in the eye of God, and in the eye of the world. There is, however, no denying the fact that many Europeans—Englishmen and Scotchmen—some time after they have lived in the Colony, alter their opinions and manners in regard to the natives of the country. A native writing in one of the local papers observes :—

"Just you mark the demeanour of a man lately arrived from Europe for the first time: he is the very essence of civility; he speaks to all men alike; he is regardless of colour to the extent of making not the least difference in his address towards white and black; the newly-arrived European is a gentleman. But take a glance of him after he has been in the Colony some months, and you see him, in nine cases out of ten, distorting his body in all forms, and keeping his head high in the air and set upon a neck as stiff as a crowbar—he has been inoculated with the prevailing poison of prejudice, and can no longer feel at ease near a black man, unless Quash, cunning Quash, should make a greater fool of him by means of repeated 'Sahs' and 'Massas,' when his heart would dilate at receiving an amount of what looks like respect, to which in his country he was totally unused.

"It is positively sickening to witness the arrogance of some Englishmen and Scotchmen when they are brought in contact with a man of colour; and all this goes to give Quash the impression that he is unjustly regarded as belonging to an inferior order of beings, and prevents him making the effort he should make to raise himself in the scale."

In regard to the colour question, I have frequently been asked by several Creole people whether the first man Adam was black or white. The following, clipped from an old newspaper, may prove an answer to my inquirers:—

The late "Dr. Guthrie, at a meeting held in Edinburgh, said that he was not sure but what Adam was black (much and long continued laughter, and cheers). He would tell them the reason why (renewed laughter). Major Denham, a distinguished African traveller, went to that country, and spent three or four years in the home and cradle of the slave race, and had got so accustomed to the dark beauties of Africa, and had got so much to admire what men called God's image in ebony, that when he reached the shores of our own land, and saw the white ladies, they looked very sickly-like to him (laughter). The celebrated Dr. Fleming, Professor of Natural Science in the Free Church College, and one of the greatest naturalists of his day, maintained that black was the right and proper colour, and that we are all bleached up—(roars of laughter)—that we were just like one of those shawls that were seen sometimes in the Cowgate—(laughter)—the colour clean gone (renewed laughter). He would give them a physical fact in connection with this. The skin that covered our bodies was composed of certain layers—one of these anatomists called the *rete mucosum*, a sort of membrane, which consisted of a congeries of cells. Now, in the white men these were very like the boxes kept in such shops as those of Mr. Knox—they were all for show—there was nothing in them (laughter); but in regard to the dark race the *rete mucosum* was filled with what is called a black pigment, and if the *rete mucosum* was not made for the black pigment, what was it made for at all (laughter)? That was rather a philosophical argument (renewed laughter). The opinion was held by some that the dark race was the old original race of man; black face and a white heart. There was many a man who had a white face and a black heart (cheers)."

8. The cry or complaint has often been that the Creole labourers will not work, and that they cannot be depended on in the work allotted to them. At the Poor Law Investigation Board held in the three counties—Demerara, Berbice, and

Essequibo—of the Colony last year (1881) several startling statements were made by the clergy and laity in regard to this very subject; but as the Report of the Commissioners is not yet published, I cannot say what the result will be. But the Rev. Joseph Ketley (a Congregational minister), having the welfare of the Creole population earnestly at heart, had been holding public meetings, independent of the Poor Law Commissioners, to ascertain how far the report is true that the black labouring population will not work. I here reproduce a correct report of the proceedings of the first meeting convened by Mr. Ketley at Wilberforce Chapel, Victoria Village, East Sea Coast, on Monday evening, September 19th, 1881, which was attended by about five hundred villagers: this will give my reader some idea of the nature of other similar meetings held by the reverend gentleman :—

4. "Mr. Ketley said, that in order to give the inhabitants of this neighbourhood, the proprietors and labourers, an opportunity of hearing what had been said with regard to the inquiry instituted concerning the large amount of pauperism now in this Colony, the present meeting was called. He had been in the Colony for four years, and there was now a greater amount of poverty than before. It therefore became a very serious question whether it should go on, or whether something could be done to stay it. He did not know whether anything would come out of the inquiry going on; but as a public teacher he thought it was his duty to give the villagers an opportunity of familiarizing themselves with what was transpiring in connection with this inquiry, and to see whether the villagers could throw any light upon this subject, and whether they could do anything to aid the Poor Law Commissioners. He would read certain statements from the *Colonist* newspaper, and then ask those of the villagers who were present as representing different localities to address him. The rev. gentleman then read the evidence of Mr. Mulligan, who, he said, seemed to have much sympathy with the Negro race. The evidence of Mr. Davson (taken in Berbice) was also read. The extracts which he had just read were a correct setting forth of facts.

"William Thomas appeared to represent the village of Ann's Grove. He stated that he had heard what Mr. Mulligan and Mr. Davson had said. He was a master carpenter. With regard to the payment of wages on sugar estates, he worked on several estates, and they agreed to give the people a certain price, but when Saturday came they did not.

"The Rev. Ketley: You mean to say they don't pay what they agree to?

"Mr. Thomas: Yes, Sir, they deviate.

"The Rev. Ketley: Is there a greater amount of pauperism now than before?

"Mr. Thomas said, within the last two years he found it very difficult to obtain work on the estates. He had to resort to the cutlass and hoe. He knew that gangs of black people had been to Pln. *Clonbrook* and applied for work, but could get none, and the few that succeeded in getting it could not earn as much as would feed them. The proprietors and managers expected the people to work for them for nothing. Work that they were formerly paid 40 cents and 32 cents for was now reduced to 20 cents. Were it not for their provision lands they would have perished. The Creole people were stigmatized as being lazy. The railway manager could prove the number of trucks that were engaged weekly to transport their provisions to Georgetown. If they were lazy, would this have been so?

"Mr. Ketley: With regard to the working of the Village Ordinance, is it favourable or the reverse?

"Mr. Thomas said in answer to this question that he was a Village Councillor of Ann's Grove. There was a grievance in the working of the present Village Ordinance. They themselves purchased the village and did not expect the Government to keep it up for them. He had no hesitation in saying that if the Village Ordinance was carried out in its *integrity* it would be more beneficial. With regard to the payment, or rather mode of enforcing the payment, of the village taxes, it was very oppressive. Household necessaries were levied on without the parties being summoned before the Magistrate, and simply on the sworn allegation of the Village Chairman; their very pots were taken away.

"The villagers here began to cry out at the top of their voices that they were much oppressed, and the rev. gentleman had to bring them to order. His reason, he said, for asking the question about the working of the Village Ordinance was because it had been hinted to him that it was oppressive, and he knew that there was a strong feeling on the matter, especially amongst the villagers of Victoria.

"Mr. Thomas continued to state that it was customary for

the villagers to pay a certain sum for the working of their villages, which they agreed to, but they never anticipated that a man's property would be sold over his head.

"Mr. Ketley: You know that you are under the law, and therefore you must submit to the law. In connection with what you have stated, have any efforts been made to represent your grievances to the authorities? In Georgetown people were constantly coming to him to borrow money to save their property from being sold out. In a village like that he believed one half of the people paid to keep up their dams, whilst the other half would not, and those delinquents should not get off. He would ask Mr. Thomas whether any representations had been made to the Government about the oppressive nature of the law.

"Mr. Thomas said, some time ago they petitioned the Government on the matter, but their grievances were not redressed. A number of them were told to wait at the Public Buildings to be heard, and they did so. The meeting was adjourned, and since then they had heard nothing of the matter.

"Mr. Ketley: Then you mean to say that they levy without notice?

"Mr. Thomas: The Chairman of the village simply writes out a document, which is signed by the Magistrate. This document is handed to a police-constable, and your property, which cost about $400, is levied on and sold for a paltry amount, without the owner being afforded an opportunity of saying anything before a magistrate.

"Mr. Ketley: Then in connection with the Village Ordinance you say it is oppressive, and the way in which it is carried out tends to cause pauperism. Is there any suggestion that you can make by which you think the labouring population can be benefited?

"Mr. Thomas said that since the introduction of Coolie immigrants into this Colony, the Creole people were not fairly dealt with.

"Mr. Ketley said he would draw Mr. Thomas's attention to Mr. Davson's statement. He said that he would at any time rather employ Creoles than immigrants, but he could not get them.

"John Lewis, who represented the villagers of Victoria, then ascended the platform. On commencing his address a general talk and noise ensued, and Mr. Ketley, after having succeeded in restoring order, said that an answer to a question put to him when giving his evidence at the Poor Law Investigation was, that there was no cohesion amongst the people; and here was an instance to-night. Their own representative was prevented from talking in consequence of voices here and voices there. They could not get on in that way.

"Mr. Lewis then stated that one of the causes of pauperism among them was the large number of foreigners introduced into the Colony by the white people.

"Mr. Ketley (interrupting): May I ask you this question—Supposing immigrants were not introduced into this Colony, what do you think would have become of it?

"Mr. Lewis: It would have been the same as in the days of emancipation.

"Mr. Ketley: Then you attribute pauperism to the introduction of immigrants?

"Mr. Lewis: O yes.

"Mr. Ketley: Well now, you know of course that truth is not always very smooth; and I am anxious to help you people in this matter; but you must look truth in the face. Here are a few thoughts which came to my mind whilst you were speaking. How is it that the people are poorer now than they were before? Continuing, Mr. Ketley said he left the Colony a youth and returned a man, when he found poverty abounding. In days gone by there were fine houses that were built by their old parents, but look at them now all tumbling to pieces. Look at that chapel—could the young people build one like it? The soil was as good, they had the same hands, the same feet and the same legs as their forefathers; and yet there was this deterioration. Of course he was aware that the Creole people got disheartened very quick; they were not as persevering as Englishmen. Another thing he would refer to was that parents did not train their children. This was easily proved by how the schools were attended. The consequences were that the children got idle and there was no discipline. Now, what was wanted at present in the Colony was something that would bring a strong pressure upon the parents to train their children. He noticed not only in Victoria, but at La Pénitence, large numbers of boys playing cricket from Monday morning to Saturday. Could men live by playing? The cause of pauperism amongst the Creoles was the lack of proper discipline. They wanted to acquire working habits and a spirit of union. Now, if they could only feel a thorough bond of brotherhood;

if they could only know the meaning of the word 'co-operation' —man to help man—they would be able to hold their meetings, and carry out schemes with success. One of the chief causes of poverty amongst them was their motto, 'Every man is for himself.' Another thing which caused poverty was because they were too rich. Now, was it a fact that they could really live upon three days' work for a week? (Cries of 'O no, Sir.')

"Mr. Ketley: Well, that is a statement which I would like to have contradicted, because it has been said so. I am obliged to work seven days, except when I can steal a holiday, and every merchant works six days.

"Aaron Adonis, representing Two Friends Village, said he had been a labourer over twenty years, and there was a great advantage taken of the people now. They were obliged to work for nothing. Work that they were formerly paid forty-eight cents for, they could only get twelve cents for now. The white people knew that they were poor and that they would be obliged to accept work at a low rate of wages. It was a practice on sugar estates for the overseer to condemn what work had been done, and when Saturday night came, although one had worked the whole week, he went home to his family without a cent in his pocket. When the overseers didn't want to pay, they simply said the work was condemned. For instance, himself and several others worked at Pln. *Cove and John* the second week in August, drilling holes a foot and a half in width, which was very hard work, and had not been paid. Sometimes they were paid half, and the balance they never got. They went to Mr. Drake, the manager of the estate, and complained. He gave them no satisfaction, but in their presence took a pen and scratched their names out of the book. They threatened to sue the estate, but never did it, as they did not like to hurt the feelings of the proprietor, Mr. Bascom. He was a kind gentleman.

"John English said he was seventy-five years of age, and was employed on Pln. *Providence* in Berbice. They were always robbed of their wages.

"Several other labourers endorsed this statement, and said that unfair treatment on the managers' part tended to alienate the Creole labourers from the White planters. Those who were willing to work were often oppressed and robbed of their legitimate wages.

"Mr. Ketley: What, then, about Mr. Davson's kind treatment of the Creoles, and the ungenerous conduct of the Creoles in refusing to agree to accept steady and continuous work, though offered on such advantageous terms?

"Mr. English: Mr. Davson is a real gentleman, but he works his estates by managers; and if we enter into contract for labour we should not get fair play from them. Many managers and attorneys get rich, and the proprietors and labourers are poor.

"Mr. James, a black man, made the following statement. He observed that Mr. Ketley said the Creole people only worked three days in the week, and that was sufficient to keep them. The Creole people were not sufficiently remunerated, for the moment a black man in any employment was getting on, or becoming rich, every opportunity was watched to put him out. He had heard it said by labourers that they could not work on an estate as they liked, as the overseers watched the pay-list very acutely to see when the wages were getting too high, and to check it. Now, why was there a scarcity of labour? It was in consequence of the amalgamation of a large quantity of sugar estates in this Colony. He felt it a public duty to speak, because he was of the African race, and anything that was said against his race he felt to the heart. He was not a labourer, but was not ashamed to labour; it kept the system in order. The Creole race was stigmatized as a lazy set, which was not true. Who could deny that many of their people rose at four in the morning to go aback as a rule? They fancied the night was too long, and yet they were said to be lazy. The bad ones made the good ones get blame; and he certainly wished that every lazy Creole could be banished. Their people had not much capital to do anything; if they had, a larger quantity of provision lands would be cultivated, and articles would be exported on a large scale, and then the Creoles of British Guyana would be better off. Now, this want of capital was owing to the non-existence of unity among their race; they did not combine to hold together as they ought. The next point was distrust. He was actually ashamed of this word. If he was inclined to lend one of his race twenty dollars, he would be afraid to do so, and would not, although he knew it would be of some use to him. It might save his property from being sold. Why was he afraid? Because the borrower would not return it. Slavery was also one of the causes of pauperism among the people. The sons and daughters found their fathers and mothers, who were slaves, poor people. This was not so with Europeans. The young generation found money at their disposal, and could put their hands in their pockets at any time.

"Mr. Ketley begged to contradict this statement, to a certain extent. There was a great deal of poverty in England. Things were quite different in England to here. These people had to provide themselves with boots, and coals, and proper clothing in winter. Here people could walk barefooted at any time. Here they could get a bunch of plantains for sixpence, which would last for the week nearly, but it was not so in England.

"Mr. James said he would now deal with the question of remuneration of the black young men who were employed professionally. If a black young man was taken into any office of rank, his employer would say, 'I will give you $30 per month.' That black young man knew he was worth much more, but could not push his claims. Let that black young man be particular with his earnings and begin to build a house, the employer (if he happened to be a white man) picked at him; he was getting too rich. He once heard a respectable gentleman ask this question with regard to a black man who was in a good position:—'I wonder what he is going to do with all that money?' He felt very queer. The general feeling was that money was not made for the black man. If a labourer got $7 at the pay table, the next week he did not get work. They must go 'thus far and no farther,' was what was generally said. The black man found that he was obliged to be cunning and work only two days in the week, so as always to get work. Referring to black men filling official positions: as soon as the black young man was turned off, a white one filled his place and immediately received from $70 to $100 per month. This was a fact, so it seemed that money was made for them and not for the black people. This was one of the causes of pauperism. Another cause of pauperism was the absence of money-lending companies to encourage commercial or agricultural enterprise, and the failure of the Government to step into the place of such companies. There were many men who would try to be industrious in planting canes, but they could get no one to assist them. If there were money-lending societies in this Colony, they would find many black men jumping up in a crack, and there would not be so many paupers on the list. The Government should say, 'Well, we want you to get out of the paupers' list; here, I lend you $500, but give me good security;' and he knew that the majority of the people would avail themselves of this offer. He must also say that the love of show or gaiety was another cause of pauperism amongst the black race, and a love for the Magistrate's office, and he only hoped that some good might result from the inquiry which was going on in Georgetown.

"Mr. Ketley said (it being now nearly twenty minutes to 11 p.m.) he could not reply to Mr. James fully. He himself had spent hours in considering what could be done to better the condition of the people. He found that the enemy of the black man was not the white man, but the black man himself. He had done many acts of charity for the black people, and he received far more ingratitude than thanks. He often aided persons and was patient, but the instant one black man owed another he was summoned; so they must not only look at the conduct of the white people, but at their own people also. It struck him that discipline was much required at present. On the School Board there was a point of dispute worthy of notice. He (Mr. Ketley) served on a School Board in England, and he found that it was absolutely necessary to *compel* parents to send their children to school. It was well to recognize the fact that to have good citizens we must develope the man. The question had arisen in the School Board as to the desirability of enforcing compulsory education amongst the villagers. He thought it was necessary to use some force by which parents should be made to say, as his deceased father used to, 'Now, you must attend to your lesson at nine o'clock, on Monday,' and if the pupil did not he was sure of receiving a caning. Discipline was absolutely necessary, and must be enforced. If two or three parents went to prison and suffered, it was better than that a whole generation should suffer. He was very anxious that they should have, in connection with their schools, a sort of industrial branch, so that the young might be taught to work, and how to drain the soil. He would also have trades taught. In England a lad was regularly apprenticed to his master, but it was not so in this Colony. At the present time, as soon as lads could purchase a jack plane and hammer, they went and hired themselves equal to the man who was equally efficient.

"The meeting then terminated."

5. A gentleman, on the other hand, well acquainted with the character and condition of the African Creole labouring population, remarked as follows:—

"It is impossible to read the report of the meeting without the conviction that the Rev. Joseph Ketley has the welfare of the Creole population earnestly at heart, otherwise he would never have run the risk of incurring odium and resentment by opening his mind so freely to a meeting attended by some five hundred people, many of them smarting under a sense of supposed wrong and oppression. It has been alleged that on sugar estates the contract to pay a certain sum of money for a given quantity of work is not adhered to. But there are two sides to the question. Does the Creole labourer in such cases carry out his part of the contract by giving the quantity and the quality of labour agreed upon? Frequent prosecutions by managers of sugar estates of labourers who have scamped their work by burying the cane tops they should have planted, and perpetrating frauds of similar character, supply the answer. Payment must be contingent on the work undertaken being fairly executed. Failing such conscientious execution, the labourer is notoriously unworthy of his hire. Complaint was also made at the meeting of the oppressive working of the Village Ordinance, and of household necessaries being levied on for payment of taxes without being summoned before the Magistrate. It is evident on the face of the Ordinance that the intention in framing it was to obviate the necessity for tortuous legal formalities. This object is effected by appointing officers under the Ordinance, in whom are vested certain powers for enforcing payment of rates and otherwise compelling the villagers to promptly meet the obligations it imposes. It is enacted in section 62 that if payment be not made in one week after notice of the assessment due on a building, share, or lot has been left on such premises, the overseer or collector may apply to the stipendiary magistrate, who upon production of the notice or duplicate may grant a warrant of distress. The assumption evidently is, and correctly, that the oath of the Overseer or Collector before the Magistrate is evidence enough of the notice having been duly served. The official has no interest in making misrepresentations for the sake of oppressing any one, while the instinct of self-preservation may cause the person proceeded against to make a false attestation. The appearance of both parties could not alter the issue; and either on the score of carrying out the Ordinance in its integrity or the allegation of injustice under the terms of this section, there is no substantial ground of complaint.

"The Creole peasantry have signally failed to apprehend their responsibilities as members of a civilized community. They expect all the protection law and good government can confer, but they object to pay for such advantages. It is by taxation alone that the funds necessary to carry on the administration of the Colony can be obtained, yet they make the loudest outcry against taxation. No people are fonder of resorting to litigation for the redressing of injury, or the settlement of disputes. But they expect their law for nothing. They are fast enough to recognize the claim of an attorney who insists on payment before granting his services, but there is no such readiness to acknowledge their liability for the maintenance of the law's cumbrous and expensive machinery. The assertion of one of the speakers that the villagers agreed to pay a certain sum for the working of their villages, but never anticipated that a man's roof would be sold over his head, shows that with all his love of litigation the African Creole has not yet mastered the most elementary principles of law and logic. It is only when a villager fails in his part of the agreement, that the law steps in to take its satisfaction. If every ratepayer puts down his quota of taxation, there will be no necessity for resorting to such forcible measures as warrants of distress. It would be idle to deny that there are occasional instances of injustice on the part of an employer; but black and white are as one in the eye of the law, which will promptly avenge the oppressed. If Creole labourers showed a more frequent disposition to carry out their contracts in the fullest integrity, it is improbable that the option of stopping wages would long be left in the employers' hands. But so long as the tendency is to evade engagements and sham work, it is an absolute necessity that a wider discretion than would otherwise be advisable should be given to the capitalist who has so much at stake. Creole labourers seem to regard the employer as their natural enemy, whereas the interests of capital and labour ought as surely to go hand in hand, as in the old slavery days, when the operative was a chattel representing a certain sum.

"It was asserted at the meeting that one of the causes of pauperism in the Colony was the large number of foreigners introduced by the white people. It is not easy to see who is to blame for this but the Creoles themselves. Previous to emancipation they constituted the only labour supply of the Colony, and if they had afterwards shown themselves to be reliable as steady labourers, there would have been no necessity for introducing immigrants in such numbers. Immigrant labour having been extensively imported, however, the question naturally resolved itself into one of competition between the two races. If the Creole has gone to the wall in the struggle, it is hardly reasonable to turn round and lay the blame upon the white employer, who had been compelled to look elsewhere for his labour supply or abandon the effort to maintain his ground. There is no such thing as attempting to keep the Creole labourer down. The laws of England and the Colonies recognize no distinction of colour. If, instead of crying out over fancied wrongs, or wasting half of the week in idleness and dissipation, a manful effort were made to better their position by steady industry, there would soon be a change from the prevailing poverty and pauperism. The spirit which regards as a solemn duty the fulfilling of every engagement would do much towards eliminating the prevailing feeling of distrust which strangles every enterprise. It is a terrible satire upon the character of the labouring classes that while the Rev. Joseph Ketley was endeavouring to impress his hearers with wholesome maxims, and point the way to their worldly advancement, his hen-roost should be robbed in his absence. Comparing the price of necessaries in the two countries, the willing labourer is really far better off here than in England. If the Creole peasantry will only rouse themselves to continuous exertion, there is no reason why they should not be comfortably housed and clothed and fed; but it is no easy matter to help a people who will not help themselves. That the African race is not lacking in enterprise and energy is evidenced in one signal instance by the career of Soley Le Black, to whom Mr. Ketley in his second meeting referred as having purchased the abandoned estate of Strick-en-Heuvel, gathered around him many followers, and established a flourishing centre of industry. It would seem, however, that his disciples were terribly deficient in the force of character which marked their leader. Mr. Ketley asked in vain of his hearers: 'Where is that centre of industry now?' And none of them could allege, though challenged to do so, that the white man had any share in its downfall."

The late Soley Le Black earnestly attempted to stir up a feeling of independence among his fellow black men, both in regard to religious teaching and in trying to rouse them to habits of industry and honesty. His life, his means, his all, were given to the good cause, and, sad to relate, he saw with his failing years that he had worked in vain. To carry on the sugar industry and procure the necessary funds he had to resort to friends in town for loans to tide over bad times, and it is well known that those liabilities bore hard upon the brave old man when he found his end drawing near. With his death the whole fabric which had engrossed his every exertion in the prime of life, fell to pieces. Strick-en-Heuvel is not the only centre of industry which has had to close up in that district. To those who remember the various chimneys which marked the sugar works of Potosi, Maria's Lodge, Vanderstein, Chantilly, Glasgow, situated between Vive-la-Force and the Sand Hills, and see now nothing but bush, with a scattered population of discontents such as attended the Strick-en-Heuvel meeting, the feeling is that of sadness, for but for the introduction of immigrants the whole of British Guyana must have followed; for in the district under consideration the natural advantages, river drainage and shipping, fertile soil and an unlimited supply of firewood, all ought to have enabled the proprietors to have pulled through. But no, the people would not give continuous labour, even when tempted with rates the payment of which soon led to abandonment. In fact the Act of 1838 had the effect of transferring the land from the then owners to their serfs in the same way as many suppose Mr. Gladstone's Irish Land Bill will cause a similar transfer of the land in Ireland, from present proprietors to their tenants. Let us hope that they may make a better use of their opportunities than Quashi has done.

Great stress has been laid upon the managers dealing harshly with the firewood merchants. Having had considerable experience of this fraternity, I can throw some light upon the seven shillings promised, and only five shillings tendered when the wood was corded. The cord ought to measure $8 \times 4 \times 4 = 128$ cut feet or $18\frac{1}{3}$ cubic feet for one shilling. Instead of the wood being according to contract it is generally only $3\frac{1}{2}$ to 3 feet long. So by the simple rule of proportion—

4 × 4	× 8 in.	128 c. feet	=	7 shillings.
4 × 3½	× 8 in.	112 „	=	6/3
4 × 3	× 8 in.	96 „	=	5/4

So that in reality the price said to have been tendered was in proportion to cubic capacity. Poetry has added a steamboat service and River Magistrates for the benefit of the scattered squatters along the main rivers, and still the cry is "want of justice," and for additional accommodation, schools, &c. So the industrious bees may expect further calls upon their energies to maintain the drones in useless existence.

The Executive have recognized the fact that two acres of land is a fair allowance for an adult Coolie to keep in fair cultivation. Apply the same rule to the Creole peasantry, and instead of scattering or encouraging them to scatter over the width and breadth of the land carry out the Polder Bill, and find suitable locations for those who really wish to be industrious, and to live within the pale, and success may be expected to attend the new departure in colonizing.

There is but little in the argument made use of by one of the speakers that the Creole is not capable of competing with Portuguese ingenuity. The law will protect all classes from fraud and imposition, and for the rest the race will generally fall to the swift, and the battle to the strong. The letter of our correspondent, already referred to, disposes, by the incontrovertible testimony of arithmetic, of the allegations of dishonest reckoning made against managers. The fact is, that the want of an "innate practical principle," the lack of co-operation, and the mutual distrust between one another, are amongst the main causes which militate against the success of Creoles as a class. There are no doubt numbers of honest Creole peasants to be found. But they form the exception and not the rule. The remarks of a speaker at Mr. Ketley's meeting are only too forcible an illustration. "Is it not a fact," he asks without challenge, "that we have robbed and cheated each other? Is it not also a fact that we do not believe, and that we distrust, each other?" Then, again, in the all-important matter of drains, the same speaker points out with only too much of sorrowful truth that nothing can be done without good drainage, but while one man dug his share of the drains, another did not. Further on, the same speaker puts the whole question of want of success in a nutshell. Want of steady labour drove the white man out of the Strick-en-Heuvel district; and now, after the lapse of thirty years, their successors only scrape the land which the capital of the white man drained and poldered. And now they are crying out for assistance from the white man. It is the old story of Hercules and the waggoner whose belief in faith was so much stronger than in works. Of what use can it be to spread out a man to the square mile when one is required for every acre, so as to attain complete success in cultivating the stiff plastic clays of Demerara? Barbadoes is prosperous, and the black man increases and multiplies with very nearly two men to the cultivated acre, and there the cultivation of the soil is child's-play as compared with Demerara. The thorough cultivation of a small piece of ground instead of the half cultivation of twice as much, sustained exertion, and a recognition of the sacredness of contract—all these must be attended to before the Creole peasantry can expect success.

6. Speaking of the Creoles of the present generation, Mr. Thomas Daly, Inspector of Villages, in his Annual Report for the year 1881, observes:—

"The Creoles of the present generation are disinclined to hard and continuous manual labour, and this tends to their wandering from estate to estate in search of such light work as *they* feel inclined to perform, and some legislation is required to prevent the wandering life to which many are becoming wholly given up. If men could be compelled by indirect legislation to elect whether they would work as labourers or as husbandmen, it would be a good thing for the country.

"In many cases where there are a hundred shareholders in a village, fifty may wish to cultivate thoroughly the village lands, while the other fifty wish to work a day on the village lands, idle the rest of the week, or else work two or three days on a sugar estate. This uncertainty renders cultivation impossible, since the combined work of all is required to keep up the system of drainage. Legislation should compel every shareholder to do his share of work upon the village lands, sea dams, drains, and roads, or provide means of having it efficiently done, under penalty of a fine or imprisonment. The result of this would be that those who do not care to cultivate their own lands would settle on the sugar estates.

"The people require to be forced by a gentle pressure into the ways of civilized men, no moral or religious teaching alone will suffice; they are fairly obedient to the law when it is known to them, and it is necessary to guide them in almost every action of their lives by rules of law. Legislation is required upon matters which to civilized men have become as second nature.

"To enforce habits of industry the Magistrate should be empowered to call upon any man brought before him to show by what occupation he is obtaining his livelihood. This I think is done in Martinique.

"The Creole population is equal, morally and intellectually, to the labouring population of England in the sixteenth century, and yet they are living under a system of law of the nineteenth century which is unsuited to them. Being without *educated* reason to guide them, they require laws to guide them, but the laws under which they are living are suited to an educated, civilized people, and are not sufficiently stringent and coercive for the great majority of the population.

"Power should be conferred on the Inspector of Villages to enable him to give orders for any work which he may consider necessary for improving the condition of a village, and internal drainage of the house and provision lots. At present the industrious man, who works his bed of land and keeps his draining trench opposite his bed clean of grass, suffers materially because his neighbour who has the next bed will *not cultivate* it, and will *not dig* or *clean* the small drains attached to his lot; the consequence is that the industrious man's ground becomes a swamp and his labour lost. From this cause many a hardworking man gets disheartened and leaves off cultivating his land. The Inspector of Villages should have power, on its being brought to his notice, either to take over the abandoned lot and lease it, or else weed the bed, clean the trench, and bring the owner before the Magistrate to pay the cost of same; in addition to which, he should be made to pay for any damage done to his neighbour's land by negligence, and in the event of his failing to pay such damages to be subject to *imprisonment*. This I am certain would have a very good effect in the villages, and would lead to increased cultivation. It may appear to a person not acquainted with the Colony as being an arbitrary measure, but I believe it will be the only way of leading the people to become more industrious in their habits.

"To the inherent suspicion and jealousy which exist in the mind of the Creole population, and the utter want of unanimity in working the villages, much of their present sad condition is to be attributed; one portion of the proprietors try to influence the Councillors to expend money in having one kind of work performed, whilst the other portion wish it expended in another way, and the consequence is, that between the two no work of any actual benefit is performed."

In contradicting many of the harsh comments that have been passed on Creoles, I have to say that our eyes are not closed to the fact that there are views held by leading planters and merchants, and we know the sarcasm we lay ourselves open to in denying the aspersions. Much of what has been said, it is believed, has been spoken by parties while having in their minds' eye the doings of individuals, and were the facts rightly placed, instead of being made the rule, it would be more the exception. If individual cases be pressed, could not it be urged that we have Creoles who have shown themselves in almost every position equal to the best? I think so. Taking the disadvantages that Creoles generally labour under, by being connected by blood with almost every nation, and the variety of feelings and ideas they are liable to be trained into, it will be seen how difficult a task it is to unite them at present as a people; and without unity, excepting by the most strenuous exertions, national prominence will never be attained. But education, though slow, marches along, and adding the soothing influence of time and age will do much to bring about changes, and those now to the fore may look to their laurels when the interests of the Creoles come to be banded together (a time not too far distant if only fair play is given), and prizes, that Creoles now neglect, will be eagerly sought after and contended for tooth and nail. Though accused of being lazy and indolent, Creoles are not; they certainly lack application, perseverance, and that tact necessary to cope with other nations who in combining nationality have shown up to the front. Happy and proud are we that many bright and promising stars are now shining in our midst as beacons for others to follow, and it is hoped, seeing how the wind blows, that their light will be so shed, as far as in their power, in the way to guide and direct those new mariners who may need and deserve their light. Had we schools established in the Colony, where sound morals, and common-sense education could be taught, our young females putting down with a strong hand frivolous and expensive ideas of living at present followed, we would soon have better homes, by having better wives, which means better mothers and children, and cheerful homes, one of the sad wants of the Colony principally felt among Creoles. Were steps taken to remedy this evil, ambitious ideas would soon be roused, as the force of desires of being of social note would soon fill their minds.

A certain anonymous writer ("Fiat Justitia"), in a letter dated June 30th, 1882, and published in the *Demerara Daily Chronicle*, of July 2nd, 1882, observes:—

"Several years ago, during my residence in the capital of one of the provinces of the Dominion of Canada, an entertainment was advertised to take place, and in promotion thereof large posters were posted about the city with full-life caricatures of the Negro. Well, Sir, next morning not a poster was to be seen in any part of the city, for during the night every one was torn down. A large amount was offered for the detection of the perpetrators, but no discovery was made and nobody earned the reward offered. Why? Because the posters were considered an outrage to public decency, and an insult to the citizens of African descent. But at the last Biennial Exhibition here an official of the Government earned twenty dollars, as a prize, by an exhibit of a series of Negro caricatures! But of all monstrous and mendacious sayings and doings in vilification of the Creoles of British Guyana, which have from time to time come under our observation, none ever exceeded the gratuitous perversion of truth with respect to our Creoles, contained in the following extract from the leading article of Thursday's *Royal Gazette*. Surely, the writer of the article was either wilfully or wofully ignorant of the facts of the case, or he dipped his pen in gall purposely to vilify the Creoles of 1838 at the instigation of some Negro-hater in order to gratify a malignant propensity, too common among a class of persons who assiduously and persistently misrepresent the real state of things for the gratification of a radical and morbid antipathy to the Creoles. The extract is as follows:—'After the abolition of slavery in 1838, the condition of agriculture slowly but surely retrograded. Estate after estate was abandoned, and the exports of the staple—sugar—sank from 75,000 to some 26,000 hhds., while coffee disappeared from the list entirely. From being labourers, the Negroes sank into the position of mere squatters, living, in many instances, in rude huts of the most primitive description, well satisfied to lead a lazy and indolent life, so long as they could procure the means of subsistence, and obtain by a spasmodic effort the necessary coin to invest in Sunday decoration, and an occasional night revel. Land around there was in plenty, and of the richest description, for a small outlay furnished them with provisions.' Against this, I thankfully quote from the last Report of the Inspector of Villages. Mr. Daly says: 'It may not be out of place to call attention to the way in which those estates that are now called villages were first purchased by the Creole population, and I beg to attach a list of those that are being worked under Ordinance 10 of 1873:—Plaisance, $39,000; Buxton, $55,000; Beterverwagting, $22,000; Friendship, $80,000; Victoria, $10,000; Golden Grove, $5,200; Two Friends, $10,000; Ann's Grove, $7,000; Nabaclis, $2,000; Good Intent, $6,400; Baggotville, $22,500; Stanley Town, $10,000; Sisters, $3,000; Den Amstel, $25,000; Fellowship, $2,000; Queenstown, $22,000; Danielstown, $16,000.' These amount, says Mr. Daly, to '$332,900, to which may be added the purchase of about 150 other estates and now settled as villages, the cost of which I consider I am understating, at $500 each, representing $75,000, thus making a total capital of over $400,000 that had been saved by the people, either before or immediately after emancipation, and which was all expended, in a few years, on the purchase of land.' Here we have the evidence of the Inspector of Villages in refutation of the *Royal Gazette's* veracious writer—that those who, the *Royal Gazette* says, 'sank into the position of squatters,' according to Mr. Daly (all thanks to him) expended in the purchase of estates a total capital of over $400,000!"

7. It has been often asserted, and many people in the Colony and elsewhere are under impression, that the Creole

labourers cannot get regular employment upon the sugar estates, and when they do they will not work. How far this statement is correct, the following letters, which were written by a planter and two others interested in the labour question, to a local paper, will show. I give the letters in full:—

"Now, if there were any substantial foundation for such a belief, it would be the duty of the Government to at once discontinue immigration until the demand for labour equalled the supply. But I am sure that if any of those who have heard the statement that Creoles cannot get work, and I allude especially to the Clergy of all denominations, will inquire into the facts, they will soon be convinced, that there is plenty to do at fair wages for all who are willing to work.

"I do not mean to say that if the 100,000 agricultural labourers all rose to-morrow morning determined to do a fair day's work for a fair day's pay, they could all find employment to-morrow, or even in a month's time, because they would have to be paid at the very least $100,000 per week, which at $40 per ton would be equal to the production of a crop of 130,000 tons sugar, rather more than the present extent of land in cultivation is likely to produce.

"But I am certain that if a law were made, insisting on each of the 100,000 labourers making a contract of service with some one or other estate by 15th December, 1881, such contract to commence on 1st January, 1882, and as is the case I believe under the Danish law, that all not 'contracted' by a certain date are taken charge of by Government and allotted to various estates as if they were immigrants, then we should find that the land in cultivation at present would absorb the services of the whole of the labourers for a few weeks, that proprietors and attorneys would make arrangements for putting in more land, and that the crop of the Colony would increase 50 per cent. in 1883 and following years.

"The Government would never have any difficulty in finding proprietors ready to take off their hands any skulking labourers who should pretend they could not get employment, and vagrancy would be abolished.

"If any of the reverend gentlemen who are informed by such vagabonds that they 'cannot get work' would take the trouble to do as one did whom I asked to cross-examine thoroughly the next man who came to him with such a story, they would probably discover, as he did, and told me, when next I met him, 'I cross-examined several people who told me they could not get work, and I invariably found that it was not '*work*' that they could not get, but something which they called '*price*,' and which as far as I could understand meant '*money without work*.'

"In conclusion, I will relate a story which was told me by the late Rev. S. A. Tanner, then rector of St. Patrick's parish, which exemplifies the above. Rev. T. met one of his parishioners, who, as usual, was in arrears with his pew-rent, and asked him why he did not bring a trifle of cash in liquidation. Parishioner at once replied, 'O, parson, I can't get any work on estate.'

"Rev. T.—'What kind of work do you want?'

"Parishioner.—'Any work, cut cane, or weed grass.'

"Rev. T.—'What price do you get for weeding grass like that?' (pointing to churchyard.)

"P.—'O, one gill a rod.'

"Rev. T.—'Very well, come on Monday and I will give you work at that rate.'

"P.—'God bless you, parson, I will come without fail.'

The week passed away, but the man did not put in an appearance. The week after the parson met him again.

"Rev. T.—'Why did you not come to weed the churchyard last Monday as you promised?'

"P.—'Well, parson, you see we Creole not work Monday.'

"Rev. T.—'Then why did you not come Tuesday?'

"P.—'Tuesday me bin go buy fowl and little bit something for make breakfast.'

"Rev. T.—'Make breakfast for what?'

"P.—'O, me cousin bin got wedding on Wednesday.'

"Rev. T.—'Then of course that was why you could not come on Wednesday; well, what were you doing on Thursday?'

"P.—'Thursday, parson, me bin a rest meself, me foot weary with dance whole night.'

"Rev. T.—(triumphantly) 'Well, if you rested the whole day Thursday, whatever prevented you from coming Friday?'

"P.—'O, parson, week no done already, what me go do them two day?'

"Rev. T.—'Well, are you coming next week?'

"P.—'Without fail, parson.'

"'And did he come?' I asked. 'Yes,' said Rev. T., 'he came on the Tuesday morning and begged hard I would give him day pay, forty cents per day, as the grass was very severe. I agreed, and during that day he worked about eight rods, and had to be driven out from under my house at least sixteen times. The next day when I went to see how he was getting on, I found he had gathered Tuesday's grass in a heap, and on it he was sleeping the sleep of the innocent. As it was then ten a.m., and he had evidently not cut any grass for the day, I woke him up and told him to be off.'

"And did not he ask for payment?

"Rev. T.—'Well, not then, but on Saturday he came with the same cry, he had not been able to get work on the estate, and he was hungry: so I gave him sixty cents for his day and a half, but I forgot or I would have stopped some for pew-rent. Of course, I paid him too much.'

"Myself.—'Sixty cents for sixteen cents' work. I should think so.'

"Moral.—Never believe any one, black, brown, yellow, or white, who says, 'I can't get work.'

"Your obdt. Servant,

"A MANAGER.

"Berbice, 10th September, 1881."

"ESTATES LABOURERS' WAGES.

"*To the Editor of the Colonist.*

"SIR,—Your weekly contemporary of last week was misinformed regarding the amount of wages paid to labourers on the estates; and I hope the Poor Law Commissioners will not adopt its suggestion—that the present state of vagrancy in the Colony is caused by the refusal of the Creoles to work for wages equal to six shillings a day. That such a statement is erroneous is known by all who are employed on estates; and your contemporary should always be certain about the truth of any information before giving it to the public. Your contemporary must in its next issue say that 'day' was written instead of 'week' through mistake, and then it will be giving a correct account of affairs. Planters are so well provided with labourers from the Immigration Department that they are not in want of Creole labourers, and will only employ them at a reduced fee. Houston, for instance, employs Creoles only to do the mechanical part of the work, which portion the Coolies cannot perform.

"Yours faithfully,

"SUPPIST.

"New Amsterdam, December 15th, 1881."

"*To the Editor of the Colonist.*

"SIR,—In your weekly contemporary of the 10th instant, the Editor informs his readers as follows:—'In several parts of the Colony, notably on the West Coast, the Creole gangs are refusing to work under a rate of wages equal to six shillings a day.' The Creole population of the West Coast, and I dare-say other places too, will be very thankful to the Editor to recommend them to those estates. I would guarantee to supply more labourers than are required, and do the work to satisfaction, if I knew the labourers would be paid every cent. Some weeks ago, a certain planter on the West Coast gave a gang of shovelmen some work to do. He himself superintended the work from Tuesday to Thursday. On Friday, he objected to the work, and said it was not what he told them to do. He drove them out of the field, would not suffer them to touch the work again, and did not pay them a cent on Saturday—lazy people, honest planter! But to return to the Editor of your weekly contemporary. Why should these people refuse to work for such fair wages? He would tell us, 'Because they are lazy.' Now this is a statement which has obtained authority without reason, and has been taken without inquiry. I do not at all mean to defend the Creoles, but all this talk about fair wages is a mere cant. That the planters have exaggerated their side of the story, and the Editor still more, I have no doubt. Some of his remarks on the black population of the Colony are only the outcome of a crass ignorance bordered with prejudice. His sixteen years' experience in this Colony as Editor has only left him the same dreaming schoolboy writ larger and more obese, and a greater dunce, writing a heap of rubbish and extravagant nonsense.

"I am, Sir,
"Your obedient servant,
"A CREOLE.

"La Retraite, West Bank, Demerara,
19th December, 1881."

The Honourable W. Russell, writing in the *Daily Chronicle* of July 12, 1882, observes:—

"I have in my time listened to excellent discourses from able men in which sections of mankind have had their faults set before them in no measured terms; but because the lecturer thus exposed to broad daylight the prevailing failings of many of his listeners, he could not be charged with being antagonistic to those whose vices he attempted to paint in plain and distinct colours; the antagonism was against the faults of which they were guilty; and if I have in my utterances in public pointed out what I consider the besetting sins of the peasantry of this Colony, it is to these sins that I am antagonistic and not to the people. I yield to no one in my wish to see the natives of this Colony assume that position which is their birthright, and it is perhaps because of my intimate knowledge of the black man, now extending over a generation, and my casting memory back to what I thought of him when I first made his acquaintance, and to think what the majority of them have fallen to—mind, I don't say all; I have in my mind's eye black men who would be a credit to any community, but unfortunately their numbers are few and far between—I have sad forebodings of the future. When I first made the acquaintance of the black man, he had not long been set free from a mild bondage which might be called military discipline, because the peculiar relation existing between the proprietor of the soil and his bondman partook of military laws, and the punishments for breaches of these laws were in accordance with the military code. Under this peculiar system the bondman had nothing to think for, all his wants were liberally supplied, and in sickness and health himself and his family were cared for and nurtured to the highest degree. His day's toil then was measured by what an ordinary labourer can now perform in seven hours, so that it was just such as to keep the labourer in first-rate physique and health. In his spare time he worked his provision plot, raised poultry and stock to a considerable extent, the proceeds of which, unfortunately, were hidden, buried in the soil. No Hand-in-Hand nor savings banks in those days for the labourer of fifty years ago to place his savings at interest. Notwithstanding, when the decree went forth freeing the bondmen, the industrious and provident had a large fund to draw upon, and to the amazement of those in power, the freedmen were in a position to dig from out of the various caches sums of money which enabled many to buy out the holdings of their masters, and, to their credit be it told, many, when they found old Massa driven to the wall, brought their all and threw it at his feet, and enabled him to stave off the time for a short season, when both master and man had to succumb to the inevitable. A country and industries, which could only be maintained by steady labour, soon succumbed to the change. The freedmen could not believe that the same exertion was necessary to maintain the cotton piece under freedom as was the case under the old regimen; they were then, as now, under the impression that the man who owned a plantation *must* be wealthy, and that no demands for wages on their part could be unreasonable; hence they betook themselves to idleness and want of thrift. Those who retained self-respect and who had invested their savings in the soil, soon found out that one man cannot work a plantation, and that it was just as necessary to maintain dams, canals, and kokers, as in old Massa's time. The cotton trees had to be pruned and kept clear of weeds, and when the time came for the cotton bombs to break out into fleecy white cotton, it was necessary to have willing hands to gather in the same. None were to be had, the high wages paid by the sugar planters withdrew all the able-bodied labourers from the cotton districts, and the new owners found themselves in a worse position than the old. Without steady labour cotton had to slide, and the remains of the half-silted-up canals, which the sea is fast regaining possession of, and the mangrove and courida swamp, inform the traveller that nature has again asserted her sway, and in another decade the seaside view of Corentyne, for instance, will be similar to what the hardy pioneers found it a century ago. This was the fate of those who attempted to continue the industry to which they had been brought up. Others, knowing that combination was power, clubbed and threw up money with a view of purchasing estates in community, and soon Plaisance, Beterverwagting, Buxton, Friendship, &c., were transferred from the old proprietors to the new. Some $300,000 was paid over in hard Mexican dollars, wheeled to the Registracy of Court in barrow loads. Soon the cotton fields gave way to tidy, well-built cottages and thriving provision beds, the system of drainage having been handed over in excellent condition; for many years that bugbear of the small settler gave no trouble, and the provision farms paid handsomely. By degrees the want of unanimity, and the loss by death of many of the old hands, led to want of attention to drainage, dams, roads, &c., the fell plantain disease made its appearance, and from that day the decline has been rapid and steady. The Government stepped in, and laws were passed which were never worked. An expensive establishment with a Village Inspector hastened the downfall; for on the villagers being allowed to get their hand into the Colony chest, it gave them a taste for borrowing, and now the cry from all the villagers under the Central Board is, 'The Governor must help us.' The official Reports of the Inspector of Villages state that 'the old industrious men who do work their farms are disheartened because of the young, idle lads stealing the provisions.' . . . .

"Now what does this mean? What is the whole position of agriculture and commerce, but the survival of the fittest? And so it must be with the labourer in this Colony. The black man had his innings. He, in the space of eight years, reduced the production of the Colony to 26,000 hhds. and general bankruptcy. An alien race, from having 'fewer personal wants,' has been able to compete with the outside world, and the position of Demerara has been elevated to its present proud position. Are we to give all this up, and for a short time pay the Creole labourer rates of wages to enable him to enjoy those extra wants, until again the cost of production exceeds the proceeds? Even philanthropy would say no to this. It seems pretty conclusive that the labourers are still short of the wants of those calling for their service, otherwise we should see far greater strides made in extending cultivation and an addition made to the few estates now bidding for labourers. With a boundless extent of fertile land, willing hands are the only want preventing extension to a fabulous area. But, happily for the Creole labourer, he is in no way tied to the sugar industry, he has the widest scope for the development of his genius and industry, if he has such. With the exception of sugar there is no tropical product which requires a large capital for plant and work. A family may cultivate and prepare, according to their power, any one of the various products which meet a ready sale for cash. Therefore there is no room for complaint against the Coolie or Chinaman, who is content with his increment arising in shape of wages from sugar. . . . . The Creole, whether black or white, has no sounder friend than I am. I tell them plump and fairly their besetting sins, and that they cannot all be peace officers and clerks, because they can stick a pen behind their ear; banish every white man out of the Colony and the circulation of money which their presence insures, and the field for educated youths could be in no way enlarged, but the reverse. I am quite aware this is most distasteful to the generation of educated Creoles, but I have the satisfaction of knowing that not a few of the good old sort endorse my sentiments, and say, 'True for you, Massa,' and even 'Justice' has to own up that it is better to give out 'devilish convictions' in preference to acting the hypocrite. I say to them, Put aside that pride which doth so fatally beset you, copy from the aliens in your midst, who have risen to fortune by sheer hard, manual labour; there is room for ten times the present population of Demerara to find ample elbow room and to spare, and instead of the present miserable exports of sugar, let us add the various articles as exports which we now import. Then British Guyana might well lay claim to being a 'magnificent province.'"

8. Whatever may be the opinions of the people in the Colony or abroad, with respect to the Creole labourers and their employers the planters, it is idle, and perhaps worse than idle, for any one in dealing with this question to indulge in diatribes on the conduct of the Creole labourers after emancipation. No doubt, if the labourers had acted differently, there would have been no necessity for the planters to resort to immigration. But it is just as likely that if the planters as a body had acted more wisely, the labourers might have been got to behave in a manner that would have left little or no necessity for immigration. But what is the use of such discussions? A certain state of things existed. For that state of things both sides were responsible and blameable. In what shares or proportions the blame is to be divided, does not signify a straw in the discussion of the present question. It is sufficient that that state of things necessitated at the time a resort to immigration, in order to save the planters, and through them to save the country. But all is changed now. The planters have been saved and are flourishing, with as much labour at their command as they can well make available. If the Creole labourers are now willing to return to steady work on the estates, and can get employment there, all the better for them and for the country at large. But the planters themselves tell us that the tables have been turned—that, whereas at the commencement of immigration their main dependence had to be placed upon the Creoles, while the immigrants supplemented the supply, now the main dependence is on the immigrants, and the Creoles are employed as supernumeraries. With such a state of things, and with sugar bringing prices that enable

estates to clear $50,000, $70,000, $90,000, and even $100,000 a year, I ask, is it not time that the planters should be made to pay for the supplies of labour which they may in future introduce? At the same time, seeing things in the Colony are not according to the wishes or expectations of my labouring Creole friends (among whom and the Indian Coolies I have laboured for the last twenty-one years), I would affectionately and seriously ask them, *Is it not better to work for small wages than to sit down and do nothing?* I remember hearing the late Rev. George McFarlane say to me on one occasion when I went to preach for him in Salem Chapel, at the Lodge Village: "A good old friend of mine used often to tell me, 'My son, it is better for you to work for little than sit down and do nothing; and even if you do not get paid directly for your labour, 'tis better for some one to be indebted to you than that nobody should owe you.'" This little piece of advice, he said, he had ever remembered and followed, and had never had any reason to regret so doing. He thought of it when amidst the greatest discouragements, and with only five bits—1s. 8d.—a week pay for a long time, he went on working, looking for better days, and he was not disappointed. Every right-minded man will admit, that under the present circumstances of the Colony it would be far preferable to work, and to work systematically and regularly, at a reduced rate of wages than not to work at all. There can be no advantage gained by refusing to work for reduced wages; it will only occasion a loss of time and exposure to many temptations, "*for Satan finds some mischief still for idle hands to do.*" If a person not disposed to work sit idle, or sleep upon the little he possesses, it will soon dwindle away to nothing, and he shall awake from his idle slumber in folly. When a man—an employer—tells another—the labourer,—"I *will* not pay," it is right for him to say, "Then I will not work for you;" but when he says, "I am *not able* to pay the price you demand for the work to be done," it is wisdom to consent to take what he can fairly afford to give, rather than cease to labour; and if this offer on the part of the employer is refused, then of course he is compelled to find others who will do the work for that price which he can afford to give. Two men, it appears, were on one occasion confined in prison to be starved for a certain number of days, for some crime they had committed: when the time of their discharge from further imprisonment was near at hand, the officer, by orders, gave each of these two prisoners the half of a loaf: *one thankfully and contentedly ate his share*, but the other *contemptuously threw his aside*. A few days after, the prison cell was opened, when the man who had contentedly eaten his half loaf was found alive; but the other, who contemptuously threw his aside, was lying dead, with the rejected half loaf near his head; and hence the origin of the proverb, "Half a loaf is better than no bread." This well deserves the careful consideration of the Creole labouring population of British Guyana.

9. The Rev. C. D. Dance, an Episcopal Church of England Missionary, writing to the *Royal Gazette*, a local journal (in 1875), on the habits of the people conducive to pauperism, observes:—

"The large portion of the Creole peasantry, comprising the descendants of the former slaves, have a pride peculiarly their own: it is indeed not pride, but vanity: it does not prevent them from being always ready to throw up their self-dependence and to take alms whenever and however offered. It it be any satisfaction to them to know it, the recent Commission of Inquiry into Friendly Societies in England reported an increasing disinclination among the working classes to contribute to them, because there is an impression that they only serve to save the poor rate. 'The rich folk,' they say, 'must keep us when we can't keep ourselves.' 'This is the tone,' says the *Guardian* of June 30, 'which the actual administration of the Poor Law has mainly helped to create.' These of our land assert their right in themselves, or derived from their parents, to claim support from the public funds, on the grounds that they are 'the Queen's people'—brought here from Africa against their wills to expend their youth and strength in enriching Great Britain by labouring as slaves in the cane-fields. They, of course, repudiate the idea that man is born to labour.

"With this reason to claim relief, must be associated other features which contribute to their pauperism. The most superficial is their want of self-respect. Then there is the low degree of natural affection existing among them. Children are pampered and brutalized according to the ever-changing impulse of the parent. In most cases, the child's first opening impressions of filial duty are afforded him by his parents sending him at a very early age to work—they eating and dressing at his expense, while the poor little fellow eats what he can get, and walks in a dirty torn shirt, whose rents, like streamers, flutter to the wind. As the child grows up he asserts his right to expend his earnings, and in the course of the controversy abandons his home. Henceforth it is seldom, even in their most abject distress from illness or age, that the parents receive a cent from their child, who has probably taken a concubine and produces fruit similar to himself, and who, with their mother, are frequently thrown upon the Poor's Fund—their father repudiating their claims to be supported by him, and asserting his paternity only when his children have arrived at an age to support the hereditary black mail which he exacts.

"An applicant for pauper's relief is seldom communicative on the subjects of family and property. It is by dint of cross-questionings that one sometimes arrives at the truth.

"At paupers' funerals one is frequently surprised at the display of silk frocks and bonnets and broadcloth coats of the most costly kinds, worn by cousins, nieces, nephews, and even sons and daughters, who have come to the burying, and are quite prepared to claim the bit of land that the pauper had disowned for the purpose of not transferring it to the Poor Law Board, and also to appropriate the dirtiest rag and even the old pot and calabashes of the deceased."

10. Though the Creole people—I mean the labouring population—may have defects, shortcomings, and other infirmities, like every other nation under the sun, they are yet, I am happy to say, a most polite, civil, and well-behaved people; and, indeed, they put to shame in this respect many who come from England and Scotland. Rude, uncouth, ill-behaved men, who call themselves gentlemen, may learn lessons from the labouring class. They are kind to strangers and others who are well disposed, but of course they will be rude and unkind to those who do not deserve their consideration and friendship. Ministers labouring among them have always found them a very obedient, loving people. Some of the members

of the different Christian Churches among them have been known to be pious and exemplary Christians indeed. A better class of Christians we need not go to Africa to find. That they are a grateful and loyal people the following interesting incident will show:—

His Excellency, Governor (now Sir) C. H. Kortright, K.C.M.G., received the following villagers of Victoria Village, on Friday the 12th July, 1878, at his residence, Belfield Villa, on the East Sea Coast, viz.:—Messrs. John Sumner, farmer; Cambridge Sumner, schoolmaster; Charles Sumner, tailor; Henry Sumner, farmer; Thomas Collins, farmer; Michael Goring, carpenter; Samuel Sam, carpenter; Newton Pool, cooper; Samuel Dodson, carpenter; John Horatio Reynolds, newspaper reporter; and Thomas Adams, carpenter. On being ushered into His Excellency's drawing-room by his Private Secretary, the following address was read to His Excellency:—"We, the inhabitants of Victoria Village, East Coast, Demerara, do most humbly beg to pay our respects to Your Excellency and family on the occasion of this your first sojourn amongst us; we all along felt sorry for not being amongst those who first welcomed your Excellency to our shores, but we feel proud of the occasion which has placed it in our reach to show our great esteem for your Excellency and family. We, in conclusion, do wish your Excellency quick relief from the effects of your late indisposition, and may you and yours be long spared to remain amongst us in your capacity as head of the Colony."

His Excellency addressed the villagers thus:—"Gentlemen, I thank you for the address you have presented to me, and for the good wishes you express with regard to my health. I am happy to say that I have already benefited by the pure sea air of the East Coast, and I hope that I may be able often to visit this part of the Colony during my residence in British Guyana. I must congratulate you on the cleanly and thriving condition of the villages of this coast, which is creditable to those with whom the management of the village rests. The state of the roads is so good, and the healthiness of the locality so patent, that I would not mind residing continuously on the East Coast." The villagers thanked His Excellency for the speech, at the conclusion of which they were furnished with refreshments, and entertained by Mr. Forbes.

11. Said a Missionary to me, on one occasion, whilst travelling together across the Atlantic, "I feel very loth to return to England from the West Indies. Whilst on my station, in charge of a Church, I have received every manner of kindness from the people, and especially the members of the Church. They were civil and courteous. Every morning they would come to the Mission House and salute me with 'Good morning, my Minister,' or 'Good morning, my Massa,' &c. Now I am going to England, but I shall not have such Good mornings and How d'yes given to me by the people."

Another Missionary, now labouring in the Colony, writing of the Creoles, says, "I am not a Creole of this Colony, but I have to confess that wherever I have moved about in it, I have, as an individual, received respectful treatment from the black people of the country; and perhaps I may regard that respectable treatment as being partly the response to my own endeavour to maintain a respectful bearing towards all. . . . . If all the lower orders of the people have become unrespectful and intolerably vulgar, there are others to blame besides the *highly polished* schoolmasters. I am the friend of all classes in this country; I am the friend of the employers of labour; and I am the friend of the labourer. I feel deeply interested in all the interests of the community; and I cannot but try to advance, as far as in my humble power lies, the interests of all. Some of the gentlemen who find fault with the disorderliness of our rural boys 'just let loose from school,' might plead guilty to the charge that when they themselves were schoolboys they were equally as mischievous, as boisterous, as pugnacious, as these rural ragamuffins. It is to be presumed that Mr. Sproston and Mr. Mulligan, or some of their friends, have, in their travels up and down the country, encountered some ruffian-like exhibitions of rudeness on the part of some of the youth of the community. Similar exhibitions may be encountered in England, and all the civilized world over; and cannot justify such sweeping denunciations of the local system of education. We have to recollect, too, that there is something mutual in manners. Respectful and dignified manners on the part of gentlemen occupying the superior stratum of society generally call forth at least some respectable recognition or response on the part of the members of the inferior strata; while harshness in the one commonly creates or educes harshness in the other. I have heard of a gentleman in this country, who undertook one day to castigate, with his stick, a Creole overseer in a sugar manufactory. The overseer turned round, collared the gentleman, and began making him feel the weight of his natural weapons. The gentleman cried for help, and declared that the overseer had become insane! Harshness educes harshness. Not long ago, I heard a black lad say, 'Everybody treats Baron Sickymore (*sic prot.*) with respect because *he* treats the poorest fellow with respect.' A decent man of colour said to me some time ago, 'I met Mr. So-and-So several times, and on each occasion I gave him as gracious a salutation as I could execute. He never returned it. I have ceased to salute; and he may now consider me an impudent fellow.'"

The Creole people are, indeed, a good hearty set of people, especially when they are a truly converted people, and connected with Christian Churches as members. A large number of them are poor, and yet they do their utmost to support their Ministers, and the cause of God in general, and have great love and respect for their Ministers and others who are in a superior position. At all events I have found them so to be. They must not be driven, but drawn by gentle means, and then my reader will find I am correct in my statement and opinion of them.

An "Eye-witness," writing in the *Colonist* of May 27, 1882, says:—

"I have often seen much display of loyalty, friendship, and attachment, but none has ever equalled the scene I had the pleasure of witnessing at Beterverwagting on Thursday, 25th inst. Amongst the passengers who left the city that day with the 12.50 train were the newly married couple, the Rev. W. E. Downer, an ex-Wesleyan Minister, and now Pastor of the Beterverwagting Congregational Church, and his bride. When they landed at the station, I was agreeably surprised to see the large number of persons who assembled to welcome them. The bride was actually bathed with a shower of roses, jasmines, and other fragrant flowers. The crowd was so great that a carriage which was in waiting to convey the party to their home could not move onwards for some time. Eventually, it was led by some one who took hold of the horse's head, whilst hundreds followed firing guns, and rending the air with their loud hurrahs, and the children, headed by the teacher, sang many beautiful and appropriate hymns. The scene was really very attractive, and will be long remembered by those who witnessed it. But it is the more pleasing when one reflects on the motive which moved the sympathy of these villagers. It was nothing more than an outburst of feeling for their Pastor, to show how they appreciated his labours amongst them. Moreover, it goes far to prove that if the Ministers of religion would cease clamouring about State-pay, and turn their attention zealously, but in a quiet and unostentatious manner, to reach the hearts of the people, they will soon find that the love which can produce such feelings will also loose the purse-strings to supply their bodily wants."

The following document also speaks for itself. It was a spontaneous tribute of gratitude, sympathy, and respect, and reflects honour on both sides,—on those whose kindness of heart prompted the movement, and on him whose sterling qualities as a Christian Pastor claimed the admiration and gratitude of those under his ministration :—

"Georgetown, Demerara, October 5th, 1881.

"Dear Pastor,—On behalf of the members and congregation of Smith Church we beg you to accept the accompanying purse and its contents of $85, as a token of esteem, and as a manifestation of sympathy on account of your recent bereavement.

"We hope you will accept the gift, and use it in any manner most in accord with your wishes, and most conducive to your comfort and welfare.

"We are, dear Pastor, yours truly in Christ,—Adam Chewitt, John Harper, James Harris, John Bagnell, Charles Wilson, Joseph L. A. Wills, George A. Smith, James Stoby.

"To the Rev. John Currie."

12. I now conclude this chapter with the following counsels

to the young men and women, whether they belong to British Guyana or to Europe:—

Never be cast down by trifles. If a spider breaks his web twenty times, twenty times will he mend it again. Make up your minds to do a thing, and you will do it. Fear not if trouble comes upon you: keep up your spirits though the day be a dark one—

"Troubles never last for ever,
The darkest day will pass away."

If the sun is going down, look up to the stars; if the earth is dark, keep your eyes on heaven. With God's presence and God's promise a man or child may be cheerful—

"Never despair when fog's in the air,
A sunshiny morning will come withont warning!"

Mind what you run after! Never be content with a bubble that will burst, or a firewood that will end in smoke and darkness; but that which you can keep and is worth keeping—

"Something sterling that will stay
When gold and silver fly away!"

Fight hard against a hasty temper. Anger will come, but resist it strongly. A spark may set a house on fire. A fit of passion may give you cause to mourn all the days of your life. Never revenge an injury—

"He that revengeth knows no rest;
The meek possess a peaceful breast."

If you have an enemy, act kindly to him, and make him your friend. You may not win him over at once, but try again. Let one kindness be followed by another, till you have compassed your end. By little and by little great things are completed—

"Water falling day by day
Wears the hardest rock away."

And so repeated kindness will soften a heart of stone.

Whatever you do, do it willingly. A boy that is whipped

at school never learns his lesson well. A man that is compelled to work cares not how badly it is performed. He that pulls his coat off cheerfully, strips up his clothes in earnest, and sings while he works, is the man for me—

> "A cheerful spirit gets on quick;
> A grumbler in the mud will stick."

Evil thoughts are worse enemies than lions and tigers; for we can get out of the way of wild beasts, but bad thoughts win their way everywhere. Keep your heads and hearts full of good thoughts, that bad thoughts may not find room—

> "Be on your guard, and strive and pray,
> To drive all evil thoughts away."

CHAPTER X.

THE WORK, PERSONAL APPEARANCE, AND DRESS OF THE IMMIGRANTS.

1. THE Portuguese and Chinese immigrants, like all other European nations, soon get accustomed to the climate of the Colony, and indeed turn their attention to work—whether hard or light—almost immediately after their arrival in it; but it is not so with the Indian immigrants. The employers or planters find that the Indian labourers on their arrival in the Colony are an indolent race of people, and are physically unable and unfit to bear their burden without some weeks' or months' preparation in the way of keeping them at light work, so that they may gradually get accustomed to do the work they have come to do. This physical disability and unfitness for work, and the difficulty on their part to get accustomed to the climate of the Colony, and the frequent attacks of Colony fever they get after their arrival, are, I believe, principally owing to their light food, which is simply rice, and currie made of dholl, and other vegetables, &c., which cannot give as much strength as animal food would, and to their dissolute and immoral habits, for it must be remembered that the greater number of Coolies imported from India to work as agricultural labourers on the sugar estates are a low and filthy lot in their habits and of an immoral character generally. Of several of them it may be said that they are more fitted to be the associates of wild animals than of humanized—if not even civilized—beings. For the first three or four months after their introduction they are, as I just stated, allowed to do little light work about the buildings and the cane-field, so that they may earn what is considered a fair week's wages at the rate of 24 cents per day, with which to support themselves. During this preparation in the way of keeping them at light work, they receive a good

meal twice a day, and get biscuits and tea in the morning. Were a man, therefore, at first only to earn as little as 24 cents a week, he would not starve in consequence. The food given to the newly arrived Coolies is generally cooked beforehand; and on some estates rations or bhatta are served out. In order to pay for this food fifty-six cents or two shillings and fourpence are deducted from each immigrant's weekly wages or earnings; but too often the estate is the loser, and the indentured immigrant the gainer, for if an immigrant, male or female, does not earn enough to pay for the food supplied, the amount short is not carried on against him or her into the next week's account, but foregone at once. When it is remembered that the Indian Coolies take a matter of from six to ten weeks, and sometimes more, of such preparation, and that the same amount of work performed by them during the whole of that time could be performed by other labourers in half the time and for two-thirds the amount, it at once shows a loss in cost of $72 to $120 on each twenty-five immigrants during the term of their acclimatization and preparation for full hard work to be done on the plantation, which after a while becomes well suited to their capacity. At the expiration of five years' term of service—save and except desertion, shirking from work, imprisonment in Georgetown and district jails, which number of days' work they must make good—each Coolie is entitled to receive a certificate of exemption from further labour on the estate to which he was bound. He is at liberty to go anywhere he pleases after that, but he generally remains and works as a free labourer on the same estate for a long time. While subject to the contract or indenture, he is bound by law to work, unless prevented through illness.

2. When the Coolies have become thoroughly acclimatized, it is no uncommon thing to see them, Portuguese,* Chinese, and

* In the reports for the year 1880 of Mr. C. B. King, Acting Immigration Agent General, we are told that the Madeirans or Portuguese, although a proportion of those sent may have been agricultural labourers in their own island, do not, as a rule, work upon the estates, so that in their case the primary object of immigration is not attained. . . . As immigration is of so much importance to

black Creoles, working together side by side on the sugar estate—doing all kinds of work, such as digging trenches, parapetting, empoldering land, making new sea dams, back dams, making kokers, sluices, locks, aqueducts, planting canes, cutting canes, preparing the field, &c. There is always a great deal of work to be done on a Demerara sugar estate. In real hard work the black Creoles surpass the Indian and Chinese Coolies.

3. In the production of sugar, the land intended for cultivation must be cleared of all bush and well drained; straight rows of cane tops are then planted closely, six feet apart. When these tops spring and have grown to the height of about two feet, the space of land between the rows (three feet between the rows, and two feet between the holes in the rows, is about the minimum) is turned up by an implement called the shovel or fork. This is called shovel ploughing, if done by the shovel; if by the fork, forking. When the plants are from four to five months old, the shovel or fork is again used to the other space which was left at the time of first ploughing. Canes planted after this mode require fifteen months before they are fit for cutting: during this interval, as occasion needs, they are cleared and kept free of grass and weeds; this is called weeding. As the canes increase in growth, the dry blades are removed. This tends to hasten growth, as it occasions a free circulation of air, and this process is called trashing. When the canes are cut, the stumps or stoles which remain in the earth spring, and the canes are said to be ratoons. At twelve or thirteen months at most ratoons may be cut; but they must be cut as near the ground as possible, because the richest juice is found in the lower joints, and after cutting them it is considered well to cut the stumps down a few inches below the surface of the ground

the Colony, and also advantageous to the immigrants themselves, . . . it is satisfactory to be able to state that the immigrants are well cared for and protected, that the feeling evinced towards them by their employers is, as a rule, one of kindness and consideration, and that every opportunity and facility is afforded them, in case of any grievance, for an appeal to either the Magistrates or the Immigration Department.

and cover them up with mould. After being cut, the canes are conveyed to the building in punts, for the purpose of extracting the juice, which is done by passing them through the steam mill, which is provided with three rollers. The sugar cane after the juice has been expressed is called megass, and after being dried in the logie the megass is used for fuel in the manufacture of sugar.

4. The juice, after being extracted, runs by means of gutters into wooden boxes, where it is tempered with quicklime. On many estates clarifiers are used, and steam being employed hastens its preparation for the pans. By means of other gutters the juice is conveyed into the iron pans, and then subjected to the action of fire. After a while it becomes of a thick consistency, popularly known as a sugar. After being allowed slightly to cool, it passes into large wooden trays called "coolers," and after being stirred it becomes hard, and when cold is put into hogsheads, in which, after remaining for eleven days, it is ready for shipment to the European markets. Rum is made from the refuse left in the liquor boxes, to which are added the skimmings from the juice while undergoing the process of boiling; to this is added a certain portion of molasses, which runs from the sugar after being put into hogsheads.

The Honourable Wm. Russell, M.C.P., speaking of the Demerara rum manufactured in the Colony, says, "It is not nearly so prejudicial to health as that dreadful compound called brandy, made from beet refuse," and "this Colony makes a good and wholesome spirit, so as to keep in check the evils which would accrue were beet spirit to gain the ascendency." Whether there is any truth in this statement of the honourable gentleman I will leave my reader to judge for himself. Large quantities of Demerara rum are certainly consumed by the labouring population and others, and the effects or results of rum-drinking contained in the following lines are what we behold in British Guyana and elsewhere:—

ODE TO RUM.

"Let thy devotees extol thee, and thy wondrous virtues sum,
But the worst of names I'll call thee, O thou hydra-monster Rum!
Pimple maker, visage bloater, health corrupter, idler's mate,
Mischief breeder, vice promoter, credit spoiler, devil's bait.

"Almshouse builder, pauper maker, trust betrayer, sorrow's source,
Pocket emptier, Sabbath breaker, conscience stifler, guilt's resource.
Nerve enfeebler, system shatterer, thirst increaser, vagrant thief,
Cough producer, treacherous flatterer, mud bedauber, mock relief.

"Business hinderer, spleen instiller, woe begetter, friendship's bane,
Anger heater, Bridewell filler, debt involver, toper's chain;
Memory drowner, honour wrecker, judgment warper, blueface quack,
Feud beginner, rag bedecker, strife enkindler, fortune's wreck.

"Summer's cooler, winter's warmer, blood polluter, specious snare,
Mob collector, man transformer, bond undoer, gambler's fare;
Speech bewrangler, headache bringer, vitals burner, deadly fire,
Riot mover, firebrand flinger, discord kindler, misery's sire.

"Sinews robber, worth depriver, strength subduer, hideous foe,
Reason thwarter, fraud contriver, money waster, nation's woe;
Vile seducer, joy dispeller, peace disturber, blackguard guest,
Sloth implanter, liver sweller, brain distractor, baleful pest.

"Utterance boggler, stench emitter, strong man sprawler, fatal drop,
Tumult raiser, venom spitter, wrath inspirer, coward's prop;
Pain inflicter, eyes inflamer, heart corrupter, folly's nurse,
Secret babbler, body maimer, thrift defeater, loathsome curse.

"Wit destroyer, joy impairer, scandal dealer, foul-mouthed scourge,
Senses blunter, youth ensnarer, crime inventor, ruin's verge;
Virtue blaster, base deceiver, spite displayer, sob's delight,
Noise exciter, stomach heaver, falsehood spreader, scorpions' bite.

"Quarrel plotter, rage discharger, giant conqueror, wasteful sway;
Chin carbuncler, tongue enlarger, malice venter, death's broadway;
Tempest scatterer, window smasher, death's forerunner, hell's dire brink,
Ravenous murderer, windpipe slasher, drunkard's lodging, meat, and drink."

And the same honourable gentleman in the same letter, dated "Georgetown, Sept. 26, 1875," and published in the *Royal Gazette*, stated, "I have long felt it to be an anomaly to see

State-paid clergymen drawing their stipends from funds raised from such a questionable source as the licences on dram-drinking, and it is with a view of removing this blot that at the last Combined Court Meeting I went in favour of dis-endowment." The servants of God, or Ministers of the Gospel, still continue to draw their salaries from this abominable source. When will a Christian Government and a Christian people and Christian Ministers wake up to the fact that it is an unholy transaction for State-paid Clergy and other Churches in the Colony to derive aid and support from such a questionable source? The revenue of the Colonial Government is increased at the expense of the sobriety of the people. If the opium traffic has called forth the indignation of the British public, the time will come when the evil of intemperance will be as great a national sin and curse as in England.

5. The process of sugar-making in this country is very rapid, if the appliances be good. An acre of canes is supposed to yield over a ton and a half of sugar, but an acre of cane ground will not give a crop more than once in twelve months. Two crops in three years is the usual average. More than 100,600 hogsheads of sugar are made in the Colony every year; and about 14,000 to 15,000 casks of molasses and 30,000 puncheons of rum are exported every year from British Guyana.

6. No doubt, for the first four or five months after their introduction, the Coolies experience rather a hard time of it on the sugar estate, and even under such circumstances some of them try to put by something out of their little earnings weekly, and before the expiration of their indentures the men become owners of several head of cattle, and their wives of goats, sheep, &c. But how do they manage to get so much money all at once with which to buy cattle? Perhaps some twenty or thirty of them will form a kind of club, under the direction or leadership of their driver, or some other responsible person on the estate. Each of the twenty or thirty men will contribute his one dollar, or two dollars, as the case may be. Ramswamy will get his twenty or forty dollars this week, Coospooswamy will get his share next week, Kandaswamy his

share the week after, and so on to the end, till every man has had his turn and full share of his contribution. The man who has received his share this week must go on contributing till he has paid up the full amount of ready cash he has received, with a slight bonus to the conductor of the club for his trouble and responsibility. With this money, and other cash savings put by, the cattle, &c., are bought. Some of the old Coolies, long resident on the estate, know too well the art of imposing on the newly arrived ones, in spite of all remonstrances and watching on the part of the overseers and managers of estates. They generally provide themselves with bags of rice, and other things necessary for the sustenance of life, and sell them at famine prices, and also lend money at heavy interest to the new Coolies, and thus make haste to become rich, and indeed in a very short time they become possessors of shops, farms, &c., and no longer desire to remain on the estate to work. Hylandum, Muniswamy Paul, Sivapadam, Pokhoye, Sukhlall, up the Demerara river, and others, are great speculators, and own valuable properties in town and country districts. They know how to make and save money, but do not spend it in the Colony. On one occasion, many years ago, the manager of a sugar estate in Berbice did not receive the money to pay the people their wages on Saturday night, whereupon several of the immigrants offered to supply the amount of money required by the manager. One Chinese Coolie brought $200, another $92.80, another $20, and another Indian Coolie $90, making in all $402.80. By this help afforded by these Coolies the people were all paid, and there was great joy on the estate. This amount of money, contributed by these immigrants in this instance of need and emergency, was not stolen, nor was it dug up, nor found on the highway, but accumulated by hard labour and patient industry. I have no hesitation in asserting that the Coolies of this Colony are quite as well off as a large portion of the labouring classes of England; certainly they are more comfortably situated and more prosperous than the peasantry of Ireland. In addition to all these comforts, they have the amplest means of redress, should they consider themselves aggrieved; and their national customs and peculiar prejudices are not in the least interfered with. Indeed, they are, perhaps, allowed too much freedom in these matters.

7. Our labouring population are in their appearance and costume as varied as they are in their speech. The Blacks and Portuguese turn out in their shirt and trousers, sometimes with and sometimes without any boots or shoes on, and the females in their petticoats and frocks, with their heads tied round with a handkerchief, and hence called "tie heads." To the black Creole labourers boots or shoes are a perfect nuisance during week days. The Coolies sometimes wear boots much larger than their feet actually require. As a rule they never wear boots or shoes at all. Even one of the Government officers connected with the Immigration Department has very strong objections to wearing shoes or boots at all, though he is a Christian. On Sundays and holidays, however, the males wear the tight-fitting coat, waistcoat, and trousers, and the abominable hat and cravat, and the females in like manner dress themselves in their very best, same as any European lady across the ocean or in the Colony, and study all the fashions in the world. Imitation jewels are in abundant use among both the male and female Creoles, and they think, I suppose, that they serve the same purpose as the real gold and silver ones. And there is also a peculiar walk called the Sunday walk, which is very different from the ordinary week day one. It is strikingly one of their peculiarities which arrests the attention of the stranger. A Barbadian can be very easily distinguished from a native Creole, for his speech and manners betray him. The ubiquitous Chinese never depart in the least from their national dress, which, indeed, it is impossible to improve for a tropical climate, whether as regards comfort or appearance. The women, among them, wear chignons and not hats, and the men wear hats with their pigtails coiled up under them.

During the trial of two Aboriginal Indians in one of the Essequibo Criminal Sessions in 1882, the Ackawois interpreter, who for the occasion had dressed himself in European garments, began to get uncomfortable under the unusual trammels, and while the case was going on, he stopped the interpretation to pull off his boots. This made him feel so comfortable that he wanted to be still more so, and was commencing to take off the rest of his clothes when he was stopped by the police. An Indian witness in the same case procured three suits of clothes for the occasion and appeared in Court in all three, determined to make a decent appearance. A more ludicrous sight occurred during the preliminary investigation of the same case in the Magistrate's Court. All the witnesses succeeded in getting some wearing apparel, save one, who could procure nothing except a chimney-pot hat and an umbrella. He, however, was equal to the occasion. He walked into Court with his hat on, and the umbrella open over his head. The effect it may be supposed was decidedly peculiar; but the child of the wood coolly took his seat on a bench in the Court and kept his umbrella open all the time.

The garments worn by the male Coolies consist of two pieces of cotton cloth or calico, which are wrapped round the middle and descend to the calf of the leg, and the other thrown about the shoulders like a Roman toga. The Mussulmen or Muhammedan labourers cultivate a flowing beard, and dress themselves in turbans or caps of white calico, loose jackets, and flowing trousers of white or particoloured muslin or calico. Gaily coloured cloths, however, are often worn by the female Coolies; a long piece of cotton or muslin wrapped round the middle, and falling in ample and elegant folds below the knees. To this garment is added a crimson cotton-velvet *ravukkei*, or jacket, with half sleeves, which closely fits the form, and covers, though not conceals, the bust. The Muhammedan females wear the green gauze *burkhā* or *mukkādu* (or the veil), which is simply done by drawing over the head the upper part of the garment. But when the men are within their own houses, it is common for them to strip themselves almost to a state of nudity, a custom which Cæsar observed among the ancient Britons.

8. All classes of Hindu labourers, men and women, particularly the married women, are extravagantly fond of silver and gold ornaments; they have an endless variety of chains, brace-

lets, anklets, necklaces, and rings: and these are common to men and women. The latter are further ornamented with rings in the nose, and *bangles*, or heavy gold or silver circlets, round the ankles, rings called *Minji* on the toes,* one of which emits a tinkling sound when the wearer is walking. It is also quite common to see men and women wear gold and silver coins around the forehead, suspended from the neck, and covering a system of network, attached to the back of the head-dress. These ornaments are worn at marriages, holidays, and other festive occasions, and on Sundays. In addition to all these, the married females wear about the neck the *Tali*,† which is either a band of gold richly chased, or a silk network entwined with silver cord. And then, as a finish, they cover their faces with a solution of saffron in water, which they think is a great improvement, and is, I suppose, intended to cover up minor defects, and hide the tinge of the countenance. The Chinese females, however, though this is not general in the Colony, are in the habit of whitewashing or whitening their faces with cosmetics, because they think that adds to their beauty. Young brides, especially those belonging to wealthy families, after their marriage, continue for several months or years to keep their faces whitened almost all the while. A respectable widow, however, is never allowed by the customs of society to use cosmetics, whatever be her age. The Chinese females, like the Indian females, are not only fond of plaiting their hair, but also of adorning their heads with flowers and various kinds of ornaments. Oftentimes females wear from six to ten or a dozen kinds or pieces of ornaments on their heads, necks, arms,

* This kind of ring or *Minji* is alluded to in the sacred Scriptures thus: Isa. iii. 16, 18, "Walking and tripping nicely (mincing) as they go, and making a tinkling with their feet." "In that day the Lord will take away the bravery of *their* tinkling ornaments *about their feet.*" The Jewish and other Oriental females were in the habit of wearing such ornaments in ancient times, and this custom is still observed by all the modern Orientals, and the Hindu females in the Colony are instances of the fact.

† The *Tali* is an ornament tied on a bride round the neck, by the bridegroom at the time of marriage; *in effect synonymous with a wedding ring.*

&c., seldom less than three. Such as these may be daily seen, and more especially on Sundays, in Lacy Town and Camp Street, &c., in the City of Georgetown. The Indian woman—especially if she is from Southern India—is literally bedizened from head to foot with jewels of all descriptions, and one may even see her on work-days hoeing in the cane-field with heavy silver bangles hanging down over her little brown feet; and what wealth she does not carry on her arms, ankles, neck, head, nostrils and ears, her husband has in the savings bank for transmission to the Emigration Agent in India, to be paid to him on his arrival or return home to his native land when his term of service or residence in the Colony has expired. There is, I must inform the reader, a general idea throughout the East that the display of jewellery on women and children draws off the "evil eye," of which they are in dread, and hence the women indulge more in an extensive quantity of jewellery than in fine clothes. Several Coolies—males and females—have gone so far as to adopt the European costume, in which they feel rather uncomfortable and awkward for a time, but soon get accustomed to it. The prevailing notion in the Colony among a certain class of people has been that unless a Coolie puts on, or makes his appearance in, shirt and trousers, he is an uncivilized being: he is a heathen man and a publican, one to be despised by the superior-looking being—the African Creole. In the manufacture of Eastern ornaments and jewels, Cassie Pattar in Regent Street, Georgetown; Joseph Henry at Enmore, and others in other parts of the Colony, make a good living; but Cassie Pattar is unmistakably one of the best and cleverest Oriental goldsmiths we have in the Colony, and he is largely patronised by many ladies in the city.

9. I have already said that almost all the Coolies we get from India are a low caste people and of an immoral character. Very few high caste Hindus, except some Sepoys and some other higher caste people, have dared to cross the "dark water" to come to Demerara. Of whatever class or caste the Coolies may be, the love of adornment with ornaments of gold, &c., we find is a trait in the character of these Orientals.

The rich and well-to-do families in Southern India especially are more profuse in their personal adornments than their sisters in the Northern portion of it. In the third chapter of Isaiah, verses 18-23, we have given a list of different *ornaments* and *vestments* which composed the wardrobe of the ancient Hebrew lady, and which the Hindus of Southern India call *Adei-abar-anan,* so peculiar to the Hindu ladies. This inventory of the wardrobe, observes Dr. A. Clarke, "from its antiquity, and the nature of the subject, must have been very obscure even to the most ancient interpretations which we have of it; and from its obscurity must have been also peculiarly liable to mistakes of transcribers." It is, however, impossible now to ascertain what kinds of *ornaments* and *vestments* were referred to in the passage. Once, however, I had occasion in the course of my ministry, to read the third chapter of Isaiah to an audience of Hindu immigrants from Southern India. One of the hearers—a sharp, intelligent Hindu,—one who had read a good deal—observed that "the man (Isaiah) who wrote that book was not a *Jew,* but a true-born *Hindu,* for he gives a faithful description of the *Adei-abaranan* of the Hindu females of the present day." Indeed, there are many respectable Hindu females in the Colony of British Guyana who wear nearly all the ornaments specified or mentioned by Isaiah. They appropriate to themselves the larger share of decorative ornaments. Upon each wrist are "bracelets" (*Asttha-Kadagam*) of great variety both in the form and in the materials—gold, silver, brass, or copper, and even of glass—which make a ringing sound, when the females walk. These "bracelets" (Exod. xxxv. 22) show great beauty of workmanship, and often are of the purest gold. Pendents of gold are suspended from the head to the forehead, called "cauls" (*Suttigal*), and from the ear to the shoulders, and rings (nose-rings) sometimes so large that they reach to the chin, and which are removed at each meal. Bands of silver encircle the arms and the ankles. On one or more of the toes are silver rings called *Minji* "(tinkling ornaments" —*Silambugal,* one of which emits a tinkling sound when the wearer is walking, to which no doubt Isaiah alludes. (See previous note.) Around the neck are strings or "chains"

(*Arangam*) of large beads of coral, gold, or glass, with broad collars—necklaces—called *Pattei* or *Karei*, set with small gems, or precious stones. The long black hair, neatly combed and made glossy with cocoanut oil, is rolled up in a tasteful manner, or broidered (or *plaited*), and placed a little in the rear of the left ear, secured with a rich gold hair-pin, or ornament, called *Sirapûshanam*. (See No. 7 below.) Their garments also are neat, gaudy, and tasteful. The jewels worn by the Hindu ladies are called their "joys" — *Santhoshams*, — and large sums are annually expended by husbands and fathers in their purchase.

The following is the list furnished by Isaiah :—

(1.) "The tinkling ornaments about the feet." This is rendered in the Tamil Version *Silambu*, and in Hindu *Ghoough-roo*, that is, a foot trinket of silver, filled with small pebbles, in order to sound when walking, or an ornament worn round the ankles with bells fastened to it to tinkle. It is the same as *Mínji*: see note on p. 211.

(2.) "Cauls" (*Suttigal* or *Nudalani*), a network jewel worn by a woman on the forehead, a pendent forehead jewel. In Hindu *Jalian*, network ornaments.

(3.) "Round tires like the moon" (*Perichindhâkku*), ornaments of gold, &c., with crescent heads, worn by women round the neck.

(4.) "Chains" (*Arangam*), a pendent: a necklace of gold or silver and precious jewels. Among the wealthier classes of people in India this graceful ornament often consists of a string of pure gold coins of one size, with a larger one in the centre, which lies upon the breast; or it may be of several strings of pearls supporting a central ornament, formed of precious stones. It is vulgarly called by the natives *Sarapalli*—a gold chain of three or four folds. In Hindu 'chains' is rendered *Jhoomka*, the bell-shaped pendent of an earring, which I do not think is correct rendering. The Tamil is preferable.

(5.) "Bracelets" (*Astthakadagam*), which are almost universally worn by men and women on the wrist. Called also *Kâppu*—bangles.

(6.) "Mufflers" (*Thalei-mukkádu*), a veil, or part of a cloth worn as a hood by females from the head down to the shoulders, or to the body. The veil worn by females differs considerably in different parts of the Oriental world. The Mussalman ladies so veil their heads and faces that their eyes only can be seen. In Hindi the word is *Goougkat*, or *barik busqa:* a veil to conceal the face.

(7.) "Bonnets" (*Sirapûshanam*), a head jewel, or ornament to fasten the hair with. The Oriental women never wear combs in their hair. A kind of jewelled hood is worn by some males and females. The Hindu rendering, *Mookoot*, means a crown, crest, diadem, tiara.

(8.) "Ornaments of the legs" (*Pádha sarangam*), anklets, or ankle-rings: little silver or golden bells worn round the ankles, or on the feet, which knock together, making a ringing sound as the wearers walk.

(9.) "Head-bands," or head-dress similar to the "horn," worn almost from time immemorial by the women of Lebanon, both Christians and Muslims, as well as Druses, with a veil thrown over it in such a manner as to leave its lower half uncovered in front. (See references to this kind of dress or ornament worn by women in 2 Sam. xxii. 8; Psal. xviii. 2, lxxv. 4, cxii. 9, cxlviii. 14.) This head-dress is rendered in the Tamil Version *Márkkachchei*, *i.e.*, a wide band or scarf passed over one shoulder and drawn on the opposite waist, so as to cover the bosom or breasts from exposure. This is a kind of veil which is folded in two equal parts, and the middle of it made fast round the waist, so that the lower half hangs nearly to the ground, while the upper half is brought over the head, face, and shoulders, and breasts, to prevent exposure. The Hindu rendering *Patta*, for "head-bands" is an ornament of the forehead.

(10.) "Tablets" [some suppose that this word should be translated *necklaces*], rendered in Tamil *Sugandaparani*, *i.e.*, perfume boxes. Dr. Van Lennep, in his *Bible Lands*, observes, "A chain is sometimes formed of large sequins, and passes over either shoulder, reaching to the hip, whence a broader chain hangs from the necklace upon the breast; it is of gold, either plain, or adorned with precious stones, and wrought with many openings, through which issues the perfume of ambergris, or the musk paste called seraglio pastilles; for Orientals are extremely fond of strong perfumes, and live too much out-of-doors to be hurt by them." The Hindu gentlemen and ladies in Southern India, I often noticed, rubbed themselves with the *Chandana paste*, and carried with them perfumed boxes.

(11.) "Earrings," which is rendered *Thâyitthar*, armlets. The Thâyitthu is a small silver box containing a charm, or talisman, to keep off the evil eye. *Bijayath*, an armlet (Hindu).

(12.) "The rings" (a general term for *Môdhirangal*), finger rings of different varieties.

(13.) "Nose jewels" (the Hebrew expression for *earrings*, and rendered in Tamil *Mûkkutthigal*, nose-rings, or jewels of the nostrils), of various sorts. Among the Hindu females the left cartilage of the nose is bored, and suspended, sometimes with a pendent called *Nidhi*. The middle cartilage of the nose is also bored and adorned with a ring called *Thongani*, or *Bulâkku*. All Oriental women are notoriously fond of decking themselves with jewellery, not only on their heads, but other parts of the body as well. They wear earrings of various forms, some of them reaching even below their shoulders, and being of considerable weight. An ornament worn by women in their ears is called *Salladeik kambu*, and another kind, made of hanging chains or globules of gold and precious stones for the ears, is called *Thûkkâm*.

(14.) "The changeable suits of apparel" is rendered *Vinôda Vasthram*, embroidered robes of great beauty and magnificence; an apparel fit only for princes and queens. *Jhoolon*, shining apparels, covered with jewels and ornaments.

(15.) "Mantles," *Sâlvei*, shawls or tunics.

(16.) "Wimples," *Porvei*, a covering garment; or cloak, or ferijah, which a Mussalman woman wears with ample folds and wide sleeves so as completely to envelope the person, and effectually conceal the form.

(17.) "Crisping-pins" (*Kuppigal*), ornaments of gold or silver of the size of a walnut fastened to the hair of women.

(18.) "Glasses," *Kannádigal*, mirrors, looking-glasses (Exod. xxxviii. 8), which, in adjusting her ornaments and arranging her dress, every woman makes use of. Anciently polished metals were used instead of glass. An Indian lady will spend hours before a glass looking at her face and admiring her ornaments. A kind of mirror called *Arsee* is sometimes used on the thumb by Hindu females.

(19.) In addition to the above, we must observe that the Eastern women dye their hands and feet with henna, the leaves of the camphor plant, which are crushed when dry, and formed into a paste with a little water. This paste is spread upon the palms of the hands, the soles of the feet, and around the ends of the fingers and toes, and bound up overnight, after which the paste is washed off, and leaves an all but indelible mark. The edges of the eyelids are also blackened with a preparation of the khol, which consists of a collyrium of antimony. Orientals admire eyebrows which meet over the nose, presenting the appearance of a bow; and when nature has denied them this ornament, they imitate it by artificial paint, which is removed in case of mourning. I have known several young females in the Colony to attend to this kind of adornment of their bodies to make favourable impressions upon their friends and beholders.

"An *ornament*, as Crates said, is that which *adorns*. The proper ornament of a woman is that which becomes her best. This is neither gold, nor pearls, nor scarlet; but those things which are an evident proof of gravity, regularity, and modesty." The wife of *Phocion*, a celebrated Athenian general, receiving a visit from a lady who was elegantly adorned with *gold* and *jewels*, and her *hair with pearls*, took occasion to call the attention of her guests to the elegance and costliness of her dress, remarking, at the same time, "My ornament is my husband, now for the twentieth year general of the Athenians." How few Christian women act this part! Women are in general at as much pains and cost in their dress, as if by it they were to be remembered both by God and man. It is, however, in every case, the argument, either of a *shallow mind*, or of a *vain* and *corrupted heart*. (See what St. Peter says in his First Epistle iii. 1-5, also what St. Paul says in 1 Tim. ii. 9.)

As there is a vast difference between the European and Oriental ornaments and vestments, I have tried to explain the list given by the inspired Prophet, to the Colonial as well as the distant reader, because nearly all those contained in this list are in use among our Indian immigrants, though called by different names, according to the languages they speak.

CHAPTER XI.

THE LANGUAGES SPOKEN BY OUR LABOURING POPULATION.

1. BRITISH GUYANA, like India—whence the bulk of our immigrant population is derived—is not only a land of idols and strange gods, but it is also a Babel of languages. The labouring population of the Colony are as varied in their speech as they are in their costume. My reader has only to visit the sugar plantations to listen to the continual rattling of the tongues of men and women in languages and dialects quite strange and unknown to him, and enough to bewilder and deafen his ears. English, Portuguese, African, Chinese, and the many languages of the East Indies, are all spoken at the same time by the people, and for a person to be able to understand them all without an interpreter or guide, he must possess the wisdom and capabilities of Joseph Mezzofanti (the son of a poor carpenter), one of the wonders of the world, who by the year 1846 had mastered no less than seventy-eight languages—nearly corresponding in number with his age, for he was born in 1774—the great Italian Linguist and "walking Polyglot," or Sir William Jones, the great Oriental Scholar, who spoke some eighteen languages. The English, however, is rapidly taking a prominent place in the Colony, and is superseding all other languages spoken by the foreigners here. It is, indeed, surprising to witness the change taking place in the thoughts and feelings of our immigrants of different nationalities, in regard to the English language, which is destined to become the one universal language of the people of the world. As this fact has already been referred to elsewhere at some length, I do not think it necessary for me to go over the same old grounds here. It is true that the early immigrants or Colonists, the Portuguese and Spaniards, wherever they went, effected more rapid changes in the countries they conquered or occupied

than any other nations of modern times, resembling the Romans in their power of impressing their language, religion, and manners on rude and barbarous tribes; and it is equally true that the English people have effected greater and more lasting changes than any other nation. Their influence is felt everywhere, and their language, in like manner, is becoming the medium of communication between different nations of the world. So far as British Guyana is concerned, the influence of the early Portuguese and Spaniards—truly wonderful conquerors and colonizers, three or four centuries ago—is seen in the words of their language which still remain in use among the Aboriginal Indians. *Sapatu*, "a shoe," *Karinha*, "a fowl," *Kaburitu*, "a goat," &c., are used to the exclusion of the real Aboriginal Indian terms. Many corrupt Dutch and English words also are in use among them and others in the Colony. The Madeirans, of course, keep up a knowledge of their national language as a matter of form merely, though nearly all of them can converse very freely in English. The Creole Madeirans of the Colony, however, do not seem to care for the language of their parents, and prefer rather to converse in English than in Portuguese: only when they want to abuse or curse, they have recourse to Portuguese, and I must say they are great adepts in it. The children of the Madeiran Portuguese, born in the Colony, consider themselves superior to their parents in intelligence, learning, and habits. We may find four or five per cent. among the Portuguese immigrants, males and females, who have come from Madeira, who can read and write their language, but the children born in the Colony all enjoy the educational advantages under the British Government which their parents never enjoyed in their beloved island home. The minds of the Portuguese also are getting more and more enlarged with regard to many things of which they were ignorant in their home, and their children born in the Colony do not seem to care a jot about Madeira. They never refer to it either directly or indirectly in their conversations with each other, or their fellow Colonists.

2. We have a few Africans in various parts of the Colony who are imperfectly acquainted with the English, even with

the Creole *patois* spoken by the labouring class of people, the Blacks, Indians and Chinese Coolies. Their lingo seems to be a perfect jargon. The descendants of the old slave population, and the present generation of the Black Creoles, never can relish the language of their ancestors, though they hear it spoken in their presence. By signs and gestures the Africans make themselves understood when they cannot express themselves in the *patois* of the people. At Nismes connected with the Wesleyan Methodist Church (Goed Fortuin Circuit) there is an African by the name of Young, who is an active, useful, intelligent, and pious man, and a Class-leader in the Church. Once or twice I have heard the man speak in public to the members of his Class: when he could not make himself understood he would use signs and gestures, and when he could not remember an English or Creole *patois* word he would use an African word. With respect to a knowledge, I mean a superficial knowledge, of the English language, I believe the Black Creole labouring population are one with the Indian and Chinese Coolies. If the Black Creole labouring population to whom the Word of God is preached by the Ministers of the Gospel, not in African dialects, not in the Creole *patois*, but in pure unadulterated English, can understand what is preached to them, then I say the Indian Coolies in like manner will and do understand what is spoken to them, especially after they have been three or four years in the Colony. Sometimes the Creole *patois*, as spoken by the people, can scarcely be understood by strangers, and by even those who had been long residents in the Colony. Strange blunders have at times been made by newly appointed officials in misinterpreting the jargon or the speech of the people. As an instance, one day some years ago in the Magistrate's Court at Leguan, a black man was brought up charged with shooting a neighbour's hog. The Magistrate, not looking at the charge, and addressing the prosecutor, asked what was the complaint. "Dis man shoot my *haag*, Sah." The prosecutor gave his evidence, then his witnesses did the same, and they all swore positively that the defendant shot the "haag." The Magistrate was convinced of the man's guilt and sentenced him to a fine of twenty dollars, adding by way of reason for the heaviness of the fine, that it was a cruel deed to shoot his neighbour's *bird;* no doubt the *hawk* was a pet bird, and on that account was valued very highly by its owner, and as the culprit was the man's neighbour and must have known how he valued the bird, his deed was the more heinous! "Me Gad," said the dumbfounded defendant, "twenty dollars for shoot a haag, and who ever heard before that haag bird? Eh! eh!!" It was some time later before the Magistrate discovered his mistake. In a similar manner some short time ago a University graduate was airing his Latin before a Coolie who had refused to understand the overseer's Hindustani. "Arma virumque cano," said the overseer. "O Massa," said the Coolie, "me poor fellow, me no sabby Inglis good." One of the Coolies standing within hearing advised the "poor fellow" to have the overseer up for "cursing" him. Among a certain class of the educated Creoles there is an impression that unless they could employ long or big words, either in their conversation or in writing, they would not be looked upon as men of education, and hence it is a frequent occurrence in the Colony for certain men of intelligence to use such terms or words as would require the necessity of appealing to a dictionary for meaning. Among the working class also a knowledge of long words of late has become quite the fashion. I remember hearing a person of this class saying on one occasion: "I thank God I am still in the prosecution of the immaculate salvation." The Barbadians especially are fond of using long words. Said a gentleman once, who was having his house papered, to the man who had brought him the patterns: "I think the colour of this one is rather high." "Yes, Sah," said the paperhanger, "it is rather high; in fact, Sah, it is a very odoriferous pattern." The Creoles, I must say, excel in the knowledge and use of big words. Sometimes, too, words and expressions used by the educated gentlemen acquire a local and temporary popularity. The Rev. Henry Moore says that "in Barbadoes, some few years ago, Bishop Mitchinson, describing the jerky performances of a certain choir in Bridgetown, used the expression 'spasmodic jets of sound,' and in a short time the phrase was in everybody's mouth, each one trying to ring changes on the words, until one might hear such lovely figures as 'spasmodic jets of meanness,' and 'spasmodic jets of extravagance.' In 1876, the then Inspector General of Police in Barbadoes thought fit to describe himself as 'poor, poor,—yea, miserably poor.' At once the expression became famous; everybody, whether rich or poor, adapted it to himself, and down to this very day the phrase is commonly heard in that tight little island. English-speaking people in British Guyana had long been acquainted with the word 'farce,' but it has devolved upon the august Court of Policy to communicate to that word some special popularity."

3. I have already in a previous chapter made some remarks on the monosyllabic language spoken by our Chinese or Celestial immigrants. The language is so difficult and complicated that it would take a man's whole natural lifetime to study it, and even then he could not be a complete master of it. (See Chapter VII., 11.)

4. I shall now direct the reader's attention to the East Indian languages spoken in the Colony, and conclude with some remarks about the Sanskrit and Tamil, the two classic languages of Northern and Southern Hindustan, pointing out, at the same time, that both these languages have lent their valuable aid in enriching the Hebrew vocabulary. I take this opportunity of stating here, that though in Chap. VII., 11, I have said that many learned scholars have thought Sanskrit was the original spoken language in the world, yet I have found there are other very able scholars in the Oriental world who deny its antiquity. Some of them go so far as to assert that instead of the Dravidian (Tamil, &c.) deriving its alphabets from the Sanskrit, the Sanskrit and Latin alphabets are derived from the Dravidians, as the Aryans brought no alphabet with them. If this conjecture or opinion be true, and I see no reason why it should not be true, then the Tamil is before Sanskrit in age, or is coeval with it in existence. As the opinions of the learned scholars on the origin of the languages and alphabets of India are various, and as yet finally undecided, I consider that one opinion is as good and valid as another.

5. The extensive territory of India may be distinguished into:—(1) *The British Dominions* strictly so called; (2) Provinces *under British protection*, and more or less dependent upon Britain; (3) *Independent States*, in alliance with Great Britain, and acknowledging her as the paramount power; and (4) A few small spots belonging to other European powers, as the French, the Portuguese, and the Dutch. The British dominions in India are divided into presidencies, vice-presidencies, and provinces under Commissioners. There are three presidencies, viz., the Bengal Presidency, of which Calcutta is the capital; the Madras Presidency, of which (*Senna Pattanam*, Indian name of) Madras is the capital; the Bombay Presidency, of which Bombay is the capital. THE BENGAL PRESIDENCY contains eleven principal divisions with fifty-six districts. THE NORTH-WESTERN PROVINCES of India (of which Allâhàbâd is the capital, including Allâhàbâd, Agra, Delhi, and Benares, the heart of the ancient Hindustan) contain thirty-six districts, under seven Commissioners. THE PANJAB (or country of the five waters) territory contains ten grand divisions with thirty-two districts. OUDH contains four divisions and twelve districts. THE CENTRAL INDIA, or INDOR, contains no less than seventy-one States. This large district includes Malwa, Bandelkhand, and other districts between the Chambal and the Jamna. The *principal* tributary States of Central India are six in number:—Gwalior, Indor, Bhopal, Dhar, Dêwas, and Jowra. THE CENTRAL PROVINCES include a great portion of the table land of Central India. Here was the kingdom of the Mahrattas, founded by *Raghuji Bhonsle I.* This is divided into four Commissionerships, in which are eighteen districts and fourteen Feudatory Chieftainships. RAJPUTANA consists of twenty provinces, of which two, viz., Ajgmir and Mairwarra are British territories, while the other eighteen States are independent, under British protection, with a Political Agent immediately under the Governor General and Viceroy, who resides at Calcutta. MYSORE (*Maisur*) which is directly subject to the Bengal Government, and in regard to military matters under Madras Government, contains three grand divisions of Nandidrug, Ashtagram, and

Nagar. THE BRITISH POSSESSIONS IN BIRMA (Burmah) comprise all the maritime districts on the east side of the Bay of Bengal. They consist of *Arakan*, *Pegu*, and the *Tennaserim* provinces, with their districts, ten in number. The Madras Presidency includes twenty collectorates or districts. Travancore, Cochin, Vizianagaram and Jeypur, and Pudukota are all Protected States. And the Bombay Presidency includes twenty-one collectorates. Within its limits are, (1) The Gaekwâr of Barôda; (2) The four Kolhâpûr Râjas; (3) The Rao of Katch; (4) The petty states of Gujarât; (5) The petty states of Câttywâr; (6) Southern Mahratta Jagirs, &c.

6. This description of the territory of India will give my reader a correct idea of the various parts from which our Immigrants or Coolies have come to the Colony, and of the various languages that are spoken by the natives of India, who may be regarded as consisting of two classes, Hindus and Muhammedans.

7. Omitting the ruder jargons of the jungle and the numerous local dialects (which would swell the list to many scores), not less than *twenty-two* independent or distinct languages are in habitual use throughout India, and these have been grammatically compared and classified. By some of the Oriental writers, these languages have been classed as belonging to three different families or groups, of which the first belongs to *Northern Hindustan;* the second belongs to *Central India,* including Hindustan Proper, and the Dakhan or Southern Peninsula, with their different provinces or Circars; and the third belongs to *the South of India.* The first family consists of the Kashmeeree, Khasi, or Purbitti, Nepaulese, Kosalese, and Dunguri; also the Palpa, Kumaon, Gurwhal, spoken in districts along the Himalaya chain. Those belonging to the second family or group are Bengali, Assamese, Maithla, Orisa or Urya, Panjabi or Sikh, Multani, Sindhee, Katchi, Gujaratti, Kankuna, Vikanerwa, Marwar, Tirhitiya, Jayapura, Udayapura, Haroti, Malvi, Bankelkhandi, Magada, Mahratti, Ranghi, Bhutiya, Gondee, Hinduwee, Hindi or Braja-Bhaka; and these are the vernaculars of the Eastern, Western, and Central Provinces of Hindustan Proper, and the

Dakhan. And those belonging to the third or *Dravidian* family, and spoken in *the South of India*, are the Tamil, Telugu (or Telinga, improperly called *Gentoo*—gentile), Canarese (or Karnata, or Cannadi), Malayalim, Tuluwu, Toda, Kota, Ghond, and Khond. As our immigrants have come from all parts, North, South, East, West, and Centre of India, nearly all these languages spoken in India are in free and constant use among them in the Colony, and only a very small portion amongst our immigrants can understand more than one language. The language of each is unintelligible to the other, though the idioms are in fact more nearly allied than English with German.

8. The Sanskrit (or *Samskradam* or *Grandam*), called by the Hindus Nâgarî or Dêva Nâgarî (*i.e.* the language of the divine, royal, or capital city, or the writing of the gods, on account of its great antiquity), is supposed to be the parent of all the vernaculars of Hindustan, together with those of Mahrashtra and Orrissa, the two adjacent countries of the Dakhan. Adelung, a great Oriental scholar, asserts with much confidence, that "the *Sanskrit* may be considered, with the exception of a few mountain dialects, as the parent of all Indian languages, from the Indus to the farthest part of Arracan, and from Cape Comorin to Chinese Tartary." Later writers or scholars than Adelung, however, suppose that the languages spoken on the northern and north-eastern provinces of Hindustan have no connection at all with the Sanskrit, but belong to an entirely different family of languages. Sir William Jones speaks of Sanskrit as "of wonderful structure, more perfect than Greek, more copious than Latin, and more exquisitely perfect than either," in which high eulogium all modern Oriental scholars fully concur. Though now the Sanskrit is entirely a dead language, and long since disused in all parts of India, it still retains a large place in the veneration of the people. In Southern India the Sanskrit or Dêva Nâgarî characters have been superseded by the Grandam, that is, letters from Tamil and Telugu, &c.

9. Whilst the Sanskrit is considered the parent of all (?) northern vernaculars of Hindustan, the Tamil, which is the

vernacular speech of above ten millions of people inhabiting the great plain of the Carnatic, "is the original source of the Malayalim, Canarese, Telugu, Mahratti, and Oorya, it being known to have attained a highly finished form some time prior to the introduction of the Brahmanical system, though, together with other dialects, having since received a large admixture of Sanskrit." The Tamil and its derivatives are supposed to belong to the Dravidian races, and have been by some scholars traced to *Scythian* parentage.*

10. The Shen Tamil possesses an extensive literature, which is held in high esteem, and is the most polished and the freest from Sanskrit admixture: the wandering Tamil *Kavirayan* poet, like the troubadour of old, is sure of an intelligent audience and a hearty welcome in every town and village in the Presidency. The Tamil, together with Telugu, is spoken from Cape Comorin to the northern extremity of the district of Ganjam, including Madras, one of the three Presidencies of British India, Vizagapatam, Vizoyroye, to the north-west point of Canara, being an area of 135,680 square miles, and a population of 22,301,687, which can read, write, and speak these languages. The Tamil is spoken also in the north part of Ceylon, and in most of the British Cantonments in the Dakhan, and by several thousands in Poonah belonging to the Bombay Presidency, and in Rangoon and Moulmein in the Bengal Presidency. Three-fourths of the Telugu and Canarese people can converse very freely in the Tamil language, though they cannot read or write it. The Malayalim and Tudu are but a corrupt Tamil: same as the corrupt English in the Colony called *patois* spoken by the labouring Creole population.

11. Besides these distinct languages spoken by the natives of India, there are dialects of the various hill tribes in constant use both in India and in British Guyana. They have no written characters, but the missionaries are endeavouring to reduce many of these dialects and jargons of the jungle into written

* If the Tamil has really a *Scythian* parentage, then it is intimately connected with the Saxons, for Saxons were all Scythians, or Goths. The ancestors of the Saxons were the Saga, Saka, or Sakai.

languages. They have succeeded in reducing similar languages of other countries, and I have no doubt that ere long these and other languages will be so systematized as to be made in some degree easy and readable. A valuable document called "A Statement exhibiting the Moral and Material Progress and Condition of India during the years 1871-2," was "ordered by the House of Commons to be printed, 28th April, 1873." From this invaluable record of progress the following is contained in the *Wesleyan Missionary Notices* for November, 1873, which I extract for the information of my reader:—

"No body of men pays greater attention to the study of native languages than the Indian Missionaries. With several Missionary Societies (as with the Indian Government) it is a rule that the Foreign Missionaries shall pass a series of examinations in the vernacular of the district in which they reside; and the general practice has been that all who have to deal with natives who do not know English shall seek a high proficiency in these vernaculars. The result is too remarkable to be overlooked. The Missionaries, as a body, know the natives of India well; they have prepared hundreds of works suited for schools and for general circulation in the fifteen most prominent languages of India, and in several other dialects. They are the compilers of several dictionaries and grammars; they have written important works on the native classics and the system of philosophy; and they have largely stimulated the great increase of the native literature prepared in recent years by native gentlemen."

I doubt not but that all the existing dialects and jargons of the jungles of India will ere long be reduced into written languages by these men.

12. The *Hindustani*, so called, is spoken by almost all the natives, in addition to their own native or caste languages, in the Northern and Central Provinces of Hindustan. It is a *dialect*, or camp language, not limited to any particular district. It is a mixture of Persian and Hindi, or the Brâja-Bhâkâ (so called from the cowpens (Vraja) and dairies in the forest of Vrinda, where Krishna was educated), and the Prakrit, which was extensively spoken in the North of India. This was the dialect adopted by the Mussalmans, after the conquest of

Mahmoud, as the medium of intercourse between themselves and the Hindus. It was originally called by the Mussalman invaders of India, *Urdu Zabân*, or "Camp Language," and by the poetical writers *Rekhta*, "Scattered," on account of the variety of languages interspersed in it. In its composition it is somewhat like *Lingo Franco*. At present it has become a principal dialect or language, and is in very common use among the Europeans and the natives of India. It is spoken throughout the native armies, and by all government officials. In fact, although properly the language of the North-West, it passes current (like French in Europe) throughout Bombay, Madras, and Calcutta: hence it has been sometimes, and very appropriately, called the *French of India*. But the intercourse of Europeans with uneducated natives of India has tended to corrupt the *Hindustani*, and thus a barbarous dialect has been produced, which is commonly called *Moors*, or, as the Madrasees are pleased to style it, the *Tulukku*. Very few of the natives of the Presidency of Madras are acquainted with the Hindustani. The *Dakkni*, or the *Tulukku*, is spoken in Madras, principally by the Patanies, Labeys, or Tulukkars, and by those belonging to the Nizam's territory, Hyderabad, and Secunderabad, in addition to their own native language, which is the Tamil. We may often find in the Colony that Indian immigrants, not being able to understand the language of each other, adopt the English, which they soon pick up on the estates. It is a fact, also, that a very large number of Indian Coolies, whose native language is the Tamil, embark at Bengal for British Guyana, and pass themselves on their arrival as Hindustani, or Bengali, or Hinduwi speaking Coolies.

13. The following will appear to my reader a striking exemplification of the diversity of languages spoken within the bounds of an Indian district, and the consequent difficulty experienced by the Missionaries in their work of preaching. A Missionary belonging to the diocese of Calcutta in charge of the Singhboom Mission, of which Chayabassa is the centre, says, "That Singhboom (and it is only one of the five districts into which the whole tract known as Chota Nagpore is divided) is itself again divided into five *Perganahs*, or sub-districts,

each having a distinct language: in Kolhan they speak *Ho*, the language of the Lurka Kols; in Dolbhoom, *Bengali;* in Barmangati, the *Santhal* language; in Powhat, *Mandari;* and in Sorikela with Karsowa, *Ooriya.*" What a medley of languages! The same diversity of languages exists even in British Guyana on the different sugar estates: each estate is a Babel of languages and dialects. The Missionary must be a wonderfully clever man to be able to understand all the languages and dialects of the different Hindu tribes, to be able to understand them all, or to be able to preach to them in their several languages and dialects. Unfortunately the gift of tongues ceased long ago with the Apostles. Very rarely a Missionary may now be found who could speak intelligently more than one or two of the languages of the people.

14. The Hebrew language in which the Old Testament was written, belongs to the Semitic stock of languages, which embraces the Indian (Sanskrit and High Tamil, two classical languages of North and Southern Hindustan; the former is now a *dead* language and the latter is still *in use* by some millions of people), ancient and modern Persian, Greek, Latin, Gothic, and German languages, and is appropriately called the *Indo-Germanic.* The name *lingua sancta* was first given to the ancient Hebrew in the Chaldee Paraphrases of the Old Testament, because it was the language of the Sacred Books, in distinction from the Chaldee, the popular language, which was called *lingua profana.* So in India, the *Sanskrit* of the North, and the *Grandaic* or *Shen Tamil* of the South, are called the Sacred or Holy languages, because in them the Sacred Books of the Hindus are written, in distinction from the common spoken languages of the country or people.

15. The Tamil (to which are cognate the Telugu, the Canarese, and the Malayalim, all spoken in Southern India, and called correctly or incorrectly by the epithet "*Dravidian*") is the living classical language of the South of India. On the one hand, the more deeply it is studied, the more close will its affinity to Sanskrit be seen to be, and the more evident will it appear that it possesses a primitive and very near relationship to the languages of the Indo-Germanic or European group.

Yet it is certainly not a mere *Prakrit*, or corruption of Sanskrit. It is a language coeval with Sanskrit, and having the same origin with it. The comparative bareness of the Tamil alphabet; its inability to indicate Sanskrit sounds without borrowed characters; the total difference in pronouns, in numerals, in many nouns, verbs, adverbs, technical terms of grammar, and similar matters, clearly indicate that the Tamil is neither a daughter, nor a derivative, of the Sanskrit. The Tamil and Sanskrit are entirely distinct from each other. The old Tamil could have done without much of the gilding which it has received. The modern Tamil, however (like the English), has become one of the most copious, refined, and polished languages spoken by man.

16. Professor Max Müller traces the Sanskrit language up to the time of Moses, and marks as descending from *Aryan* source the now spoken dialects of Hindustani, Mahratthi, and Bengali. He considers that Sanskrit was the spoken language of India for at least some hundred years before Solomon; and Bournouf has since proved the ancient Persian language of Zend and Sanskrit to be very nearly allied. In like manner I think the pure, high (Shen) Tamil of Southern India—the only living classic language—may be easily traced up not only to the time of Solomon, but up to the time of Moses and Job of the patriarchal dispensation.

17. It is very evident that the Hebrew language has borrowed or introduced into its vocabulary several Tamil terms or words, as the following examples will show:—

(*a*.) The word "*peacocks*" (1 Kings x. 22; 2 Chron. ix. 21) is in the original Hebrew *tucciyim* (and in Greek *tuones*), which is of foreign origin. On this word Dr. W. Smith, in his *Dictionary of the Bible*, Vol. XI., p. 763, makes the following observation:—"There can be no doubt that the Hebrew word is of foreign origin. Gesenius cites many authorities to prove that the *tucci* is to be traced to the Tamil or Malabaric *togei*, 'peacock': which opinion has been recently confirmed by Sir E. Tennent, who says, 'It is very remarkable that the terms by which these articles (ivory, apes, and peacocks) are designated in the Hebrew Scriptures, are identical with the Tamil names by which some of them are called in Ceylon to the present day,—*tukeyim* may be recognised in *tokei*, the modern name for these birds.' Thus Keil's objection 'that this supposed *togei* is not yet itself sufficiently ascertained, is satisfactorily met.'" The word "ape" which in Hebrew is *Koph* (and in Greek *Kebos* or *Kepos*) is also of Shen Tamil origin. *Kavi*, or *Kapi*, is but another word for *Kurangu* (ape, monkey, of the long-tailed species), which means *swift*, *active*. And the word "ivory," which in Hebrew is rendered *Shen habbin*, is either of Sanskrit (*ibhas*) or High Tamil (*ibham ; ibham ruppa*, the tusk of an elephant, ivory) origin. The Hebrew *Shen* I believe is a slight alteration or corruption of the Tamil word *tandam* (an elephant's tooth), whence *tandi*, an elephant. With the exception of this reference to ivory, there is no other mention made of elephants living in Palestine, as they did not form a part of the fauna of Syria.

(*b.*) The word *Behemoth*, an animal known to the patriarch Job, is mentioned only once in Job xl. 15, which in the margin of the Bible is rendered "the *elephant*, as some think." But what kind of an animal was this *behemoth?* Dr. W. Smith, to whom I have already made reference, in his first volume, page 181, observes: "Various conjectures have been hazarded as to what animal is meant, the principal authorities being in favour of either the elephant or the hippopotamus. Among those who adopt the elephant are Drusius, Grotius, Schultens, J. D. Michaelis, &c., while among the advocates of the rhinoceros are Bochart, Ludolf, and Gesenius." I, however, venture to state and maintain that the word *behemoth*, an ambiguous term referring to the *elephant* or *hippopotamus*, which in the English Version is left untranslated, is not, strictly speaking, a Hebrew, but a foreign Tamil word introduced into the Hebrew vocabulary. The following probable derivations of the word may not be uninteresting to my reader, especially if he is a Bible student :—(1) The Tamil words *Bagadu*, *Bôdhagam*, mean an elephant: also the terms *mattham*, *matthagisan*, *matthavâranam*, and *matthügünan*, mean an elephant, a furious, irritable elephant. The word *mottham* means largeness, stoutness, bulkiness. The Hebraized compound word *behemoth* is equal to the old Tamil word *bagamath*, or *bagamoth*, which means an elephant of a large size, furious and irritable, and ungovernable in its disposition and practices. (2) The Tamil terms *Vayamá* (or *Bagamâ*), *Vayam*, and *Vâmanan*, mean also an elephant, or water elephant (hippopotamus). The word *Vayam* means water as well as elephant: hence water elephant. The Hebraized word *behemoth*, even in this second derivation, is equal to *behema*, *bagama*, *Vayama*, an elephant. There are in the Tamil language some eighty (80) terms or synonymes for an elephant: *Bagamoth*, *Peruma*, *Pondei*, *Madogayam*, *Vayaman*, &c., and the very shape or form of an elephant on paper makes the word *Bayama* or *Vayama*, corresponding to the Hebraized *Behemoth*. Though the elephant was not a native of Syria or Palestine, Job and the people in his days knew enough of it, and were sufficiently acquainted with the animal, its nature, and its powers.

(*c.*) The word *Almug* (1 Kings x. 11, 12) or *Algum* (2 Chron. ii. 8) in the Hebrew form, retained in our English Version, was a costly and highly scented or perfumed timber introduced by Solomon from Southern India—Ophir. *Algum* or *Almug* is only a slightly altered or corrupted form of the Tamil words *igam*, *ingam*, *anugam*, *anukam*, the same as *Chandana*, or *Sandana*, *tree*, which is still highly prized in the East for making musical and other instruments. The Anglicized word *Sandal* (which is a corruption of the Tamil word *Savandilei*, generally known in India as the Trincomalee Red Wood), or *Savandilei* tree, is also a highly scented tree, but not *the* (real) algum or almug, or chandana tree, evidently imported by King Solomon.

(*d.*) Moses, in Gen. xi. 31, says, "They went forth . . . . from *Ur of the Chaldees*, to go into the land of Canaan;" and St. Stephen, in his apology before the Sanhedrim (Acts vii. 4), interprets this word *Ur* to signify the land—"The land of the Chaldees" (*Ur Chasdim*, the country of Terah). Bertheau derives the word *Ur* from the Zend root *Vare*, "country," meaning a place of residence, with which the translation of the LXX, *Choraton Chaldaion*, also agrees (See Dr. Kurtz's *History of the Old Covenant*, Vol. I., p. 167). I, however, maintain that this word *Ur* is entirely and purely a term of Tamil origin, and the *U* should be pronounced long, as *Ur*, or *Oor*, which means country, land, village, place of residence. The word in Hebrew is not used in its contracted, altered, or corrupted form, from the Zend root *Vare*, as Bertheau supposes, but is introduced into its vocabulary in its real, unaltered form *Ur*. The "Ur of the Chaldees" is equal to the Tamil form "*Chaldēyū Ur*," i.e., the land, country of the Chaldees. Compare this word *Ur* in Gen. xi. 31, with "*Ar* of Moab" in Isa. xv. 1, which means the city or country of Moab. In Gen. iv. 16, we read of "the land of Nod on the east of Eden." Some suppose Nod to mean China, and others Tartary: but all this is false. The word Nod means *flight*, *vagabond*, *wandering*, and the Hebrew exactly corresponds to the Tamil word or root *Nada*, to walk about, wander about; and the passage may be, according to Tamil idiom, rendered, "He went and dwelt in the land of his wandering on the east of Eden." The Tamil word *Nâdu*, country, or uncultivated tract of land or ground, is also equivalent to the Hebrew Nod, and the passage would be better perhaps if rendered, "He went and dwelt in the land of that uncultivated part of the ground east of Eden." The Hebrew word *Nod* and the Tamil word *Nada*, or *Nothu*, exactly correspond in meaning. The Hebrew word *Kinoor* for harp in Gen. iv. 21, is in Tamil *Kinnâram*, or *Kinnâr*.

(*e.*) In Nehemiah x. 1, we have the *Tirshatha*, which is not at all a Hebrew word. Dr. A. Clarke in his Commentary on Ezra ii. 63, makes the following remark on this word *Tirshatha*, applied to Nehemiah. "Some suppose the word to be *Persian*, but nothing like it of the same import occurs in that language at present. If, as Castel supposed, it signifies *austerity*, or that *fear* which is impressed by the authority of a governor, it may come from *ters*, FEAR, or *tersh*, ACID, the former from *tarsidan*, to FEAR, or DREAD." I am of opinion, however, that both Dr. Clarke and Castel were wrong in their statements or conjectures as to the supposed derivation of *Tirshatha* from the Persian. The word *Tirshatha* is neither Hebrew nor Persian. It is altogether a pure Tamil word introduced into the Hebrew vocabulary. *D(Th)êsâthi*, or *D(Th)êsâthipadi*, means *the chief over the land, lord over the country; king, governor.* The word *Dêsâthi*, or *Thêsâthi*, has been evidently altered into *Têrshâth*, or *Tirshatha*, thus giving it a Hebrew or Persian twang or turn. There is another Tamil name, *Thêrchchittan*, exactly corresponding in sound and in meaning with *Tirshatha* of the Bible, *governor, prince, prime minister.* If this derivation of the term is not conclusive enough to the ordinary student of the Bible, I may have recourse to another elegant Tamil word or term, *Th(D)urei*, which means a *master*, a *prefect*, a *governor of the town* or *province*, a *gentleman;* and at that rate the compound Tamil word *Dureisâth*, or *Thureisâth*, the *Tirshatha* of the Bible, will mean a *prefect* or *governor managing all the affairs of a kingdom, and having all the cares and welfare of the people at heart, and who is faithful in the discharge of his varied duties.* In either case the word *Tirshatha*, I maintain, is a pure Tamil word.

18. I can very easily give some one hundred other instances of this kind from the first chapter of Genesis down to the last chapter of Malachi, proving, or rather showing, that the classic language Tamil can be traced up to the time of Moses, the leader and lawgiver of the people of Israel, yea, to the time of Abraham, and before him to postdiluvian patriarchs. The Hebrew name of one of the patriarchs, *Peleg*, *Phalec*, or *Palag*, means *rent, cleft, cutting, splitting, division, separation* (for in his days, about one hundred years after the flood, *the earth was divided* among the sons of Noah), and is equivalent to the Tamil *Pelagu, Pilavu.* In Sanskrit there is no term corresponding to it of the same or similar import. Dr. Clarke says that the oldest people now existing next to the Jews are the Hindus. The Tamil and Gentoo laws of Southern India in regard to certain ceremonies and practices in use will throw a good deal of light on the circumstance mentioned in Genesis xxix. 26.*

* A learned work on civil and canon law of Ancient India mentions eight species of marriage. 1. When the girl is given to a Brahman without a reward; 2. When she is presented as a gift, at the close of a sacrifice; 3. When two cows are received by the father in exchange for a bride; 4. When the girl is given at the request of a Brahman; 5. When money is received in exchange for a bride; 6. When a marriage takes place by mutual consent;

I may, however, in conclusion observe, that the words which are common to all the Shemitic group of languages are very numerous. There are many which are found in nearly all the languages of the Aryan group. The occurrence of the same words in different divisions of languages, without any evidence that the words were imported after the tongues had been formed, points to a primitive tongue from which all have been originally derived; and the Sanskrit, not the *Hebrew*, is supposed by many learned authors or writers to possess that honour. And if the Hebrew is a derivative language, then there is not the slightest doubt that it has equally derived several terms or words from the Sanskrit and Tamil (coeval with the Sanskrit) to make its vocabulary full and complete. There is not a Brahman (except those who have studied in English Universities in Calcutta and Madras) in the whole of

---

7. When a bride is taken in war; and 8. When a girl is taken by craft. In addition to these, there is another, not indeed to be found in the Smrittis, unless it be considered a variation of the Gändharva-vivähah, but sanctioned by the Puranas and frequently alluded to in the heroic poems. It is peculiar to princesses, and consists in calling together by heralds, deputed to proclaim the beauty and accomplishments of the lady, an assembly of kings and princes, from whom she personally selects him she wishes to prefer to her bed: it is thence called SWAYAM VARAH, *her own choice*. But of the eight species of marriage we have mentioned, those actually in practice in the present age are the first principally, the third and fourth in a less degree, and, notwithstanding it is condemned by the lawgivers, the fifth very generally: instances of the seventh may occasionally occur, and the sixth, the marriage of lovers, is the constant theme of the poets in India as well as in other countries. The third form of marriage, called *Aesh*, may recall several cases mentioned in Scripture; Gen. xxxiv. 12; 1 Sam. xviii. 24-26. The fourth, *Gandharva*, may throw some light upon Gen. xxxviii. 12-18. The seventh form, upon Deut. xxi. 10-14. The eighth, called *Peishach*, upon Exod. xxii. 16.

Two Coolies on a certain occasion waited on me. The case to be decided was a difficult one: each asserted he had spoken the truth, and nothing but the truth. To confirm the statement made by each in a sacred manner, *he lifted up his hand above his head and called upon his God to witness to the truth of the assertion or statement made by him*. This was the most primitive kind of oath-taking, and I think reference to this kind of oath-taking is made in *Gen.* xiv. 22, which see.

India, however learned or accomplished in Sanskrit or Tamil, that has any idea or knowledge of the Hebrew to derive any words to enrich their vocabularies. The Hebrew has many terms from the Sanskrit and Tamil.

NOTE.—See my *Guyanian Indians*, Section V., Nos. 7-9, Section VIII., Part I., Nos. 8-9, where the subject of this chapter is treated on.

CHAPTER XII.

THE CHARACTER AND MANNER OF LIVING OF THE COOLIES AND CREOLE BLACKS IN THE COLONY.

1. THE Coolies are, as a whole, intelligent, and some of them carry it in their physiognomy. They are cunning too, and, as might be expected, some of them are very vicious. To be more clear, in many we may find temperance, frugality, hospitality, obliging manners, mildness, and submissiveness; while in others we find falsehood, duplicity, apathy, selfishness, avarice, sensuality, and dishonesty. The remarks made by a Missionary in Trinidad, with respect to the Coolie immigrants there, may *in toto* be applied to the immigrants in British Guyana. "Several of them," observes the Missionary, "have been hung for murders of most atrocious peculiarities. It has struck me that, however amenable to law all men must be who live in civilized society, these unfortunate beings can hardly be held responsible to the usages and rules of civilization and Christianity, of which they know positively nothing; hence the greater the responsibility in the proportion to our agricultural necessities of instructing and winning over to a gentle, loving, attractive Christianity (subduing and elevating) a class of people who have decidedly all the susceptibilities for the acquisition of knowledge, and for being touched by the appeals of redeeming mercy; a people, like ourselves, fallen, but who may be raised and blessed by a potent religion, in the light of which, even in the estimation of the converted Coolie Indians, the false religions by which they have been heretofore misguided and held in bonds to sin are worthy only of contempt." I said that the Coolies are intelligent, and so they are. Those who have read the history of India—ancient as well as modern—will admit that these people, at least their

forefathers, have very largely contributed towards extending our knowledge of nature in mathematics, astronomy, mechanics, and other sciences, such as arithmetic, geography, algebra, &c. Need I mention the names of Kapila, Goutama, Vyasa, and others, contemporaneous with the pre-Socratic thinkers of Greece, and indeed with Zoroaster in Persia, and Confucius in China; and attempt to describe the nature and contents of the following learned works:—*Nyáya-Sûtra-Vritti*, *Tarka-Sangraha*, *Bhôsha-Paricchêda*, *Vaishê-Sheka-Sûtras*, *Nyáya-Lilâvati*, *Tarka-Bâsha*, *Agastyâs' Sutras*, *Tolcâppiamby*, *Tiranatûmâkkini*, *the Nannool*, *the Kural*, *Nâladinanûru*, *Naishdadham*, *Sivaga-Chintâmani*, &c. Many of the Coolies in the Colony are correct accountants, and we have sometimes felt surprised to find them master simple questions in arithmetic with the greatest facility and expedition. Their children, too, possess a capacity for learning and knowledge by no means inferior to the young of other lands.

2. The Coolies of British Guyana are, on the whole, avaricious of dollars and cents. They, like the ancient "Cretians, are always liars, evil beasts, slow bellies." The remarks made by the Rev. William Arthur, in his *Mission to the Mysore*, may be properly and strictly applied to the immigrants in British Guyana. "The Hindus," he says, "have a natural apathy, which is increased by the joint influence of the caste system, the doctrine of transmigration, and other barbarous and painful penances. Caste severs the cord of brotherhood, transmigration shuts the heart against all their fellow-sufferers, and the barbarous penances deaden their compassion, harden their hearts, and make them little better than beasts which perish. These three, combined together, make them remarkably cold of heart. They will not go out of the way to torture or murder human beings like unto themselves; but, if revenge or the hope of gain stimulates them, they will do so to the utmost pitch, and as unmoved as if they were cutting sticks. Their revenge once roused is unsparing and unchangeable. Coolly, and yet furiously, they will pursue their unfortunate victim to do the dreadful deed in silence, unknown to any one else, if possible. They will spend their last cent at law rather

than fail to ruin their victims." This description is true of almost every Coolie immigrant in the Colony; but, with proper management, discipline, and kindness, the Coolies become excellent servants, and prove themselves faithful and trustworthy towards their masters, the planters and proprietors of estates. We read of the faithfulness and good behaviour of many of these very labourers to the late East India Company. Until the Mutiny of 1857, these traits of character were the theme of universal praise; and, if need be, I could also mention the names of several of these labourers on the different estates in the Colony who have been found faithful, trustworthy, and diligent, and, in consequence, have been raised to higher positions by their employers.

3. As to temperance, I regret that I cannot say that it is a striking virtue of all the Coolies of the Colony. The Muhammedan Coolies, of course, consider temperance a part of their religion, and hence it has become so much a habit that practically the rule is never transgressed. The Chinese Coolies, though not given to drinking propensities like the Black Creoles, Portuguese, and others, yet are great opium consumers, in which unfortunately the Blacks and Indian Coolies also greatly indulge. Though the Hindu religious laws proscribe all kinds of drinks that inebriate, yet, since their arrival in the Colony, the Coolies have been, and still are, exposed to every kind of temptation and vice, and especially to intemperance. The Portuguese have their grog or rum shops in every direction, in town and country, and especially on the estates, and are persistent in their attempts to lead them astray. They sit and watch at their shop-doors "to call passengers who go right on their way," and frequently do they succeed, "but they know not that the dead are there, and that their guests are in the depths of hell." On Sundays, especially, the Portuguese grog-shops are opened on the different estates, and large quantities of rum, brandy, and other intoxicating drinks are sold to the Hindu and Chinese Coolies, and these poor, silly, simple ones drink to excess, and when drunk they fight and make a noise. This Sunday drinking unfits and incapacitates them for their Monday tasks, and becomes one

great incentive to idleness and crime, and a fertile source of want. Not the Coolies only, but the very Creoles, with all the advantages they possess, give themselves to strong drinks on Sundays in country places, especially on the different estates, and in due course become thieves, liars, and drunkards, besides being incorrigibly lazy. Besides the spirituous liquors sold in the Portuguese shops, some of the Coolies, who belong to the *Shànar* caste, make their living by extracting from the cocoanut-trees (which are in abundance in the country) a kind of juice called toddy, or *Kallu,* and selling it to their countrymen. They bestow great labour upon this particular craft. The vessels are changed twice a day—morning and afternoon —and the juice, when fresh, is delicious; but, when kept for two or three days, or when exposed to the sun for three or four hours, it ferments and becomes strong and sourish. Many of them like to drink it when in this state, for then it intoxicates. The cocoanut-trees, too, after a while, become barren and die.

It is a notable and startling fact that in this Colony ninety-nine rum shops out of every one hundred are owned or kept by the Portuguese, and it is also a fact known as well to the police as to others, that in many of the grog shops in Georgetown traffic is as untrammelled on Sunday as on any other day in the week. So bold and reckless have the sellers become through their repeated successes in the Police Court, owing to the difficulty in getting a conviction, except by aid of informers, that some of them make no attempt at concealing the fact that rum can be had on sale at their shop on Sunday. From the time the morning breaks till late at night, the entire Sunday is desecrated by the bands of dissolute men and women rum-laden, that quarrel and fight around and in the shop, and rend the air with their shockingly profane conversation. And this weekly repeated scene is within hail of a police station. The rum shop is on one hand, and the police station on the other; the publican is conscious and cares not that the police know he is illegally selling rum; the police know the man is doing a roaring business, and yet there is not the slightest attempt to put a stop to it. For the respectable inhabitants in the neighbourhood of these pandæmoniums, we have real sympathy. They look forward to the Sunday not as a day of rest and peace, but as a day of clamour and ugly noise, during which their ears are sure to be assailed with language actually frightful in its profanity, and shocking in its lewdness. And they have no redress. They may petition the Government on the subject, but what then? The chances are that the petition will be laid over ungranted; the Town Council, the guardians of city propriety, take no interest as a body in putting a stop to the evil; the City Commissary has been so heartily abused for receiving the testimony of avowed spies, and his attempts at bringing the offenders (as we have said already) to punishment have so often been thwarted, that he has fallen into a state of apathy regarding the evil; and the police pass the noisy shops with as much complacency as if they were passing the door of a chapel. The only remedy that offers itself is the determination by our worthy Police Magistrate to convict on satisfactory evidence of a sale having been effected, without the necessity of producing the rum in Court, &c. A few heavy fines, if they did not stop the habit entirely, would at least compel the offenders to have some respect for public decency, and sell their goods with as little display as possible.

✓4. The Coolies are easily provoked. Sometimes about ten or twelve of them may be found sitting together and talking on different subjects. Peace and concord may be thought to exist. But not so. One wrong word or expression, one wrong movement of the eye or mouth, produces instant discord. That the Coolies are quarrelsome in their disposition is a fact which cannot be denied by any one that has any dealings with them. In fact, it is a national habit of theirs. Sometimes the simple quarrel leads to fighting, and ends in their being summoned before the local magistrates and punished. "We can't help it, it is habitual to us," is the ready excuse given by them when they are spoken to about their quarrelsome disposition. They will call upon their gods for everything, and curse and swear at a furious rate when they get into a passion. They never for one moment think it indecent to make use of the most disgusting language, accompanied by violent and fearful gesticulations, even before their children. But the women excel the men in these bad qualities. The Creole black women, whether in the city or in the country, are equally as bad, if not worse. Their expressions, attitudes, or postures, &c., &c., are such as modesty compels me not to describe. The Chinese vocabulary is full of curses, oaths and imprecations. The vilest of language is used by them when cursing anybody. For the sake of the merest trifle they will create quarrels and disturbances. The Coolies and blacks are emphatically a quarrelsome people. The Portuguese and Chinese are not so. One would think they are great cowards. In connection with this subject I may mention that the Coolies as a nation are fond of loud talking, or using vehemence in speaking. Talking together at the top of their voices, and a great way above anything of the kind we have ever heard, is quite natural to them. Apparently they are quarrelling, but such is not the fact; they are only giving their opinions or deciding a matter. Indeed, it is an incessant tempest of grating gutturals, which sets one's teeth on edge: and, in addition, head and shoulders, hands and feet, the whole body, in fact, is wrought up into violent action to enforce the orator's meaning.

5. The Coolies, among other evil practices, are addicted to that kind of licentiousness which is principally owing to constitution, climate, and the institutions of the country from which they have come. Though this is the case with the men, it is not so with the females, for the women of Southern India are more chaste and temperate than those of the North. We have females in the Colony come from both of those provinces, and as they are indentured servants they are often obliged to labour in the fields with their male relatives and others; and crowds of them may be daily seen, and especially on Sundays when they have no work, bathing together and washing their wearing apparel publicly in trenches connected with the sugar estates. Such scenes are witnessed by many; nevertheless, we, as well as others in the Colony, have noticed their trying to avoid every indelicate exposure. They would in fact sooner die than abuse their liberty. This is their general character;

but yet instances of misconduct in the unmarried, and of conjugal infidelity in the married, do sometimes occur (and more frequently among the Northern Indian females), as the result of circumstance and temptation. We must bear in mind also that the great majority of women imported from Calcutta are very loose in their habits: they were bad in Calcutta, and so they will continue to remain in Demerara; and hence so many glaring instances of infidelity and misconduct on the part of the married and unmarried females. Example, whether for good or evil, has great power over people, especially the heathen Coolies. There is a great paucity of women (Oriental) in the Colony at present, and the disproportion of women to men is very nearly 49 to 100, and to this are attributable the many murders which are committed, and the many disturbances which arise among the Coolies. And till this want is supplied, we shall hear of murders and rumours of murders in every direction in the Colony; and nothing else, I believe, except the abatement of the cause, will check this great and sore evil. Several years ago His Excellency the Governor, Sir Francis Hincks, had a long conversation with me on the subject of brutal murders committed by the immigrants in the Colony. I gave the opinion I have just expressed, and strongly recommended His Excellency to put himself in correspondence with the different Auxiliary Missionary Societies in India who have large numbers of orphan girls in their several schools, with a view to import a ship-load or two of female immigrants only, so that every labouring Hindu may take unto himself a wife, either according to the Christian, or according to his own country's religious custom. The Governor thought it was a good plan, but a few days after my interview with His Excellency, the Rev. E. B. Bhose, Church of England Missionary to the Coolies, was in a similar manner consulted. What opinion that reverend gentleman expressed to the Governor on the subject I never could learn. We still, however, continue to receive from India only limited numbers of Coolie females. In looking over some of my old papers I find that on one occasion the ship *Wiltshire* (1,461 tons) carried to Trinidad 606 souls, viz., 217 men, 206 women, 76 boys and

55 girls, and 52 infants. There was an equal proportion (within a fraction) of men and women. This is what is wanted for British Guyana.

6. At a meeting of the "Court of Policy," held on March 20, 1882, the subject of the disproportion of Indian Coolie women was discussed; when the Hon. William Russell remarked, the immense advantage derived by the immigrants themselves from immigration to this country was a very strong argument for asking the Secretary of State to use his influence with the Government of India to induce them to withdraw from the Bill all the unnecessary restrictions which it was proposed to place upon immigration. The fact was that anything that would tend to check immigration from India would be a direct tax upon the immigrants already here. Dependent as the Colony was for labour upon immigration from India, it would cease to be a sugar-producing country if labourers could not be procured from thence. It was, therefore, the interest not only of the employers, but of the immigrants themselves, that the cost of introduction should be reduced, so as to enable the planters to add to their labour supply and increase their cultivation. To remove all restrictions, and allow free competition in the collection of immigrants, would be a direct benefit to the Indian community in this Colony. It would be to the advantage, not of the planters alone, but of the immigrants, that immigration should be relieved of all unnecessary charges, because, if the cost of introduction were reduced, higher rates of wages might be paid, and the Indians, as the recipients of the larger portion of the money paid for labour on sugar estates, would derive the greater benefit. He was not one of those who joined in the outcry sometimes raised about the Indians hoarding up their savings and carrying away money out of the Colony. On the contrary, he held it to be a good sign when immigrants were able to provide back passages for their families, and return to their native land with a competency, to show their fellow countrymen what they had gained by emigration to this glorious country of the West.

The Hon. Dr. W. H. F. Smith, Attorney General, said it

would be well also to request the Secretary of State to bring to the notice of the Indian Government the difficulty that was experienced in obtaining female immigrants. It was of the utmost importance that a due proportion of the sexes should be established, and it was some time ago suggested that it might be possible to induce the Indian Government to offer facilities for the emigration of widows, and other females, who were prevented by Indian customs from marrying in that country. If the Government of India could have been induced to remove any restrictions upon, or impediments in, the way of emigration, on the part of such women, it would have been of great service to this Colony, by increasing the proportion of marriageable women among the Indian population; but the Government of India reported that there were difficulties in the way which could not be overcome. It was a matter which should be again brought prominently to the notice of the Indian Government.

The Hon. P. H. Nind, Auditor General, said the Indian Government appeared to regard emigration as a sort of excrescence upon their system of government, as something which they merely tolerated, were not bound to assist and promote. He did not regard this as a statesmanlike view of the subject. Having regard to the density of the population of many parts of India and its periodical decimation by famine, the Indian Government should promote emigration to countries such as this, where the condition of the immigrants was so greatly superior to their condition in their own country. He thought the time had arrived when the cost of immigration might be reduced by abolishing the free return passage. It did not exist in other parts of the world, and there was no reason why it should continue to exist here.

His Excellency Lieut. Governor W. A. G. Young said he should forward the report to the Secretary of State by the next mail, and would, at the same time, direct his Lordship's particular attention to the points which had been referred to, especially that with reference to increasing the number of women. He could only express his own regret that the endeavour to bring to this Colony widows and other women who could not marry in India resulted in failure. The Indian Government took a long time to consider it, but finally reported that there were obstacles in the way. It would be remembered also, that upon another occasion, when the complement of immigrants in one season was short, the Court passed a resolution asking that the number might be made up by a greater proportion of women, but it was not possible to give effect to the recommendation.

7. Jealousy, one of the strongest passions of human nature, prevails extensively among the Coolies. I have never met with a more jealous set of people than they are. But why should they be so jealous? Jealousy indicates or denotes a suspicion of conjugal fidelity. The Coolies are jealous of their wives. I believe this is entirely owing to the degraded manner or condition in which the females are kept; and this state of inequality of women leads to serious evils. The men, of course, will attempt to justify the consequence of such a condition; and when the women do wrong, there is no end of inflicting punishment upon them. The men are obliged to govern the wives with the utmost strictness, or they would not only ruin their husbands but themselves also. The rod and blows are freely laid upon them, especially when they have, or imagine they have, cause to suspect the fidelity of the wife. Scores of instances have been brought before our Courts, in the city of Georgetown and elsewhere, in which the husbands have been charged with brutally cutting and wounding their wives with intent to murder, and instances in which the husbands had killed the wives outright for this cause. A dreadful murder of this kind was committed in Trinidad not very long ago. The following are the particulars of that tragedy, extracted from one of the Trinidad papers:—"One Mahabil, a Coolie shopkeeper in St. Joseph, entered, in February last, into a somewhat peculiar kind of bargain with a fellow-countryman, by which, for a consideration of twenty-five dollars, he purchased the latter's reputed wife, he, the seller, being then about to leave in the return ship for Calcutta. This strange bargain seems to have been so far carried out that the woman, with her two children, a boy and girl,

respectively aged six and eight years, was transferred to the buyer (Mahabil), but the seller, having changed his mind, did not leave for Calcutta, but remained in the Colony, and ultimately became the clerk of Mahabil, living in the same shop. It would appear that recently Mahabil conceived a great jealousy for this former husband; this suspicion being confirmed by the disappearance of the woman with her former husband and the two children. Learning in the early part of the week, that the woman, man and children were living in St. James's, he went there on Wednesday last. The wife stating that she would return if Mahabil would give her all of his former wife's jewellery, Mahabil agreed, and Mr. Jardine, the solicitor, drew up an agreement to this effect, and which Mahabil signed, and left in Mr. Jardine's possession. On the next day, Mahabil returned to Port of Spain, to the store of Messrs. E. H. Fitt and Co., where he had been dealing for the last ten years, and begged Mr. Smith, a clerk in that firm, to come up to St. Joseph and ask for money, and he, Mahabil, would deny having any, and give him his wife's jewellery to hold in payment. Mr. Smith did not go up to St. Joseph that day, and he, Mahabil, that same night murdered the man from whom he had bought the woman, and also the woman and her two children. Persons living in the vicinity heard a row in the shop, but no particular attention was paid to it. Next morning (Friday) a clerk was sent from Messrs. E. H. Fitt and Co. to St. Joseph, and he returned, stating that he found the shop closed, but could learn nothing of Mahabil. Next morning (Saturday) Messrs. Fitt's clerk, Mr. Smith, being at the Port of Spain Railway Station, saw Mahabil arrive by the train, and at once called him, and asked him if he did not know that Mr. Fitt had sent the day before, as he had requested, and the clerk had found his shop closed. Mahabil replied, that the shop was shut because he had gone to Frederick Estate to collect money, that he had the money with him, and that if he, Smith, would go to the store with him he would pay it over. Mr. Smith went with him to the store and remonstrated with him about his behaviour; Mahabil begged him to go with him into the back store, and there he handed Smith twenty dollars, and told him that Mr. Fitt must send and take charge of his shop, confessing, at the same time, that he had murdered the woman he bought for twenty-five dollars, as well as her former husband and the two children, and that their bodies were in the shop, the body of the man in one room, and the woman and two children in another, and begging Mr. Smith to 'save' him. Mr. Smith's feelings may be better imagined than described. The police were communicated with, and Mahabil was taken into custody. The police were dispatched by the half-past one o'clock train to St. Joseph, the shop was broken open, and the bodies found as stated by the murderer, cruelly and foully murdered. The body of the man was cut to pieces, and the other three bodies otherwise mutilated; the weapon used by the murderer was a cutlass, and was found outside of the shop." In this country, as well as in Trinidad, of course, legal proceedings are immediately instituted respecting the murderers; but in their own country, murders have seldom been dealt with judicially by the English Courts, and the cruel shedder of blood has escaped punishment. I have known or seen in India, as well as in British Guyana, the wives literally closely confined, watched with jealousy, and everything valuable belonging to them kept under lock and key by their husbands. I confess there is very little married or conjugal happiness experienced by men and women of this class. In too many instances marriage is looked upon as purgatory. When the first wife dies, the widower has to consider a long while ere he can make up his mind to marry a second time. What will the reader say to the following Hindu's story?—"A poor Hindu, having been released from the cares of this world, and from a scurvy wife, presented himself at the gate of Brahma's paradise. 'Have you been through purgatory?' asked the god. 'No! but I have been married.' 'Come in, then, it is all the same.' At this moment arrived another man, just defunct, who begged of Brahma to be permitted to go in also. 'Softly, softly! have you been through purgatory?' 'No; but what of that? Did you not admit, a moment ago, one who had not been there any more than I?' 'Certainly; but he has been married.' 'Married! whom are you talking to? I have been married twice.' 'O, pshaw,' replied Brahma, 'get away! Paradise is not for fools.'" On one occasion a jealous and noisy wife, chiding her husband, told him, that if she was dead he would marry the devil's eldest daughter, if he could get anything by it. "That is true," replied the abused husband, "but the worst of it is, *one cannot marry two sisters, and you are one of them.*" It, of course, ended in a terrible fight.

"Her face is wild, her head is thick,
Her tongue keeps up a clackety-click;
Minds every one's business but her own,
Is a nuisance abroad and a pest at home."

8. I have stated the opinion of a Missionary in the beginning of this chapter, about the murders committed by the Coolies. He says: "However amenable to law all men must be who live in civilized society, these unfortunate beings can hardly be held responsible to the usages and rules of civilization and Christianity, of which they know positively nothing." Among very many good people, the opinion prevails that there is truth in the old saying. "The worst use you can put a man to is to hang him." We have had many cases of Coolie murderers tried in the Colony, and the sentence of "life for life" passed upon them, and put into execution. It is well known that stoical indifference to death is a marked trait in the Coolie character: practical experience as well as books teach us this indisputable fact. Let death come, no matter with what accompaniments, to the Hindu in his deep-rooted belief, it is but a passage to an elysium—a heritage of bliss for ever. The Coolie cares very little whether he is hanged or shot: in short he cares very little for the deprivation of life; and therefore he does not spare his hand in his onslaught upon human life. Some years ago, his Excellency the Governor, Sir Francis Hincks, asked the co-operation of all those coming immediately in contact with the Coolies, a request which, of course, was complied with most heartily, and his views were, and are still, publicly and privately made known. But what has been the result? They are as bad and listless as they

ever have been. The Coolie murderer is hanged, but this infliction of the death penalty ceases to have terror for the culprit, or an influence to deter his compatriots from the commission of the crime for which the offender suffers death. Instead of hanging the Coolie, who can hardly be held responsible to the usages and rules of civilization and Christianity, of which he knows positively nothing, might he not, upon conviction, be sent back to his plantation, and there, under prescribed restrictions, work out a term of labour designated by the Court, say for life? He might have extra tasks imposed upon him, work apart, be kept closely confined, and be deprived of pay. It strikes me that some plan of that kind would be very desirable, for thereby justice would be subserved in two ways, viz., the planters' interest would be consulted, while, at the same time, the supremacy of the law would be vindicated, and the comrades of the offender made to realize by his presence among them under punishment that they cannot thieve, and cut, and stab with impunity. I shall refer to this subject again in a future chapter.

9. The Coolies understand pretty well how to beg. From the first of January to the thirty-first of December this is their daily occupation. Many of the Coolies who are able and strong enough to work and earn their living, being encouraged by their countrymen in this disgraceful life, instead of working, go about the streets, and wander from estate to estate, begging. Sometimes these supposed poor beggars become richer and wealthier than their brethren who have to work hard to support themselves and their family. When the time arrives for the departure of the Coolies to their native country, the so-called beggars present themselves *as candidates for departure for good*, having in their possession large sums of money to carry away with them. Mr. J. T. Cullandar, a Wesleyan schoolmaster, at Bourda, Georgetown, told me a short time ago, that an aged Coolie who appeared very helpless, and who went about in his neighbourhood begging from house to house, having gathered a decent sum of money, left the Colony for India, in the ship *North*, in August, 1882. This professional beggar apparently possessed nothing beyond

his *bobba*, and yet he was saving up his daily earnings to carry away with him to Calcutta.

10. Fortune-telling is a superstition which prevails very much among the Orientals; and it is commonly practised by the Coolies in the Colony. In fact this is another form of begging. On Sunday mornings, especially, some of the fortune-tellers may be seen parading the streets, and visiting the different houses of their countrymen, with bags hanging down their shoulders, in which the presents are put, and *Kudu Kudukei* or small drums in their hands, which are beaten with the thumb and forefinger, to keep time whilst their imagination is busy with the invention of some foolish but taking falsehood. These fortune-tellers drive a brisk trade with the Coolie females who desire to know what destiny awaits them. Fortune-telling is carried on to a greater extent on the estates than in town. These professional beggars — Indians and Chinese—of whom we have a large number—follow out their trade faithfully as they did in their own countries, before they came to the Colony. They never care to work, and always cry out that the times are hard, and no work to be done; and that they can't get sufficient money for the work done, &c. These begging and fortune-telling Coolies are in addition to their idle habits very trickish and cunning. One of them, not long since, when he was detected forging an order for goods, and was remonstrated with by his meek and loving Pastor, answered plantively, "Boss, honest man no good this country." But the latest instance of their advance occurred in Essequibo, where a Coolie entered a shop and ate and drank until he was full. The shopkeeper then asked for payment. The Coolie laughed at him, remarking that "he eat um plenty, he drink um plenty, he belly full, no body can't take um from him; he go to gaol, he don't care a dam." No educated and refined Englishman could have shown more disregard or contempt for his creditors,—which shows what a fine healthy influence the ordinary Briton carries with him wherever he goes.

11. A Hindu in the Colony seems to lead a secluded life. *He is not as happy as he should be.* He cares not for what we consider some of the comforts of life. His dwelling is plain

and is not set off with a fine display of expensive and gaudy furniture. High tables and chairs, and other necessaries, are not only out of place, but in the way at all times, and many of these, the females think, are a great nuisance and encumbrance, for they do not know in the Colony how to use them, or to take care of them. Some, however, since their arrival, have learned to use spoons and forks; but in general they have neither knives, forks, nor spoons. Their fingers serve all the purpose for which spoons and forks were invented. As their meat is always cut up in small pieces, or cooked until it is ready to fall to pieces, knives and forks are useless. The Chinese can never do without their chop-sticks, for they serve the purpose of knife, fork, and spoon. The Portuguese and black Creoles on the different estates and villages, I have repeatedly observed, make use of their fingers in the room of forks and spoons. Sometimes only an iron spoon (table or large spoon) is used when they eat their simple meal. Reader! if ever you visit their dwelling in this country, you will be surprised to find things contrary to your expectations. You will find their homes in a state of confusion and disorder, *topsy-turvey*. You will find, perhaps, a bedstead in one corner, on which the husband, wife, and children (if any) sleep. The bedstead, or *khatola*, or *palangiri*, serves them for the *visipalagei*, used in their country, and when a Coolie wishes to remove from one estate to another, or from his cottage to another part of the same estate, he piles all his kitchen and household gear upon his *khatola*, then takes up his bedstead on his head, and walks out as coolly and comfortably as possible to his new residence. (See Matt. ix. 6.) Many of the Coolies make their own cots of pieces of bamboo tied or nailed together, and others spread their mats or *viriyolei*, made of cocoanut-leaves, or the East Indian mats, on the floor, or on the ground, while others again sleep on the bare ground, taking a piece of stone or brick for their pillow, like Jacob of old, at Bethel, on his way to his mother's country. In another corner of the house you will find all their kitchen utensils, and not improbably a bundle of grass or a heap or bag of plantain skins to feed their cows with; and in another part of the room you may find all their wearing apparel, either in a trunk or bag, or thrown about formed into a bundle. Many of the poorer classes of the Portuguese and blacks occupying small rooms or chambers are no better or worse than the Coolies. A calabash, a coal-pot, a saucepan, and two or three other nick-nacks are all the furniture, &c., which many a poor Creole possesses. In the same chamber which the Portuguese or black occupies, you will find pigs, fowls, goats, plantain skins, salt fish, potatoes, plantains, &c., side by side, occupying a place also. As the houses are all built of wood, they are obliged to be careful, and some of the *housewives* take great pleasure in keeping their dwellings clean; but some, to their shame and dishonour be it said, are so lazy and dirty, that they will not trouble themselves about the cleanliness of their homes, or their bodies, or their clothes.

12. Some of the free Coolies have their own dwellings in town, but there are others who have no dwellings at all. But how and where do they sleep? The dried leaves of the palm or plantain trees form their beds, their shelter some old building or umbrageous tree. They think of *Sivan* and go to bed—"*Sivne endru paduttukkol.*" They are not afraid of snakes, or scorpions, or centipedes, which we have in abundance in the Colony. Their slumbers are heavy and sweet. The piece of calico cloth which they use as a garment, or a cloak, becomes in the evening or bed time their only covering. And how beautifully does this custom of sleeping in their ordinary clothes illustrate that law of Moses for the protection of the poor—"If thou at all take thy neighbour's raiment to pledge, thou shalt deliver it unto him by that the sun goeth down; for that is his covering only, it is his raiment for his skin: *wherein shall he sleep?*"

While on this subject, I may remark, that in addition to the dwellings (including large logies, of two and three stories, long ranges of buildings of two stories, detached ranges of cottages with double apartments above and below, and detached double and single cottages) generally situated in the vicinity of the manager's residence, and provided for the immigrants by the proprietors of estates or their attorneys, they build their own wattle and daub cottages. Such cottages are found almost on every other estate in the Colony, and are of small dimensions. The walls are of wattles, covered on both sides with clay. The floors are of clay, well smoothed over with a composition of clay and fine sand, and besmeared with a solution of cow dung, which gives the surface a smooth appearance. The walls on both sides are also besmeared with the same solution. The roof is always thatched. The doors and the windows are of very small dimensions. Every such cottage has a thick and substantial clay hearth, which is constantly kept in use. The immigrants build these cottages in imitation of their country mud houses, at their own cost, and they are generally much prized by them. Sometimes the materials for building such cottages are provided by the proprietor or manager. In visiting these cottages, especially in places where several of them take their standing in regular succession, we are often reminded of India, with its mud-walled and thatched houses of the natives. Wherever an Indian Coolie or Portuguese, whether in town or in the country, builds his house or cottage, he is sure to have a paling or fence put round his house, so that he might have an enclosed yard for garden and other purposes; but if a Creole black is fortunate enough to build a cottage, he will never think of enclosing it, but leaves it open as a thoroughfare, *pro bono publico*, nor will he put himself to the trouble of having a flower garden in the front, or a kitchen garden in the back part of his house or cottage. In fact he does not care to have the trouble and botheration in such matters; and yet he feels jealous, and becomes spiteful when he sees his neighbour the Portuguese or Indian Coolie in better circumstances than himself.

13. As to the kind of food used by the labouring population there is great variety. The black Creole likes his plantain (boiled whole, and sometimes pounded and made into *Foofoo*), and salt fish, and hence the expression of the words, "salt fish and plantain the Demerarian's delight." The black Barbadian likes his Coocoo (made of Indian cornmeal boiled) and fish and eddoes; the Portuguese likes his mess of cabbage, pumpkin,

potatoes, cornmeal, pork, and salt fish; but the Coolies principally live on rice and curry, a wholesome food which is generally prepared by the *woman of the house*, during the absence of the husband. When both the husband and wife go out to work in the field together, on their return the wife prepares the repast, while the husband goes to sleep or visits his *matties*. Should there be a daughter in the family, during the absence of the parents, her duty is to fetch water, wood, and prepare the food, which is done to their liking. They take care to have their food cooked clean and nice. They do not eat any and every thing. There are some among them who have never tasted meat (beef) at all, from the day of their birth: it is an abomination unto them as human flesh is to us, and they even profess to know a flesh eater by his scent. The killing or murder of a cow (for eating) is, according to Hindu theology, (though the Vedas fully show that the ancient Hindus killed *pashu*—cattle—to eat them, and so may all the Hindus now, if they like, kill and eat them; but ignorance and prejudice lead them to regard the killing of cows by Europeans and others for food as) something incomparably worse than the murder of a man; and the salvation of even a few of these holy animals from a brutal death at the hands of an irreligious Mlech, would procure righteousness enough to blot out the sins of thousands of mortals. This is really, soberly, the belief of the immense majority of Hindu Coolies around us. But they are fond of mutton; and sometimes pigs, fowls, and some kind of fish constitute their principal meat diet. They have their own gardens on the estates, and grow their own country vegetables, such as *Snake gourd*, *Bitter vegetable* (Pavalkâi), *Drumstick vegetables* (Muringei), *Agatie*, &c. Rice, as said above, is their and the Chinaman's staple food, which is boiled either in an earthen vessel, or in an iron pot, or saucepan. In another pot is cooked a piece of mutton, chicken, or fish, *tempered* in ghee (or butter), to which is added a composition of the following articles or ingredients, called *masalei*:—red pepper, or Chili, coriander, saffron, cummin, garlic, onion, tamarind, made liquid in cocoanut milk or pure water, which is prepared according to the taste and custom of the person, and proves a delicious accompaniment to their rice or other food. Curry made by the Calcutta Coolies is not so hot as that made and eaten by the Madras Coolies; it is so hot, that no European, except one long accustomed to it, can venture beyond a few spoonfuls. Rice and curry as food is much prized by Europeans and other native residents in India, and in this Colony also it is patronized by several respectable families. Curry-making is so simple and easy that it has become a proverbial expression among the Coolies that "if there be three and five even an ignorant woman can prepare curry." [The five kinds of savoury substances are *pepper, dill, cardamum, garlic, asafœtida.* The three kinds of fruit are the *plantain* (banana), *mangoe* and *jaca.*] To the curry may be added the delicious pickles or chatines, and other condiments, enough to tempt the appetite of any epicure.

14. When the food or meal is ready, the man of the house and his male friends wash their hands and feet, according to the *Vishnu Purana,* which says, "He who eats without performing ablutions, is fed in hell with filth; and he who repeats not his prayers, with matter and blood;"—and then sit themselves asquat on their heels to eat the food set before them. Before a Coolie eats, he places a small quantity of the prepared food before the idol or god of the house to propitiate his favour. This done, he mixes his rice and curry with his right hand, and rolling a small quantity into a ball, tosses it dexterously into his mouth, great care being taken not to allow any to fall into the *vati,* or *kopei,* or *elei,* or plate, since such mishap would defile the remaining mass.

The author of the *Padma Purana* asks, "What woman would think of eating till her lord had had his fill?" This custom is strictly observed by the Coolie women to this day. They never eat with their husbands, brothers and grown up sons: they serve the men, and after they have eaten, the women regale themselves with *what is left,* which is frequently very scanty, commenting at the same time on what this man and that woman said; what nice curry such an one can cook, &c. The men, too, seem to think that it is highly improper for women to sit down and eat with them. It is against their religion, and the foolish and ignorant women think that it is their *taleiezuttu* (head writing) destiny.

The meal over, his thirst quenched by water again brought to him, the Coolie retires to his couch, or goes to his neighbour's house, there to chew betel and nut or smoke his pipe,—"the pipe of peace," the *hukka* or *sungan*, passed from one to the other—and thus lounge the hours away until the time for retiring arrives, which is usually from eight to nine o'clock. When he sets to work, it is for necssity, not choice, to satisfy a demand, not to gratify an inclination. In the place of the motto, "Labour is itself pleasant," he would substitute this, "*Work* when you *must*, be *idle* when you *can*, eat, drink, and be merry." The Hindu females since their arrival in the Colony have learnt a bad practice, which they never dare do in their country. The practice I refer to, in addition to chewing betel and nut, is *smoking. They like their short clay pipes, and can't get on without them.* Rising at dawn, the Hindu goes to the trench, or takes the water into his own yard, and there, with religious care, he cleanses his teeth, performs his sacred ablutions, imprints the emblems of his faith upon his forehead, arm, and breast, visits the idol of the house, or faces the rising sun, before which he falls down, takes his morning meal, and prepares himself for the duties of the day. The Hindu Shastras direct that men shall eat at two o'clock in the day, and again at one in the night; but this law is set aside by the immigrants in the Colony, though but two meals are taken by them generally. The domestic conversation turns chiefly upon the business of the family, the news of the country, religious ceremonies, marriages, narratives of heroines and gods, *mischief-making, and injuring others.*

15. A few years ago, one Sunday morning I found myself in the house of an Indian Coolie on Pln. Clonbrook, on the East Sea Coast. There were about ten persons in the room, and the master of the house was getting ready the simple meal to set before them, during which time I kept up a religious conversation with those present. When everything was ready, the master piled the rice and curry on one broad leaf plate. They all took their seats according to age, forming a circle.

To the right of the master there was placed a vessel of gravy, made of bitter greens and other vegetables, and a penny loaf of bread, bought at the Portuguese shop. Before the food (set before the persons) was touched, the master took the loaf in his hand and divided it into equal portions. He then dipped the pieces into the dish of gravy by his side, and gave to each person before him, expressing the hope that all ill-feeling, &c., existing in their breasts towards each other might for ever be forgotten, and never be referred to again. The master gave me a piece also, which I was compelled to take to show that I had no ill-feeling against any of them, and that I loved them, and studied their temporal and spiritual interest and welfare. After this they set to eating the food before them. These people had never read the New Testament, and were therefore ignorant of the facts mentioned therein. This circumstance, however, gave me a literal illustration of the fact mentioned in John xiii. 26: "Jesus answered, He it is, to whom I shall give a sop (morsel), when I have dipped it. And when He had dipped the sop, He gave it to Judas Iscariot, the son of Simon." The Hindu Coolies are in this instance, as well as in many others, living illustrations or proofs of the truths mentioned in the sacred Scriptures.

16. I have already, in the previous pages, referred to the character and manner of living of the black Creole labouring population in the Colony. I shall now further add a few more particulars, showing how they live when left to themselves without any interference on the part of the Government, or the planters of sugar estates. Lying north of Anna Regina, the last police station on the Essequibo coast, is a district extending some ten or twelve miles towards the Pomeroon, and having a resident population of about 6,000 souls. These live on the sugar estates, in villages, and are scattered here and there on Government lands. One settlement, known as Lima Dam, appears a sort of "no man's land," as, whenever "Quashie" or "Sammy" can collect a few boards and troolies, he erects his castle, and squats down as perpetual owner. The pigs wallow in the stagnant trenches round the huts, while their owners may be seen basking like lizards in the

sun. A little further north is a village called Danielstown; for six months of the year a vast swamp, it might strike an uninitiated observer as a remnant of the Lake Dwellings of ancient times. This village forms a sort of City of Refuge to the outcasts of the County. The visits of policemen are like those of angels, few and far between, not that their presence is not often urgently required, but the amount of energy required to track an offender in the village is not possessed by the average policeman, and their distance from the police station renders the villagers, like the Gentiles, "a law unto themselves." When a new Magistrate is appointed to the district, the villagers, to use an Eastern allegory, "take the length of his foot," and their subsequent free fights and drunken rows are regulated by that measurement.

The village is possessed of three rum shops, and the rails of the bridges leading to them are invariably ornamented by the ablest youths of the village, squatting there, day after day, with a calm indifference to the cares of life, and a patience worthy of emulation. Their elders bask in the sun, but not under the shade of the palm-trees, as the only trees of that description grow in the yards of the better class of Portuguese, and the average villager only visits them by the "pale moonlight."

An entertainment in great repute in the villages is what is known as a "tea-fight." This is generally supposed by the outside world to consist in drinking tea to the sound of slow music. Some one has said, "Music hath charms to soothe the savage breast," but if the author of that saying could hear the sounds produced by a "tea-fight" band a "wee short hour ayont the twal," he would find music was a science capable of great development, and that the charming sounds produced by a collection of old drums is not necessarily soothing. The "tea-fight" orgies seem to continue for a series of days and nights, but the palm, *par excellence*, belongs to the individual who becomes most rapidly oblivious of mundane affairs.

The village is generally in possession of a "merry-go-round." The air of importance with which an old Negro bestrides one of the horses, while his "keeper" of three score years and ten reposes elegantly in the carriage behind, is well worth seeing. A black gentleman treats his neighbour's sweetheart or wife, as the case may be, to a ride, and of course a fight follows, which usually ends in a general *mêlée*. The parsons object strongly to these merry-go-rounds, as on Sunday the mysterious brown paper contains no valuable offering, sometimes not even a coin of the realm.

By-the-bye, referring to this "merry-go-round" business, a certain would-be Creole reporter, writing to the Demerara *Argosy*, of May 20, 1882, says (and I give his letter word for word, as written),—

"SIR,—Trusting these few words will not fail to give general satisfaction, and remove all doubt from our mind, Mr. Editor I am happy to say that the Merry go round reach us early this week, I mean reach Mahaicony, it cause the population to leave there houses, to sleep in the open air all night, the oldest is to be found there, and the youngest leaving there children without food, to pay there fees, and sunday when they go to servis in time of collection they fail to give there contribution. But go to the Merry go round you will fine them with dollers, for there savings. Mr. Editor our Wesleyan Chaple was in building for meny years gone, but the Revd. could not rise a pound from the members. But has soon as the Merry go round enter the village they have hundreds of pounds to give to Idals, Mr. Editor, and Saturday lass the rains fall like hail, the Society of the Merry go round are still keeping there social intertainment, to there members, Mr. Editor the bright round moon is shining down on all this and the weet air of April is breathing over it, oh what a scenes for God and Angels to look upon."

The occurrence of a funeral is an event of great importance in the village. The garments then displayed are astonishing; the ladies' boots and hats being "too awfully utter." I met an old Negro, the other morning, looking as if he stood very much in want of a B. and S. "Well, old man, what's the matter?" "O, Sah, me daughter bin dead a town—Da letta bin lie a Pos Affis ten day afo me a heary—so me bin keep one lilly wake." Such a good excuse for consuming bad rum could not be passed over.

Fish abound everywhere. The villager can open his door, throw his cast-net, and haul in a collection of fish. These, with a few plantains got from some neglected patch of ground, put him at ease on the score of provisions. One week's steady labour will supply him with clothing for a year. He is very fond of renting an acre of ground to grow provisions. He weeds a few square yards, puts in a few plants, erects a shelter with a few sticks, and covers it with grass or other convenient material. And now the ambition of his life seems to be reached. Day after day he goes manfully to his ground, with his hoe and cutlass, squats under his shelter until the sun is well down the horizon, and then returns home with an approving conscience. I have known whole fields of provisions in this partially cultivated condition, completely swamped out, because the owners of the different beds would not clean their drainage trench, which one hour's labour on the part of each man would have accomplished.

The only four-footed animals the villagers seem to possess are pigs. The village pig is a perfect study. Its snout is nearly as long as the rest of its body, and has doubtless grown so in vain searchings after food. If it were not that necessity has made them expert catchers of fish, they would run a poor chance of surviving. They catch crabs, not in the cunning way the fox is said to do by lowering his tail into the water, and allowing the crabs to hold on, but by digging them out, which their elongated snout enables them to do to perfection. They turn up the ground thoroughly, and a manager in the district, when labour was scarce some years ago, took advantage of this fact, and had his front fields tilled by them, "as hath been said or sung."

The villagers, as a class, are very thriftless, and never lay by anything for a rainy day. While one Creole out of every hundred does not possess a cow, a savings bank account, or anything in the shape of jewellery, there is scarcely an immigrant labourer of two years' standing, on a sugar estate, who does not possess one or other of them; and a very large number, all three. And the Creole cannot say he lives so much more expensively than the Coolie, as far as necessary food goes. The plantains, fish and rice, which form his great staple, can be procured fabulously easy; but the rum shop, two or three days' idleness every week, and general want of application, handicap him heavily, and are the correct causes of his from-hand-to-mouth existence.

17. We have another instance at the villages of Buxton and Friendship of the laziness and utter worthlessness of the Creole peasantry. At Friendship there is a draining engine which is available for draining Buxton, the two villages being contiguous. The back lands of both villages are as good as any lands in the Colony, and an offer has been made by the proprietors of Pln. Nonpareil, that if the villagers are desirous of planting canes in their diseased and worn-out plantain lands, they will crush the canes and purchase the juice at $3 per gallon (regardless of polariscopic indications). This would pay the farmers better than a few bunches of diseased plantains, and would also put their lands in order for the production of plantains at a future time; but the lands are there yet to be seen covered with para grass of a most luxuriant growth. A few acres of the new empolder land of Friendship have been planted with canes (and well they are growing too), but Mr. Daly, in his report, should not have made the person by whom these canes are planted the exception to his rule "that the Creole labourers are lazy," because the man by whom these canes are planted stands on entirely a different footing, inasmuch as he is not a labourer himself, but employs *others* to till the land, of which he is a lessee, and if he did not do something to obtain the wherewith to pay his rents (to the Government, whether on behalf of the village and for its benefit I trow not), then he might be put to a little more inconvenience than he would like. But even with this fine example before them the villagers still keep their lands overgrown with para grass in the hope that some day soon a splendid lot of plantains will come forth spontaneously. The villages entire are little better than pigmires, with all the high rates imposed, and the excellent draining engine to pump off the water with. The draining engine cannot work, however, without steam, and this cannot be generated without fuel of some sort, which

cannot be obtained without money, and this latter is wanting, because the villagers will not pay their rates as they ought—perhaps more than half pay, but when the estimate of expenditure is made it is expected that all the rates would be paid up; but if this is not done, where is the money to come from? Nothing would make a labourer work on Monday, and on Tuesday they only turn out to look at the work and ask the price. Then they go away and come on Wednesday and mark the work, or work for an hour or two, and they are off again, but not without asking for what they call "feaud," which is an advance in the shape of cash, or a "good" to the Portuguese shop, when they go and get their salt fish and a "little schnapp." Now here are only Thursday, Friday, and half of Saturday to complete a week's work in, and when they get 10s. to 15s. wages on Saturday evenings they spend it in the rum shops.

18. These are real facts which I have here mentioned, and I know they will not meet with the approval of three-fourths of the labouring Creole population, and my statements will not escape criticism.* There are, however, honourable excep-

* A good sound healthy public opinion does not exist in the Colony, no matter what subject comes to the fore; for we are all of us led to form our opinions from those to whom we look for support, so that, as a rule, if we feel that our opinions would clash with those of our supporters, we are, sad to say, liable to suppress them or to go with the power that rules. Our actions and words are supposed to be guided by self-interest, which is everything in this peculiarly constituted Colony, in some shape or form, and an adverse opinion or criticism on any particular scheme or action, political, religious, or ecclesiastical, is for the most part met with such unpleasant consequences either in a business or in a social point of view that you desist after having made one trial of your critical powers. I am sure to meet with the severe displeasure of many in the Colony, and perhaps, too, not experience the same kind cordiality hitherto shown to me by my numerous friends. It is a well known fact, however, that men alter in coming to this Colony: the restraint common to home life to such a great extent disappears, that the same man is an entirely different being in Europe to what he is a few thousands of miles away from it. He sees the iniquitous injustice, oppression, and advantage taken in too many instances, but he dares not express his opinion; he must go in with the public opinion, though that might be damaging and injurious enough, if he wants to live in peace and friendship, and curry favour.

tions; hard, plodding villagers in the Colony, who do not countenance such things, are to be found in the three Counties of the Colony. I have no hesitation in saying that, as a general rule, the agricultural labourers in the Colony have never received that meed of encouragement which might have resulted in the improvement of the whole class. They have been too much regarded as mere labour machines. Not very long ago, certain elective members of the Colonial Legislature enunciated the extraordinary doctrine that the people—the labouring class—had no right to be educated. They look upon our education system as a farce, a waste of public money, and productive of harm amongst the people. The children of the Indian, Chinese, and Black Creole Coolies or labourers have no right to be educated at the expense of the Government; and besides, of what use will education be to them? Education should be confined only to a certain few. To spend money in educating the masses of the children of the labouring population, is to waste it. We do, indeed, live to hear such opinions freely exploded by the sapient legislators in the present enlightened age. Do away with educating the children altogether, for it is an expensive item, and the Colony cannot afford it. But when Colony money, says some one, "is to be squandered on any pet scheme of theirs, or in granting heavy salaries to some needy adventurers, to their own friends or relations; the Colony is then supposed to be a mine of weath, from whose perennial fountain streams of gold and silver flow in inexhaustible supply. Can the Colony afford to pay TWO HUNDRED THOUSAND DOLLARS TOWARDS IMMIGRATION, wrung from its impoverished exchequer, the direct object of which is to enrich the plantocracy, and enable them to live luxuriously and sumptuously? I had thought that immigration was only supported from the Colony's treasury when the estates were on the verge of ruin and to save them from such a fate, but that it was never intended to be a charge on the Colony in perpetuity. All principles of political economy point in the other direction, when, from year to year, the Colony is called upon to vote large sums of money which directly benefit only the few at the expense of the many. It is well known that clearances of twenty, thirty, forty and fifty thousand dollars, and sometimes more, are annually made by many plantations, and it is hard that the Colony should still continue to subsidize to so great an extent this system. Whatever subterfuges, masks or disguises the plantocracy may adopt, the reason of their objection to the education of the people is quite patent. Ignorant though the people may be, yet they have sense enough to see that the planters fear an educated public opinion among that class which they would gladly keep in darkness, lest with knowledge come power, and 'the hope of their gains be gone.' It is nonsense to talk of the Coolie not desiring education, or wishing to impose that belief on the community. It was most amusing to hear these men mutually felicitating one another that at last they had arrived at the same conclusion, to put as many difficulties as possible and raise as many objections as they could in the way of educating the masses. Whatever may be the qualifications of the 'blacks,' at whatever expense those qualifications might have been acquired, the 'black' man is 'accursed,' not because he is ignorant, unintelligent, uneducated, but because he is 'black.' The legislators who denounced the education of the blacks as 'a farce' spoke correctly, because what advantage, let me ask, was it to a 'black' to be educated either at the expense of the Government or at the expense of his parents, when there was no opening for him in any situation in which his capacity and capability could be tested? 'Gibeonites' the blacks have been, and 'Gibeonites' will they remain to the day of final doom. Mr. Russell should be deemed, at least, an honest man for giving 'utterance' to his convictions; but what can be said of those who take the 'black' man by the hand with Joab-like grins, with hypocritical cant, with hollow and insincere professions, and then stab him under the fifth rib? Mr. Russell's pronounced antipathy to the 'black,' and blustering utterances of his hatred, as emanating from an open enemy, may be considered a blessing when compared with the insidious but odiously plausible professions of pseudo-negrophilists. They may attempt to throw dust in Governor Irving's eyes, but they cannot deceive an enlightened community, who are perfectly cognizant of their policy. Why, was it not the other day the Coolies demanded that in connection with their free settlement at Essequibo schools must be established? Forsooth! the elective members of the Court of Policy have convenient memories. I would remind our rulers, that as long as the people see that the Colony is in a position to expend thousands of dollars annually on immigration, extracted from the taxation of the people, they will never be cajoled into believing that the Colony is unable to educate their children, who expect to live and die in the Colony, and are not simply adventurers seeking a temporary field for the exercise of their talents. Why is it that so little was said about the two hundred thousand dollars to be abstracted from the Colony purse for immigration? Why was it that the matter was so lightly passed by? Is there no independent reformer in the Court? The time has come when this ancient form of government, the Court of Policy, and Combined Court also, should be swept away, and a more liberal form of representation and government be instituted in its place. A single chamber, half elective from a wider constituency than the present, and the other half nominees of the Crown, would be infinitely preferable to this present form of government."—*Daily Chronicle.*

CHAPTER XIII.

HOSPITALITY, COURTEOUSNESS, AND SOME RELIGIOUS AND NATIONAL CUSTOMS OF THE IMMIGRANT POPULATION.

1. There is a large number of people in the Colony, and very unfortunately among them some respectable and intelligent persons too, who look upon their fellow subjects the Indian Coolies as semi-savages, or semi-civilized barbarians. What can these poor heathens around them know? Simply nothing at all. They are an ignorant, illiterate people, come from a barbarous country. They are not so wise or clever as the Creole gentlemen and ladies, I mean of the labouring class of our people. According to their notion or idea of things in general, no ladies or gentlemen are to be found in any other country, or among any other class of people. All persons coming to the Colony from India are simply *Coolies* or *Motiyon*, porters, day-labourers, burden-carriers. "*A lady—black lady;*" "*a gentleman—a black gentleman;*" "*a woman—a white woman;*" "*a man—a white man,*" are expressions or epithets which often fall upon the ears of a stranger visiting the city of Georgetown, or the Colony of British Guyana. "*You, gentleman, with the crabs;*" "*You, lady, with the plantains;*" "*You black* (or *coloured*) *lady! You hear dis white woman* (or *white man*) *a-wanting of you,*" &c., are terms restricted in their application to the black Creoles, males and females. And when an Indian is addressed it is "*You Sammy;*" "*You Coolie,*" &c. However, there is no use contending about the terms and their limited application. I allow my Creole friends to enjoy their opinion in this respect! Why shouldn't there be "black gentlemen" as well as "black ladies?" Are they not addressed as "ladies" and "gentlemen" in public meetings? Of course they are! We have also in the city of Georgetown "Chin-chin ladies,"

a term applied not only to the natives of China, but even to the Creole paramours of male Chinese.

2. A very poor and unfavourable opinion is formed of the Hindus in general, not only by the ignorant class of people, but unfortunately by the educated classes also, from the ways and manners of the lower orders of the Indian Coolies around them. One may as well take the scum of the English people —the rude and unwashed throng—to form an opinion of the better educated and more refined natives of England. Not the lower orders, but the upper classes, are the people to whom we must look before we can form an opinion. Even among the Creoles of the Colony there are many well educated and refined persons, than whom a community can desire no better members. And so among the East Indian Coolies in the Colony, there are some who were never Coolies at all in their own country, but to better their circumstances they shipped themselves as such and came to the Colony to work on the sugar estates. I knew many gentlemen and gentlemen's sons in Australia who went out there from England, Scotland, and Ireland, not to trudge about the streets of Sydney, Melbourne, &c., with the hands in the pocket, but to work hard as labourers, and make an honest living, and better their temporal circumstances. Whatever may be the defects and blemishes seen by the people of the Colony in the Coolies around them, I have no hesitation in saying that I have found a large number of them to be a very hospitable and courteous people. They surpass every other nation in this respect, if not in anything else.

3. Among the ancient Europeans the rites of hospitality were regarded as under the immediate protection of the gods, of Jupiter especially, thence called the *Hospitable* (Xenios), and the people were taught to believe that the different deities resorted to the earth, in order to try the disposition of the different individuals, and were frequently entertained in the guise of strangers. Ovid, too, mentions the story of the metamorphosis of an extensive country into a lake, on account of its inhabitants refusing shelter or protection to Jupiter and Mercury, who appeared in the guise of strangers. Fables

similar in substance and intent are narrated and believed by the Hindu mythologists. It is narrated of *Anna-purna*, Parvati, that she in the character of *the goddess of abundance* (whom the Romans, it is worthy of notice, worshipped under a similar title, corrupting *purna* into *perenna*) and in the guise of a stranger applied for shelter, but was cruelly driven from the door of the parsimonious inhabitants of Cāssi (Benares). In like manner, one Māren of Ileiyānkudi had for a long time been in the habit of supplying all who came to him as guests with food: the Most High, for the purpose of trying him, permitted him to fall into extreme poverty. At this time Iswaren came in the middle of the night well drenched with rain in the form of a Jangamer (a religious person of the Saiva sect), and sought his hospitality. As Māren was totally destitute of all means of affording speedy assistance to the stranger, who was hungry, he went out, in the midst of darkness and rain, and, plucking a quantity of sprouting rice-seed, which had been newly sown, returned and delivered it to his wife, and, having no firewood to dress it, pulled down a part of his dwelling for that purpose, and placed the food (rice) thus prepared before the Jangamer. The god, who had requested food in this shape, greatly pleased at this action, resumed his proper form, appearing as the bull-borne Deity, and carried Māren of Ileiyānkudi with all his family to *Keilāsan* (the heaven of Siva). The Hindus have great faith in such tales, and they are always ready liberally to supply food and other necessaries to those who come hungry to them, in order that they may become illustrious guests of gods, and attain to eternal bliss. The Hindu Coolies of British Guyana, I am happy to say, are not in any degree behind their countrymen in India. They are hospitable, and are always ready to entertain strangers, guests, friends, relations, or neighbours, according to their power and means at command. If possible, they would very much wish to build public establishments called *Sāvadi* (from *Sā*, food, and *Adi*, foundation) and *Sattrum* (from the Sanskrit root *Sad*, sit or rest), for the daily supply of food and other necessaries to those who are strangers or visitors from a distance.

4. It is against the religion of the Vedas for a Hindu to

show himself inhospitable and uncourteous. Hospitality is the chief duty of the domestic order, and includes both the *reception of the stranger* and *guest*, which is a religious rite, and the free, full entertainment of ordinary guests, friends, relations, or neighbours. Hence the Hindus take great pleasure in erecting, for the accommodation and support of the pilgrim or traveller, the *travellers' bungalows*, or Sāvadies, or Sattrams. Many such public establishments abound in Southern India. These establishments differ from the inns and caravansaries, common in other countries of Asia, by invariably providing at their origin for the daily supply of food and raiment to strangers, more particularly to Brahmans, Pandārams, or Pilgrims, and Yogees. Sometimes also schools for teaching the Veda, or the languages, are attached to them. Besides these public charities the rite of hospitality, as a religious observance, is considered as fulfilled by occasional feasts given to religious persons according to the sect of the party. In addition to the public entertainments, the private ones are almost invariably connected with some religious solemnity, or with some circumstance the memory of which it is wished to retain, such as marriages, births, and deaths, the commemorative ceremonies to ancestors, appointments to public stations, or the readmission of a disqualified person, after the performances of the proper Prāyaschittam, or expiation, to full communion with his caste. In the last case, it becomes imperatively necessary on the part of the offender to give a public feast, and to invite all his friends, who had forsaken him, in order to eat with him. This act is the sign of the entire remission of his offence, and of his complete reconciliation with his fellow caste men. The following instance may perhaps, not inappropriately, illustrate this, though, as relating to manners rather than sentiments or opinions, it is somewhat foreign to the intention of this notice. The mother of a female child of the Brahman caste, who had been finally degraded for some crime, was inadvertently permitted by the family to retain and nourish her daughter for some time after her expulsion. This circumstance was, at first, overlooked, and in due time the girl was wedded to a respectable young Brahman. A few months after the marriage, the friends of this Brahman, coming to a knowledge of this blemish in the education of his wife, advised, or rather almost forced, him to put her away; but he was very unwilling to consent to this, for he was passionately fond of his wife. An assembly, therefore, of Sastris, learned in laws, usages, and ceremonial rites, was convened, from whom a favourable decision was obtained, and a mild prāyaschittam prescribed. A public feast was given by the young Brahman, to which most of his fellow caste men were invited, and the female was restored to all her social and conjugal rights, and was appointed to serve the water which is sipped from the palms of the hands while reciting a prayer, both before and after meals, the salt, and the pickles, of which all present partook.

5. Hospitality among the Hindus is not confined merely to friends and immediate strangers and neighbours. I remember some time ago witnessing an interesting circumstance of hospitality in the city of Georgetown. An Indian Coolie travelled on foot all the way from Berbice to Georgetown, with the intention of going across the river to the West Bank. He was much exhausted and tired from his long journey. He saw a well-to-do Hindu Coolie in Bourda—a shopkeeper—a perfect stranger to him. He, however, said to him, "Friend, I am on a journey, I am come to your house now, you must shelter and entertain me for a few days, and then I shall take my departure." He invited himself. The house was at once opened, and the stranger made comfortable during his stay with the shopkeeper. This circumstance threw some light upon the fact mentioned in Luke xix. 5, where the Saviour invited Himself to become the guest of Zacchæus. Cases of this kind often happen in British Guyana.

6. I have said enough on this subject. A few words on the courtesy of the Coolies now demand our attention. The Hindus are a polite and courteous people. The Hindu moralist expresses this virtue in beautiful language, and the following are a few of the stanzas translated into English:—

"The grace of fair humility, the grace
Of courteous words, do all far more adorn
Than do all other ornament."

"O wherefore useth he discourteous words
Who knows full well the sweets of courteous speech?"

"Discourteous speech, when courteous may be used,
Is like the sickly appetite which culls
Fruit immature, leaving the ripe untouched."

A cold observance of the forms of hospitality, without that kindness of manner and cheerfulness of temper from which social intercourse derives all its zest, is justly considered as destructive of its most essential quality, and as depriving the act of its beneficial effects on the relations of this life and the expectations of the next.

When a Hindu meets you on the road, or wishes to honour you with a visit, he comes near the house, and asks (*Sahib ghar men hai?*) whether the master is at home. Receiving an answer in the affirmative, he appears before you in a respectful attitude, and, bowing low, lifts his hand in a graceful sweep till the fingers touch the forehead, or sometimes, his arms outstretched, makes his *Salām*;* but some who have since their arrival in the Colony adopted the English costume, and all the children of Hindu parents born and brought up in the Colony, take off their hats and make a very polite bow, or touch the forehead with the fingers. Sometimes some of them make their *Sāshtāugams* and *namaskārams* by bowing and touching your feet and their forehead in three rapid successions, or in bending still lower, grasping your feet and placing their hand on the crown of their head. They are not wanting in thankfulness for kind acts done to them. "You are my father and mother;" *tum mêrâ mâ bôp-tâi tagappar-hain*—"You are my (*ratchagar*, or *baebâo*) saviour"—are the expressions of gratitude and thankfulness common among them.

7. It is indeed extraordinary that in so opulent a language as the Greek no term should have been found to express courtesy or politeness. Aristotle, on whose authority this fact rests, describes it as "the intermediate habit between

* *Salām*, *Salamun alaikun*, means, "The peace be on you." It is equivalent to "Good morning" or "Good evening," &c., and is identical with *Salem* mentioned in the Holy Scripture.

T

flattery and moroseness, between that disposition which inclines the feeble-minded in all cases to sacrifice their own opinions in deference to others, and that by which men are excited to contend for the mere sake of contention." (*Ellis.*) In all modern languages the idea is conveyed by many synonymes of various derivation and shades of meaning; but in no case liable to be compounded with either of the extremes, severity or rudeness. The Tamil, the genius of which is to hint rather than to define the signification of its words, selects generally a single idea to indicate a class or series; and the Tamilians accordingly comprehend under a phrase, expressive of their principal characteristic, *Inchol* or *Iniyakural, pleasing speech,* which admirably applies to acts of civility, meaning *courteous conduct, polite attention.* The highest expression of courteous adulation in the language is, Dēvarīr, which is the Sanskrit or Grandaic-Tamil term Dēva, *God,* declined in the second person plural, or the honorific singular, and literally signifies *Ye gods,* and is equivalent to "Your Majesty." The courteous manners of the Hindus in general, we have no room to question. In India, in the Colony, and in other places, the Hindus have been and still are, not an inhospitable and rude people, as some suppose, but a very polite people. The national courtesy is indicated by various idiomatic expressions, suited to the different classes of persons addressed. The languages of the East exceed beyond comparison those of Europe in minuteness of distinction and strength of hyperbole. Thus, if a Hindu in the Colony, or even in his own country, is asked, "*Are you well?*" he will reply, "*By your favour, Sir, I am well,*" or "*By God's grace and your favour, Sir, I am well.*" To one whom he wishes to praise he will say, "*You are religion incarnate,*" or "*You are a sea of excellent qualities.*" Similar complimentary expressions are also employed in directing letters. Such a style of courtesy is universal among the natives of India, and their languages admit of such expressions. To some, perhaps, it may appear as if the people had been taught to address their superiors in regular prescribed forms, but such is not the case. Even the most ignorant among them are familiar with such and similar expressions of courtesy or politeness. In contrast to them, many of us must hang our diminished heads.

8. As to the practice of giving and receiving presents among the Chinese, though very difficult for a foreigner to understand, the Chinaman thoroughly knows its consequence, and therefore cannot be actually deceived. The Chinese, like all other nations, like to make a grand show or parade when they wish to make presents to a friend or neighbour. Too frequently the supposed presents sent to a person or friend, are not meant to be kept or retained by the person to whom they are sent. For instance, one offers a present to another, secretly desiring him not to accept, saying, "You must take it, I brought it on purpose for you; if you do not accept it, I will think it very strange," &c. Sometimes if three or four (or more) articles are sent to a friend as presents, he must take only one, or send all back by the messenger to the sender with thanks. If the whole of the presents offered or sent be retained by the receiver or friend, he would be regarded by the sender of the presents and his family as deficient in good breeding, as destitute of politeness, or ignorant of the customs of society. When a Hindu Coolie, or Creole, or Portuguese, or any one else sends a present to a friend, he means it from his heart, and means well, and wants to cultivate his acquaintance and good opinion of him. Not so John Chinaman.

9. Among the courteous or polite customs of the East Indian population of the Colony, I may mention the following interesting circumstance, which will throw some light upon a similar custom referred to in Judges iii. 19. About ten years ago I received a letter from a Christian Indian from one of the West Indian Islands, with a request that I should make it my duty to see his relative in Demerara, who was well-to-do, and mention the matter to him personally, and bring the misunderstanding existing between them to an end. When I called to see the person referred to in the letter, I found him busily engaged transacting some business matters with some of his country people. A chair was offered to me on my entering his house, with a request that I should sit down and wait a little till he had finished his business with the people. I told

him, however, I was in a hurry, as I had to go elsewhere, and had a "secret" errand from a relative of his at a distance which I wanted to communicate to him. On hearing this the people at once walked out of the house, leaving the master of the house and myself alone. He (N—m) rose from his seat and requested me to follow him into his "bedchamber," which also was soon vacated, for his wife and children went out of the room, out of the house, into the yard. There in that room, "the secret chamber" of the master of the house, unheard by any other person, I told my errand contained in the letter above referred to, and left him with many salutations or *vandanams* on his part for the message delivered by me. This is another instance among many others from which we may learn that the Indian population by whom we are surrounded and with whom we come in daily contact are a class of people whose customs and manners throw a flood of light upon the Eastern manners and customs so frequently referred to or mentioned in the sacred Scriptures.

10. We may see on the forehead, arms, and hands of the Coolies, especially of the females, certain painted figures or representations and patterns of the most ancient art, called tattooing. All Orientals have a passion for this description of painting, and the women especially think that it heightens their beauty. Moses, who was an Oriental himself, instituted some such custom. He says: "And thou shalt show thy son in that day, saying, This is done because of that which the LORD did unto me when I came forth out of Egypt. And it shall be for a sign unto thee upon thine hand, and for a memorial between thine eyes;" or "for a token upon thine hand, and for frontlets between thine eyes." (Exod. xiii. 8, 9, 16.) Sometimes the Coolies—especially the Madras females and men—thus mark themselves as religious tokens, and each of these marks or paints has some idolatrous or superstitious signification. The process of imprinting these marks on the hands, arms, foreheads, legs, is painful, and yet the individual who desires to have these marks put upon him or her endures the pain calmly. I have seen this done both in India and in the Colony. A number of needles are bound tightly together in

the shape of the desired figure. The skin being punctured by these needles, certain mixtures of colouring matter are rubbed in, and the place is bound with a tight bandage. This is called *Patchei Kuttal.* This custom has become so universal, that even the Christian Hindus, and Europeans in India, have the operation performed on them.

11. There are certain other emblematical marks in use among the Indian Coolies of the Colony which need a little explanation. Parading through our streets may now and then be seen men and women with certain marks upon their foreheads, necks, and arms; but these paintings or marks do not make them look beautiful, nor are they intended to make them look ugly, and yet they cannot walk about the streets without them. I have often been asked by many of my respectable friends what these painted marks mean. Hinduism or Brahmanism, which is the most subtle, complex, and debasing system of religion ever put forth, and assumes Proteus-like a thousand shapes, has divided its votaries into different sects, devoted to the worship of particular deities. The principal of them are the *Seivás*, the worshippers of Sivā; the *Vishnuvites*, the worshippers of Vishnu; and the *Saktas*, the worshippers of the *Saktis*, *i.e.*, the wives or female associates of the Hindu Triad. Of the latter, Devi, the consort of Sivā, has by far the most numerous train of worshippers. Durga and Ganēsa, also, have their particular sects. The Hindus who wear the three horizontal red, white, or yellow marks or lines (parallel with each other) on their foreheads, are the worshippers of Sivā;* and those who have them in perpendicular direction but inclining together at the base like a trident, are the worshippers of Vishnu, and those who have one single dot, or one horizontal, or one perpendicular line on their forehead, are the worshippers of the Saktis. These marks do not point out their caste, as supposed by some, but

* In some parts of Southern India Brahmans who wear the three horizontal lines are daily ridiculed by the vulgar thus :—

"To the Sheep and Cow two horns (God has given).
To the Iyangra Brahman three horns (the devil has given)."

their religion, and indicate strong attachment to Paganism in preference to any other creed. And hence one of the first and most absolute requirements of a Christian convert in India, or in the Colony, is the removal of these marks of the devil, and the *sacred ashes*, made of cow-dung, with which they rub or besmear themselves.* This custom, universal among the natives of India, is the first and foremost which attracts a stranger's attention. And it was this custom, to a great extent, that first attracted the attention of the early Christian Missionaries when they gained a firm footing in India. Retiring into a *Choultry*, or Sāvadi, during the heat of the day, they would begin their discourse or address after this fashion: "I can see that you are people that do not know the true God, because the marks on your foreheads show that some of you are worshippers of Vishnu, and others of Sivā." The worship attached to Durga, Sivā, or Vishnu—the popular or favourite gods of the modern Hindus, is of recent date, and receives no countenance from the Vedas, and, indeed, there is no reference whatever to such a worship in the Vedas. Brahma, however, is represented as having four faces, and afterwards developed into a triune divinity—*tirumurthi*—composed of a creating power, *Brahma*; a preserving power, *Vishnu*; and a destroying power, *Sivā*. Though Brahma has no temples erected for his worship in a formal manner, he is still regarded as god, and worshipped as such. To Vishnu and Sivā endless temples are created—all possible forms and shapes throughout India, and from these two have proceeded endless *avatars*, or incarnations, or manifestations, all worshipped as gods. The Brahmans are the teachers or priests, *Gurus*, of the whole system. To them principally the people look for instruction in religious matters, &c. We

* This Hindu heathen custom of rubbing the ashes made of cow-dung, so prevalent in India and British Guyana, appears to be alluded to in Mal. ii. 3, where the prophet speaks of spreading dung upon their faces. It is remarkable also that in India and in the Colony gods are sometimes made of cow-dung. The Israelites, whilst travelling to the promised land, saw some gods of the heathen made of dung. The word in Deut. xxix. 17 translated "idols" is in the original "dung gods."

have in the Colony of British Guyana a few who call themselves Brahmans, who left India as emigrants to work on the sugar estates as Coolies, which they have never done, and never will do, so long as they can impose upon the credulity of their fellow countrymen with the supposed fact that, being *Gurus*, they dare not work on the sugar estates as Coolies. The laws of Manu tell the people that they must honour the Brahmans, no matter how bad, vicious, and ignorant they may be: they must almost worship them, and consider them as next, if not actually equal, to the gods. Even kings are warned not to provoke a Brahman to anger: "For," says the old law, "the Brahman could easily destroy his sovereign, his elephants, and everything belonging to him." The poorest people must cheerfully contribute something towards his support to secure his favour or goodwill, and hence a Brahman, whether at home in India, or abroad in British Guyana, among his countrymen, is not likely to want. Many of the planters or proprietors of sugar estates in the Colony perhaps are not aware that this is the principal reason or cause why so many able-bodied fellows do not work, and that these are the fellows who give them so much trouble, and prove themselves to be ringleaders, now and then, on the different estates. The Brahmans have often been soldiers, *sipahees*, not the Kshatryas, though they strictly belong to the soldier caste; and these Brahman soldiers, who are priests or teachers as well, lead a lazy, miserable life, and eke out a living from the hard earnings of the poorer but really working class of our immigrants. The Brahmans in the Colony I find are not high caste men, for these will not readily consent to leave their native land to go abroad, especially to such places as British Guyana, Trinidad, Jamaica, &c. I was very much surprised only a short time ago, to find in St. Lucia's Census Returns for 1881, that nearly all the Indian Coolies in that island were put down as Brahmans. If all were priests, where were the laity? Priests could not teach priests, and priests could not do any work on sugar plantations to support themselves with, for it is against their creed. I am sure it was a mistake made by the Census takers. As among the Hindus, so among the

Brahmans also, there are various castes of them who refuse to eat with one another, but then these castes are not the same as that described in the Shastras. These castes are only internal distinctions, each exhibiting a perceptible difference of character and appearance. Some of these Brahmans have had their minds enlightened since their arrival in Demerara, in regard to the truth and importance of the Christian religion, and a few of them have cast aside their sacred thread, *poonool*, or *Jano*, and the *poita*, the badge of their divinity, and have become Christians since their arrival in the Colony. John Bansalal is connected with Friendship Wesleyan Chapel; Thomas Deendial has removed from Georgetown to Berbice, and is connected with the Wesleyans there; whilst John Ganessa, with his wife, married in Georgetown Trinity Wesleyan Chapel, left the Colony in September last year (1881) for Calcutta, with a promise to return. There are some others of this class of immigrants connected with the Episcopal Church of England in the Colony. They are a very hard and difficult people to be got at, to make any impression for good on their minds. All the good impressions made on the minds of the bulk of the Indian Coolie population of the Colony, in favour of Christianity, are very easily caused to be set or thrown aside by these wretched impostors. Several of these *Gurus* have come to me, from time to time, with the hope of getting letters of recommendation or petitions written to the Government, praying for support to carry on their religious worship in the Colony. In every instance they were made to understand that the Government of the Colony being a Christian Government it could not and would not countenance, sanction, or give its aid or support to propagate or promulgate the erroneous and idolatrous doctrine and worship of Hinduism and Muhammedanism, while, at the same time, the Government of the Colony or the Christian Missionaries never compelled or forced any of the Hindu Coolies to become Christians.

CHAPTER XIV.

CASTE DISTINCTION AND OPPOSITION TO GOSPEL PREACHING AMONG THE HINDU COOLIES.

1. ONE of the most formidable barriers to the propagation of the Gospel among the Hindus in India is caste,—a word, the full import of which it is impossible for any European to understand—which not only makes them look upon the Christian religion with no favourable eye, but is the fruitful source of all the deep-rooted prejudices. "Caste is woven into the whole daily life of the Hindu, and forms by no means a small part of his very existence. The keeping of his caste is the highest virtue—the breaking of it, his greatest crime. A man may commit murder, theft, and a whole host of unnatural crimes, it matters not, if his caste is not broken; but if he takes food with a man of another caste, he is driven as a vagabond from his home and friends. He may lead a blameless life, his integrity may be unquestioned, his conduct may be unimpeachable; but let him violate a caste-rule publicly (privately, he may do it as much as he likes), and he is driven forth as unclean, as an *out-caste*." According to the Brahmanical teachings, "no person can receive him (the miscreant) into their houses, or hold any intercourse with him; every one agrees to cover him with ridicule, contempt, and disdain; to be seen with him would be deemed a crime worthy of reprehension; the woman to whom he was betrothed would not be allowed to marry him; all denounce him as the veriest vagabond, and his parents and friends must be the first to disown him, and shower curses upon his head." How great an amount of moral courage and firmness of mind must that man, whether in British Guyana or India, possess, who, with the certain prospect before him of losing his caste, yet dares to become a Christian! When Mr. North, for instance, was Governor of

Ceylon, some of the chiefs of the island actually refused to enter his carriage along with him, because the coachman was seated on the driving-box above them. This feeling of caste prejudice, however, is gradually disappearing in India through contact with Europeans and their descendants, and in Ceylon it is by no means so strong as it is in India. Even in British Guyana it is slowly, and yet surely, disappearing, for the people (the Coolies) are not so immediately and directly under the sway or influence of the priestly Brahmans.

2. The word *Jat* (which frequently denotes sex) is, however, considered by all classes of people in India to refer to the *distinction of caste*, and accordingly it has become a generally received opinion among the Hindus, that mankind was originally distributed into four distinct classes or species: the *Brahmans*, who sprang from the head of Brahma; the *Kshatryas*, from his arm; the *Vaisyas*, from his loins; and the *Sudras*, from his feet. Agreeably to this supposed origin, to the first was assigned the office of teaching and guiding; to the second, of ruling and bearing arms; to the third, the pursuits of commerce and agriculture; and to the fourth, subjection to the first three. The distinctions in caste, however, vary according to localities. In Ceylon the agriculturists belong to the highest caste, and the washermen (*dhobies*) to the lowest, being an employment universally despised, even the poorest natives of other castes objecting to wash their own clothes or garments. In British Guyana, however, Leila, who belongs to this caste, actually refuses to wash and iron the clothes of his fellow country people. He is a noble-looking man for a washerman, and some members of his family belong to the Wesleyan Methodist Church in the Colony.

3. At the present state of India it is impossible, however, to suppose for a moment, that the great bulk of the Hindu population is really descended from this scanty and polluted origin. The majority of the existing castes have nothing at all to do with the primitive four, or with the Shastras which describe them. In many cases they denote only the trades of their members, which, like political offices, usually become hereditary in India. There is a goldsmith's caste, a barber's

caste, and an oilman's caste; the weaver, washerman, and sweeper have their caste; even the aboriginal Shánárs of Tinnevelly (of whom we have many in the Colony) assume the appellation and make a caste for the cultivation of the palmyra (and cocoanut) trees. In these instances the caste is clearly a sort of guild or craft, only constituted by birth, and admitting of an apprenticeship from without. In other cases, especially in the Dakhan, caste is the acknowledged distinction of race or nation. The natives call themselves of the Malabar caste, the Gentoo caste, and so on. There is even a caste for thieves (Kallars), which probably represents some original race; and the Thugs, who worship Káli by assassination, call their fraternity a caste, though admitting Muhammedans into its numbers. In fact, the caste feeling is strongly shown by the Mussulman population throughout India; and (contrary to all religious theory) the Hindus assign to it a higher position in society than to some of their own inferior classes.

4. In the Colony, too, we have *Brahmans* from Calcutta and from the Dakhan, called *Bengali*, *Gentoo*, and *Tamil* Brahmans. They, however, do not belong to the highest class or rank of Brahmans of India; for the latter will not readily emigrate nor mix themselves with the lower classes or castes. One of our first converts in 1866 was a young Brahman of the *Gentoo* order, who had been acting like a priest on some of the estates in the Colony. We have also about twenty other castes acknowledged by the Hindu immigrants; and there are likewise some in the Colony who have come from the northern part of India, such as the "hill tribes," or puharrees, who acknowledge no caste whatever; they care nothing for the Hindu deities, and they have no idols or images of any kind. They simply believe in the existence of, and offer prayer to, "*Bwado Gosaee*," which in their language means the supreme God.

5. As observed above, caste presents more formidable resistance to the success of the Christian religion in India than even superstition itself. "Superstition," observes the Rev. Dr. Caldwell, Church of England Missionary (and now Bishop) of Tinnevelly, India, "loses strength and disappears as enlighten-

ment and civilization extend; but caste is so deeply rooted in the Hindu mind, that no amount of intellectual enlightenment compels it to quit its hold." As in India, so in British Guyana most of the Indian immigrants belonging to the upper classes are regular caste men; and though its influence on the minds of some of them is so slight as to present no serious obstacle to the Missionary, yet, on the whole, they are afraid to lose their caste, as appears from a circumstance which I shall mention presently. Our books are dreaded as devices to draw them into the Missionary's caste, which is by them called the Christian caste.

6. Although such a thing as caste is still observed by many, if not nearly all, of the converts or native Christians in India, and it so prevails that even Christian piety does not in all cases succeed in eradicating it, yet the Christian Ministers do everything in their power to put down this gigantic obstacle to the spread of the Gospel in India. It is also customary in that country for Hindu Christians—persons from different castes—to sit down together to eat the same curry and rice, prepared and served by men, some of whom used to count themselves of high caste, the Mission families also uniting with them. This is done both as a test of caste principle, and to promote kindly feelings toward each other. In British Guyana, and also in Trinidad, we have a few Hindu immigrants converted to Christianity who belong to different castes. The ex-Wesleyan Missionary, Dr. Horsford, some years ago put the converts to a similar test, and refreshments were partaken of by the Hindus joined by several other persons; and at the early Christmas service the Asiatic brethren assembled in the chapel. In a similar manner a few years ago several of the converted Coolies belonging to different castes, Calcuttians and Madrasees, used by appointment to meet in my residence in Georgetown, to eat and drink the good things of this life at my own expense, but which practice I had to discontinue for want of funds, as I could not afford to spend some thirty or forty dollars per annum, besides making provision for them on Sundays when they came to service from different estates. The quarterly gatherings of the Christian Coolies used to be

a season of great joy and gladness, and we partly realized the blessing pronounced in the 133rd Psalm—"Behold, how good and how pleasant it is for brethren to dwell together in unity!" Before their conversion to Christianity these Coolies would not have sat down together, to eat and drink, and to enjoy each other's company. But Christianity does what philosophy and science cannot!

7. About eighteen months after my arrival, one of the Hindu labourers in this Colony, belonging to the *Vellálan* caste, nearly lost everything he possessed for losing his caste by eating in a Pariah-man's house, but money alone enabled him to regain it. The following are the particulars of this circumstance extracted from my journal, dated May 31, 1863:—"A great crowd of Hindu labourers was already gathered. A high caste immigrant had lost his caste by eating in a Pariah-man's house, and they were assembled to settle this case. In their sight a great and horrible crime had been committed, and a great insult was also brought upon the culprit's fellow caste men and other higher caste people. The poor Hindu was surrounded by haughty men, ready, with one voice, to anathematize him, and put him out of society and existence by shameful, dreadful, and cruel treatment; but the power of life and death being withheld from them, they could not stone or whip him to death. Fortunate it was for the poor fellow that I made my appearance unexpectedly among the number, to allay their commotion, not by force of arms, but by soft words and sober talk. A solution of cow-dung was also ready at hand, to baptize him withal, as soon as he was condemned. I spoke to them about the folly of caste, appealing to their earliest religious works which do not teach such a doctrine, and finally told them that if they would not let the man go in peace, I should complain to the *Kumpanyár* or *Sircar* (Government authorities), which would bring them into serious trouble. They all heard, and, after half an hour's grumbling and loud talking, they agreed to let the man go. But the headman, who got up the affair, not being satisfied with this kind of treatment of the prisoner, said to the people, that if the *loser of caste* was to be readmitted into their society or caste, he must pay down a certain sum of

money to make a feast to the gods, to propitiate their favour and smile. The man consented to give them thirty dollars to regain his caste. He was then set at liberty and readmitted into the fraternity." An instance of a man having his tongue burnt with a gold pin or pen for losing his caste, may be mentioned; but this one instance is sufficient to give the reader an idea that caste distinction still prevails in British Guyana among the Hindu immigrants. And yet, as all the Hindus in the Colony have money (and money is their principal god), anything can be done for money. Caste once lost can be regained by money. I was glad to learn from the late Rev. W. O. Simpson's speech that the Brahmans in the Madras Presidency were getting to be wiser every day, and to find out that caste is all "bosh."

8. Loss of caste, as I have already stated, is, as a rule, accounted by the Coolies of British Guyana a most grievous dishonour, an unpardonable sin, and the inferior and spurious castes are equally sensitive in this point with the higher. The rules, too, which regulate the penalty are as capricious as they are irrational. A high caste Hindu labourer is defiled by eating in a Pariah-man's house, and another is defiled and takes the rank of a low caste by becoming a Christian, and yet it seems strange that in the railway carriage the Brahman, Kshatriya, Pariah, and Sudra are seen side by side, enjoying the comfort and economy of this mode of travelling to the different sugar estates without offence to their conscience. The black caste—*Kâlê* or *Karoon jât*—the Negroes, are, in the estimation of the Indian Coolies, people of the lowest or the most degraded caste, not fit to be associated with. They belong to *Ibliss*. And yet they come in contact with them in every possible manner, on the sugar estates, and in the villages. Caste distinction, I say, still prevails in the Colony, but its influence is very slight on the minds of the bulk of the Coolie population. Persons who are ignorant of the usages or customs of the Orientals around them in the Colony often arrive at the conclusion that because some of the Coolies eat, drink together, and sometimes intermarry (being only a provisional arrangement), they do not observe caste rules, and thus it becomes

extinct. This is a great mistake. The Vedas allow certain licences or privileges to persons leaving their native country for a distant land, which they readily avail themselves of. A woman of a low caste may be taken in a kind of marriage by a higher caste Hindu in British Guyana, but a high caste or respectable woman will not be given in marriage to a man who is a Chamar (cobbler), or any other inferior caste. All such temporary marriages hold good whilst they are in Demerara, but when they arrive in India there is an end to such marriages. The women go one way, and the men another way. Some of the more serious or thoughtful among the Coolies, however, inquire if there is really such a thing as caste, and (being open to conviction) when their inquiries are respectfully met, they go away perfectly satisfied. The question generally asked is, "How many castes are there, and if it is right for a man to give up his caste?" This question I have always answered in two different ways:—(1) There are but two *castes* in the world, male and female: these were the only two castes which God made in the beginning. Here the word *Jat* (generally translated, "caste") means "sex"; thus *An jât* or *purush jât*, and *Pen* or *stri jât*—male sex and female sex. (2) A second reply is—God, the Creator of mankind, has not made this distinction, for the Christian *Bêd* (religion) says that "God hath made of one blood the whole nation of men for to dwell on all the face of the earth, having determined the times before appointed, and the bounds of their habitation: that they might seek God, if haply they might feel after Him, and find Him." We may therefore conclude that the black man, the red man, and the white man are children of one common parent, and bow to the Divine Authority; that Eve was the mother of all the sons of men; that Shem, Ham, and Japheth were the three sons of Noah, and of them was the whole earth overspread, and hence we are all brethren of one family. Again, no uniform theory on this subject is to be found in the Shâstras. In the *Väyu Puràna* we learn, that there were no castes, orders, varieties of conditions, or mixtures of caste. The *Maha-Bharat*, after describing the castes by their colour, adds, in express terms, that "there is no distinction of castes: this whole world is formed of Brahma, it became separated into castes in consequence of works;" and one of the philosophers himself (whose writings the learned Hindus very much admire) has sung:—

"What, O wretch, is caste? is not water an accumulation of fluid particles? Are not the five elements and the five senses one? Are not the several ornaments for the neck, the breast, and the feet equally gold? What then is the peculiar quality supposed to result from difference in caste?" The Christian, or the follower of Jesus Christ, alone belongs to the highest and noblest caste in the world, and when a Hindu becomes a Christian, he does not lose his caste, but becomes a member of this great caste, and, in fact, gains a caste and a name in the family of heaven.

9. Caste is, indeed, a direful foe to all generous and noble feeling. It binds in chain of adamant, never easily broken, a large portion of our fellow creatures of like passions with ourselves, saying to them loudly but firmly, "Ye proceeded from the feet of Brahma; ye are created for servitude." Our blessed Saviour mentions a very striking fact in the tenth chapter of St. Luke, which is full of instruction. While the generous and noble-hearted Samaritan who bound up the bleeding sufferer is strongly recommended and held out as a pattern to some, the proud, presumptuous priest, and the priest-like Levite, who would let the poor sufferer die of his wounds, are condemned, as a warning to others. A Brahman would sooner see a Sudra, or any one else, die than give him food, or administer relief, if, in so doing, he must touch the body or clothes of the despised and rejected Nazarene.

10. The golden rule of our blessed Saviour—"Whatsoever ye would that men should do to you, do ye even so to them," should be written in letters of gold on the door-posts and on the walls of every dwelling of the Hindus. Caste, I say, is a serious evil; and it is this cursed, horrible thing that prevents the Christian teacher from gaining that free and friendly intercourse with the Hindus so very necessary for the spread of the "truth as it is in Jesus." All Europeans, and other foreigners, are considered by them as belonging to the lowest

class or caste, and are, therefore, stoutly forbidden that social intercourse which secures an occasion for giving a personal direction to his public instructions. A beef-eater is detested and abominated by them, and counted a Mlech. A high caste Sepoy in India has been known to throw away his meal to the dogs and to the birds of the air, because the space which he had cleared for cooking it was defiled by the shadow of his European officer accidentally passing by. A Miss Monelle, an American lady physician in Lucknow, found herself in one of the zenanas belonging to the Nawab. The Begum was very ill, but Miss Monelle dared not practise till permission was given. The Nawab asked the lady physician if she could not relieve the Begum without medicine. The lady could not promise to do so. "Will you promise, then," said the Nawab, "that the medicine will positively cure her?" This again Miss Monelle could not do. Then fell from the lips of the Nawab a final sentence which was twofold: a sentence for the doctor, of bitterness, for the patient, of death. "To take medicine from a Christian would break caste, and since you will not promise to cure her, she must die." This young and beautiful creature died of caste. On another occasion a woman of sixty, dying with chronic dysentery, actually refused to take medicine from the hand of Miss Lore, another lady physician. The old woman would not risk her caste. Not one drop of liquid from impure hands should pass her lips. A single pill she did accept, but never another. She died of caste. But fortunately such things as these do not occur in Demerara. And as the Hindus are, by the Providence of God, permitted to sojourn in this country of Bibles, Christian Sabbaths, and Christian Ministry, they will gradually "cease to do evil, and learn to do well." They will get more and more enlightened as the light of the Gospel breaks upon them, and they will learn that there is no truth in their human institutions, which only tend to ruin them. May God hasten this time!

11. The question might be asked, and indeed has been asked by some: Are India and Ceylon the only countries in the world where caste distinction has existed for so many

centuries? Are there no other countries where it did not exist some time or other? Does not the Bible seem to countenance this distinction of caste among the people of the earth, &c.? If we turn to the Bible, the Sacred Scriptures, or the *Shastras* or *Bêd* of the Christians, we find therein stated, that in the antediluvian world, though the record is brief, there was a division made of families according to the occupations or professions pursued by them. We have these seven classes specified:—(1) Agriculturists, Gen. iv. 2; (2) Shepherds, Gen. iv. 2; (3) Citizens, Gen. iv. 17; (4) Nomads, Gen. iv. 20; (5) Herdsmen, Gen. iv. 20; (6) Musicians, Gen. iv. 21; (7) Artificers, Gen. iv. 22. Cain and Abel, the two sons of Adam, were divided in their occupation or calling, for Cain was a tiller of the ground (agriculturist), and Abel was a keeper of sheep (shepherd). The occupational and professional distinctions did not sever the brotherhood, the family tie, as the Hindu caste system does, and is calculated to do. These distinctions merely show that mankind were, and are, dependent upon one another: the artificer could not clothe himself with the metals, nor could the musician subsist upon the mere melody of his instruments, &c. The only distinction marked out in the Bible, bearing on the subject, probably, is that which speaks of the *moral* and *religious* condition of the people —"the sons of God," on the one side; and "the daughters of men," the children of an evil generation, on the other. We have also the expressions "rich and poor," equivalent to patricians and plebeians, but these social or "caste distinctions," if I may be allowed to use the expression, have nothing whatever to do with the perversions of corrupt minds to suit their own ideas, nor do they in the least countenance caste in the sense in which it is generally understood by Hindus and others. Caste makes mankind to belong to different species. Caste has existed in India and Ceylon for several centuries, and every one knows the mischief it has done. It is the system of caste, with its terrific denunciations against all who dare to abjure the national faith, and attach themselves to the creeds of strangers and foreigners, which hinders the people from becoming Christians even in their temporary home, the land of their adoption, British Guyana; and it is this system of caste among the Hindus which prevents the unity of action essential to the success of any enterprise, and which gave free scope to foreign invaders to have their own way in India. The caste of India has been, and still is, very different to that which existed among the Egyptians, Colchians, Iberians, Medes, Persians, Etrurians, and even among the Peruvian and Mexican Indians of the New World. The Egyptians had the power to change their caste, which is impossible among the Hindus. The Chinese also have a kind of distinction between the shape and size of the feet of women which constitutes a caste among them. In England, too, among the Saxons the three classes of society were strongly divided by the law of caste that no marriage could take place between persons in the different ranks. Nobles married nobles. They were extremely jealous of their race; and the severest penalties prohibited intrusions of one rank into the other. Happily these dark days of differences, distinctions, and prejudices are passed away. There is no caste, strictly speaking (unless I make the "Lords" and "Commons," the "Patricians" and "Plebeians," two castes), in England now. Even in British Guyana and the West Indies, where there was so much caste or prejudicial feeling against the innocent and greatly wronged natives by the opulent race, it is now fast dying out. In Demerara especially moral and religious character, educational advantages, good training, &c., are of little or no account, but persons possessing hard cash, lands, houses, &c., no matter what their colour or complexion or nationality, are by money-hunters sought for, and their company courted. Money puts an end to all prejudices.* Not so, however, in India among the Hindus.

12. In the previous chapter I have made some remarks about the Brahmans in the Colony, and the secret way in which they try their utmost to oppose and set aside the teaching and preaching of the Christian Missionaries to the Coolies. Besides these Brahmans we have some others in the Colony,

* See Chapter V., Number 5.

who, on certain occasions, act as priests, or *Gurus*, or *Pujaries*. They are more generally known under the epithet "COOLIE PARSONS." These "Coolie Parsons" pay their monthly, quarterly, half-yearly, and yearly visits to the different sugar estates and Coolie villages; and when they do, it is to perform some religious ceremony or service, offer some sacrifice, &c. They get large sums of money given them by the people whom they visit. I remember, on one occasion, at a sacrificial service held one Sunday forenoon on Plantation Farm, the Coolies raised the sum of one hundred dollars to give the officiating priest for his religious services to them that day. On another occasion, a similar service was conducted by one of these Coolie Parsons on one of the East Coast sugar estates, and the people readily and cheerfully raised about sixty dollars, which they gave the priest. In India, however, the *Gurus* or Hindu priests travel in great state; and receive large contributions from their disciples. One of the late Rajahs of Tanjore—in the Presidency of Madras—is said by Buchanan to have given his Guru or spiritual adviser 250 pagodas, or four hundred and forty-one dollars and twenty-five cents (£91 18s. 6½d.), when that personage honoured him with a visit. Such high caste Brahman Gurus will never condescend to cross the dark waters to come to Demerara. I knew a young Brahman some ten years ago on Pln. Ruimveldt, East Bank of Demerara, whose name I cannot remember just now. He provided himself with a copy of the Hindui New Testament, which he used in the place of Ramayanam, or the Bedas, and read from it to the people—his disciples especially—and performed the different religious ceremonies according to his country's custom. I often used to have interesting conversations with him on the book he possessed and the religion that book taught. He was a good man in his way, and a great admirer of the life of Christ and the religion taught by Him, but he was afraid to abandon his ancestral religion, and make open confession of Christianity. One thing, however, I did not approve of in him, and that was, whilst reading out of his Hindui New Testament to the people, whenever he came to the name "Jesus," "Christ," or "Jesus Christ," he substituted

"Ram," "Krishn," or "Ram Krishn." He had received some instruction in Calcutta in the English language from one of the Wesleyan Missionaries. What became of this young Brahman I cannot tell. Probably he has left the Colony and returned to India, as he did not care to live or remain away from his home and friends. Baldeo, another immigrant, belonging to the Brahman Caste, who has been in the Colony some fourteen years, has carefully read both the Old and New Testaments in the Hindi language, and is convinced in his mind that Hinduism or Brahmanism is false, that the Brahmanical teaching about caste is not true, for the Christian Shastras plainly show that in the beginning of the world Parameswar created only two persons from whom all nations of the earth are descended, that the avatars or incarnatians of Krishn were utterly useless, and no good whatever has resulted from any of his incarnations, and that the Christian Bêd is the only Satya Bêd which is destined to root out or destroy the various forms of religion in India and become the one only true religion of the world. He has no particular desire to return to India, as he has no friends there who would care to see him. He would like to become a Christian, but not just now. I have conversed with him several times on his delay in the matter, but, alas, I find he lacks moral courage. The work of a Christian Missionary to the heathen Hindus, whether in India or British Guyana, or elsewhere, is indeed most trying, discouraging, and difficult. He labours hard, he exerts an influence for good, he makes some favourable impressions by faithful and plain preaching upon his hearer's mind, he hears expressions of approbation in regard to the doctrines of the Christian religion, and yet in ninety-eight cases out of one hundred he is doomed to disappointment. I, however, trust that Baldeo will ere long see the necessity of altogether abandoning his ancestral creed and making an open confession of Christianity.*

* Since this was written and published in the *Colonist* newspaper, Baldeo changed his mind all at once, and left the Colony in the ship *North* in August, 1882, for India.

13. The pride of the Hindu infects not merely the higher castes but every caste. From the highest to the lowest the same spirit is manifested—"Stand by thyself; . . . . for I am holier than thou." The Coolies as a whole look upon the Europeans and their descendants in the Colony as well as in India as *Jati-héen*, persons void of caste. Closely connected with this is their prejudice against the "Cross of Christ." It is to them, as it was to the Greeks, "foolishness." And hence it is not an easy matter to convert a Hindu to the Christian faith. Preaching to our Indian immigrants is not an easy work. I believe all our Indian Missionaries experience this. Our hearers are of almost every variety of character and disposition. Some are so blindly attached to their creed, that if an argument is brought against it, they at once raise the charge of blasphemy, and substitute invective for argument, and passion for reason. Others, with less bigotry and a cooler temperament, are equally pugnacious. From the beginning to the end of our preaching they are on the look-out for objections. It is not indeed difficult to secure sometimes smaller and at other times larger congregations to hear what the preacher has to say, but it is almost impossible to convince the hearers of the folly of their idolatry, castes, and superstitions, and to impress their hearts with the truths of Christianity. Their minds are full of errors, and their mouths are quick to utter everything which is against the doctrines of Christianity in support of their own system of religion. They raise difficulties where ordinary people fail to perceive any, and wrangle over them when they have nothing more to say than what has been said a dozen times before. Some who appear quiet, earnest, and patient listeners without servilely acknowledging the truth of statements that do not at once commend themselves to their understandings, freely assent to all that their reason approves, allow it its due weight and value, and with Berean nobility of mind show themselves ready to inquire "whether these things be so," and sometimes honestly enough tell me in a straightforward manner, that they shall not embrace Christianity. "Walk in the religion and caste of your forefathers," is their favourite proverb.

14. In preaching to the Coolies, whether on sugar estates, in the yards, villages, or in town, publicly, in large numbers or in small numbers, or privately in their houses, we (that is, myself, the Missionaries of the Anglican Episcopal Church, and the Missionary of the United Presbyterian Church) meet with endless objections brought before us again and again by the same people, who had received answers on former occasions. The objections of course are ridiculous, and in order that my reader may know the nature of them, I shall now place before him a short list of these objections extracted from the *Wesleyan Missionary Notices*:—

(1) "'Where is *your* God? Have *you seen* God? *Show* us your God, and then we will believe your words. Is not the same God living in the bodies of men, beasts, birds, and everything? Who is the author of both good and evil? If God did not wish some persons to go to hell, why did He make them? We worship the idols because we believe that the all-pervading God is existing in them. Show me in what part of the body the soul abides. What does the soul do when you are sleeping? How did sin come?' or literally, 'Who made the sin? Has man the liberty of committing sin? There is nothing in the power of man. All the words you utter would be highly acceptable, if the name of Jesus were only omitted; we will then take you as our *gurus*. We are delighted to hear your preachings about God, but the word Jesus poisons the whole. Have *you* got *your sins* pardoned? Are *you* quite free from sin? If not, why should *we* hear the words of a fellow-sinner? If you say that we should not love the world, and the things therein, why did you not strip off your dress, and give up every pleasure in the world? Are you united with God, *i.e.*, one with Him? Can you make a black dog white? How could a man live if he did not lie? Is it right to forsake our own father and take another in his stead? Is it proper to receive the new religion, leaving our own? Have you seen heaven and hell? Nobody knows about the world to come. What will you be in your next birth? Why did God forbid Adam to eat of the fruit, if He knew that Adam would eat it? If men are not governed and rewarded by the merit and demerit of a former birth, why are some wretchedly miserable, while others are extremely happy? If the Creator is just and good, why are some created blind,

and deaf and dumb, &c.?' By these they mean to refute God's omniscience, existence, justice, &c.

(2) "On another occasion a discussion took place between a Brahman and the preacher; the substance of it is as follows:—

"A Brahman sat with us and inquired, 'Why do you tell us to forsake our gods?' 'What gods?' I asked. 'Our gods are,' replied he, 'Narainswamy, Narasimhaswamy,' &c. 'Have they,' asked I, 'human bodies and natures, that they may be called by such names? and have they divinity to be reckoned as gods?'

"*B.* 'If our parents have worshipped such gods, ought we not also to imitate them?'

"*P.* 'If they have done right consistently with the will of God, you ought to and must imitate them; but if they have done anything contrary, you should follow the will of God, rather than your parents. His will is revealed to you: you must forsake your idols.'

"*B.* 'What is the reason for doing so?

"*P.* 'If you kindly give attention to my words, I will just explain to you the four following reasons:—

"'1st. Idolatry is against the commandment of God;

"'2nd. It does not and cannot exhibit the nature and attributes of God;

"'3rd. It is the mother of every vice; and

"'4th. It brings the fearful curse of God upon all its believers, both in the present world and in the world to come.'

"To prove the last point I refer to the destruction of many of the ancient countries, such as Babylon, Nineveh, &c., and the present villages and towns.

(3) "A discussion followed on caste. One of the Brahmans asked whether caste was a lie. A reply being given in the affirmative, he appealed to the Shāstras. A few quotations from the Shāstras, proving that they contain false doctrines and contradictory statements, inflamed the ire of the boasting Brahman. He affirmed loudly, not in the best of tempers:—'You Pádres may say what you please, and convince the ignorant of our nation of the untruthfulness of our sacred books: but never will you be able to get us to believe that caste is of man's invention. God Himself made men Brahmans, Kshatriyas, Vaishyas, and Shudras, from His face, arms, thighs, and feet.' On being told that God is a Spirit, and consequently without bodily form, even according to the teaching of the Shāstras, he left us, saying to the people,

'Don't listen to them.' In the evening we preached in the Petta to a large congregation of Hindus and Mussulmans. My discourse was founded on 'Search the Scriptures;' the *unity* of the Divine nature, the duty of all men to worship the *one* God, and the necessity of escaping from *one* hell, and of winning *one* heaven, being topics dwelt upon for a few minutes. A Brahman, seeing the drift of my remarks, called out, 'Don't you see the Pádre will tell you that there is only one true Shāstra? God is One, all must serve Him; there is one hell, and there is one heaven. Don't you see that from these truths the Pádre will infer that there is only one Véda?' And, turning to the Mussulmans, he said, 'Off with you, your Koran is false.' And, addressing his own people, 'The four Védas, six Shāstras, and eighteen Purānas, are lying fables. Christ's Véda is the true one.' Whilst the Brahman was thus talking, we continued to preach. Finding that he could not succeed in making us cease from proclaiming the truth, he remarked personally to me, 'Let us talk together on the Hindu Shāstras.' I told him that I should be glad to do so, if he would listen to my sermon first. He consented. My sermon being finished, he said, 'You have anticipated all the questions I intended to ask respecting the true Véda, and have shown us that inasmuch as the Supreme Being is one, and our Shāstras teach us that there are three gods,—Brahma, Vishnu, and Shiva; that, inasmuch as God is eternal, and our Shāstras teach that the triad, though not eternal, are gods; that, inasmuch as God is holy, and our Shāstras teach us that He is the Author of sin, I agree with you in saying that they are false, Salám.'

✓ (4) "The Rev. F. De W. Ward, in his *India and the Hindoos*, mentions the following incident:—'A Missionary in Bengal, being asked by a philosophical Brahman, "What do you preach here?" replied, "We teach the knowledge of the true God." "Who is He? I am God," said the Hindu. "I thought," said the Missionary afterwards, "that it would be an easy matter to confute him, but I soon discovered my mistake." "This is very extraordinary," said I, "are you then almighty?" "No," he replied, "if I had created the sun I should be almighty, but I have not." "How can you pretend to be God if you are not almighty?" "This question shows your ignorance," said he; "what do you see here?" pointing to the Ganges. "Water." "And what is in this vessel?" at the same time pouring out a little into a cup. "This is water likewise." "What is the difference between this water and that of the Ganges?" "There is none." "O, I see a great difference: that water carries ships, this does not. God is almighty; I am only a part of the Godhead, and therefore I am not almighty; and yet I am God just as these drops in the cup are real water." "According to your representation God is divided into many thousand portions; one is in me, and another is in you." "O," said the Brahman, "this remark is owing to your ignorance. How many suns do you see in the sky?" "Only one." "But if you fill a thousand vessels with water, what do you see in each?" "The image of the sun." "But if you see the image of the sun in so many vessels, does it prove that there are a thousand suns in the firmament? No! there is only one sun, but it is reflected a thousand times in the water. So likewise there is but one God, but His image and brightness are reflected in every human being." The Missionary, instead of stopping to point out the falsity of the comparison, preferred trying to touch his conscience. "God," he continued, "is holy, are you holy?" "I am not; I am doing many things that are wrong, and that I know to be wrong." "How, then, can you say that you are God?" "O, I see," said the Brahman, "that you need a little more intellect to be put into your head before you can argue with us. God is fire; fire is the purest element in the creation; but if you throw dirt upon it, a bad odour will arise; it is not the fault of the fire, but of that which is cast upon it. Thus God in me is perfectly pure, but He is surrounded by matter. He does not desire sin; He hates it; but it arises from matter." In this way the conversation' (says Mr. Ward) 'continued long, but at the end the Missionary found that he had made but little progress in convincing his opponent.'

(5) "A man met me in the neighbourhood of Lacytown one afternoon, and said, 'Sir, if your God be true, why has He made one rich and another poor? You go about like gentlemen, eating, drinking, and having much to enjoy, and we are poor hard-working men.' This is either a profound question or a trifling one in the mouths of foolish men. It was the latter, in this instance, for the persons in whose hearing this question was asked were those who assumed that if they embraced Christianity it must be for some material benefit. The only reply to such is a question of the same genus. I said, 'Can you tell me, Sir,' (pointing to a cocoanut-

tree in the yard) 'why God has made cocoanuts to grow on this tree and not mangoes?' He looked at me, and then at the people, and remarked, 'I cannot answer that question.' I added, 'Neither can I reply beyond this, that God made it so. It is a part of His wise beneficent arrangement. The potter makes out of the same lump of clay vessels of honour and dishonour. The clay has no more right to say to him, "Why hast thou made me thus?" than we, poor ignorant, vile creatures, to ask our true Merciful Almighty Creator.' . . . . Another man asked me, how old the Christian religion was which I preached, and whether the other religions professed by Hindus now prevailing were not very ancient? I replied by asking whether he would eat the fruit of a poisonous tree because it was old, in preference to the newly-grown sugar cane. A third inquired what (temporal) benefit would those derive who embraced Christianity? I quoted a common proverb among them, 'Is a reward needed for eating sugar cane?' Another man asked me, 'What is the difference between your religion and ours? You have pictures and images in your church; you burn lights, and we do the same.' I gave him to understand that I was a Protestant and not a Papist. One can well imagine the reasons why so many Coolies find their way to the Romish Church, and take their children with them."

Such are the people I have to labour among, and contend with. At times my heart faints, and I am constrained to exclaim, "With men this is impossible, but with God all things are possible!" The same God who has blessed the efforts of His servants to drive away the heathen darkness to *nirwana* from Fiji, and such other places, shall, in due time, do the same in British Guyana.

CHAPTER XV.

THE VARIOUS TRADES, OCCUPATIONS, OR PROFESSIONS OF THE IMMIGRANTS AND NATIVES OF THE COLONY.

1. Although "caste like a deadly poison" rankles in the heart of every Hindu, yet the *Brahman*, the *Kshatriya*, the *Vaisya*, and the *Sudra*, with various sub-divisions under each general class, are freely permitted to accumulate wealth. The following from the Tamil Version of the Barodam will show by what modes they are allowed to accumulate wealth :—

"The herds of kine should by skilful management be protected from hunger; those employed in servile duties should discharge them with fidelity, and, not neglecting the orders of their superiors, should in all their conduct avoid deceit and falsehood: these occupations will give gold, jewels, and ornaments, success, long life, fame, pleasure, virtue, the delights of love and other enjoyments, and, besides all here enumerated, will afford stores of rice and all other grain: these are the modes in which the four castes may, in the practice of their duties, accumulate wealth." "Of whatsoever caste or employment a man may be, he should accumulate wealth without swerving from virtue; with his wife and his kinsfolk, he should perform with zeal the prescribed duties towards the gods and towards his ancestors; to his occasional guests, after they have entered his respectable dwelling, he should distribute food with kindness, and, having paid due attention to all others, he should take his own meal; above all things he should be conspicuous for never coveting the wife or the wealth of another. These rules apply equally to all the four castes."

And what do the Hindu Coolies belonging to the different castes in the sugar-growing wealthy Colony of British Guyana? Treating with the greatest indifference the above rules, they both by fair and foul or false means accumulate wealth, sport their gold watches and chains, and literally cover their wives and daughters from head to foot with different kinds of ornaments, and when they leave the Colony for their native home —India—carry away large sums of money, and astonish their friends on their arrival there. "*Tirei Kadal Odiyum tiravyan tedu*," *i.e.*, "Go even on the tossing sea, and search after riches." So Avvey, a woman of great learning, has said. And this is being religiously and scrupulously obeyed by nearly all the Hindu Coolies in the Colony.

2. All the Immigrants in the Colony are of course looked upon as Coolies or day labourers, and so they are, for on their arrival they are expected to go and work in the cane fields with their shovels, hoes, and cutlasses, which they readily do, thinking that it is their *ta lei ezhuttu* or *ta lei vidi*, *i.e.* destiny. In their own native land they were doctors or physicians, clerks, schoolmasters, teachers, sirdars, shop or bazaar keepers, etc.; but these caste or trade distinctions they are compelled to lay aside for a time in British Guyana, and turn out with a good will to do the work expected of them by their employers who are *no caste people*. My reader must remember that the different trades professed by the Hindu Immigrants have direct and immediate reference to the existing castes in India; thus, one who belongs to the doctor's caste or profession dares not in his country think or presume of becoming a lawyer; a person belonging to the lawyer's caste dares not become a clerk; a person belonging to the merchant's caste or trade dares not become a doctor; a person belonging to the dhobi or washerman's caste dares not presume to become a schoolmaster, etc. Our Coolies try as much as possible to keep up the same distinctions in the Colony also, especially after they have completed their term of service on the sugar estates, when they are free to leave them and go wherever they please. I shall now mention a few of the trades or occupations of the Indian Coolies in the Colony, with some remarks upon each:—

(1) Doctors.—India abounds with these empirics and quacks, and some of them are found in Demerara also. According to Hindu custom and notion a man belonging to the *doctor's* caste can be nothing else than a doctor or a *Veidhya* all the days of his life; and he is supposed to know all the

different kinds of diseases in the world and be able to cure them. Be he learned or ignorant, he must be always ready to give suitable medical advice and directions to those who apply to him. Dr. Royle says that the knowledge of medicine among the Hindus is more ancient than the Greek. Their medicinal preparations are chiefly compounds of herbs, of which an immense number are employed; hence physic, decoction, and other medicines obtained from the bark, wood, roots, fruits, flowers, of different plants or trees, are freely used in all cases. The native doctors know too well the use of minerals, particularly mercury, and boast of being able to prepare it better than Europeans, and profess that when their prepared mercury is taken in small doses monthly along with sulphur it renews youth. They believe that sulphur and mercury, mixed in various proportions, are the base of all metals. The homœopathic system of medicine, a supposed modern invention of the Germans, has been known and acted upon from the earliest period, both in India and Ceylon. Dr. Davy says, as they have a horror of dead bodies, and object to dissections, they know nothing of anatomy, but practise cupping and bleeding, and amputate with a knife heated to a dull red, a method formerly practised in Europe. According to the physiology of the Hindus there are in the human body 72,000 pulses, the three principal of which are *the windy*, *the bilious*, and *the phlegmatic pulse*, 4,448 bones, and 4,448 diseases of various kinds, with 35,000,000 of hairs on the human body. The treatise called *Janma-Chakra*, by *Nandi-dêvar*, gives the details of this system. Peacock flesh, among the Hindus, is considered a remedy for contraction of the joints. Bezoar stones, a smooth, glossy, dark green concretion, found in the stomachs and gall-bladders of animals, commonly in monkeys', are in great repute all over India and Ceylon as an antidote to poison. In cases of fever fasting from one to ten days is the remedy recommended. Medicine and entertainment, the Hindus say, are only for three days, that is, during three days a medicine is to be taken in order to know its effects, and a guest in like manner may remain three days in a family without offending the rules of hospitality. A patient, generally speaking, is never bled, for the life is in the blood. In fact the doctor and the patient depend as much upon charms and prayers for restoration, as upon physic and decoction. The physician expects to receive his fee before prescribing, which varies according to the ability and circumstances of the patient. The following recipe from *Agastyar*, a learned native physician of Southern India, may not be uninteresting to those who are suffering from blindness: "The tusk of a swine, the breast bone of a cock, silver, and the claw of a tiger are to be rubbed and mixed together with honey; this mixture, put in the eye of a blind man, will enable him to see the little star in the north, *Arundadi*, near the Great Bear, *i.e.*, he will recover his sight." Several funny stories or anecdotes are current among the Coolies of the Colony, showing the skill and cunning of the native physicians of India. One is: A certain man, having a pain in the stomach, went to a *davâji-sahib*, and said, "For God's sake, doctor, give me some physic, otherwise I die from a pain in the stomach." The physician asked him what he had eaten that day. The man replied, "Merely a piece of burnt bread." On hearing this, the doctor said, "Let me look at your eyes;" then, having called his disciple, said, "Bring me the medicine for the eyes." The sick man, on hearing this, screamed out, "O, doctor, is this a time for your joking? I am dying from a pain in the stomach, and you talk of medicine for the eyes; what connection is there between medicine for the eyes and a pain in the stomach?" The doctor replied, "I wish, in the first place, to make your eyes sound, for it is evident that you are unable to distinguish between black and white, otherwise you would never have eaten burnt bread."

I have not only seen Hindu *davâji-sahibs* or *veidhyas* in the Colony, but I have also seen Chinese and Obeha doctors who have succeeded in making a living. Of the Chinese doctors one used to live up the East Sea Coast at Plaisance Village not many years ago, and there are two or three still in George Town who continue to discharge their professional duties among their countrymen. I remember a circumstance which transpired in Australia whilst I was there in the year 1855, in connection with the death of a Chinaman who had been visited by a Mongolian M.D. in the earlier stage of his illness. At the post-mortem examination some interesting facts were elicited which the reader will see for himself in the following account, which I give entire as published in the *Melbourne Argus*. The same kind of Chinese doctors we have in British Guyana, who need looking after by those who know their profession too well:—

"CHINESE PRACTICE OF MEDICINE.

"Whatever claims the Celestials may have to earlier information and enlightenment on many of the arts and sciences, that of medicine does not appear to have been sedulously or successfully cultivated. We of course were previously aware that Chinese doctors resided amongst their countrymen, and gathered their fees as diligently as their Caucasian brethren, but as to what their mode of practice might be, or whether it in any manner approaches that of the duly qualified, we could only guess. Some light, however, has been thrown on the subject at an inquest held on an unfortunate Chinaman on Friday last. There were no suspicious circumstances about the death, which occurred from natural causes, or rather from what the medical man who made the post-mortem examination termed 'water on the chest,' but the information elicited on the occasion from a Chinese doctor, who attended the deceased in the earlier stage of his illness, as to Chinese practice, is worth recording. We may observe that this was not brought out in evidence at all, but was voluntarily communicated in reply to questions from a European medical man, who had occasion to be present. It may be relied on as strictly correct, and not furnished for the purpose of ridicule or deception, the source from which it emanates rendering such impossible.

"The first question put to the Chinese Esculapius was respecting the examination necessary to qualify a medical man, and to entitle him to practise in China, and the reply was that no examination whatever was needed, the only condition being that every aspirant to medical skill should serve three years with a Chinese doctor, when he received a certificate, and could follow in the footsteps of his tutor without further trouble. As to dissecting, or acquiring any knowledge of anatomy, that was unheard of, the Chinese idea being that the sooner corpses are disposed of the better, scientific study notwithstanding. Their surgical practice appears to be on a par with their anatomical research; for if this member of the Chinese surgical and medical profession is to be believed, it is customary, in case of fracture, to let nature take its course, and amputations are unknown, the only remedial means adopted being an attempt to truss the limb or limbs into shape, with or without bandages, we did not learn, and then trust to chance for the cure. As a matter of course, in case of compound fractures requiring amputation, the patient dies, and therefore wooden legs must be an unknown institution in the Flowery Land. In pursuing the inquiry, it was asked by the examiner on this occasion what the uses of the heart were, and what position did it occupy. The Mongolian M.D. pointed to the centre of the chest as its situation, and explained that 'it was a thing for thinking,' that a man having a good heart 'would be able to do his work well,' and that on the goodness and health of this organ depended a capacity for making bargains, or whether a man did his business rightly or wrongly. On this account the object of Chinese medicine was to keep the heart, on which so much depended, in a sound condition, and also to purify the blood. The next question, in some measure arising out of the latter answer, was—what quantity of blood the human body contained; and a characteristic reply was given to the effect that as Chinese practitioners had never let it out, or practically solved the problem, they did not know, and had no idea. He knew where the lungs were placed, and pointed out their position tolerably accurately, but as to their use he admitted himself at fault, in fact his belief was that they were as it were—just to cushion the heart. The pulse, with celestial as barbarian doctors, is held to be a test of sickness or health, though beyond this bare fact the deductions drawn from its beating bear no analogy whatever. For example, our Chinese curer of ills considers that if the pulse is strong, quick, and bounding, the patient is either in a perfect state of health at the time or on the royal road to recovery. The M.D. of Europe looks on this state in most cases as indicative of high fever. Again, whilst the European would consider the lowering of the pulse as a sign of safety in inflammatory cases, the Celestial on the other hand regards it as the symptom of approaching dissolution. It is certain that in this case the old adage respecting the harmony of doctors is exemplified, but we confess our predilections for the European usage and theory. But as singular an idea as any in connection with the human body is that held by Chinese physiologists respecting the

"I am compelled to narrate a shameful story which occurred in this village yesterday, about ten minutes before the mid-day service began.

"The minister was on his way to church when he saw a throng of spectators in a communicant's yard. Thinking there had been a sudden death in the family, he inquired the cause of the mob. How sad and disappointing it must have been to him to learn from the landlord that vials of Obeah had been found buried in the yard by a brother-communicant with whom he had a quarrel!

"From this, you and the readers of this paper will know what characters are here who form the greater bulk of the villagers. Let me, therefore, ask the legislators to put the police after these sons of Belial. Let me call upon the ministers and people of all Christian denominations to remember this benighted class of people in their prayers; and last, but not least, let me ask you too, Mr. Editor, to give your word in season towards extirpating this wicked devilish superstition from the minds of these miserable people in a Christian land."

The Editor of the *Royal Gazette*, in his issue of June 16, 1877, stated :—

"A letter from Essequibo over the somewhat vague signature of 'an Essequibo Correspondent,' which we received to-day, gives an account of a case of Obeah, in which 'a decent young man with long fine beard by the name of Lewis Kennedy,' professed to be able to cure a young woman living at *Reliance* Front who had the 'Phyts.' Kennedy came to the patient about ten o'clock at night, and took out a lot of shot, sand, and a brass cross out of the girl's stomach, and was about taking out more articles when some shot fell out of his shirt sleeve, and the people standing by, perceiving they had been duped, called in the police and gave Kennedy in charge. He was taken before the magistrate, and on pleading guilty was committed to Suddie Gaol for one month."

A correspondent at Hope Town, West Coast of Berbice, writes as follows, under date February 27, 1882 :—

"I learn this morning that 'CARRION CROW,' the great Obeah doctor, and a terror to the people in his neighbourhood,

X 2

is dead. I sincerely trust that with all his supposititious belief he was able, like the prodigal, to say before his death, 'I will arise, and go to my father.'"

(2) WRITERS, CLERKS.—The books of the Hindus are made of palmyra, talipot, or cadjan leaves called "*Olei.*" A number being cut the same length and breadth and placed over each other, with a piece of thin wood or ivory above and below for covers, a string runs through a hole made in the covers and all the leaves at each end, which are thus strung together, something like window blinds. The olei or cadjan *sevadi*, or *postak* books, are of various lengths and thicknesses, but the breadth of all is about the same; some of the larger ones are nearly three feet long, two and a half inches broad, and contain many hundred leaves, with eight or nine lines of writing on each. An iron pen called *Ezhuttâin* is used to inscribe or mark the characters required on these leaves. Olas are also used for keeping accounts by shopkeepers in various parts of India. When rolled up into a kind of ring and secured with wax, these olas were formerly sent through the post-office as letters. Pliny (xiii., 21) remarks "that the most ancient way of writing was on palm leaves, hence the term *folium*, or leaf, applied to books;" and Prescott, in his *History of South America*, says, "The Mexicans, before the arrival of the Spaniards, used the leaves of the aloe for writing on, made into books shut up like a fan." I have seen several of these ola books in the Colony which the Indian immigrants brought with them. Cassie Pattar (*Cassie the Rock*, as his name signifies) in the City of Georgetown has several of them in his possession, and they are written in Telugu, Tamil, and Grandam, or Sanskrit characters, and some have hieroglyphical characters or lines which none but the trained or initiated ones can decipher. My only regret is I cannot place before my reader some of these inscriptions, which are indeed curious. In many of the native schools in Southern India children are still taught to write on the ola in addition to writing on paper with pen and ink. Reed pens are still used by the Indian letter writers in

the Colony. Many who were letter writers in their country have been sadly disappointed in not being able to employ their time as such since their arrival in the Colony. When asked, "To what caste do you belong?" "I am a letter writer (scribe) by caste," is the ready reply given. The Hindu letter writers are of no service at all to the merchants of the Colony, for they cannot (except those who have been taught in our English schools in the Colony) write or copy a letter in English. In the Immigration Office several of the Creole Indians who could read and write the English language, a few of whom were trained by myself, are employed as clerks or copyists. A few of the native Hindu scribes or letter writers, as Gobindass, Prabhudass, Bhalader, Rangar, Muttuswamy, &c., in Lacy Town, or Bourda District in the City of Georgetown, and others in the country districts, find occasional employment among their countrymen in writing letters and reading them to those who could not read for themselves. The following story is told of one of the letter writers: A certain man went to a Hindu letter writer or scribe, and requested him to write a letter to be sent to a friend at a short distance from his neighbourhood. The writer in reply said, "There is a pain in my foot." The man said, "I do not wish to send you anywhere: why are you making this unreasonable excuse?" The scribe answered, "You are speaking the truth; but when I write a letter for any person, then I am always sent for to read it; for nobody else is able to read my handwriting." And this incident reminds me of a similar circumstance with which perhaps the reader is acquainted; viz., that the writing of many authors is trying to the eyes, ay, and even the pocket of the poor "comp." Montaigne and other writers were often unable to read their own MS. Can we wonder that the "stupid compositors" were unable to decipher them? The posthumous works of an eminent authoress cannot be published, as no one living can read her writing. Mr. Sala says that as editor of a magazine he gave offence to many literary persons because he could not master an antipathy to cramped MSS.; and I believe many good things are thrown into editors' wastepaper baskets because the writing is repulsive. Some great men write slovenly on old envelopes, wrapping-paper, handbills, &c., and I have seen paper utilised in this manner.

Persons belonging to the *Pariah* caste among the Coolies are generally employed to carry letters or notices of deaths, marriages, births, &c., to the different sugar estates and villages in the Colony, and hence these letter or message carriers are by them called *Anjarkârar.* Both letter writers and letter carriers among the Coolies get large presents given to them for the work done. As far as reading and writing is concerned, I think I can confidently say that there are more people—between 45 to 50 per cent.—among the Madras immigrants, who can read and write their native languages, than there are to be found among the Calcuttian Coolies. On some of the sugar estates, and in the city also, there are some of these Oriental or Eastern schoomasters who spend a little time in teaching the children of their countrymen to read and write their native languages. The children of course are taught to write with their forefinger on the sand before them. This custom of writing is referred to in John viii. 6, 8. After this kind of writing on the ground or sand, they are taught the use of pen, ink, and paper. The Creoles, above all, are very fond of writing letters to their friends and others, and their style of writing, composition, spelling, &c., is very peculiar to themselves. I have many letters in my possession, but the original of which unfortunately I cannot place before my reader. The following, however, may not be uninteresting :—

(*a*) "BROTHER STEWART'S BROTHER CHESTER.

"TO THE EDITOR : DAILY CHRONICLE.

"Sir,—Permit me a space in your valuable colum. On sunday 30th April 1882 a sabbath school anniversary was held on Plantation Leonora West Coast, they were many children present two hundred who formed a gathering, also many of the children from Anna Cathrinna Village who were entertained in a satisfactorary manner by those of aforesaid place. The worthy superintendent Revd. N. B. Stewart of the British Methodist Episcopal Church being present and the way the children replied to questions interrogated from Saint Matthew gospel third chapter he was oblidge to distribute to them reward tickets for their proficientcy. Cakes Gingerber, &c., &c., &c., were given to the children which were prepared by many of their benevolent parents who deserve groat credit for the charitable way in which they have acted.

"I remain your Obdt.

"svt. I. A. CHESTER.

"Preacher in charge of Anna Cathrinna Circuit, 1st May, 1882."

(*b*) The following affecting application for the loan of four dollars must have produced the money at once. I wish I could learn to borrow in such flowery language; I might make an honest living by it:—

"RESPECTED SIR,—I most respectfully beg that you will pardon me with regards to my undertaking moreover for my approaching so far into your existance of humanity Nevertheless I prayeth your participation with sympathy toward the delicacy of my position all arriving from long standing physical effects on the system of your undersigned, which effects has materially reduced me into extreme wants and piculiar conflicts Compeling me therefore to entreat graciously the faviour of you of the loan of $4 00 which amount including what due by my wife I shall pay at the earliest opportunity as a strict duty. I prayeth your approbation with regards to the solicitations made herein as in duty bound will ever pray."

(*c*) Here is a polite note asking a favour:—

"24 of September 1881.

"Mr. AusBourn Esqouir I umble Ask you the Favour of lending me Fow of your Lamps for A Burth Night My Neast to-morrow evening Night I Will Roturn them Thusday Morning you shall Have them Sir if you so please Sir so Grant me the favour Sir I Will Bee much A Bloige to you Sir."

(*d*) The following "letter" of application was received by a manager in Berbice. It will do for the Letter Writer, as being a fine specimen of how a manager ought to be addressed when a favour is wanted:—

"Honoured Sir—Your most obedient servant the bearer most humble beseech your dignity as it lie in your power for a few days work, for having for a week working at Pln. —— and leaving there on Sunday night to go to Geo. Town and unfortunately I was robbed out of 25 dollars not leaving as much to pay my passage down. I will ever acknowledge Your Superiority if you could have compassion on me as to give me if no more than this week work, I will to get the work work a few hours on trial surely if you would give me some you will satisfy with it. I am the Bearer your obt. Servant."

(*e*) The following letter is from a loving husband, working far up the river, to his wife in town, and is worth reading as an example of the regard that husbands, as a body, manifest for their devoted help-meets. If all the articles he asks for himself were duly purchased, the six dollars must have been economically spent:—

"My Dear girl I have taken my pen in hand riting you these few, hoping to find you well as it leaves me well at present, you must go to the Bass and he will give you 6$ six dollars, you must buy two flannens for men and you must buy two yards and a half of cotton and a half yard of marsell and get a shirt make for me, you must send the flannen as quick as you can and dont forget some Rum and you must send some Seamans pills, I have nothing to send for you yet, you must keep heart, Babie say howdee, if you are hardup send and tell me and I will relieve you, you must go to the post office and book for me and see if any letters from home, now must bear in mind what I told you when I was coming away, mind I am trying best if you dont it will not be my fault, you must do what I told you, tell everybody howdee

"Now you must send some coffee and spice coaco envelopes thread and send the flannen as quick as you can for it is a plenty of water work, you must not buy them so thin for they wont stan the water, these is all torn up, I will send something for you next month tell Siss howdee and I will send some thing for her next month although I dont no her"

(*f*) The following must be very gratifying to the Gospel ministers of the Colony to see to what good uses their instruction in Divine things is put:—

"Golden Fleece, 27th Dec. 1881. From a son to his Father. My Guide from Heaven's decree.—Dear Father—As I am obliged and authorise again and again to let you know that I have return home standing and waiting to received your call I humbly begs of your assistance in helping me with a few bits to defray my expenses at the East Coast B. V. Wagting Village and I will be up in Town this week and be down as early as ever for I am told of my vissions several nights past and months too I wont let you know any thing untill I return again to you. Please to deliver to my Brother the answer should you like to see me before I leave the coast you can say everything is shone to me nothing is hidden I am now redeem as a son and you to me a Father, oh how stupendous was the power, that lead me with a word and every day and every hour I will lean upon the Lord my God add his blessings upon yourself and each off your household for Christ's sake yours days and months are now prolong from this untill he who your trust is on would hasten us to our eternal home of Glory no more I am great deal better by the help of Providence Amen only waiting to your call,—I Remain Dear Papa yours humbly and obedient son and servant my for life time ever and ever Amen."

(*g*) The following may be regarded as a prize application for a situation. The document also has an historical interest, the writer claiming to have been the first—the very first—carpenter who began work in Columbia District:—

"Honoured Sir!—hopeing you well, I have attempted to write you, trusting that your gentlemanship will do no less than complying with my most ardous request,—Sir, I the person, York Aleyne Norville of whom at present you might be at a loss for, But with my feeble introduction you may fully recognise me, asks of your generosity and hospitality to give me a recommendation to Mr. Choppin, who is now Clerk of Works, at the Public Work department, so that I may be re-employed, as you know I was the first the very Carpenter who began, that work when it was then known, by the Name of the Columbia district, who afterwards was sent to the Public Buildings, the which I was again brought up to you by Mr. Sullivan (Mason) and Mr. Blank Superintendent, and lastly was sent for at the present named New Law Courts, as Sub, Foreman Carpenter, and as there was not anything doing in that Course as you fully knows, I have been of long doing scarcely anything, and as there is a recent Beginning and I am unknown to Mr. Choppin I humbly bow at your knees for an introduction, as no other would tend to lead me so far, your credential I have with me at all times to show which will satisfy you, and if any further be wanted you may be sure of them from the two Mrs. Volkmars Mr. Thompson and Mrs. Howard (Masons) And Mr. Frost Carpenter, But you is preferable above all other,—, and I trust that as I have asked your reliable gentlemanship, most Honoured sir, you will do not less than comply with my most emergent, but particular request whilst I remain your Humble and Obedient Servant YORK A. NORVILLE.

"Or, I also beg you if there is anything in your present place that you will render me your services truly trusting that you will do so."

This same person wrote a letter not very long ago to the Rev. D. Wright, Superintendent Minister of Georgetown Circuit, in which he uses far-fetched expressions that would puzzle the best scholar in the world to make out the sense or meaning.

(*h*) A black Creole labourer belonging to my Mutual Improvement and Bible Class, in connection with Trinity Wesleyan Church in Georgetown, wrote the following Essay, which, in due course, found its way into the columns of the *Colonist* newspaper. It is printed, word for word, as written by the individual. The subject of the Essay is "MUTUAL IMPROVEMENT:"—

"To Comprehend the Substance of the tirm in hand it is Necessary to take them not only in their Active Sense but also in the Passive. The tirm Mutual in its Active Sense tends to direct the Social Mind to the Grand point or aim which Mankind was designed.

"From the earliest period or time Mutualete have elevated its Self and have found a place in the hearts & hands of those who favoured her with a Self observeing and penetrateing view. The Studant who possesses a Social Mind Makes the Man for Society; Mutualete Speeks for herself in the Mind and actions of a Studant whose gayges is Set in the line of improvement, in the acts of Giveing or recieveing He is humble especially to those with whome he may have to do with; He is dilligent and Active to show Mutual Kindness to all in his reach, As he Asume the Seat of eminence the direct principal of his Mutual affections indeed or in buisness will produce in him a dislike to egotism or egotistic ambition and pride, if He be a Merchant, by the influence of his Commercial Ability and restitution of Spirit in his Sphare of life, He will endeavour to show Mutual Kindness or improvements to advance the condition of his fellow Citizens around him, improvement is the Key to the history of a man's life,—he will endeavour to Show Mutual power and Sympathy. Improvements is the Active power that Sways the Royal Scepter on the battle field in the day of battle and desolation: What gave assent to lord Nelson's fame and lord Buonapartes dispare; Successful improvements, although the Heroic Warrior fell with tryumphant victory in his hand and a graceful testomony in his Mouth as he Comanded Saying lay Me down where I May die in peace let the earth take My body, and heaven my Soul. What is the Strength of Mutual improvements in a Nation, What is that which Makes the distinction between Man and Man when drawn in a line together; What is it that gives to us the Distinctions between the Barbarion Man and the Civilize Feegeian, What is it that Subdues Nations and yield the power of their reasons in harmony together and establishes the treasure House of a Mutual Improvement amoungst themselves. I humble Asert, it is the powerful Claims and boolwerk of vitual religion which have estabilished life and unity into the Mind of Savages. The reciprocal Act of benevolence have influence Men to improve themselves for Society. Fidelity or Heroic loyalty points out the Channel for improvement in a Man's life and Carrictor; his zealous ambition will offer him a Seat in the Congress of Kings and in an elevated manner Compell them to offer him a hearty hand of fellowship and gratitude.

"In the passive Mutualete Speeks for herself in the life of Kings who with ambition and zeal for his Kingdom and people endeavours to lay hold of reformation by a Strict performance of his duty to God and Man, As he Keeps before his eyes the grand view of Mutual improvements which tends to elevate Men from God to better yielding a valuable attention to them, both in their Nature and in their principal, improvements refines his Morals, extends his Sympathys, brakes down Selfishness and produces a thorough progress wheather He obtains it in his youth or in old age; improvements Calls upon ManKind individually to take a Standard for the Celestial band, to renovate and exercise their talents, when practical improvement shall worke out for them the soundest experience and in a Speial manner guiard them against ingratitude to God and Man. While the interchangeing virtues of the Narritave on debate reciprocally does not affict each other but to promote the honour of their Creator's design. And Now Mutualete offers to us a course of direct Gratitude to God; as it is ours in return to him for the influences felt and received, And it is also Nessary to devote our thanks to him for those whome He have blest with the gift of Literature and learning and perticularly etirnal Bliss May those receive whose Sympathy it is to impart the gift they have received to those whose neede it is. And from the designes and influences of this presant and practical gathering of "ours. May be eagendered in its Self, to establish and promote the virtue of Mutual improvement not only limeted in its Sphere but also to the Political World. And alike the Venerable John Wesley who have Given us a pattern for Mutual improvement who after receiveing additional Gifts which brought tranqulity and Joy to his Soul. He tryumphantly went forth as a Gospel Heroe Scatering as it is widely Spreadeing the Gospel of the blessed Saviour, it is to be observed that all government of Actions is to be obtained by Knowledge, whilest love and obedience brightens the affections for the Master. And to sum up these imperfect remarks i May adapt the language of the Cellebrated Poeit when He Joyfully invites you to raise your eyes and tune your Songs, the Saviour lives again: Not all the bolts and bars of death the Conqueror Could detain. "Ye Servants of God your Master proclaim, and publish abroad his wonderful Name; the Name all Victorious of Jesus extol; his Kingdom is glorious, and rules over all. E & O E.

"D—— B——."

(*i*) The following further illustrations of Creole odd notices, &c., may not be uninteresting to my reader.

On the Albany Police Station wall the following notice was stuck up:—

"Forage supplied to public officers will be charged at the following rate, &c., &c."

"Until I saw this notice," says a traveller in one of the local papers, "I was always of opinion that the forage used by public officers when travelling was generally ham, eggs, cold fowl, &c.,

sprinkled, in the case of teetotallers and good templars, with a dash of whiskey or brandy. I was not aware that they had descended so far in the scale of the animal kingdom as to be in the habit of partaking of oats, bran and hay, and probably this is the reason why so many of them are intractable."

The following was stuck up elsewhere, evidently written in Italian:—

COTTA
GE TO
LÆT.

On the Le Penitence Road I saw a sign-board with the words on it:—

UPS
TEARST
OLET (quite original).

The following order was once sent to a large firm in town:—

"One pond of corns, haf pond of cros shougur; half pond of sed tram; one penny of hamman drop; and one penny of gom marabeek."

The store assistants not being Greek scholars, it took them some time to discover that the articles required were currants, crushed sugar, citron, almond drops and gum arabic.

The following was sent by a female to a dry goods store in Water Street:—

"Mister clurk please will you be kind enuff to change the shuse for me I his the pirson that baught to pear of boots on one pear of shuse this very shuse so please to change it for other pear of shuse the shuse his not number four his number 3 but pleas to send number four for me."

Notwithstanding Mr. Benson's care and industry, mistakes occasionally will occur amongst his clerks. One of them sent a message to a gentleman in Georgetown to say that his telegram to a certain manager had not been delivered, and this is how it was rendered:—"The manager of pln. ——— is underlivered. The manager is not at home and the overseers refused to receive it." Whether the clerk thought the manager had rather too little liver, or what, I cannot pretend to guess.

The following is a *bonâ fide* copy of the advertisement bill of a recent rural entertainment :—

"A. Maggical proformments Wil bee held hat plantation ——— School room by. D. L. Shakespair hat 16 sents. A Card to the oversairs wish to take acard thay Can have thiss For all gentlemen hat 16 sents each gentle Men."

The Local Census returns on this last occasion afford instances of eccentricity or ignorance, calculated to entertain or amuse the public :—

"One citizen gives his name as 'JOHN,' head of the family, 'is a male,' and then under the column of 'Rank, Profession, or Occupation,' he puts down—'Can't get nothing to do for the last six months and can't pay house rent; has got a "keeper" and 4 children; they in Barbados, but is coming to Demerara.' The column of 'Rank, Profession, or Occupation' is filled in with some somewhat peculiar information. For instance, one person's occupation is put down as 'sickly' one is an 'invalaid,' another is 'Cuck,' while one admits he is an 'Idler,' and another ambitious person claims to be a 'Scoller.' One says he is a 'Farmer but sick of a cough,' and one one-year-old inhabitant's occupation is entered as a 'Sucker.' The column devoted to a return of Deaf and Dumb, Blind, Imbecile or Idiot, and Lunatic persons, is not less interesting. One man says he has no 'infurrities,' the next man on the list writes 'dito,' while a neighbour says he is 'romatic.' Another says he has 'Know or flections,' which means that he has no afflictions; while one citizen puts down as an affliction that he was 'Black from his birth,' another, that she is 'Cob in complexion,' and a third, that she has 'a Black mother and a Portuguese father.' An East Coast resident says that he was born at 'Larry Sophenear,' this being his way of spelling *Le Resouvenir*. One man returns himself as having been 'born near town and is belong to the Weslen Church.' A gentleman employed in working a punt, after entering his name and occupation, enters his wife's name and then discourses :—'Is my wife. Is a Female. Not married yet, but will married she in May. She is dimesticated in close washer. She is not himflicted, is got two Boy children for JOE in Barbados, but two is dead. Is got two for me, they cant read nor right yet.' "

The following written by the Coolie himself from Calcutta was received by a gentleman in the city, on the 5th of March, 1880:—

"To The J. HALLIDAY, Auctioneer,
19/1/80 Calcutta

"Sir,

"I beg to inform you that on my arrival all my hopes been decayed because I found my mother is dead and the money I brought all been robbed, only I have got rs. 50 by me and I don't like this country, I shall soon be there till the month of June, positively, now I conclude with my best compliments to self and Mrs. also love and kisses to the children and with all good wishes.

"I am,
"MOHOMED HOOSAIN."

(3) GOLDSMITHS and IDOL-MAKERS.—A Hindu goldsmith is one who understands his work thoroughly, and in a Colony like Demerara is sure to find constant employment for his craft, since there are so many Hindus who are all fond of decorating and adorning themselves from head to foot with gold and silver ornaments. The reader will find a long list of these ornaments given in Chapter X. The goldsmith carries his implements wherever he goes. His furnace is an earthen pot, an iron pipe his bellows, while his crucible is made upon the spot, and thrown aside when no longer needed. Although the instruments employed in manufacturing these ornaments are simple and rude, yet some of the most beautiful productions are the result. This is not all. As it was in the days of the Apostle Paul, so now. We have yet in Ephesus—Demerara —Hindu Demetriuses, who make gold and silver shrines and idols for Diana and her worshippers — which employment brings great gain to the craftsmen. Although the goldsmith has frequent calls from almost all the Hindus in the Colony, to bore holes in the ears and noses of children, men and women, and to attend other ceremonies, yet he is denied the privilege

of whitewashing his house, and tying wreaths of flowers to his gates at the time of marriage ceremony or any religious festival. My reader, however, must not suppose that the various caste rules existing in India are strictly observed in British Guyana: most of them are set aside *in toto*, and some only partially observed. I have known in Demerara some immigrants belonging to the Rajpoot caste, and some who call themselves Brahmans, do what other caste people would not dare do; and yet when the question of caste is raised, and if they could gain anything by it, they would most strongly advocate it, and anathematize every one who would not stick to his caste principle. Periannan, or Joseph Henry, as his Christian name now is, was a great idol-maker and goldsmith on several of the sugar estates on the East Coast, and was greatly patronized by his country people wherever he went. Though he still continues to be a goldsmith, he is by no means an idol-maker. He has abandoned idolatry, and has with his wife and children become a Christian. He calls himself an idol-destroyer.

Though I have lived in the Colony very nearly twenty-two years, I have not seen any Portuguese goldsmiths, nor have I seen any among the black Creoles. We have a few French goldsmiths in the city: in this list of course I do not include the well-known establishments of Messrs. T. M. Sargent & Co.; B. V. Abraham, &c. The Chinese goldsmiths are found in almost every part of the city, and are doing well.

(4) Cattle-minders and Milkmen, who tend cattle for different respectable people in town and country. The Coolies are particularly fond of cattle, and these are almost the first thing they buy in the Colony. The milk trade to a large extent belongs to them, and they make large profits by selling this needful accompaniment of a morning or evening meal. The wet season (or weather) is highly favourable to the milk trade, and offers in its conveniences a striking contrast to the troubles and hardships the milk-sellers experienced during the long dry season. One poor fellow was obliged to water his milk with water from the trench, and one day, when charged with this, as a matter of course, he denied all knowledge of such an

abominable practice. He told the lady, "Beerebmetogad, Missy, me never did such a ting." The lady said, "Well, Sammy, how is it I found these little fishes in the milk?" (producing two tiny spawn.) "Missy," said the ready heathen, "dont bex, it must be cow do so. She drink too much trench water, that make she milk have fiss!" On another occasion an Indian Coolie milkman was sitting sheltering himself under a large umbrella, his milk-can beside him, when he thought he might employ the time to advantage. So he opened the can, and holding the umbrella in position, he allowed the accumulated water to drain from one point of the umbrella into the milk. After doctoring his stock as much as it could stand, he put on the lid and soon after went forth to sell his fine fresh "milluk." The Portuguese milk-sellers are no better in their tricks in connection with this trade. The Coolies principally, and the Portuguese to some extent, are the people who go about from street to street selling milk. It is a degrading business or trade for the "black gentlemen and ladies" to have anything to do with. "I am not a heathen Chinee, or Coolie, or Portuguee, to walk about the streets of Georgetown with a milk-can on my head, or in my hand, selling milk," is what they say. I have never known the Chinese to use milk in their tea, which is their only drink, morning, noon and night, and therefore I think they do not care to have anything to do with cattle.

(5) There are among the Indian Coolies of British Guyana *Interpreters*, who attend the different courts in town and country to explain or translate words and sentences used by the non-English-speaking Hindus to the Magistrates and other gentlemen whose native tongue is English, and who therefore cannot understand the Eastern languages. *Grass-cutters*, who go a great distance to cut grass in order to supply their customers. *Confectioners*, or *mittai-sellers*, who make different sweetmeats, principally composed of sugar, molasses, flour, and spices, of which all native Indians, Portuguese, Chinese, and black Creoles, adults and children, are excessively fond. These mittai-sellers find themselves on the public or estate roads, with a lot of other commodities, as cakes, buns, bread, &c., which

they readily dispose of. *Fishermen*, a hardy, industrious, but illiterate class of persons, who find a ready market for their commodity in Georgetown. These fishermen are principally Madrasees, and their headquarters are in Upper Water Street, Kingston Ward, near the Light House. *Singers*, whose trade is to sing from house to house, on the estates and sometimes in town, and get large sums of money given them. *Water-suppliers*, who are generally females employed on the estates, to give a cup of water, now and then, to the working men. Some of them consider it a privilege and a work of charity to be thus employed, for by that means they get rid of a load of sins, and become fit subjects for *Sivalögam* (heaven of Siva). In India, the Hindus go sometimes a great distance to fetch water, and then boil it that it may do the less harm to travellers when they are hot; and, after that, they stand from morning till late at night in some great road, where there is neither pit nor rivulet, and offer it, in honour of their god, to be drunk by all passengers. The Hindu females fancy, although hired by the estates to supply water to the workmen, they are doing a good work in giving water to them who are weary and thirsty. And how beautifully does this instance of giving water illustrate the following Scripture: "And whosoever shall give to drink unto one of these little ones a cup of cold *water* . . . he shall in no wise lose his reward." The last occupation of the Hindus that I shall mention is *story-telling*. There are several immigrants in the Colony who are adepts in that work. They can invent or make their own tales—always new—so as deeply to interest the hearers. And how finely does this story-telling occupation illustrate the genius of the Athenians and strangers of old, mentioned in the Acts of the Apostles, who spent their time in nothing else, but either to tell, or to hear something new!

(6) OTHER TRADES.—There are more than I am really able to mention, and nearly every one of them is more or less connected with caste. *Carpenters*, who know no other tools than the plane, chisel, wimble, a hammer, and hatchet. Several carpenters among the Chinese also, but none among the Portuguese who have come from Madeira. *Blacksmiths*, who

set up their forge before the house of the person who calls them, will with their pincers, hammer, mallet, and file, "turn out" articles which will bear comparison with the like productions in any English market. Besides estate and town (belonging to the Task Gang) labourers, we have *Shopkeepers*, who do a large and extensive business. Their shops are largely supplied with East India stores, such as rice, grain, ghee, chintz, &c., &c., and the owners of these shops are getting rich fast. *Washermen* (dhobi), who in their country used to make sad havoc of the clothes put in their charge by beating them upon a flat board or stone till cleansed, and then pounding with a mallet till made smooth and fit for use, are by the higher caste immigrants employed to travel to different estates and yards, and give publicity to their friends and neighbours of the birth and marriage of children. They are also employed to build *pandals* (sheds) for marriage purposes; to tell the neighbours and friends the time such and such a marriage will take place; to make themselves useful at the marriage ceremony in dyeing cloths for the bride and bridegroom, and to spread cloth or garments (Matt. xxi. 8), before the funeral, on the ground, so that the company preceding and following the procession may leisurely walk on it. This last is a common practice in India, and it has been done in the Colony also, especially on Plantations Enmore and Great Diamond, when the deceased had been a well-to-do fellow.

Among the Creole blacks the real number of artisans or mechanics, who have any right to the term in the true meaning of the word, is very limited; and it is to be regretted that in a Colony like British Guyana, where the people are apt to learn and tolerably quick to apply, when they give care and attention, there is not a greater number of thorough workmen to teach their handicrafts and become examples to the rising generation. A youth who has been two years with a carpenter, bookbinder, blacksmith, or mason, arrogates the title to himself without any compunction, and frequently, whilst he is learning from an indifferent teacher the rudiments of his trade, he sets himself up as a master of his profession. There is hardly a single trade that can turn out half a dozen men who would be certificated by any English master workman or tradesman for possessing a thorough knowledge of it. These are the men, however, the Colony has to depend upon for building houses, stores, &c. To obviate this evil, and to raise our working population to a higher standard, I suggest that the governing body of our Colony seriously take the matter in hand and introduce the European system of apprenticeship, which means binding by law a youth to an employer for a certain term of years, the employer in turn to give a *bonâ fide* guarantee to the parents or guardians of the youth that he shall be taught the art and profession of the business as carried on by his employer, and that during that period of his service he shall be remunerated by his employer (as at the time of his apprenticeship shall have been agreed to) according to scale and ability or terms of service. By this system the youth will receive a much better and more practical knowledge of his trade than heretofore, and be a competent workman at the expiration of his service. The artisan class will be then raised to a higher standard, greater respect to their employers will be imbibed by them, and better moral and more dutiful feelings engendered. The best trade, however, in the Colony among the Creoles and others, and the most patronized, is tailoring, and this arises from the love of dress, which is inherent. Several of the Creole young men employed in Water Street stores and elsewhere as clerks, &c., are good and well disposed in their ways, but then they need consistency, steadiness, or stability in what they do and desire after. Learning a useful trade is out of the question: it is degrading to them; not worthy of their notice. They are not like English boys or youths who work their way up from the lowest position, but they all want to become clerks and professional men and masters all at once without working their way up gradually. Perhaps a youth who has been only five or six weeks or months in a cloth or dry goods store will profess to know as much as, if not more than, a person who has been in business seven or eight years. Ask a youth to take or carry a parcel out to any place in the city, he will look round for a porter or Coolie to carry it for him. Carrying a parcel would degrade him perhaps in the estimation of some of his friends. There are some Creoles, however, in the Colony, to their honour be it said, who have raised themselves to high positions by dint of perseverance, stability, and consistency of character, diligence in business, strict honesty and sobriety, and well do they deserve the respect and confidence of their employers. The youths of the land are as tractable as any to be found in any other country, but they need the exercise of patience, humility, obedience, and other virtues, to enable them to look forward to a bright future. The great hindrance, however, to progress on their part is, they do not seem to lay any particular value on the amount of intelligence and ability they possess, and hence they live void of nearly all the comfortable enjoyments of life. Certain gentlemen of this city, and more especially the Ministers of religion, have time after time offered their valuable services to preside over associations for their social and intellectual welfare, and which have been heeded too for a short time in one or two cases, but to no purpose whatever, for as soon as they have attended for a couple of weeks they become weary, and hence the result is that instead of doing any good to their country as was looked forward to, they hinder society with vice and crime and leave a black mark for those that are to come after. Some as a rule prefer to attend accursed schools of drunkenness and rioting, and there, night after night, they are to be seen over the counters pouring out orations of blasphemy and shame; others are to be seen brawling in the streets at unreasonable hours with stringed instruments and flutes, disturbing respectable citizens and shattering their own constitutions; such is the use that they make of their precious time.

In an extensive Colony like British Guyana, in which we have a mixed population, the parents need all the wisdom and tact to enable them to train up and educate their children:—

"1st. *To be true—to be genuine.* No education is worth anything that does not include this. A man had better not know how to read,—he had better never learn a letter in the alphabet, and be true and genuine in intention and action, rather than, being learned in all sciences and in all languages, to be, at the same time, false in heart and counterfeit in life.

Above all things teach the boys that truth is more than riches, more than culture, more than any earthly power or position.

"2nd. *To be pure* in thought, language and life, pure in mind and body.—An impure man, young or old, poisoning the society where he moves with smutty stories and impure examples, is a moral ulcer, a plague spot, a leper who ought to be treated as were the lepers of old, who were banished from society and compelled to cry, 'Unclean,' as a warning to save others from the pestilence.

"3rd. *To be unselfish.* To care for the feelings and comforts of others. To be polite. To be generous, noble and manly. This will include a genuine reverence for the aged and things sacred.

"4th. *To be self-reliant and self-helpful*, even from early childhood. To be industrious always, and self-supporting at the earliest proper age. Teach them that all work is honourable, and that an idle, useless life of dependence on others is disgraceful."

(7) AGRICULTURE, though the *last* mentioned in this list of the various trades or occupations of the Immigrant Coolies and others, is *not the least* to which the Hindus pay their attention. It stands foremost among the pursuits of native Hindus throughout India and in the Colony also. I have already referred to this subject, and therefore need not say anything more about it here. The implements used by them are the same which have been in use throughout India from time immemorial. They are of the most simple and primitive kind, such, indeed, as no European artisan would use in forming the rudest structure or the coarsest fabric. Similar implements have been manufactured by our Indian immigrants in the Colony, and used by them, in cultivating or preparing the land for growing rice. Speaking of the agricultural propensities of the Coolies, and the implements used by them in cultivating the land, the Honourable W. Russell says:—

"It is now twenty years since two Coolie men applied to me for a couple of fields in front of Edinburgh for paddy planting (16 acres), which I granted; seeing them potching the land with hoes, I suggested a pair of oxen, and the use of implements of English and American construction.

They jumped at the suggestion, and soon a pair of oxen was to be seen at work, not with any improved implements though, but yoked in the rudest fashion to a crooked stick very nearly resembling the Egyptian ploughers represented in ancient hieroglyphics. This system of tillage was entirely new to me: the oxen worked in fluid mud to above the knees, and with the crooked stick and a scraper made by dragging a plank on edge, the whole surface was reduced to the consistency of mud, such as is seen on the fore-shore. In this state it was considered fit for the rice plants, and in a few days the two fields were covered with sickly drooping tufts of rice, which, in course of a week, became as green as a well-kept lawn; a couple hand-pickings of weeds was all the work bestowed on the crop until it was ready for the sickle, and the heaviest rice crop that I have ever seen rewarded the farmers. A second and a third stubble or rattoon crop were reaped from the one sowing, after which a luxuriant crop of grass covered the fields, making it superb pasture. I had no chance of finding out the cost of production; but from what I have seen of rice planting, where the land is prepared by manual labour, I should say there can be no comparison; and if rice growing here is ever to compete with the East, it must be done with the assistance of animal power; for even with the overgrown population of the East all the work of preparing the land is done with that aid, hence cheapness of production, although the land on which the rice is grown is heavily taxed for local purposes, as well as by the Government of India."

[See my "*Guyanian Indians*," where this subject is referred to.]

CHAPTER XVI.

MARRIAGES, AND MARRIAGE CUSTOMS AMONG THE PEOPLE OF THE COLONY.

1. "WOMEN all happiness from wedded love
Derive, and by it blessed foretaste on earth
The joys of heaven."

"The wife maintains the glory of the house;
All other glory, if she fail in this,
As if it were not is."

"What is deficient with a virtuous wife?
If in the wife defect, then what is all
This world can give?"

So says Tiruvalluvan in his Kural *on the virtues of a wife.*

"Marriage is honourable in all men," and is universal. It was instituted by God Himself in the garden of Eden, for the prevention of uncleanness, the propagation of mankind, and that the parties so contracting might be mutual helps and comforts to one another; and was also sanctioned and countenanced by our Blessed Lord Himself in Cana of Galilee, as we learn in the second chapter of St. John's Gospel. The Hindus believe, that in obtaining a husband (*i.e.* by marriage) women obtain here the supreme bliss of the world inhabited by the gods. The conjugal state is the proper sphere of women, and it is for their sakes that the laws by which it is regulated have been instituted; for, however various, their purpose is the same, all being intended to restrain the stronger and to protect the weaker sex. Marriage is the condition that nature has assigned them, and from which spring their usefulness, their happiness, and their glory: it is no hyperbole, therefore, to say that wedded love, with respect to women, creates a paradise on earth.

2. As I am to speak on Hindu marriages only, I must say

something on the qualifications required in a woman that is to be married. Men of all ages, countries, and classes study this subject ere they undertake such a step. As regards female beauty, I may safely say that no country furnishes a style of female beauty superior to that which is found among the higher circles of Hindu society. Even Circassia, which is noted for the beauty of women, is far behind. I have seen some of these Circassian beauties, and I readily admit that they are beautiful and lovely creatures,—and I was going to say angels; but almost all the different travellers in India—Ward, Clarke, and others—have unanimously given preference to the Hindu ladies. Almost all the Hindu authors express themselves in fascinating terms on female beauty. But after all beauty is only skin deep, and soon fades away. And as regards the virtues and qualifications required in a woman, I shall produce a few appropriate quotations from the Hindu writings, and beg the readers to judge for themselves. "To every household duty fitly trained, the wife should to her husband be in all a helpmate meet." "She must not be of a family where the prescribed acts of religion have been omitted, or a family in which there have been no sons, or a family in which the Veda is not read, or a family that has been subject to disagreeable ailments of any kind. Her form must be, so far as possible, without defect, she must have an agreeable name, she must walk gracefully, *like a young elephant*, her teeth must be moderate in size and quantity, her lips must be like the leaves of a mango tree, and her voice like the *sound of a cuckoo*." "When I have lost a woman who excelled in the knowledge of housewifery, who performed rightly all domestic duties, who never transgressed my word or my door, who chafed my limbs, and, never slumbering until I slept, arose before I awoke; alas! alas! how can my eyes again know sleep?" As to mental and moral qualities, the Hindu female's are not deemed of sufficient importance (exceptions there are, however) to deserve a place in this enumeration of desirable qualities in a bride. As her only duties are to cook food, clean the house, fetch water, and take care of the children, it matters little to the Hindu whether his wife is amiable or morose, wise or ignorant, engaging or repulsive. Subserviency to the inclinations of the stronger sex is her supreme duty. But inattention to the first duty of a housewife is reckoned among the greatest defects of women, and is accordingly severely reprehended; thus, "The woman who, bold in opposition, threateneth blows, is as death; she who resorteth not to her kitchen betimes in the morning, is an incurable disease; and she who, having prepared food, grudgeth it to those who eat it, is a devil to domestic happiness. Women of these three descriptions are a destroying weapon to their husbands."

3. "A woman" (says Cornelius Agrippa, a Doctor of Divinity, aged twenty-three, who wrote a book entitled, *The Nobility of the Female Sex, and the Superiority of Woman over Man*, at Dole, in the year 1509) "is the sum of all earth's beauty, and her beauty has sometimes inspired even angels and demons with a desperate and fatal love. . . . . Her very structure gives her superior delicacy. Even after death nature respects her inherent modesty, for a drowned woman floats on her face, and a drowned man upon his back. The noblest part of a human being is the head, but the man's head is liable to baldness; woman is never seen bald. The man's face is often made so filthy by a most odious beard, and so covered with sordid hairs, that it is scarcely to be distinguished from the face of a wild beast; in woman, on the other hand, the face always remains pure and decent. For this reason women were, by the laws of the Twelve Tables, forbidden to rub their cheeks, lest hair should grow and obscure their blushing modesty. . . . . Benediction has come always by woman, law by man. We have all sinned in Adam, not in Eve; original sin we inherit only from the father of our race. The fruit of the tree of knowledge was forbidden to man only, before woman was made; woman received no injunction, she was created free. She was not blamed, therefore, for eating, but for causing sin in her husband by giving him to eat; and she did not that of her own will, but because the devil tempted her. He chose her as the object of temptation, as St. Bernard says, because he saw with envy that she was the most perfect of creatures. She erred in ignorance because she was deceived; the man sinned

knowingly. Therefore our Lord made atonement in the figure of the sex that had sinned, and also, for more complete humiliation, came in the form of a man, not that of a woman, which is nobler and sublimer. He humbled Himself as a man, but overcame as a descendant of the woman; for the seed of the woman, it was said, not the seed of man, should bruise the serpent's head. He would not, therefore, be born of a man; woman alone was judged worthy to be the earthly parent of the Deity. Risen again, he appeared first to woman. Men forsook Him, women never. No persecution, heresy, or error in the Church was begun with the female sex. They were men who betrayed, sold, bought, accused, condemned, mocked, crucified the Lord. Peter denied Him; His disciples left Him. Women were at the foot of the cross, women were at the sepulchre. Even Pilate's wife, who was a heathen, made more effort to save Jesus than any man among believers. . . . . Aristotle may say that of all animals the males are stronger and wiser than the females, but St. Paul writes that weak things have been chosen to confound the strong. Adam was sublimely endowed, but woman humbled him; Samson was strong, but woman made him captive; Lot was chaste, but woman seduced him; David was religious, but woman disturbed his piety; Solomon was wise, but woman deceived him; Job was patient, but was robbed by the devil of fortune and family; ulcerated, grieved, oppressed, nothing provoked him to anger till a woman did it, therein proving herself stronger than the devil. Peter was fervent in faith, but woman forced him to deny his Lord. . . . . All evil things began with men, and few or none with women. We die in the seed of Adam, and live in the seed of Eve. The beginning of envy, the first homicide, the first parricide, the first despair of Divine mercy, was with man; Lamech was the first bigamist, Noah was the first drunkard, Nimrod the first tyrant, and so forth. Men were the first to league themselves with demons and discover profane hearts. Men have been incontinent and bad in innumerable instances, to each man many wives at once; but women have been continent, each content with a single husband, except only Bathsheba. . . . . Only bad husbands get bad wives, or if they get a good one, are sometimes able to corrupt her excellence. . . . . Our prisons are full of men, and slain men cumber the earth everywhere, but women are the beginners of all liberal arts, of virtue, beneficence. Therefore the arts and virtues commonly have feminine names. . . . . Plato and Quintilian so solicitously urged a careful choice of children's nurses, that the children's language might be formed on the best model. Are not the poets, in the invention of their whims and fables, ... surpassed by women? . . . . . Are not philosophers, mathematicians, and astrologers often inferior to countrywomen in their divinations and predictions, and does not the old nurse very often beat the doctor? Socrates himself, the wisest of men, did not disdain to receive knowledge from Aspasia, nor did Apollos the theologian despise the teaching of Priscilla." So much for woman, her beauty, and her superior qualities; and now for the engagement, courtship, and marriage, wife-beating, and other incidents connected with a married life in British Guyana.

4. Engagement and courtship, people say, are pleasant things indeed, previous to real marriage. Among the Portuguese Coolies or immigrants courtship is carried on at a distance, and the couple engaged to be married are never, or are very seldom, allowed to go out for a walk together without a third person, and that, too, some brother, or sister, or perhaps the father or mother accompanying, and yet with all this precaution now and then some dreadful misfortune happens. The Creole blacks, or their descendants, carry on courtship in an open manner, like any civilized European nation. There is a good deal of truth in the following matrimonial paragraph from *Life Illustrated*:—

"Choosing a wife is a perilous piece of business. Do you suppose there is nothing of it but evening visits, bouquets, and popping the question? My dear simple young man, you ought not to be trusted out by yourself alone! Take care that you don't get the gilt China article, that looks exceedingly pretty on the mantel-piece until the gilt and ornament are all rubbed off, and then is fit only for the dust-pile. A wife should be selected on the same principles as a calico gown. Bright colours and gay patterns are not always the best economy. Get something that will wash and wear. Nothing like the suns and showers of matrimony to bleach out these deceptive externals! Don't choose the treasure by gas-light or in a parlour sitting. Broad day-light is the time—a kitchen the most sensible place. Bear in mind, Sir, that the article once bargained for, you can't exchange it if it don't suit. If you buy a watch and it don't run as you expected, you can send it to a jeweller to be repaired; in the case of a wife, once paired, you can't *re*-pair. She may run in the wrong direction—very well, Sir; all that is left for you is to run after her, and an interesting chase you will probably find it! If you get a good wife, you will be the happiest fellow alive; if you get a bad one, you may as well sell yourself for two shillings and sixpence, at once. Just as well to consider all these things beforehand, young man!"

Perhaps my reader may not know how to approach a young lady with whom he has fallen in love, or address her on the subject nearest to his heart: if so, I shall take the liberty of placing before him one or two letters, quite original in character, and he may be guided by them, and know how to write love-letters if he has a mind to do so. Here is a copy of an ardent love-letter, which, as a change from the ordinary style, may be preferred by corresponding lovers to the forms in the English manuals:—

"Maden, with Love and respect I have the pleasure of writen you these few lines hopen that they may be succesfull I have now make my application of courtship for I could keep it no longer but explain it for when ever I remember thee my love strikes with a kind of gigantic Dignity into my mind which cause to applied ah yes yes my dear my yearn for thee I cannot at present write you any more with my spirit but to beleve and to be shure of one thing that you would not be deceved by me my duty and love to you remain ever my worthy compair yours with the utmost sincerity."

The annexed is a warm epistle, quite the thing for Valentine season:—

"My Dear beloveing, in expressing love i hope you Will be no to much anoid for my come away yesterday because is the same thing i told you about them old people they fret with me when we meet last night so do my beloved dont angry with me for not write try and do as you promise because my father ask me were me been me told him the truth me were stop at your mother place but what he said to me that you dont wrote them so do man you must and write them no danger than this week believe me my dear love dont be afair of me as you said yesterday that I dont love you but believe my word is true my heart also is faithful believe not one decieveing in me all to you i look upon, my father said that if you did write them me could go to you mother place and spend three weeks; you be plese to send me an immediate answer for me, i will be looking for your dear sweet answer do my love dont be angry with me you try and wrote and then i will took great pain an come were you are. I enclose this letter with true an sincere love and with one dozen kiss am your dear love."

5. Courtship, however, as a term and usage, is not found in the Oriental Vocabulary, and is a strange and harsh word to the Hindu or Chinese mind. The Hindus look upon it with horror. Marriage, which forms the foundation of domestic society, is contracted at an early age, and as an obligation of religion. Hindu maidens are invariably betrothed and wedded, to husbands twice, three or four times older than themselves, before the age of puberty. The parents who neglect this their duty in procuring a suitable husband to their daughter, although she may be too young to be capable of or to inspire love, are under the penalty denounced in the following text:—"The giver of a Gaurí (a girl of eight years of age) obtains the heaven of the celestial deities; the giver of a Róhini (of nine years), the heaven of Vishtnu; the giver of a Kanyà (of ten years), the heaven of Brahma; and the giver of a Rajaswali (above ten years, when the signs of puberty appear) sinks to hell." Well, then, may the Hindus be anxious about their daughters' future prospects. We may illustrate this by the following instance, contained in one of the East Indian papers before us:—

"I saw to-day," says the writer in the *Indian Reformer*, "a Brahman youth of sixteen years of age. Observing his pensive appearance, I asked him,—'Brother, why do I see you sorrowful and melancholy? Have your parents rebuked you

enjoy no peace till I have fixed upon a husband for my daughter; so let me go to-day, I'll come and see you some other day.' So saying the Brahman son departed."

The Hindu parents consider it as much a part of their duty to provide suitable partners for their children, as to feed and clothe them. In British Guyana, too, we have witnessed marriage contracted at an early age. But such marriages too generally produce disappointments, serious disturbances, annoyances, and end in separation, or death of the woman or her male friend, or *mattie,* with whom she has fallen in love in mature years. The following case of threatening, or attempting, to murder a Coolie child-wife was tried at Belfield Police Court, East Coast, before Mr. F. E. Dampier, Magistrate, on Tuesday, March 21, 1882:—

"THREATENING TO CHOP HIS WIFE.—Bhotah, indentured immigrant on Plantation *Hope*, was charged by Mr. Munroe, deputy manager, with using threats towards his reputed wife Babooneah. Mr. Munroe stated that the reputed wife, a little girl, complained to him in the presence of the prisoner, that during the night he held her down and tied up her mouth so that she could not make an alarm, and severely beat her. He had good reason to believe that the prisoner might carry out his threat. The girl on being brought into Court was asked by the Magistrate if she knew what an oath is, and she said yes. She was about seven or eight years of age. The defendant had threatened to chop her to pieces in the presence of Mr. Munroe, if she did not return his jewellery. Sentenced to one month's imprisonment, and to be transferred to another plantation."

Managers, Doctors, and others, who have opportunities of judging, know that as far as the *wife's* age goes there are hundreds of parallel cases in this Colony, and yet the authorities who would do their utmost to punish a planter, who has given a Coolie a thrashing, although he may well have deserved it, will calmly sit down and contemplate this atrocious wrong without the slightest attempt to suppress it.

Is there no way of punishing the aiders and abettors of these "marriages?" The poor little wretched girls are not free agents in the matter; the sin and the shame lie with the parents, the priest, and the *husband;* the latter is liable under the Criminal Law, but, to judge from the past, it would appear that the Coolies are to be allowed openly to violate this portion of the law, and the protection which it affords to the women of all other races in the Colony is to be denied Coolie women. Truly our Immigration Office can "strain at a gnat and swallow a camel." Does it never strike them that if the childhood of these girls were better looked after, there would be fewer cases of wife-murder among them? Whatever India may do in allowing or tolerating early or infant marriages, British Guyana most assuredly should not only discountenance such abominably immoral practice, but put an end to it by all means. Many young persons have applied to me from time to time for the performance of such marriages, and I have in every instance refused to have anything to do with it. Such marriages as these, which always end in murder, I look upon as social blots, and the sooner they are removed will be the better for the people themselves and the Colony also.

6. Whilst I am on this subject, and before I proceed farther with my description of marriages in the Colony, I may state that the very Immigration Office Authorities seemed to think that the "Heathen Marriage Ordinance" was defective, requiring revision and amendment. All immigrants desirous of being legally married had to come to Georgetown (whether from the County of Berbice or Essequibo or from any other part of the Colony) to attend before the Immigration Agent General or his first sub-agent; and now the amendment is, heathen marriages can be celebrated by all the sub-agents in any part of the Colony, and they have full power to sign and issue certificates of marriage. The marriage ceremony gone through by them is a perfect farce, and is not calculated to make much impression upon the minds or consciences of the couples who get married by the sub-agents: at least the Coolies have repeatedly told me so. Further, the "Heathen Marriage Law," Ordinance 10, 1860, s. 11, provides for the punishment of men guilty of enticing from their husbands women married pursuant to the Ordinance, but no provision has been made

for the protection of the rights of men whose wives have been married to them under any other law, as, *e.g.*, by a Christian Minister. The whole Ordinance requires revising and remodelling, and provision should be made also to recognize the marriages celebrated in the Colony by the Hindu priests, or Gurus, called "COOLIE PARSONS."

7. Before a marriage takes place among the Hindus of Demerara, one or two months' notice is given to friends and relatives at a distance. According to Hindu custom, it falls on the washerman (*Vannân*) to go from estate to estate, and from village to village, where Hindu labourers are located, and tell them the place, the day, and the exact hour when such and such a marriage will take place. After this public notice, any of them knowing cause or just impediment why such and such a man should not be joined together in matrimony to such and such a woman, or *vice versâ*, they come forward to declare it to the friends and relatives of the bridegroom or bride, as the case may be. But the Christian Hindus have their banns published, a custom very different from the above, and which is English-like. Very seldom marriage between parties is objected to among the Hindus. When the appointed time has arrived, and the marriage is duly solemnized by the *Andi* or *Pûjâri*, the bridegroom, attended by his friends, conducts his bride home, but not as a rule by night, as is done in India, in grand procession, with torches and fireworks, beating of tom-toms, playing of music, and great rejoicings.

Among the Coolies of Demerara, whether Christian or heathen, there is a marriage custom in use called the giving of *Parisam* or *Sparida*—nuptial present—to the newly-married couple. The *Tambulam*, or plate, is put in a conspicuous place, where it may be seen by the invited guests, to whom betel and nut have been sent, or the plate is handed round by some person appointed, and soon that plate is heaped with a large sum, between 300 and 400 dollars, which is handed over to the bride and bridegroom. The same kind of collection is expected to be made in every marriage, whether the parties to be married are well-to-do or not. In some instances the Creole people have adopted this plan in the city and country.

When the bride and bridegroom, and all the invited guests, have taken their seats at the bridal table, and before the cake is cut, a speech is made by some one, and then the plate is handed round, and a collection is made to meet the expenses of the cake, &c.; the balance, of course, goes into the pockets of "Mr. and Mrs. Bride," so that they may have a few dollars with which to begin life or housekeeping.

The forms of marriage ceremonies among the Hindus of Demerara vary, according to the places or countries from which they have come. Thus, while the Hindus from Southern India tie the *tâli* (an ornament answering to the marriage ring) round the neck of the bride, the Hindus from the northern districts of Hindustan adopt quite a different custom. Among the Bengalis, for instance, the marriage contract is solemnized in a very simple manner. No *tâli*, or ring, is worn by the married females to distinguish them from the unmarried. At the time of the marriage the bridegroom impresses upon the forehead of the bride a straight line with vermilion or red ochre, and this red line indicates that she is no longer a single but a married woman. And among the Mussulmans or Muhammedans, marriage contract is solemnized, after the customary interchange of presents, by reading the first chapter of the Ku'rân, called the *Fatiha*. But, unfortunately, there is not a copy of the Ku'rân to be found in the whole Colony in their possession. The so-called *Coolie Parsons* (a term used by them and Hindus for their Kâzis, Moollahs, or Priests) substitute something else in its place. At the marriage itself (called *Shaddi* or *Nikha*) the bridegroom repeats certain formulas, with the five Creeds, the articles of belief, and the prayer of praise, after which he joins hands with the proxy or *vakil*, for the bride (whose presence in person is contrary to Mussulman notions of delicacy), and their faith is plighted in a prescribed formula. Prayers are then offered by the *Coolie Parson*, who concludes by sending some sugar candy to the bride, with a message that she is married to such a person. She is then conducted by her female companions and friends to her future home. The Coolie converts and a few heathen Hindus who get married in Christian sanctuaries in this

Colony, instead of tying the *tâli* round the necks of their wives, or impressing a vermilion line on their foreheads, adopt the European custom of putting the ring on the fourth finger of the left hand.

In commencing marriage ceremonies, great attention is bestowed by the Hindus in determining the "lucky day." The idols of the house are consulted, sometimes by sticking flowers, which have been wetted, against the cheeks or breast of the image or idol, accompanied by a short prayer that, if the union is to be auspicious, the right-hand flowers may fall first. When the indications are favourable, a time is appointed for the marriage rites. These are numerous, tedious, and, in some cases, far from delicate. We shall mention a Hindu marriage which we witnessed a short time ago in this country, to which we were invited by both the bridegroom and the bride's friends. A large pandal (a kind of shed) was erected, extending the whole length of the yard of the bridegroom's house, which was tastily decorated with evergreens, flowers, &c. While the preparations were going on, some of the company were enjoying themselves outside the bridegroom's house, under the pandal. A large *mêdei*—a square seat made of clay hardened—was erected, beautifully and tastefully decorated with flowers and gold and silver leaves, and washed over with a solution of saffron-water. A little god, called *Pulleiyar Swamey*, made of cow-dung and clay, with a few pieces of grass and flowers in its head, was placed in one corner of the mêdei, and Vêlan Andi was hired to make the necessary preparations for celebrating the worship of this hand-made idol god, and also for the performance of the marriage ceremony. Presents of money, and other things, were offered to this god, which, of course, were appropriated by the Andi after the wedding ceremony. The bride and bridegroom, dressed in silks and satin, attended by their friends, proceeded from their house to the mêdei, and, after worshipping the idol by prostrating themselves before it, they went round the mêdei in regular succession about ten times, each time invoking the Pulleiyar god to be favourable to them. This tedious and trying affair over, the Andi, who sat all the while by the side of his hand-made god, ordered the bridegroom and bride to ascend the mêdei, and worship the god and himself. This being done, the bridegroom and bride washed the feet of the Andi and kissed them, and tasted the water in which the feet of the Andi were washed, as a sign of respect and religious honour. While the couple to be married were prostrating themselves before the god, the Andi stood up and blessed them, and, sprinkling a solution of saffron-water upon them, and upon their friends and upon himself, after a few more incantations, he commanded the two to rise up and go round the mêdei with him, in solemn silence, about six times. These senseless ceremonials being over, he told the bridegroom to tie the tâli—the marriage knot—around the neck of his bride, which was a general signal for the tom-toms and timbrels to be put into motion, and, amid the general stir, the happy couple retired to their house, having received blessings of their relatives and friends. Shortly after this, the feast commenced, and continued throughout two whole days.

8. On another occasion I was invited to a grand wedding ceremony in Camp Street, Georgetown. Chakrachetty, a wealthy Indian Coolie, had an only son whom he greatly loved, and whose marriage it was I called to witness. The yard where the father and son lived was tastefully decorated, and a large and wide pandal erected, under which some three hundred guests, or persons invited, could easily find shelter. The father, who has since with his son and daughter-in-law returned to India, went to great expense in furnishing everything which was necessary. Several sheep and fowls were killed, and large caldrons containing rice and currie were bubbling. The Priest who was to officiate on the occasion was busy with his preparations, &c. Each chosen guest invited had a *Kâvi vêshti* (a splendid garment) given, and when I put in my appearance at the door of the house belonging to the bridegroom, where the father was, I received the greatest respect that could be shown, and was by the father and the son led to a seat under the pandal, whence I could see everything, and hear everything. All the special guests had reserved seats just beside and behind me. The master of

ceremonies for the time being, by the order of the Priest, proclaimed that the stars had been consulted, that everything was favourable, and that the time had arrived when the marriage ceremony must commence. But just before the bride and bridegroom were led by the selected parties on the mêdei, where was an altar erected, and Pulleiyar waiting anxiously to be propitiated, an unfortunate circumstance happened, which threw some light upon a certain portion of the Scripture in Matt. xxii. 11-14. The father of the bridegroom, coming out of his chamber into the pandal yard, spied a man in the corner among the chief guests without the *Kâvi vishti* on, furnished to every guest. He went up to him and said, "Friend, how did you manage to get in here without the garment I have furnished for my son's guests?" and then called a friend of the bridegroom and ordered him to take the culprit out, and send him about his business, as he was only an intruder, and came in uninvited. When this little disturbance was at an end, the service, or ceremony, of marrying the couple began, which lasted for nearly an hour. When this was over, the tom-toms and timbrels, &c., struck up, and many danced and played, till they were called to the eating and drinking feasts, in which, however, I did not join. At about twelve in the night a conveyance in the shape of a palankên was brought in, and the bride and bridegroom were paraded through some of the streets of Georgetown, with lighted torches and the beating of tom-toms, to the great annoyance of many of the principal residents of the city. In some cases I have known fireworks to be used. Thus these Orientals try to keep up to some small extent the customs and manners of the country whence they have come to Demerara, and at the same time throw a good deal of light upon portions of God's Word, where references to such customs are to be found.

9. Among the black Creole labourers, whether in the country districts or in the city, when a marriage takes place, it is a lively scene: I mean among those who can afford to make a display. They must and will have a regular turn out, in carriages, balls, and feasts, though two days after the marriage they may not have a penny with which to buy bread, nor have

a bed to sleep on, nor even common chairs or tables. Those who have it not in their power to make this display, will borrow (in too many instances without the probability of paying back) money enough from their friends to enable them to do so. Some, again, who have been living in concubinage for years, will live on perhaps in that state till they can see their way clear to get the wedding suit, the wedding ring, the parson's fee, and sufficient to keep up a feast. Many rich jokes may be told of Creole labourers and Creole weddings.

Who that reads the following note will say that the Creole labouring man is indifferent to the moralities and conventionalities of modern life ? It would be unkind to be hard upon the writer of the note for postponing his marriage until he had fairly established a hope of perpetuating his name in the land, for no doubt he has been misled in this matter by numerous examples amongst the Christian nation who acquired and populated and are now evangelizing the Colony. We sincerely hope that the manager (a worthy deacon) to whom the letter was addressed, advanced him the three dollars which he required to "met up the Minister":—

"January 14th, 1879.

"Dear Sir,—I have Writeing this Polite Note to you my Employer, I hope it his none offences Sir, I humble beg you if you please to lend me $3 dolars, please. I am gawin to get Married on Tuesday Coming sir, and the Money it his not enough to Met up the the Minister sir. I am humble beg you if you please to Assist me to lend me sir, I am humble beg you very hard, will Return it back to you only let next week past, I will pay $1.00 every week untill I have finish with you my Employer. I am humble beg you sir do. My wife she his very far gone that I am Want to Married shortly before she confind, and My Name his call out 2 Sunday already, I haven not the Means to reach the Minister, and to finish take out the Clothes, I am humble beg you sir do if you cannot believe me sir, tell the Overseer let he stop $1 every week from me, please, do I am humble beg you Sir do."

There was a "house" wedding in a village near Mahaica not long ago at which everybody was so drunk before the clergyman arrived, that he had some difficulty in getting the party into anything like order and in singling out the bride and bridegroom; and, after all his trouble, when the ceremony was ended it turned out that he had married the wrong woman. "Don't fret, Passon, don't fret, no 'casion for vex," said the accommodating husband, "this wan sa do as well."

There was a marriage at Plaisance some time ago, and a very merry marriage party; but of a sudden the bride had to retire, and the bridegroom found, a few minutes later, that he could attend to both the Registration matters at the same time. And with evidence like this staring them in the face the enemies of the Creole race say that they, the Creoles, have no thought for the future.

The following is the latest style of Marriage invitation:—

"Mr. William Negrocop and Miss Marian Jacob Will be hapy of yow company to their Selebration of their Nupitol on — May 1881 at 12 oclock Blanting Burge church from their to their Residnce, Demamstil Village."

Our Portuguese Colonists do not make such fuss and show when they are to be married as our native Creole friends do. But fashions are certainly observed by Portuguese as well as Creoles. Splendid and costly dresses are worn by the bride and bridegroom.

10. For the first few days or weeks after marriage the husband and wife live very happily and peacefully together, enjoying the honeymoon; and after that is over, too often misunderstanding and squabbles are sure to occur, in the best regulated families. The following lines beautifully describe this state of things:—

"THREE DAYS AFTER.

"'My precious popsy-wopsy, love,
I'm going out,' he softly said,
And she upon his manly breast
All lovingly reclined her head.
'You will not leave your birdie?'
'I will not, darling, rest content;'
And then they kissed a dozen times—
'Bye-bye!' 'Ta-ta!' And so he went.

"THREE WEEKS AFTER.

"'My dear, I'm going out to-night;
Pray, don't sit up—I may be late.'
She laughed a pretty little laugh;
'O, never fear, I shall not wait.'
Then, having lighted his cigar,
Above her in the chair he bent,
And kissed her somewhat languidly
A single kiss—and so he went.

"THREE MONTHS AFTER.

"'Irene, I'm going out to-night'—
She does not raise her eyes
From Mrs. Blankwhite's latest tale,
Nor does it cause him much surprise;
He hums an Offenbachish air,
And pins upon his coat a rose—
'I'm going out.' She coolly says—
'Why don't you go?' And so he goes.

"THREE YEARS AFTER.

"'Yes, Mrs. C., I'm going out!'
''Twould be a blessing if you'd stay!'
'I wish upon my soul I might!'
'You horrid wretch!' 'What's that you say?'
'I only wish I was a man.
Your insults then I'd soon resent!'
'I wish you were, and not my wife!'
And, followed by the broom, he went."

11. Since marriage was first instituted, it is probable that quarrels between man and wife have been of frequent occurrence, and it is equally likely, more especially in the barbarous ages, that blows have been resorted to as a settlement of disputes that may have arisen. So long as the warfare waged is merely wordy, the fair sex has an undoubted advantage; but where physical force comes to be employed, the tables are turned, although instances are on record, where brawny dames have had the advantage in these encounters, and vanquished their lords and masters with a prowess worthy of the paladins of old. Still, cases of this sort are the exception and not the rule, and it is generally the wife who is the recipient of the hard knocks.

The practice of wife-beating is an ancient one, and by our

ancestors was viewed with more toleration than modern civilization seems inclined to accord it. Some versificator of old declared that—

> "A woman, a dog, and a walnut-tree,
> The more you beat them, the better they be,"

and some moderns are still to be found with faith undiminished in the truth of the old fashioned-couplet. Indeed, in the present day the practice is very prevalent among the uneducated in that "right little, tight little island," which so many of us are proud to call our mother country. So much has it been on the increase of late, that a correspondent of one of the leading London daily newspapers has felt himself called upon to offer an explanation of it; and his views on the subject are worthy the attention of those who interest themselves in the temporal and moral welfare of the working classes at home. These latter, we learn from his communication, do not keep pace with the advance of the nineteenth-century civilization; rather indeed do they seem to retrograde. According to the views of the gentleman we are quoting—"If the man is growing more and more ruffianly, you will find, I think, that the woman is growing more and more provocative of his brutishness." Indeed, the writer, who speaks from his own experience of a manufacturing town in England, thinks that the balance of guilt inclines to the softer sex. He attributes the absence of proper domestic education to the employment of women in factories, and considers that, thrust as they are early on the world to gain their own living, they acquire independent ways and a habit of flirting which unfit them for the proper performance of their duties as housewives. They prefer an outdoor life to the calmer joys of home; and they are, he asserts, as unfit to bring up a family as to command an army. This absence of domesticity on the part of the women drives the men to the public-houses for amusement and distraction; the wives cultivate the society of male acquaintances, and are perfectly willing to be treated by them to strong drinks, and to share their amusements. As a sequel to this, quarrels ensue, and not unfrequently the gaol is reached by means of these family differences.

This may be perfectly true of the particular district of which the writer discourses, although for our part we are not inclined to credit such wholesale depravity; rather would we believe that men and women in the humbler ranks of life are as good and pure as those who arrogate to themselves a superior social position.

Still even in a rank of life from which one would imagine brutality to be precluded by education, cases of disgraceful violence are but too common. A glance at any London daily in the column devoted to the report of the proceedings of the Divorce Court will convince any one of the truth of this assertion. We read but too frequently of delicate women being subjected to the unjustifiable violence of those whose duty it should be to protect them; of cases where the violence is not the result of a sudden outburst of ungovernable passion, but the climax to a long steady course of ill-treatment, the outcome of an unquenchable hatred. For cases like this it is difficult to account, but that they do occur is indisputable. A case of this nature has been inimitably described by that great master, Charles Dickens, whom we who gain our livelihood by the pen will always regard as little short of a demi-god, in his description of the marital relations between Jonas Chuzzlewit the younger and his wife. His description of the scene where the ruffian, on his return from a dinner party, and flushed with wine, strikes his unoffending wife, is probably as fine a page as any in his writings. The manner in which the consistent vindictiveness and meanness of the repulsive scoundrel are elaborated is a supreme effort of art, and its minute examination into the worst traits of a thoroughly bad man shows the miraculous insight of the master into human nature.

There can be no doubt that Charles Dickens depicted Jonas Chuzzlewit, like all his other characters, from the life; and as such a man has once existed, there is a possibility that men with similar dispositions may be still in existence. We trust for the credit of human nature that they may be few and far between, but when they are found they should be avoided like the plague.

12. The Hindu and Chinese husbands often enough beat their wives unmercifully for every trivial thing, but I am happy to say that among the Portuguese wife-beating is a rare occurrence. The black Creole women, however, have a strange idea that unless their husbands to whom they are lawfully married, or their "men" with whom they live in cohabitation, and that too in a shameless public manner, beat them, horsewhip or cow-hide them, from time to time in a brutal manner, they do not show much love or affection to them, the wives or "keepers." The following strange case of wife-beating, for instance, was tried before Mr. G. H. Hawtayne, S.J.P., at Belfield Police Court, on Tuesday, March 2, 1880:—

"Thomas Greaves was charged by Mr. Inspector Butts with having assaulted his wife Ann, at Ann's Grove Village. The wife and husband occupied different apartments in the same house. On the night of the 24th ult., the defendant (as he alleged) read three chapters from the Bible, prior to lying down, after which a thought occurred to him that he should 'make friends' with his wife, so he went to her bedside, and begged her 'to turn,' but she would not, and he became enraged and beat her into fits. Dr. Dalton stated that he attended the wife at the request of the defendant. Her throat was a little swollen, and there were a few scratches on her shoulders. He thought she was more or less excited.

"The defendant said he regretted very much that the matter had been laid before the public. Himself and wife had a struggle, and he flogged her with a strap.

"Mr. Hawtayne: 'You must have used some violence to the woman. Wife-beating is becoming very prevalent amongst you people. You read three chapters of the Holy Gospel and then lashed your wife. All your religion doesn't do you much good.' Fined $15, or six weeks."

And the two following cases, tried before Col. Foster Foster, S.J.P., at Providence Police Court, on Thursday, July 3rd, 1879, which I shall mention, will give my reader an idea of a model wife and a woman's temper:—

"A man named Nathaniel Damon appeared in answer to a

summons, at the instance of the Rev. David Smith, to show cause why he should not be adjudged to support his wife Matilda Damon and two children, their support being at present chargeable to the poor funds. It turned out during the hearing that the defendant was not to blame for the cost of supporting his family, but that the blame was to be attributed to his wife, who left his house without any cause. The Magistrate, addressing her, said he supposed Mr. Smith in bringing this matter into court was not aware that he was adjusting the details of a little device on her part to prove unfaithful to her husband to the letter. She had left her home, he supposed, because it was not good enough for her. No doubt she wanted to live in a pile of buildings with floor packed upon floor, till the topmost story almost reached the sky, and ascending stairs which would never end, in short, a sort of 'Jacob's ladder.' It would be excruciatingly absurd for him to give a decision against the defendant, and he would advise the woman, who had an assumption of boldness in her face that was surprising, and eyes sparkling like a tigress's, to return to her husband and try to prove a model wife. On leaving the court the woman muttered something about impartial justice, and she was brought back into court and informed if she uttered another word she would find herself in the wrong box, where he guessed she would get very little support from her husband."

"Jane Aundlack, a woman of violent temper, was charged with obstructing P.C. Chester, 524, while in the execution of his duty. It appeared that the officer had prosecuted the woman some few days ago on a charge of assault, which resulted in her dismissal, but she evidently was not satisfied with this, and meeting him on the road while he was escorting a number of prisoners from Providence to town, she rushed up to him in a menacing manner and threatened him with violence. On being asked what she had to say in defence, she said the officer had an old grudge against her, and that was why he brought her up. The Magistrate inquired of the prisoner if she meant that her statement was to be construed into an insinuation that the officer had told an untruth, and upon her replying in the affirmative, the magistrate said he believed that she was lying, which the defendant rejoined was also an untruth. This latter remark seemed to have kindled the ire of the Magistrate, who, addressing the defendant, said with fierce emphasis, 'If you dare either by expression or gesture insinuate that you are being unfairly dealt, with I will show you what power I have, you savage. You don't lie, I suppose. You scorn and scout it, ay. That is what you would have me believe, but I, on the contrary, fancy it is a sort of inward nature with most of you black people, and I fancy some of you can put it on thick too.' The defendant here attempted to speak, but was checked by the Magistrate who commanded her to hold her tongue, and ordered her to pay a fine of ten dollars or undergo imprisonment with hard labour for thirty days. The defendant said she had a further defence to make, and asked the Magistrate to hear it out, but his worship replied that he would not trouble himself to do anything of the kind, and ordered her to be taken down."

It is a common occurrence in Demerara to see wives and husbands wrestling, fighting, and perpetually rowing in the presence of the children and others. Sometimes the whole night is thus taken up by them, and the neighbours consequently have little or no rest during the sleeping hours. Saturday evenings mostly are thus spent by them, when the lords of the creation, and the masters of the women, can spare a few shillings in the cursed stupefying and intoxicating grog. On such occasions one would be inclined to think that all the demons in hell were let loose to have their fun of rowing, and quarrelling, and beating, and kicking each other. Solomon, speaking of a contentious woman, says, she is like "a continual dropping in a very rainy day;" "It is better to dwell in the wilderness, than with a contentious and an angry woman;" and speaking of the contentious man he says, "As coals are to burning coals, and wood to fire; so is a contentious man to kindle strife." The women and men of Demerara, especially among the black Creoles, are indeed very contentious. The woman scolds, screams, and curses her husband in a style quite original. She would rush into the room, then bound out of it, and fly round the house like a fury, throw off her upper garment and be ready to fight, tear or pull her hair, beat her breast, wring her hands, and scream at the top of her shrill voice. It would indeed puzzle even a Petruchio to tame such a shrew.

The Hindu law, in a case like this, is repudiation. It is thus expressed in the Nídisàram:—

"A wife given to constant strife, who stealeth her husband's property,
Or taketh part with his enemies, who converseth with strange men,
Who eateth before her husband or resorteth to the houses of others,
Such a one should be *put away*,* although she have borne ten children."

13. On the subject of divorce the law of the Smrïttis coincides with the common law of England in considering marriage once contracted as indissoluble. The word *tyágah* (which we have already named) means exclusion from the bed and from sacred rites, not the utter rejection (divorce) of a woman guilty of any heinous offence; and this is the sense given to it by Hindu commentators. Accordingly a Hindu cannot, on any account whatever, divorce his wife; but if she be unfaithful, or so incorrigibly wicked as to have been finally degraded, he may, to preserve himself from contamination, repudiate her. But, even then, he must provide her with food, raiment, and habitation, for though excluded from society, so long as she wears the *táli*, she is his wife, the marriage can never be dissolved. Once *paired* can never be *repaired*. Among some Brahmans, the singular custom exists of performing the funeral rites for degraded females, as if they were actually deceased. In such case, the outcaste usually becomes entirely estranged from her family, and seeks support elsewhere; if, however, she be married, her husband may by law, notwithstanding the custom, be compelled to maintain her. Adultery among the Hindus is punished with death. Instances of this description have been repeatedly brought before our Courts, and parties guilty of murder have undergone the extreme penalty of the law.

* The original word or term is *tyàgah*, and describes precisely that species of divorce to the extent of which the common allows the canon law to operate; that is, to separation *mensa et thoro*, which is expressed, almost literally, by the Sanskrit, *upab, hóga dharmacárayoh*, the latter term here meaning the preparation of the daily meals, the rites of hospitality and other domestic duties.

14. While on the subject of Hindu marriages, I take the opportunity of mentioning a custom or usage which is practised by some of the immigrants from Southern India. It is true the Hindu code permitted such a usage to the inferior castes, but, although it has ceased among the Hindus in India, it has been revived in this Colony to a certain extent. The practice I refer to is this:—When a husband is impotent, or incurably diseased, or superannuated, he lends or transfers his wife to a kinsman or other person of the same caste, for the procreation of children. When by this cohabitation or intercourse any child is born, it is called CSHE TRAJAH (from two Sanskrit roots, *a field* and *born*), because the offspring resembles the produce of a field, which belongs to the owner of the soil, not to the casual cultivator. Sometimes, too, by special agreement between the parties, the two fathers have a joint right in a son of this description; he is then called *the son of the wife having two fathers*, and succeeds to the estate of each. In this enlightened age, of course, such a practice or usage as this will be publicly censured and cried down; but what was the state of society in ancient Rome and Greece? Cato, of Utica, gave his wife Marcia to his friend Hortensius, *according to the old custom of the Romans*, and received her again on his death, after she had borne him several children. In Greece, also, it prevailed: the heiresses, when their husbands were impotent, were authorized to resort to the next of kin for aid in continuing the family. At Athens, Socrates transferred his wife, Xantippe, to Alcibiades. In Sparta, the loan of the wife, both to citizens and strangers, was strongly recommended, if not enjoined, by the laws of Lycurgus. Herodotus mentions a similar custom among the Agathysses of Scythia, B.C. 484. Humboldt found it in one of the Canaries; it is said to exist at Guyana, in South America, and was common in Britain at the time of Cæsar's invasion. True, such things were done in the dark ages, but now the state of society and morality in these places is different.

15. The Mussalmans we know are allowed by the Kuran four wives, but additional wives or concubines are added, by wealthy persons, apparently without limit or law. But though

polygamy is permitted by every Hindu code, and in every age, to all classes, yet the practice of it among the natives of Southern India is by no means general; in fact, it seldom happens, even among the wealthy, unless the profligacy, barrenness, or incurable disease of the first wife renders it expedient. And in a country like Demerara, where women are so scarce, the Hindus cannot by any means contrive to keep a harem. There is such a scarcity of women here, that many a man among them has to live and die without experiencing a life of wedded bliss or wedded misery. But, to return to the subject, I may observe, that when a second marriage takes place during the lifetime of the first wife, she is always considered as the mistress of the family, all religious ceremonies are conducted by her aid and under her protection, and all household affairs are under her exclusive management. The other wives, who are denominated *secondary* or *auxiliary wives*, are considered as her younger sisters, from whom, as to their senior and superior, all deference and respect, and even service, if required, is due. In England, and in other countries where English laws prevail, persons guilty of bigamy, trigamy, and polygamy, are severely dealt with or punished; but, owing to the institutions and customs of the country perhaps, the Hindus who are guilty of such gross offences are not punished in British India! In this country, of course, immediate steps would be taken if such a thing as polygamy or trigamy was brought to the notice of the public. It is, indeed, shameful and disgusting to see a man have a plurality of wives, but what shall we say of the women who have a plurality of husbands? There is many a Coolie woman in the Colony who has more than one husband. The black Creole female belonging to the labouring and poorer class will not think of getting married to a man till she has lived with some half a dozen men, and had children by each of them. This is what the Ministers of the Gospel in the Colony have to contend against. Although this is a fact which could be proved, I do not mean to say that this degrading practice is so carried out as to be exposed to the public, or cause her paramours to suspect.

16. I have, I think, given my reader a sufficient idea on

Hindu and Creole marriage ceremonies, and now before I close this subject, I beg leave to lay before him the true condition of the female sex among the Hindus, and two instances extracted from my *Journal*, dated July 11th, 1861, and May 24th, 1863, of a man and a woman going out in search of a wife and a husband, respectively.

"It is indeed difficult to ascertain the amount of married happiness enjoyed in the privacy of Hindu life. The female sex is certainly in a much lower social position than the other. Women are neither treated with respect, nor regarded as equals by the men. We see enough of this in this country. The men denounce them as weak and inferior in the most unqualified terms. They are not even allowed to call their husbands by their names; and if they did it is regarded as a sin that cannot be forgiven. If the husband or the brothers accompany their female relatives anywhere, they walk before, and the women follow at a respectful distance. In the lower orders, women assist in agricultural labours, and are not unfrequently seen staggering under heavy burdens, while *my lords* walk at their ease. It is common also, in this class of society, for the men to beat their wives; as also small boys to lord over both mother and sisters in the most insolent manner, in which they are encouraged by the father. 'Among the higher classes of Hindus, much deference and personal attention are shown to mothers and elderly female relations. The Hindu annals record the deeds of noble ladies worthy of all admiration; and their drama often attests a high conception of female character.'

"*Man in search of a wife.*—'Where do men usually discover the women who afterwards become their wives?' is a question we have sometimes heard discussed. Chance has, undoubtedly, much to do with these affairs; but then there are other important circumstances. It is certain that few men make their selections from ball rooms or other places of public gaiety, and nearly as few are influenced by what may be termed 'showing off' in the streets, or any allurements of dress: and the same may be said of the women. I do not, however, intend to make further comments upon this subject, but will simply state two instances which came under my own notice. On a Thursday morning, about ten o'clock, I was conversing with Mr. S. I—— of the Immigration Office, previous to our going on board the ship which brought some immigrants to this port. A few

Coolies from the estates and town, having heard of the arrival of this vessel, came to the office to make inquiries about it. Several of them wanted to go on board, among whom was a fine, healthy, strong-looking man. At first he stated that he wanted to go and see a sister of his whom he expected by that vessel, but afterwards he contradicted himself and said that he was on the look out for a wife. He did not altogether like the single life he was leading, and therefore was anxious to go on board in the hope of getting a woman who would become his wife. After a hearty laugh, I entered into conversation with him, and he told me that he would give anything to get a wife —a countrywoman of his. The man went on board, but whether he succeeded in finding a wife or not I cannot tell.

" *Woman in search of a husband.*—While riding up to Plantation *Herstelling*, one Sunday forenoon, I met a fine-looking young woman on the road crying, and in great distress. I dismounted from the horse and entered into conversation with her, thinking that she had been ill-used by one of her countrymen. I felt very much for the young woman, when I heard her pitiful tale. Her father got drunk on the previous night and was robbed of the little money he had, and on the following morning very early, wanting money to get more drink, he went to her for it, when she refused him. He got very angry and went away, swearing that he would be the death of her. About eight o'clock that morning he went to some of his friends and bargained to sell her for ten or twelve dollars. He returned home and called her to him, and commanded *her to go and live with such a man.* But she refused to do it. He then beat her most unmercifully, and being afraid to live with her father any longer, she had run away. I asked her what she intended doing, and where she was going: to which she replied, 'Sir, I am going down to town, to see if I can find a man of my own caste, who would make me his wife, and support me, and deliver me from my cruel and drunken father.' From further conversation with her I discovered it was her determination to find or meet with a husband that very day. After explaining the nature of the Colonial law respecting Hindu immigrants, I strongly advised her to go back to the estate whence she came, which advice she took and returned. This account is both painful and amusing. The woman in due course found a husband, to whom she got married, according to her country's custom, and lived happily together with her husband, though both had to work hard for a living."

CHAPTER XVII.

THE "TAZZIA" AND OTHER FESTIVALS OF THE IMMIGRANTS.

1. AMONG the festivals observed by the Hindu Coolie Immigrants I may mention the much-famed *Sheddal* or Hook-swinging festival, which was practised several years ago in Berbice and Essequibo Counties. The Government, however, very wisely and judiciously put a stop to it, and now it has ceased altogether, and I sincerely hope that ere long all the Eastern festivals in practice in the Colony will be put a stop to. The Sheddal is a beam about forty or fifty feet in height, across the top of which is placed a transverse pole of smaller size, to each end of which is tied a rope, one end of which trails upon the ground, while to the shorter end are attached two iron hooks, strong, pounded smooth, and sharp pointed. The devotees are retained in an adjoining place or temple (as I may call it) until the fitting time arrives, when one of them is led out, preceded by pujaries or priests, musicians, drummers, and male and female relatives and other friends. The devotee approaches the upright pole, and lies upon his face while the hooks are thrust under the flesh on either side of the vertebræ below the shoulder blade, and is then hoisted up in mid air, where he swings round and round from ten to thirty times, according as strength allows, or vow makes necessary. Twenty or thirty may sometimes go through this ceremony in succession, manifesting total indifference to pain. This they do to obtain *Sivalögum* (or heaven of Siva). After the devotees undergo this painful and torturing ceremony, they retire and keep at home for some days—their co-religionists say, to propitiate the favour of the gods—and many valuable presents are given them by their friends.

2. The Dasserah, or the *Durgah Pujah*, is held for nine days, in honour of the victory gained by Durgah, the wife of Siva,

over the giant Maghisan. This festival is not carried on to such an extent in this country as it is in Bengal or Madras, where Durgah is considered to be the favourite deity. An image of the goddess made of straw and clay represents her as possessed of ten arms, each grasping a weapon, with one foot on a lion and the other on the prostrate giant. This terrific idol is worshipped for three days, and then cast into the Demerary, or Essequibo, or Berbice river or sea; after which mutual embraces and salutations are exchanged among the people. This festival is kept about the same time as the Tazzia festival.

3. Year after year the inhabitants of British Guyana are afforded the opportunity of witnessing, at their own doors, certain pseudo-religious ceremonies, which, to be seen in all their glory, must be viewed on the banks of the sacred Ganges. On these occasions mobs of Coolies, with their gaudy ("tadjah" or "tajah" or) "tazzia," flaunting flags, and barbaric music, take possession of the principal streets, to the unmistakable annoyance, not only of those whom business or pleasure forces to pass in their direction, but equally so of the quiet inhabitants, in front of whose windows the crowd assembles.

The Tazzia festival is properly called the (*Allah*, or) *Mohurram*, which signified a "feast." This feast is observed with devout fasting for thirteen days, during which period the Muhammedans, especially the *Shiites*, abstain from every description of work, from strong drink, and from nuptial festivities. Some even (as well as the other sect, the *Sonnites*) deny themselves the use of a bed, of meat, fish, &c., and are devotedly engaged in erecting or making *tazzia*. The *tazzias* (of all sizes, according to the wealth or poverty of their bearers), as they are called, are made from the precious metals and bamboo, and are papered inside and out with costly and tinselled paper, intended to represent the funeral chapel of Hosein. The Chinese sometimes have been employed to build these gaudy temples, and indeed they give the Coolies far better temples than they themselves can make. This feast is not so rigorously observed in the Colony as it is in India, and the principal part of the ceremony is not kept up here. The origin of this feast may be given in a very few words. There is a tradition current among the Mussulmans of India and the Turks that the ancient Islam Prophets observed a feast on the tenth of the month Mohurram, which Mohammed continued with some additional ceremonies. The anniversary of this grand day is now chiefly remembered on account of the death or martyrdom of *Hassan* and *Hosein*, the two sons of Ali; and the prophet's daughter Fatthima. Ali was murdered by the Caliph, who also caused *Hassan* to be poisoned, and *Hosein*, after suffering the most severe trials, was thrown down a precipice on the tenth day of the Arabian month "*Mohurram*" by the order of the King Zuzeed, and it is to commemorate his death and the persecution which the prophet's family underwent that this annual festival is now held.

The tazzias I have already referred to are considered sacred and holy on account of their containing the *Ullams*, or representations of Hosein's standard; the *Nal*, or the imaginary shoe of the horse on which he fought; the *Neesa*, on which his head was borne by his enemies; *Rast-hath*, or the right hand with the five fingers which was cut off during the battle; and the *Purmêshl-reg*, or a handful of sand, designed to represent the grave; the whole are deposited in a very neat coffin—*Janazah*—garlanded with beautiful flowers, and covered over with a white (*malmal*) figured muslin. After the necessary preparations, the tazzias are lifted up by more than four men, who consider it a great honour to be thus employed, and taken three times round what is called the plain of *Karbela*, a raised mound—the supposed scene of Hosein's fall, or the grave which contained the loved ones—and rested there for more than an hour. While they rest the Coolie parson makes *fâtiha* or *namas*—prayers—and performs additional accompaniments to the ceremonies. Several sit rouud and weep for a while, and then they fall on each other's necks and cry aloud in the Eastern style—that is to say, they first place their head on the right shoulder of the person they were embracing, and then on the left. Cakes, sugar, milk, and money, are laid as offerings on Karabolla, and ghee lamps are also lighted by the females who take part in such proceedings. None but those belonging to the *true faith* and a few intimate friends are allowed to come near and witness the scene. The tazzias are again borne on shoulders and carried in procession with the shouts of *Shah* (King) *Hassan! Shah Hosein! Dhoolla! Dhoolla!* (bridegroom) *Holl Dwast!* (alas, my friend) and *Rhuerho!* (stop, stop) repeated again and again, at the top of their voices. At the repetition of the two last words the procession suddenly stops, and the people begin dancing before the funeral chapel, shouting out with all their might, *Shah Hassan*, &c. Some of the male Coolies dress themselves like tigers (called *Puli Vêsham*), &c., and skip about before this chapel, and others engage in fencing. While all this is going on, another set of Muhammedan females and others, at some distance, may be seen beating their breasts and tearing their clothes and making loud lamentations. This festival is regularly observed on almost every estate in the Colony. And when the grand procession of the tazzias is over, the *taboots*—coffins—are stripped of their fineries and thrown into the water, in obvious imitation of the Hindu practice with the Durga idol. But when this festival happens to occur at the same time with the Hindu Dasserah, the collision of the two sects of religious worshippers creates no little disturbance. Violent conflicts occur in the streets. Sometimes, too, the passengers and others are stopped on the roads and prevented from pursuing their journey. Thousands can bear testimony to this state of things as they existed a few years ago in this Colony in connection with these festivals, and even now in Berbice, Essequibo, and in other places, similar scenes are occasionally enacted. The warlike demonstrations which generally follow the throwing of the tazzias into the rivers or creeks in the Colony are to show that the followers of the Prophet are ever ready to fight his enemies, and never will forget the persecutions his grandsons *Hassan* and *Hosein* suffered at the hands of the "unbelievers"—Kaffirs—until their deaths have been avenged. It is during these passages of arms that frequently some Muhammedan Coolie works himself up into a perfect state of frenzy, and attacks any European or Creole who is not a believer, and therefore not a true friend of the Prophet and his family.

In June, 1866, a Tazzia case was tried in Essequibo Court. The following are the particulars of the open assault:—Mr. Robert Bunburry stated that on the afternoon of Friday, the 25th of May, 1866, he was returning from Bush Lot to his house. He found a Tazzia at *Coffee Grove*, and three others at *Hampton Court*. A number of Coolie men came up to him and said he must get off his horse and walk. He told them that he had passed the other Tazzia by the side of the road, and he would do the same in this case. He then proceeded on his way, close by the trench, when Bahaal, the defendant, came up and took hold of his horse's bridle, and attempted to back it into the trench. Witness told the man to let go the bridle, and struck him with a switch which he had in his hand—he could not say whether it was on the body or on the face that he struck the defendant; but defendant returned the blow with a stick which he had, and the blow fell on witness's arm. Witness jumped off his horse, held defendant, and called out for a constable. The defendant Leeree came up and struck witness with a stick. Other Coolies then came up, and took the two defendants away. Henry Stephen, a witness, confirmed the foregoing statement in the main; but he did not see the second defendant strike the complainant. James Farrington gave similar evidence to the last-named witness, and added that when the complainant ordered Bahaal to let go the bridle, Bahaal said if the complainant would not come off the horse, he (Bahaal) would lead the horse by the tazzia. Ragmut, for the defence, said, seeing the complainant coming along the road towards the dam where the *Devonshire Castle* Tazzia was, he went to complainant and begged him to dismount until the Tazzia had passed. Complainant refused. Witness then called to the defendant Bahaal to take complainant's horse's bridle, and lead him past the Tazzia. Complainant refused, and said to Bahaal, "Loose the horse." Complainant then struck the horse and Bahaal. Witness then went close to the Tazzia. The magistrate dismissed the case, observing, at the same time, that the Tazzia was sanctioned by the Government, and consoled the complainant with the information that he was not the only person who had been obstructed and assaulted at that particular ceremony. Some years ago, two gentlemen of the Mahaica district (Messrs. Collin Smith and James Smellie) were dragged from their vehicle and nearly murdered by the Coolies, for attempting to pass on their way while the idol and its votaries were in possession of the highway. Not long ago the West Coast was the scene of a most scandalous outrage arising from the same cause; and every now and again we hear of breaches of the peace and murderous assaults committed by the Coolies as drunken interludes to their religious ceremonies. And another circumstance of this kind, which ended in a sanguinary affray, at the Tazzia festival, will be found in the "Missionary Notices" for August, 1867. I make no comment upon this state of things in the Colony, but simply mention the facts, and leave the reader to form his own opinion.

The Coolies in this country contribute very largely indeed to get up the Tazzias and other festivals every year. Every man, woman, and child gives something handsome towards them. Some thousands of dollars are spent annually by the Coolies belonging to the different estates, besides the profusion of offerings presented during the ceremony. The following facts may give some idea to the reader about Hindus' giving. In India, at the celebration of the Durga festival, a wealthy native has been known to give eighty thousand pounds' weight of sweatmeats, eighty thousand pounds' weight of sugar, a thousand suits of silk, a thousand offerings of rice, plantains, and other fruits. On another occasion, a wealthy Hindu has been known to have expended upwards of £30,000 sterling on the offerings, the observances, and the exhibition of a single festival, and upwards of £10,000 annually ever afterwards to the termination of his life. In this country, too, the well-to-do immigrants give largely and liberally towards the celebration of the Tazzia festival. I know several estates in this Colony where immigrants have spent from eight to nine hundred dollars per year. This is a large sum indeed, but not so large when compared with the Indian figure. I have no doubt the immigrants would spend more if they were in a position to do so.

It is indeed a great pity that the Coolie immigrants are thus allowed to carry on all their heathenish abominations in a professedly Christian country like British Guyana. Although we would very much wish to see these things at an end, yet we do not believe that any act or interference of the Home Parliament or Colonial Government will put an end to them. The preaching of the Gospel alone must put an end to them.

4. In former years, it was a common occurrence for two processions of devotees belonging to different estates to give battle on the public road, to the annoyance and danger of the general public. To such an extent had the Tazzia nuisance arrived, that the Government was obliged to interfere, and make the most stringent regulations for its observance. Now, the business of the Tazzia is conducted on the various estates in an orderly way, under the care of a driver or head man who obtains leave from the Magistrate to have a procession, and becomes responsible for the conduct of the people under him. The black native population on the different plantations seem to be getting as fond of the annual show as the Coolies themselves are, and they follow the gaudily-dressed temples in thousands with all the appearance of religious fervour that marks the natives of the East. The Ministers of the Gospel in the different country districts entreat the people from the pulpits to give no countenance to the worship of idols; but the blacks find the Tazzia procession to their taste, and decline to be dictated to in matters of religious belief. Some time during April of 1873 there was actually a Creole Tazzia procession, down the coast of Essequibo, got up by some wicked people, who were afterwards justly punished by the magistrate for their wrong-doings. The following is the account of it given in the *Royal Gazette* of April 19, 1873:—

"The news from Essequibo of a Creole Tadjah, originated and observed by black natives, which was celebrated at Pln. *Sparta* during last week, is a warning note to clergymen and other moral teachers to prepare for a crusade against a new religion, which promises to find great favour with the Creoles in the country districts, who have had the opportunity of witnessing and admiring the Tadjahs belonging to the Coolies. For two or three years back we have regularly drawn attention to the love which was springing up in the bosom of our native population for the 'Tadjah,' and the evident desire they manifested to join the ranks of its worshippers; their passion for it has already broken down the very thin barrier of their Christianity, and they now appear as worshippers of a 'Tadjah' belonging exclusively to themselves.

"This is having the tables turned, with a vengeance. Philanthropists, Ministers, and others fondly thought that the intercourse of Coolies and Creoles would be the means of bringing large numbers of the former within the pale of the Christian Church; but they never dreamt that it would be the means of thinning the Church's ranks of members, even though they be thoughtless and unprincipled ones. If the 'movement' gains ground, and the blacks remain faithful to their new creed, we may look soon for a missionary combination amongst our localized Coolies to import some able priests to aid in the conversion of the unenlightened; and by-and-bye their petition will be going into the Court, praying to be allowed to participate in the benefits of concurrent endowment."

An anonymous writer, signing himself "Sodom and Gomorrah," from Mahaica (a very populous village, and generally known in the Colony as the "Wesleyan Methodist parish"), in a letter dated February 27th, 1877, and published in the *Royal Gazette*, speaking of a Creole Tazzia procession, says:—

"I happened to be in Mahaica Village on the day of the 'Tadjah Procession,' held by the Creoles of the different villages, and to my utter surprise and disgust I was shown the 'molten image' with paraphernalia that qualifies the God of their imitation—Mohamet. Before the 'altar' of this unknown god, there (to my horror and burning indignation) grovelled the sons of the soil whose creed from childhood was Christianity, and whose parents are followers and leading members of the two churches to be seen not one hundred roods from the scene of their performances. Against both the peace and goodwill of the respectable portion of the community, these reprobates were allowed to have things all their own way, and unsupported by Coolies, Chinese, Africans, Barbadians, and Portuguese, they conducted this most scandalous and disgraceful exhibition. I thought how appropriate it would be if the fate of one and all who had fallen before the altar and worshipped the 'Idol,' were to be like the fate that attended the Prophets of 'Baal' in their like endeavours. I would strongly recommend, as a preventative to a like occurrence, an Act of the Legislature, with no less a punishment than a smart application of the 'cat-o'-nine tails.' This, I am sure, would effect in a single instance a radical cure and prevent all further violations of the laws of God and mockery of mankind."

It is, however, deeply to be regretted that Christians like ourselves, though unhappily in but too many instances having but slight knowledge of the tenets of their faith, are easily led away and actually take part in the heathen ceremonies which they see practised around them. It is a common thing to see the tazzias carried by the black men hired for that purpose by the Coolies, and I have also repeatedly seen the respectable Creoles and European planters not only countenance these festivals by their presence, but also give the immigrants large presents and then encourage them in their wickedness. This much is certain, that Christians who attend on such occasions give those who invite them the idea that idolatry is a trifling matter, a harmless amusement, instead of a sin of the deepest dye. How awfully and truly may the words of the prophets Jeremiah and Ezekiel be applied to this class of Christians! "Thus saith the Lord, Learn not the way of the heathen, and be not dismayed at the signs of heaven; for the heathen are dismayed at them." "And ye shall knowthat I am the Lord: for ye have not walked in My statutes, neither executed My judgments, but have done after the manners of the heathen that are round about you." The heathen Coolies are brought here to till our sugar fields, and it becomes the solemn and responsible duty of the Christian, instead of countenancing or encouraging them in their vile practices or learning their ways, to set before them a holy, pious, and Christian example.

5. The Chinese or Celestial Coolies also have their annual lantern processions in the City of Georgetown. These processions are intended to show that they are fully alive, even in a strange and distant land like Demerara, to all to which they have been accustomed in their beloved home, and that they have not forgotten the way to celebrate their New Year holidays. In town this year (1882) they have had a lantern procession in the evenings, the lanterns,—which were made of thin coloured paper formed very ingeniously in the shape of huge fishes and nondescript animals, and lighted up with many candles,—having a very striking effect. The procession marched to the sound of anvils, gongs, cymbals, and other kindred melodious instruments, and was attended by crowds of the "unwashed" natives. The Chinese "visited" the Governor, the Sheriff, the Immigration Agent General, the Inspector General, Mr. DeJonge, Mr. Abraham, Mr. Fresson, and other well-known citizens. It is not every man, however, who would like to have a 200 yards' procession of paper lanterns paying him an evening visit. The black people in certain districts have followed the example of the Coolies, and have a Tazzia procession every year. We shall doubtless see a Creole procession of lanterns at an early date. Only, Quashie will have to employ the Chinese to make the lanterns.

6. The Portuguese have their regular *fêtes* also in various parts of the Colony, which are great nuisances to a Protestant country. I am a Protestant, holding liberal views, and having no undue prejudice against the Roman Catholic body. But I must confess that I cannot but feel it an injustice to my fellow Protestants and to myself to be compelled to support their religion, especially those forms and observances which are to the Protestant mind offensive and repugnant. On Sunday, the 4th of June, 1882, there was a general *fête* along the East Coast, the trains were filled with persons, who, under the sanction of the Roman Catholic Church, were bent on violating the Protestant observance of the Christian Sabbath. No civil law was broken, but the higher law, in which I believe, was decidedly violated. I am taxed to pay for the support of a church which sanctions this violation! These

fêtes are not religion at all, they are simple dissipation, and yet, under our present system of state endowments, Protestant Christians are sanctioning the violation of the Christian Sabbaths.

7. The last religious ceremony of the Hindu Immigrants, to which I draw the reader's attention, is death. "The wages of sin is death." "By one man sin entered into the world, and death by sin; and so death passed upon all men, for that all have sinned." "In Adam all die." Hindus, Muhammedans, Christians, all must die, for "it is appointed unto men once to die, and after that the judgment." Death comes to the Hindu, as "the king of terrors," with all its natural repulsiveness and gloom unalleviated by the bright hope of a happy future. It comes to usher him in an instant—in the twinkling of an eye—into the awful presence of the ever-living God. If the Hindu dies with calmness, without murmuring, it is because he is under the influence or effects of some narcotic or poisonous drugs which render him insensible, and in a state of unconsciousness his existence terminates. "Resignation," such as the Christian feels in sorrow's darkest hours, is foreign to the creed, as it is a stranger to the heart, of an idolatrous Hindu. Hence, when a friend dies, the mourner uses language of reproof, to us most strange and repulsive. Instead of raising his weeping eye upward, with the language of the Patriarch, "The Lord gave, the Lord hath taken away, blessed be the name of the Lord," he turns to the lifeless form with words of upbraiding and censure. "Why," exclaims the weeping widow, "why, O my husband, hast thou forsaken me? What did I do to drive you hence? Was I not a faithful wife? Was I not attending to all your household affairs, cooking your food, taking care of your children, defending your character? O, why did you desert me thus cruelly, my departed one?" The mourning women beat their breasts in sorrow with a force which is terrible and alarming, and then, putting their arms on one another's shoulders, droop their heads in the centre, and weep most furiously and bitterly. According to the Oriental custom, the people and relatives in the house of the dead neither eat nor bathe so long as a corpse is lying

ere. The funeral procession is formed in a way which is peculiar to themselves, and somewhat strange to those who are not accustomed to the manners and ways of these Orientals. When the deceased is laid in the grave, and the grave is closed up, they return homewards, and ere they enter their dwelling they perform the necessary ablutions to purify themselves and their garments from pollutions contracted by the touch of the dead person, or by mixing up with those who were polluted. How sad and solemn does this appear to the Christian mind!

The Hindus observe certain funeral rites which are burdensome and expensive at the death of their friends. The corpse is bathed, shrouded, and buried, if possible, the same day, or the next day at the latest. The funeral obsequies terminate in a great feast. It is also a custom, among some of the immigrants here, on certain days, to send, *in the name of the dead*, large quantities of cooked rice, and other food, to all the friends and neighbours, however numerous; and sometimes presents are made to their poor. This custom, I believe, explains the twenty-sixth chapter and fourteenth verse of Deuteronomy: "I have not eaten thereof in my mourning, neither have I taken away aught thereof for any unclean use, nor given aught thereof for the dead." On the day when one of their number dies, crowds of relatives, friends and neighbours assemble, for all of whom refreshments must be provided; they also must be entertained as long as they choose to remain. Some time ago, a very singular funeral took place on one of the estates not far from the city of Georgetown. A so-called Coolie Parson, from the East Coast, died suddenly, when on a visit to some of his friends residing on the estate referred to, and his countrymen resolved to give him a grand burial. Funds were quickly raised for the purpose, one man contributing as much as ten dollars, and others five, six, and eight dollars respectively. The coffin was decorated, and gaily adorned with gold and silver leaf. A large body of Coolies assembled to escort the remains of the deceased to his last resting place; eight so-called Coolie Parsons attended the procession; eight singers and eight drummers were employed.

Incense was used on the occasion, as was also perfume in great abundance, not only for the dead, but for those accompanying the funeral; beer and spirits were poured out in large quantities as libations, and money was also thrown into the grave. Before and after the procession moved on, passionate exclamations in the houses of the friends of the deceased were distinctly heard. Such exclamations were confined almost exclusively to the female mourners and the mourning women. They wept, tore their clothes, smote their breasts, and lay upon the ground; really it was a distressing sight to behold. When the bereaved mourners were exhausted and tired out, mourning women were hired to keep up the bitter lamentation and woe. This custom of hiring mourners corresponds with the ancient custom of Jeremiah's day—"Consider ye, and call for the mourning women, that they may come; and send for cunning women, that they may come; and let them make haste, and take up a wailing for us, that our eyes may run down with tears, and our eyelids gush out with waters."

The husband of the beloved one has been carried and deposited in the house which is appointed for the living. One scene of woe is over, and another of misery and wretchedness remains to be seen. Seated on the ground or the floor in the centre of a room is the bereaved one; a young woman scarcely twenty, or twenty-five, or thirty, dressed as if for bridal. Cruel mockery! Flowers and jewels—her *santoshams*—adorn her person; her face is covered with a solution of saffron in water, which gives her countenance a yellow appearance; her clothes are all newly purchased, and around her are seated her female relatives. All wail and mourn, beat their breasts and heads, tear their hair, and throw ashes over their persons. This continues for seven days. On the eighth day the flowers and jewels are removed from the bereaved one. Her jacket, instead of being taken off in the usual way, is forcibly rent at the back. The tâli, or marriage token, is severed from her neck, and henceforth she is regarded as a widow indeed. After this, oil is rubbed on the heads of all the mourners, and they bathe and eat; and thus ends the public mourning. But who can picture the hidden grief of the poor out-caste widow, ever after regarded as a thing of scorn?

Christianity enjoins the visiting the widow in her bereavement and afflictions; but *Hinduism* teaches that widows are to be regarded as the dross of human existence. She cannot marry a second time; she is a widow for life, but she may live with any one of her own class, and bear children, as is frequently the case in this Colony.

CHAPTER XVIII.

RELIGIOUS CEREMONIES AND SUPERSTITIONS OF THE LABOURING POPULATION.

1. The Hindu Immigrants in the Colony practise to a very great extent all their country's rites and ceremonies. It may be truly said of them, they are a ceremonious or religious people. The number of Hindu or Coolie festivals, including the monthly observances of the sun's passing from one side of the Zodiac to another, is *one hundred and fifty-five*, which are differently esteemed among different classes, and in different localities.

2. The birth of a child, for instance, is observed with a variety of superstitious ceremonies. The Shastras prescribe a drop of honey to be given to the infant immediately on its birth, but this ancient usage has fallen into disuse, and is only observed by the higher classes or ranks of Hindus. The Muhammedans or Mussulmans, too, do occasionally adopt this usage. Instead of the honey, the immigrants sometimes use syrup or sugar water. When a male child is born, the priests are consulted a few hours after its birth. These learned men (for so we must call them as a mark of honour) for the mere purpose of obtaining a few dollars, profess, or at least pretend, to reveal beforehand, by consulting the "*position of the heavenly bodies,*" the future prospects or good and bad luck and qualities of the infant man. A *chembu* (copper pot) of water, a large quantity of rice, and other presents are placed before the officiating priest; the parents, male and female relatives and friends, and others interested in the child, apart from each other, sit round him; and he, after repeating a few prayers invoking the assistance and guidance of the gods, looks round on all the company, and then at the presents set before him (and if insufficient cries out for more), and then on the parents of the

child and its relatives. This part of the ceremony over, he nexts asks the father of the child to cut or divide the *olei book* (made of Palmyra leaves, which he holds in his hand) in two, with a piece of string attached to it, and then proceeds to read out in the hearing of all parties everything good and bad concerning the infant. The priest performs his illusory task very cleverly indeed, so as not to be doubted by any one present. If the male child is born to good luck, he is petted and cared for by the parents and other male relatives, which latter are expected to give him a piece of coin, silver bangle, clothes, &c., &c. A great feast is made, friends are invited, and the day or the night passes off with great rejoicings. The giving of presents to male children among the Coolies in the Colony is a fixed rule. Every visitor is expected to give something; if he does not, he is looked upon as a shabby, mean fellow. This custom of giving presents to children, males and females, is universally observed in the Colony by both the Portuguese, Creoles, and others, and even in such a matter mistakes are sure to be made, as the following incident will show:—

"A lady on the West Coast prepared a cake for some of her little friends in the city and left it overnight on the table, ready for the estate's messenger in the morning. The messenger, according to instructions, went for the cake, and found lying beside it a bottle which the nurse had left there by mistake. Arguing that both the bottle and the cake were for a Christmas present, he carried them both to town; but fancy the surprise when the bottle was opened and found to contain —castor oil! Until the explanation arrived on the following day, the mother of the little cake recipients was under the impression that the present of the bottle was a gentle way of reminding her that, with children, castor oil and Christmas cake are closely allied."

At a ceremony which I attended in Lacy Town, to look on for information, I observed about one hundred immigrants present, and at the close of the ceremony about fifty dollars were contributed, which the priest took for his trouble, as also other presents, such as rice, ghee, fowls, &c. Such ceremonies as these are never observed at the birth of a female child.

The birth of a daughter, in fact, is generally accounted a calamity rather than a blessing. Very much like the Bok Indian (aboriginal native of this Colony) the Hindu father and husband refuses to speak to the mother or see his child; and the friends, relatives, and neighbours, *particularly the females*, upbraid the innocent wife, and condole with the unkind husband, as if he were very cruelly treated by his partner in life, his better half, the wife. Worse than this, I have known one or two instances in this Colony in which the husband has sent his wife away because she has borne him no sons. This fear of being discarded by the husband produces in every Oriental wife intense desire to become the mother—not of daughters, but — of sons, not a whit less vehement than that of Rachel.

While on this subject I shall take the liberty to place before my reader, for his information, the Hindu laws respecting male parents and children. "For five years he (the male child) should be treated like a prince, for ten years as a slave, but, when he has attained to the sixteenth year, a son should be treated as a friend."—*Ni disaram.* "Her father protects her in infancy, her husband in youth, and her son in old age; no woman ever possesses independency."—*Manu, the Hindu Law Giver.* We see from these extracts that the law is very favourable to the male children. As soon as a male child is born, he becomes a co-partner with his father in the family estate; and at the age of sixteen he is at perfect liberty to demand the delivery of his share of the paternal property, and when that is obtained, he becomes perfectly independent of his father and family. But with regard to daughters the Hindu code has not been sufficiently regardful. It has not placed infants of the female sex, as it has the male, under the protection of their parents' fears, and the preservation of the former, therefore, is a matter of cold duty, not, as in the case of the latter, of anxious solicitude. Hence daughters are not looked upon as blessings from God, but as pests and curses. Even the Demerara Hindus, though living in a Christian country and under Christian laws, look upon the birth of a daughter as a *domestic calamity.* No rejoicing attends her natal hour, as does that of her brother, and she shares not the blessing which is invoked from the Divine Benefactor for his prosperity and happiness. With regard to sons only, the poorest Hindu father in this Colony is ready to respond to the Psalmist's exclamation: "Happy is the man that hath his quiver full of them."

3. All nations are in the habit of giving names to their offspring; but mostly the names conferred upon children have some reference to the circumstances connected with their birth. We have many instances of this sort in the Bible. For instance, we read that when Leah called her eldest son *Reuben*, she said, "The Lord hath looked upon my affliction;" and thus we find to the end of the list. Such was the ancient Oriental custom in this matter, and it is the same in modern times. The Muhammedan as well as the Hindu immigrants, like their brethren in India, observe the custom of naming their children on the tenth or twelfth day. The Mussulmans generally join the name of the Divine Being to one of His attributes or to some other word, in order to make agreeable names for their children. Thus Abd Allah—*servant of God;* Ameen ed Deen—*faithful in religion*, &c. But when the Hindu immigrants give names to their children, all the priests from different estates are invited to attend, and a great feast terminates the whole affair. The *Vishnu Puràna* says:—"Ten days after the birth, let the father give a name to his child, the first term of which shall be the appellation of a God, the second of a man. . . . . A name should not be devoid of meaning; it should not be indecent, nor absurd, nor ill-omened, nor fearful; it should consist of an even number of syllables; it should not be too long, nor too short, nor too full of long vowels, but contain a due proportion of short vowels, and be easily articulated." This rule only applies to the Brahmans, who are the teachers of the Hindu religion, and possessors of all the Vedas and Puranas. But the poor ignorant Coolies of this Colony know nothing, see nothing, and hear nothing of their sacred books; and yet the custom is duly considered and practised. Some of the Hindu children who attend our schools have such names as these:

Gopaul, Ramaya, Chinna Swamy, Peria Swamy, Gungamma, Kaliyamma, &c.

In some cases the name given to a child refers to something peculiar in the child, and sometimes, when children are grown up, they get a new name, because of some great event or circumstance connected with their life. There is what I may call a regular change of names. The Black-eyed Beauty, The Fish-eyed One, The Swan, Gold, The Precious One, The Only Pearl, The Meek One, are the meanings of some of the names of the Hindu females, and The Daring One, The Tiger-Hearted, The Persevering One, The Cunning Fellow, Blackman, Redman, &c., are the meanings of some of the names of the Hindu males.

4. We very often see in print, and hear of persons having queer or curious names, and these persons have received these peculiar names in curious ways. For instance, says the *Exchange*:—

"Mr. Kansas-Nebraska Bill, of Connecticut, received his name when there was a great excitement in the States on the Kansas-Nebraska bill question. Master Endymion Garfield Chester was recently christened at Milwaukee. Six names were put in a hat and his parents drew two. Miss Mazin Grace Brooks is a resident of Kansas City, Mo., her pious mother having named her (by ear) out of the hymn-book: 'Amazing grace, how sweet the sound!' The late Mr. Lewis Hamilton, of Kentucky, left five children: Mr. London Judge Hamilton, Master Southern Soil Hamilton, and Misses Avenue Belle, China Figure, and Hebrew Fashion Hamilton. Miss Mary Germanic Vanderbilt Phillips was christened on the *Germanic* in May last, Mr. Vanderbilt standing sponsor for her mother's doctor's bill. Mr. Arthur Wellington Waterloo is an ex-army surgeon in England. Michael Sir Shephard lives at Elford, England. When his mother was bidden, 'Name this child,' she curtsied and replied: 'Michael, Sir,' and Michael Sir it was. An old Irish song records a parallel case, where a dog, answering to the name 'Dennis,' was making himself too busy at the christening, and had to be checked by the mother, with the result described:—

"'What's his name?' says the priest; 'Down, Dennis,' says she;
So Down Dennis Balgruddy they christened me."

An anonymous writer in the *Argosy*, speaking of the origin or derivation of the names of the Creole Negroes of the West Indies, in a style rather felicitous and peculiar to himself, says:

"The predilection which Negroes have for grand names, alluded to by Marryat in one of his novels, is well known. In some of the West India Islands even darkie has a play-name, or name for common every-day use, which is, as a rule, short, and, so to speak, handy. Their baptismal names, on the contrary, are lengthy and romantic, being borrowed from the pages of 'standard novels,' or from the heroes and heroines of 'penny dreadfuls.' In the olden days, Shakespeare was greatly resorted to as a sponsor; and sable Hamlets, Othellos, Romeos, and Macbeths abound among the older Negroes. Often in the desire for a polysyllabic name its uncomplimentary or inappropriate character is overlooked, and hence some more or less worthy people are found whose names bear the prefixes of Mendacious, Abnormal, Abdominal, Ananias, &c. One man I know, christened Hobbledehoy, tries to conceal the unfortunate name by a strong accent on the second syllable. I have even known a Camomile Brown.

"'Massa,' said a respectable dark gentleman to a Registrar of Births, &c., 'Massa, me make you for know dat for me wife confine Tuesday gone, and she gie me twin, both of dem boys, and me ax you be so kind as gie me name for dem.'

"'Well,' said the Registrar, 'let us see, I think you have better call one "Waverley" and the other "Guy Mannering."'

"'Tank you, me massa, dem name fustrate, but me beg you write dem on a crip (scrip) of paper, else me no member dem.' The Registrar did so, and Mr. Pompey went away rejoicing. Some weeks after, the following conversation was overheard between Pompey and a friend:—

"'Well, buddie (brother), and how does dem two picknie get on?'

"'Fustrate! hearty,' replied Pompey.

"'Dey is christened yet?'

"'O yes! dey baptize last Sunday at chapel.'

"'And what name you gie dem?'

"'Well, me friend, for tell de troot' me scarce able for get my tongue round de words, but de name well handsome. Ah! dey call um "Waberley" and "Guy Maddering," someting so.'

"'Eh! me fadder!' said Pompey's friend, 'where ebber you get dem name?'

"'Registrar gie um, and write um down for no make mistake.'

"'And parson take um?'

"'Yes, me friend. Fust he say he nebber hear "Guy Maddering" before, but he know "Waberly" been one pusson as write plenty good book, so he speck praps dey been brudders, and so he receive de name for me picknies and dem.' The 'parson' no doubt was one of the locus preacher tribe whose reading did not extend to Scott.

"Two black girls, labourers on a friend's estate in the island of ——, returning from work, met on the road. They had but a scanty amount of clothes, but each had a baby in her arms. There was some quarrel between them, and a wordy combat ensued. At its close one damsel turning away said, 'Well, I don't want no more discoorse wid you, Miss Teráza.'

"'Me make you for know, marm,' retorted the other girl, 'that for me name no Teráza, but Tereesa.'

"'Well, me dear,' was the reply, 'Teráza else Tereesa, both de same, for me name a better name than for you own, for me name Diana de Goddess of Chaste;' and Diana strutted off with a swing of her tattered skirt and toss of the head that would have become a duchess.

"A Negro often takes as his 'bragging' or 'play' name that of his master, and in their social gatherings these names alone are used, while the gait and manner, or any other peculiarities of their employers, are also imitated.

"Servants and labourers are addicted to bestowing on their offspring the names of their masters and mistresses, and often when, as is the custom in some of the Colonies, a son takes as his surname the Christian name of his father, the result is embarrassing. For instance, if Mr. Brown Robinson's groom, Jack Cæsar, calls his son 'Robinson Cæsar,' the latter, when he has a boy, will probably christen him as 'Brown,' and the child is known not as 'Brown Cæsar,' but as 'Brown Robinson,' so that proper-minded persons are apt, on finding the aristocratic name to be borne by a small coloured boy, to shake their heads, and make edifying reflections on the morality of the original Robinson.

"This mark of respect or of admiration for the name and sometimes the rank of a superior was curiously exemplified some years ago in, as I think, Jamaica, where the wife of a black military labourer marched up to the font with her infant, and in the presence of a scandalized congregation gave its intended name as 'George Frederick Augustus Snodgrass Adjutant.'"

The late Rev. Henry Bleby, in his *Missionary Father's Tales*, Third Series, gives the name of a fugitive or runaway slave as "Shadrach-Meshach-Abednego-Hannibal;" and the Rev. M. C. Osborn, who paid a visit to British Guyana in the fall of 1878, in a speech he made at the Exeter Hall Annual Missionary Meeting in 1879, said, speaking of his work in Jamaica, "I several times administered the sacrament of Holy Baptism, and I am credibly informed that a good number of little male darkies, *in esse* and *in posse*, will at a future time be known by the name of Marmaduke Osborn; and I should not be surprised if some are called 'General Secretary,' and others go down to posterity as so many 'Deputations.'" I do not know what has been done in Jamaica, and the other West Indian Islands the Reverend gentleman visited. So far as the Colony of British Guyana is concerned, I have not heard of any one as yet being baptized, or named, "Marmaduke Osborn," or "General Secretary," or "Deputation."

Very frequently when I baptize adult Indian Coolie Immigrants, I give them some Scriptural names, and sometimes the names of those persons who stand sponsors, or godfathers and godmothers, and the same thing is done by the other Missionaries who labour among the Coolies, and by other Ministers also. The following incident connected with the baptism of an Indian Coolie is of rather an amusing character:—

"Two neighbours, a proprietor and a middle-aged maiden lady, had a desperate quarrel over a disputed right of way. They had not gone to law, but from being excellent friends they had become bitter foes, and the small society of the parish was deeply interested in each phase of the dispute. Mr. P—— employed on his estate several Coolies; and two of them, a driver or superintendent, Sahye, and his wife Jebuseeah, having become converted to Christianity, were about to be baptized. Sahye appiled to his employer to be his sponsor, and Jebuseeah, who was a *protégée* of Miss W——, obtained permission to take her name. The unhappy feud between the sponsors prevented the double ceremony taking place on the same day, as nothing would induce the one to meet the other under any circumstances; and so the Coolies were baptized on different days.

"Of course, a marriage according to the rites of the Church was to follow; and one fine Sunday, when the quarrel between Mr. P. and Miss W. was at its climax, the congregation in the church were astounded at hearing the banns of marriage published between Philip James P——— widower and Arabella W——— spinster. The gentleman and lady rose simultaneously as if to forbid the banns; the greatest excitement prevailed; when their eyes met, it flashed across their minds that the banns were those of their Coolie *protégés*, a smile lit up the face of each, and the incident was the means of a mutual explanation, and afforded an opportnnity for a happy adjustment of the disputed right of way."

5. Ear-boring is another ceremony which is kept up by the Coolies when the child is about one or two years old. Letters whose edges and corners are stained with saffron are sent per express messengers to the friends and relatives on the different estates, requesting them to attend the *ear-boring* ceremony on the day appointed. Sunday (being a free day to all the immigrants, and a day in which they can enjoy themselves in worldly and sensual pleasure) is generally the day fixed by the Andi for such a ceremony, which is generally well attended. Large sums of money are also spent on the child who has his or her ear bored. The whole ceremony concludes with a grand feast, which is generally given by the father of the child or his nearest relative.

6. In connection with the birth, naming, &c., of the child, there are a few things which must be guarded against, such as the *evil eye, evil saying*, and the like. "Is thine eye evil, because I am good?" seems to refer in a very striking manner to the Hindus who believe in the malignant potency of the evil eye. Should a child be pretty and attractive, he is then in danger of being narrowly looked at by strangers, and every time the child is thus looked at, some god or idol must be invoked to neutralize the influence of the evil eye, or the child would not thrive.

So also with a good milch cow. Should a Hindu possess a fine cow, and you express a favourable opinion about it, he or you must immediately spit on it, or the evil eye will ruin the cow, and it will not give as much milk as it was accustomed to give. While a house is in process of construction, there may be seen near it a pole stuck into the ground, upon which is placed an earthen jar, covered with white spots, or a flag fastened to the pole, having for its design to "*keep off the evil eye,*" which would otherwise be harmful to the builder or the owner. So completely are they under the power of a ridiculous superstition. And should a man in future years become weak, and poor, the exclamation is at once heard, "See how sharp people's teeth are! He is ruined entirely because people could not bear to see his happiness."

7. The Hindus are a very superstitious people, and the disposition manifests itself in a variety of ways. Against the mysterious source of evil (evil eye) above mentioned, there are countless charms and counter-charms employed by them. People of every rank and station in society, and of every creed and sect, among the Hindus here provide charms for themselves, their children, their houses, their cattle, and even for their gardens. Amulets are hung round the neck, or hid away in the bosom; and their dwelling houses and gardens have mysterious signs drawn upon them, to guard against the evil eye. The sacred rupee, or piece of silver (a coin dedicated to the guardian Iman), is tied on the arm, or suspended from the neck, to avert evils, to defend from sickness, accidents, from the malice of enemies, from the evil eye, in short, from every kind of calamity. The forehead is sometimes marked with *tikha*, or curdled milk, as a propitious omen, on beginning a voyage or journey.

8. As to superstitious practices, not the Indian and Chinese Coolies only, but the very Portuguese, Blacks, and other respectable inhabitants of the Colony are addicted to them. The following case of superstitious practice by a Portuguese was tried at Belfield, Mahaica Judicial District, on Tuesday, March 14, 1882, before Mr. F. E. Dampier, S.J.P.:—

"Francis Ferreira was charged with using insulting words to one Joseph Thomas, at Ann's Grove Village. The complainant is Village Councillor, and on the 12th inst. was engaged superintending the removal of a house from a certain lot at Ann's Grove. After the house had been removed the defendant proclaimed that a quantity of money which he had concealed in the house was stolen by some one. In order to discover the offender, he adopted a practice which is common to the Creole people, viz., the book and key. The complainant was invited to defendant's room where he found a large number of persons gathered. As he entered the room, defendant, who had a key tied between the pages of a Bible, cried out, "By St. Peter, by St. Paul, is Mr. Thomas stole this money?" The Bible which was held between the fingers by the key, immediately fell on the name of Thomas being called, and he was declared to be the thief. The magistrate addressing complainant said there was no evidence that any insulting words were used; all the complainant's witnesses simply proved that a book and key were used, which he did not care much about. He must therefore dismiss the case. The complainant said he was provoked to break the "bridge" of peace, and he knew he would have broken it.

9. Speaking of superstitions, I may say that the following, handed down by tradition, are fervently believed in many parts of America, and in the Colony of British Guyana.

White specks on the nails are luck.

Whoever reads epitaphs loses his memory.

To rock the cradle when empty is injurious to the child.

To eat while a bell is tolling for a funeral causes a toothache.

The crowing of a hen indicates some approaching disaster.

When a mouse gnaws a hole some misfortune may be apprehended.

He who has his teeth wide asunder must seek his fortune in a distant land.

Whoever finds a four-leaf trefoil shamrock should wear it for good luck.

Beggar's bread should be given to children who are slow learning to speak.

If a child less than twelve months old be brought into a cellar, he becomes fretful.

When children play soldiers on the roadside, it forebodes the approach of war.

A child grows proud if suffered to look into the mirror when twelve months old.

He who proposes moving into a new house must first send in bread and a new broom.

Whoever sneezes at an early hour either hears some news or receives some present the same day.

The first tooth cast by a child should be swallowed by the mother to insure a new growth of teeth.

Buttoning the coat awry, or drawing on a stocking inside out, causes matters to go wrong during the day.

By bending the head to the hollow of the arm the initial letter of one's future spouse is represented.

Women who sow flax seed should, during the process, tell some confounded lies, otherwise the yarn will never bleach white.

When women are stuffing beds, the men should not remain in the house, otherwise the feathers will come through the tick.

When a person enters a room, he should be obliged to sit down, if only for a moment, as he otherwise takes away the children's sleep with him.

Among the Creoles I observe that until the ceremony of baptism is performed on an infant, a Bible is always placed under its pillow. A horse shoe is nailed on the door to secure the inmates from the attack of hogs or witches. On the death of a relation the children are crossed over the coffin before it is taken from the house to the burial; should any one sneeze at the time of this performance, it indicates the death of another near relation. Among the Coolies the cat passing across the road is a bad omen, the business begun is obstructed. The chirping of a lizard from the south of any person is a favourable omen. The flight of a heron, from right to left, across the path of a person first setting out on a journey, is inauspicious. If at the time of a person getting married the dog growls or barks, or a cat rushes in, it is a sure sign of the marriage being an unhappy one.

10. One great superstitious abomination practised and believed in by the black Creoles of the Colony, and other West Indian Islands, as Trinidad, Jamaica, Hayti, &c., is Obeahism, which seems to defy all the efforts of the Legislature to stamp it out. The law does not trifle with offenders when they are brought under it and their offence is brought home to them; but it is very seldom that an Obeahman is publicly catted for practising his abominable and diabolical calling, and yet it is patent to every one who takes any notice of the habits and customs of the labouring Creole population, that their belief in and their fear of the Obeahman are strong and deeply grounded. It is the people's childish fear of the impostor that constitutes his main safety. Imbued with the superstitious feelings of their ancestors, they firmly believe in the Obeahman's power to work evil for them, and, weak-minded and timid as they are, they hesitate to place themselves in antagonism to what they consider to be supernatural powers that are able to deprive them not only of health but of life itself. The Obeahman or Piaiman (from the Caribi word "*Puiai*," which signifies a sorcerer, and equivalent to the Tamil word *Pcy-Karan* or *Pey-Pidittavan*, literally devil-man, one possessed of the devil) is consulted in cases of sickness and adversity. If the patient is strong enough to endure the disease, the excitement, the noise, and the fumes of tobacco in which he is at times enveloped, and the sorcerer observes signs of recovery, he will pretend to extract the cause of the complaint by sucking the part affected. After many ceremonies he will produce from his mouth some strange substance, such as a thorn or a gravel-stone, a fish bone or bird's claw, a snake's tooth or a piece of wire, which some malicious Yauhahu is supposed to have inserted in the affected part. As soon as the patient fancies himself rid of this cause of his illness his recovery is generally rapid, and the fame of the sorcerer greatly increased. The Obeahman, generally speaking, is deformed, ugly, with a lot of wrinkles on his face, and altogether a frightful object. Some folks go even so far as to believe that the Obeahman can transport himself from place to place at his pleasure, like an unseen spirit; and hence

they dread him. Nor is the dread of Obeah confined to the uneducated classes; it exists in the minds of men and women who have received a liberal education, but who, instead of labouring to defeat the impostor's power by ridiculing it or exposing its contemptible nature, pay it homage, and in some cases call in its aid to help out their special purposes. The following account, taken from the *Royal Gazette* of Georgetown, Demerara, will give my reader some idea of what Obeahism really is:—

"It is useless to look to the lowest class in the country to rebel and throw off the Obeah yoke as long as their superiors in position and general advantages are content to remain in bondage, and Ministers and others who are bent on eradicating the evil should direct their crusade, in the first place, not against the lowest grade of society, but against a higher class which provides the Churches of the Colony with the great bulk of their members. When this class has been brought to see Obeah in its true light, then it will be easier to prevail on those at the bottom of the ladder to laugh at the threats of the Obeahman; but until then the Ministers' efforts will be almost in vain.

"In the meantime the profession goes on flourishing, and provides a large and regular income to a number of blackguards who are either located in some district populous enough to support them, or who perambulate the country on the hunt for work, which is seldom hard to get. It is seldom their prosperity is interrupted, but occasionally a man is found sensible enough to lay a trap for the scamps, and then the Magistrate's Court becomes the means of giving the general public some idea of the ceremonies performed during the working of the magic, and the articles that are necessary to render it effective. Such a case has just occurred in Berbice. A policeman received notice from a man that an Obeahman was going to practise at his house that night. The policeman concealed himself where he could see and hear everything that was going on; and after the magic was performed, he arrested the magician himself. The evidence given in the Court, one would think, would suffice to break the power of Obeah without one word being added against it. As is usual in these cases, the Obeahman pretended he had been hired to kill the man in whose house he then was, for which deed he was to receive six dollars; it being understood, of course, that if the

Obeahman was to receive six dollars for killing, he ought to be paid at least double that for disappointing his customer, and letting the intended victim live. To make the bargain binding, the Obeahman then called for a tumbler, into which he poured some of the contents of a bottle; he then called for another tumbler and poured some of the bottle's contents into it also; he then called for a third tumbler, but he did not pour anything into it. He called for a looking-glass and six bits, a pair of scissors, a reel of black thread, a razor, five pins and two needles, and arranged these articles on a table before him. He then called the man whom he was engaged to kill, and putting his hand on the victim's stomach muttered something which nobody could understand. Whether the spell was complete at that stage we cannot say, but the policeman stepped in and arrested both the magic and the magician, and seized the whole of the household articles which were being made such a mysterious use of. The ludicrous ceremony thus disclosed in Court is, no doubt, a fair specimen of the performance by the generality of Obeahmen in presence of their believers; and it shows how deep-rooted and firm the superstition must be in the minds of the people, when such childish, silly, and contemptible forms can awe them. In this case the victim had sense enough to know that the Obeahman was a law-breaking rascal, and that the jail was the best place for him; but he is a great exception to the ordinary run of his class, who would not dare to betray the presence of the Obeahman, for fear of the awful consequences that, in their opinion, would be sure to follow. The light way the Obeahman talked of being engaged to do murder is, in a manner, very amusing. He was engaged at six dollars to murder the man in whose house he was; but this was a cheap job; for in the course of conversation he stated that he was engaged to go to Lochaber that night to throw a man into the boiling tache, for which he was to get forty dollars. The policeman, in arresting him, thus spoilt a good night's business, and interfered with the magician's income; it is to be hoped the law will see its way clear to indemnify the Obeahman for this loss by providing him with free board and lodging for some time, and with such other attention as the ordinance regarding the practice of Obeah recommends. It is humiliating to think that a superstition of pins and needles should, after fifty years of freedom, flourish as bravely as it did in the days of slavery." *

* See Chapter XV. under *Doctors*.

The following I extract from a recent number of the *Berbice Asylum Journal*:—

"That a firm belief in Obeahism is widely diffused amongst the people of this Colony any one who is brought into intimate contact with them is not long in discovering. This belief is not one in Obeahism only as a mode of secret poisoning, a materialistic and gross view of the craft, but in it as a form of enchantment, after the style of that of which we read in the *Arabian Nights*. By its means it is believed that the fortunes of men can be made or marred. When any one wishes to wreak his vengeance on his enemies without danger to himself, it is to the Obeah doctor he applies. An incident which took place a few years ago at the Asylum so strongly illustrates both the belief in Obeah and its mode of working as to be worth relating. One morning the senior attendant, a fair-skinned, almost white, man, and one of fair intelligence, made a complaint that an attempt had been made to Obeah him. He said that early that morning an Obeah bottle had been found upon the doorstep of his cottage, and as he was the first person likely to pass it, it must have been intended for him: although he made the complaint, he was loud as usual in his expression of unbelief in Obeah. How could he, a Christian, believe in such a thing? At the same time he showed great reluctance to bring the bottle, and only did so after a good deal of pressure had been put upon him. He treated it much after the same manner as one can suppose an infernal machine is handled when its character is known. It was afterwards found out that he had, before leaving his cottage that morning, looked out of the window, and saw the thing of horror upon his doorstep. At once a hue and cry was raised to bring assistance from outside, as no one dared pass it. A woman living near came and undertook to exorcise the demon of the bottle, which she did by performing the usual rites of invocation, and a liberal application of salt and water. When examined, this terrible thing was found to be an ordinary eau-de-cologne bottle filled with a heterogeneous collection, after the approved style of necromancy. Here were—

> "Eye of newt and toe of frog,
> Wool of bat and tongue of dog,
> Adder's fork and blind worm sting,
> Lizard's leg, owlet's wing,"

or their local equivalents. Conspicuously standing above the cork was a hair, certainly much like one from the head of the attendant who complained, and its presence was said to act as a guide to direct the mischief towards him. The bottle was afterwards used as a test of the belief in Obeahism amongst the attendants, and its effects were very marked. The application of the test was made in this manner. First came the question—'Have you had anything to do with this Obeah business? Do you believe in it?' 'O, Sir! how could I believe in such a thing?' 'It is a good thing you don't believe in it, for then you will be able to tell me what you think of this.' On which the bottle suddenly appears. The abrupt start, the tremor, and change of complexion, in one instance a bolt made for the door, showed that the heart did not confirm the denial made by the tongue. The bottle is still in existence, but its contents have dried up, so it is feared that its virtue may have departed from it."

11. All the dances carried on or practised by the black people in the Colony are more or less connected with Obeahism and superstition. The songs sung and the attitudes adopted at the time of these dances, which are generally kept up in dark nights and in dark places, are indecent and disgusting, and very much resemble the orgies of devil-dancing, practised by the Shanars of Tinnevelly in South India. The Tchibounga, the Comfoo, the Racoon, the Joe and Johnny, the Somma-Somma, the Shiloh, the Shake-shake, the Drupoid, the Water-Mamma or Mermaid, the Meringa, and other dances are all thus connected with the practice of Obeahism. The Aboriginal Indians of the Colony, in like manner, have some dances peculiar to themselves. When a male member of the tribe dies, they hold a festival called *Macquarie*, and a dance called *Mocquarie* for his memorial; and when a female dies, they have a dance called *Hauyarie*. They have also the dances called *Bimmith*, the humming-bird dance; *Hicuhrie*, the turtle dance; and the *Hanorah*, the crane or heron dance. But the most immoral and vulgar dance among them is called *Shah-coco-lih*. When, however, this dance is to be held, all the strangers and the modest girls or women present at the entertainment are duly notified, so that they might retire, so as not to witness the disgusting scenes.

I am inclined to believe that the ancient dances about which we read were of the same kind or stamp, and hence the ancient Christian Fathers, aroused by the indecent dances of those days, gave emphatic evidence against any participation in the dance. St. Chrysostom says, "The feet were not given for dancing, but to walk modestly; not to leap impudently like camels." One of the dogmas of the ancient Church reads: "A dance is the devil's possession; and he that entereth into a dance, entereth into his possession. The devil is the gate to the middle and to the end of the dance. As many passes as a man makes in dancing, so many passes doth he make to hell." Elsewhere, these dogmas declare: "The woman that singeth in the dance is the princess of the devil; and those that answer are like his clerks, and the beholders are his friends, and the music is his bellows, and the fiddlers are the ministers of the devil; for, as when hogs are strayed, if the hogs'herd call one, all assemble together, so the devil calleth one woman to sing in the dance, or to play on some instrument, and presently all the dancers gather together."

However strongly the lovers of dance and public balls may advocate the practice as a harmless amusement, there is no denying the fact that dance is the devil's bait, and the ball room or dancing saloon has been the downfall and the ruin of many a respectable female, and has sent thousands to an eternal perdition.

In British Guyana, especially among the vulgar, there is frequently an entertainment held in the evenings called "The Dignity Ball." Each individual who wishes to attend it and have a dance in the room must pay a certain sum at the door. Sometimes a few stray respectable characters find themselves enjoying the sport with the unwashed throng of the community of the city of Georgetown. There is also another institution, of a pseudo-religious character, which is largely patronized by the natives especially in country districts, and that is the "tea meeting." Instrumental music is allowed in these tea meeting gatherings; the people sing heartily and lustily enough to the sound of the music. Only sacred (or, as some are pleased to call it, "secret") music is allowed, and every thing goes on well for a time, but by-and-bye the musicians ("musicianers") play a sacred march, and the friends take up the musical strain by keeping time with their feet or by marching round with a limitation of the number of hops in each bar of the music. Sometimes the Ministers of the Gospel also take part in dancing entertainments connected with their Sunday and Day Schools, as the following, reported in the *Argosy* of November 6, 1880, will show:—

"On Monday, the first of November, a service was held in the Church of St. Mary the Virgin, Beterverwagting, East Coast, for the day and Sunday scholars of the juvenile and infant departments. The programme was as follows:—

"*Processional.*—Hymn 194 (Ancient and Modern); *Opening Sentences.*—By Rev. W. CHRISTOPHER, of Beterverwagting; *The Lesson from* Matt. xix. 13—26.—By Rev. McDONALD, of Christ Church; *Venite.*—Psalm cl., to Grand Chant.—Te Deum in D major.—Ring the Bells of Heaven (Sacred Song).—The Seven Joys of Mary (Choral); *Address from* Matt. xix. 14.—By Rev. THOS. FARRAR, Rector of St. Paul's; *Anthem.*—Benediction by Rev. T. Farrar; Recessional 299 of Hymns A. & M.

"The Chant to Psalm cl., Ring the Bells of Heaven, and The Seven Joys of Mary, were sung by the children with great taste and accuracy, qualified as they have been by the skilful training of the Rev. Christopher.

"The address was short and easily grappled by the children, and showed the skill of the Rector, who handled the subject in a homely way; but he made a serious blunder when he asserted that in the Bible we have two books written by Timothy.

"After the service was concluded a procession was made round the village, with drums and fifes from Eve Leary Barracks accompanying. The Sergeant-Major who presided over the band, did his utmost to enliven the party for the whole day.

"The company reassembled for refreshment in the schoolroom, after which there was general dancing in the school-yard, where the clergymen tried all they could to further the enjoyment of the people. It was laughable to see the youngest clergyman affecting the cavalier to an old toothless granny in waltz and quadrille. Only one clergyman did not try to dance, owing to an accident. He was rushing down to the spot, the centre of the dance, as lightly as he could, when down he went; earth and his haunch met with a fearful crash audible at a great distance off; every one felt sorry for him, but he started back brushing and scraping in such a pretty way that a smile played upon the faces of many. He came out no more for the day, but took to his 'corner sweet.' Upon inquiring I heard it was the Rector, but I don't believe it.

"Children and parents sought their homes only after they saw that the Sergeant-Major was safely seated in the evening train on his way to town.

"It is seldom we see such an exhibition of good feeling between the clergy and the people as was made on Monday last, and every one prays here for the long life and happiness of such gentlemen as the Revs. Williams, Hay, McDonald, and Christopher, who do great honour to their spiritual head our venerable Lord Bishop, by their activity and care for the interests of the Church, and who bind the hearts of the people to them by laying aside upon occasion that misanthropical niceness so popular in this nineteenth century."

12. In addition to all the ceremonies above mentioned, I may say the Indian Immigrants have other amusements, such as *theatrical exhibitions*. These they keep up in regular succession; and the *maistry*, or headman of these exhibitions, gets large sums of money as the fruits of his toil. All the deeds of Krishna, Rama, Siva, Durga, and others, are exhibited in scenic representations. These entertainments are held at night, and are often continued until the morning, the spectators being affected with grief or joy, according to the drama performed. Many of the scenes portray vile events in the life of the horrid Krishna, and produce the most pernicious and mischievous effect upon the morals of the spectators, especially the young, of both sexes, to whom the drama proves a curse and ruin. Some of these performances are periodically held on Plantations Enmore, Great Diamond, Farm, Cane Grove, &c., and in Georgetown, Essequibo, and Berbice.

CHAPTER XIX.

CRUEL HABITS, ETC., OF THE LABOURING POPULATION.

1. In his *At Last*, speaking of the Trinidad Coolies and Negroes, Mr. Charles Kingsley observes: "We have almost daily proofs of the Coolie men's fondness for their children; of their fondness also—an excellent sign that the *morale* is not destroyed at the root—for dumb animals. A Coolie cow or donkey is petted, led about tenderly, tempted with tit-bits. Pet animals, where they can be got, are the Coolie's delight, as they are the delight of the wild Indian. I wish I could say the same of the Negro. His treatment of his children and of his beasts of burden is, but too often, as exactly opposed to that of the Coolie as are his manners. No wonder that the two races do not, and it is to be feared never will, amalgamate; that the Coolie, shocked by the unfortunate awkwardness of gesture and vulgarity of manners of the average Negro, and still more of the Negress, looks on them as savages, while the Negro, in his turn, hates the Coolie as a hard-working interloper, and despises him as a heathen; or that heavy fights between the two races arise now and then, in which the Coolie, in spite of his slender limbs, has generally the advantage over the burly Negro, by dint of his greater courage and the terrible quickness with which he wields his beloved weapon, the long hard wood quarter-staff—the hockie-stick." This description is true also of the Coolies and Negroes of Demerara.

2. I would not, however, attempt to argue that the people of British Guyana are more heartless and cruel towards their domestic animals than are the people of other countries, for I do not believe they are. Such atrocious practices as the "manufacture" of goose liver by a process which must entail

great suffering on the bird, the "horning" of cattle, the plucking of live fowls, the bleeding of calves to death so as to acquire whiteness in the meat, the blinding of canaries to make them whistle better, and so on, are peculiar to the advanced civilization and great refinement of European countries and are unknown here; but though we as a Colony can plead innocence of nearly all forms of what may be called scientific and deliberate cruelty, such as those enumerated above, there is no denying the fact that there is much unreasoning brutality practised towards the domestic animals that minister to our wants and convenience. Our lower classes are so indifferent to the physical condition of themselves and their children that, until they are educated into it, it would be unreasonable to expect them to show more consideration for their animals than they show for themselves. They ill-treat, over-drive, and abuse their beasts of burden, not because their moral nature is so depraved and vicious that the contemplation of the pain they inflict gives them pleasure; in the majority of cases, it is because they do not give the nature of their action a thought. A boy, a mule-driver on an estate, anything but cruel in his disposition, will walk behind a punt-mule from the field to the mill, and ply his long heavy whip on the animal's quarters, without a moment's intermission; not because the mule is lazy and requires the lash to quicken it up, but because the lad has fallen into the habit and regards it as part of his duty. And so it is with the cab and cart drivers in the city and villages. The "evil is wrought for want of thought."

3. Touching on this very subject I remember reading somewhere an incident which, if practised by the cart-drivers, mule-drivers, and others of Demerara and elsewhere, will be to their credit and honour. In one of the London timber-yards there was a carter who was noted for his kindness to the horse which was under his care. He was deeply attached to it, and the handsome creature appeared to be equally fond of him. Such was the command that this carter had acquired over his horse, that a whip was unnecessary. He had only to walk a little in advance, when, after a kind word or two, and the simple

pointing of the finger, the noble animal would draw his heavy burden much more readily than those which were cruelly lashed with the whip. O that more kind words were used in the management of horses, donkeys, and mules, and fewer lashes of the whip! These and other animals, like human beings, are more easily *drawn by kindness* than *driven by cruelty*.

4. One of the most revolting forms of crime by two black Creoles, investigated during one of the Criminal Sessions three years ago, was entered in the calendar as manslaughter of an orphan boy (black) named Clarke, in the month of May, 1879. The following particulars I extract from the *Royal Gazette* of August 23rd, 1879 :—

"The persons charged with the crime, a black man named Brutus and his wife, were shingle cutters on a wood-cutting grant in the Hianira creek, Demerara river, who, when in town in January, engaged the boy Clarke to go to the grant to work under them at the trade. Clarke, whose sobriquet was the singularly appropriate one of 'Poor Boy,' was fated to undergo on the grant such an amount of physical suffering and misery as we hope falls to the lot of few persons within the jurisdiction of the Colony; but the revelations in the present case are frightfully suggestive of what in our ignorance may be going on day after day close around us. Poor Boy was evidently not in very good health when he reached the Hianira, for immediately after he arrived on the grant he was found to be troubled with sores on his toes and swollen feet, which prevented him working as he wished to do, his disposition being anything but unwilling or indolent. Having been engaged by the Brutuses as their servant to work at shingle making, it was to them a disappointment and annoyance to find that the lad could not always go out to work, and could do but a very limited amount of work on such days as he managed to reach the shingle field, the more especially that whether he worked or not they had to feed him, that is to say, to give him food enough to keep him alive. It is hard to understand why, when the boy's uselessness as a shingle maker became apparent to his employers, they did not do as they did later on,—send him back to town in one of the punts which were continually trading to and fro, unless we are to suppose that the unfortunate wretch was retained purposely to be starved and tortured. To the woman in particular, Poor

Boy appears to have been an object of the most inveterate hatred, and her heart never appears to have been touched by a thought of the boy's helplessness and misery. The man was disposed to be kinder to the lad, and one of the witnesses testified that on more than one occasion when the husband was interceding in the lad's behalf, the wife turned upon the husband and gave him a beating. This brute in the shape of a woman used to strip the lad naked and weal his back with bush rope, until his screams 'for murder' were heard ringing over the grant. Occasionally for one, two, three, or four days at a stretch she would keep him without food; and it was told in the witness-box how she fell foul of a Portuguese lad who was cook for the grant-holder, because he had taken pity upon Poor Boy and given him some victuals. The victuals she tore from the starving lad's hand and scattered over the ground. Week after week this diabolical treatment continued, until at last Poor Boy's state had become so deplorable that it was clear he could stand the starvation and the bush rope only a very limited time longer. The wife and her husband then decided to send him back to town, and arranged with a punt captain to give him passage, telling the captain to drop the lad on the first stelling he came to. The captain told the Court that when the prisoners asked him to give the lad a passage, he told them he could not take him unless they first cleansed him a little, for he was in such a filthy state it was almost impossible to stand near him; and to give emphasis to his description of the lad's condition, the captain said he had so much difficulty in getting hands to engage to work the punt to town, that he asked the prisoners to take the lad back to their house, but this they declined to do. Dr. Leary's description of Poor Boy's condition when he was brought to the Colonial Hospital accounted for the puntmen's refusal to go in the punt with him. On the surface of his body were over a score of sloughing wounds, the result of the woman's cruel beatings; both feet were attacked with gangrene, and one had almost dropped off the ankle. No human skill could work a cure in such a frightful mass of sores and putrefaction, and the wonder is that the lad did not perish on the grant, under the hands of his torturers. He died the day after he was admitted to the Hospital. The jury found both prisoners guilty and recommended the husband to the merciful consideration of the Judge. The man was sentenced to six months' imprisonment, and the woman to two years. Considering the horrible and persistent cruelty which the woman displayed in her treatment of the Poor Boy, the general feeling is that her sentence errs greatly on the side of leniency."

The following horrible description of another diabolical crime committed in the County of Berbice this year (1882), will give my reader a sufficient knowledge of the depravity of man :—

"Mary Rose Alfred (interpreted) sworn said :—I am both deaf and dumb, but I can babble a little. I know the prisoners in the dock, likewise Emma Benjamin and Frances Johnnie. I remember on Saturday night, 13th May this year, about 10 o'clock, I was selling fried fish and bread at De Cunha's Liquor Shop Bridge. I saw Mrs. Ferrell dressed all over in black, her daughter also dressed in black; both of them went down China Lane towards the Back Dam. Frances Johnnie went up Davson's Lane towards Water Street. She asked me to go with her to the High Bridge, where a girl had gone for a frock. I did not go, so she went alone. At 11 o'clock she returned and found me at the same place, she told me that 'Half-a-hand Bosy' had given the girl a blow on the side, and the others she went with beat the girl about the body. She would not tell me the name of the girl. Myself and her were alone when she told me this. After they had beaten the girl, she said, they stripped her and each of the men violated her; they cut her breast off, and her private parts they also cut; they cut her all about the face with razors; her finger rings, earrings, beads and shawl they took away, and gave to a lady at the Winkle. After this had been finished they tied her 'hand to hand' and dragged her to the river side towards the High Bridge. In returning the three men walked Middle Road, homewards, and Mrs. Ferrell and daughter the Back Dam Road. The Monday after I had told the policeman and inspector, Frances met me and said that 'I had too much mouth.' On the said Saturday night (13th) I called a policeman to relate the story to him; but he pulled away his hand from me and said he couldn't understand me. The very night I saw Bosy going up the street with a big white painted stick. Bosy heard when Frances was telling me the story, so he tried to flog me, but did not get me. I ran towards a policeman for protection, Bosy then walked quickly away."—*Berbice Gazette*.

A mother—a black woman—only about three years ago, in

Golden Grove Village, on the East Coast, was seen to strip her daughter naked for some fault she had committed, and then to beat her unmercifully in a brutal manner publicly in the village, and then to rub in Cayenne pepper and salt on the wounds inflicted by this heartless mother on the body of her own offspring. The following are the particulars of this diabolical act, tried before Mr. Hawtayne, S.J.P., extracted from the *Royal Gazette* of Saturday, February 22, 1879. It is a kind unfortunately only too common in the West Indies:—

"A woman named Maria Hercules, Golden Grove Village, was charged with 'peppering' her own child Maria, a girl of about nine years of age. The evidence proved that the girl returned from school with her dress torn, which exasperated her mother, who first gave her a thrashing, then prepared a mass of bruised peppers, which she rubbed into the girl's eyes and other delicate parts of her body; having done which, she pitched the girl out upon the dam. The victim of this awful treatment was called as a witness in the case, but denied that her mother had so treated her. The case, however, was too clearly established, and the Magistrate sent the woman to jail for three months with hard labour.

"We have always regarded it as a defect in the law that there is no special punishment provided for those male or female brutes who inflict the excruciating agony of 'peppering' upon children; and the punishment of all others best calculated to act as a deterrent to the crime would be two or three applications of the peppers to the offender after the fashion in which he or she had applied them. But for its comparative leniency as compared with the peppers, we would recommend the use of the lash."

Such cruelties are not to be seen practised by the Indian Immigrants. They are fond of their children, and they are also fond of their animals, and are kind to them.

✓ 5. We have, however, in this Colony dreadful wife murders, committed in cold blood by the male Indian Coolie Immigrants. The crime of murder instead of decreasing seems to be increasing year by year. We are literally surrounded by a set of bloodthirsty ruffians, and no Indian woman's life is safe. From the numerous instances of murders committed every month or week on the different sugar estates by these wretches, it would appear that they care very little or nothing at all for the consequences. Hanging does not in the least deter them from repeating or perpetrating the dreadful crime. I have already made some reference to this subject, and thrown out some hints or suggestions in Chapter XII., Nos. 7 and 8. Considered as a crime, the murder of a Coolie woman is not more heinous than the murder of any other woman or of any human being, but when we consider the fact that this terrible crime or butchery of women is committed by one particular class of our fellow colonists, it becomes a very serious question, and every civilized individual shudders at the thought that such a dreadful state of things should be allowed to continue in a Christian Colony like British Guyana without some more definite step being taken to put a stop or check to the perpetration of the crime. However desirable it may be to get the Coolies to abandon all class prejudices, and cease regarding themselves as people who may not amalgamate with the other nationalities which abound in the Colony, yet in a case like wife murder there ought to be some special criminal laws for them, and this change from their being hung up like dogs on the gallows would not in the least harden their prejudices or encourage in them a dislike of the Colony and their fellow Colonists. What does the reader think of the following, which I extract from the *Royal Gazette* of January 7, 1873?—

"The three Coolies who were convicted of the murder of Mr. Payne, the overseer of Pln. *Success*, were executed within the Georgetown Jail, on the 28th ultimo. The men were attended by the two jail chaplains; but they refused to take any interest in the chaplains' exhortations. It is said that by way of showing their contempt of our religion and the efforts being made to benefit them by it, they preferred a desire to have a dance before they were hanged. It is painfully evident, more and more so as each instance of capital punishment succeeds the other, that hanging has no terror for the Coolie, and that he looks forward to it not with a feeling of horror, as to some dreadful ignominious punishment, but with a feeling of satisfaction and delight, believing that it is the means of introducing him to that state of sensual beatitude which awaits him in the next world, should he reach that world unmutilated. The intent of the law is thwarted, and society has not that safeguard to protect it against bloodshed in the fear that the hangman's rope is suppose to exercise over the evil-minded. To render capital punishment a deterrent from murder to the Coolie it will be necessary to resort to mutilation of the body, so that his prospects of future bliss may be blighted, and death may have some horror for him; but the change in the mode of capital punishment for Coolies, even if it passed the Court here, would almost surely be rejected by the Home Government on the ground that it was un-English or on some other ground equally unreasonable."

"Another Coolie wife murder has been committed, this time on Plantation *Aurora,* Essequibo. The victim was a mere child of ten years of age, who had been married to her husband by a Roman Catholic priest. In open daylight, and before witnesses, the husband dragged the girl to the door of his house and with a cutlass ruthlessly butchered her, whilst their friends and acquaintances looked on as if the offence were quite an ordinary domestic occurrence, such as might occur soon in any of their families. After killing the girl, the man marched off to the police station, carrying the cutlass with him, and gave himself in custody, confessing his crime. He stands charged with the crime of 'wilful murder.'"

6. In July, 1878, I addressed a letter to the editor of the *Royal Gazette* on this very subject, which, with a slight alteration and some further additions (made by me in another letter published in the Colony) I now place before my impartial reader:—

"About four years ago (August 7, 1874) a letter written by me, signed 'ONE OPPOSED TO HANGING,' appeared in the columns of your journal, and since that, others have expressed their opinions in a similar strain, both in your journal and the *Colonist.* We have seen no changes since 1874. The Coolies still continue to hack and butcher their fellow creatures of the weaker sex—their wives and reputed wives—in a merciless manner, and we look on, pass our opinion, and then hang the murderers, hoping in vain that there will be an end to these murders. I was going to say, wholesale butcheries. Almost every week witnesses a dreadful murder committed by these Coolies. The cutlass is never idle; it is constantly employed in doing some damage to precious lives. We have tried 'hanging,' but hanging has not taught them any good lesson. It has not in the least deterred these cruel-hearted fellows from repeating or perpetrating cold-blooded and brutal deeds. They look on the execution of their countryman, who has been unfortunate enough to bring himself to the gallows, with the same apathy as they would look on a scene in a native play. Some even go so far as to regard the execution of a father, or brother, or uncle, as a decree of fate in which they have no part or concern. This stoic indifference, so characteristic of all Orientals,—Hindus, Chinese, Turks, Arabs,—is fostered, if not originated, by fatalism which is part of their religion.

"It is a well-known fact that to a Muhammedan the loss of the beard is as grievous and disgraceful as it could have been to the Israelitish ambassadors, who, after their beards had been shamefully taken from them by the Ammonitish king, could not make their appearance in the metropolis, but obtained permission to tarry at Jericho until their beards were grown. To say of an Oriental, 'I spit on his beard,' or 'I spit on his face,' is the *greatest verbal insult* one can inflict; and to do so, the GREATEST ACTUAL ONE. Some have been known to prefer death, and many would prefer blinding or mutilation, to the loss of the beard, or being spat on the beard or on the face, so intolerable is the disgrace, so intense the shame. The following from the *Institutes of Manu*, the great Hindu law-giver, will throw some light upon this *spitting on the face*, &c. (and I hope, Mr. Editor, you will pardon me for the plainness of language contained in the *extract:* it is not mine: the original has it so):—'He who raises his hand or a staff against another, shall have his hand cut; and he who kicks another in wroth, shall have an incision made in his foot. . . . *Should he spit on him through pride* (on the face of course), *the king shall order both of his lips to be gashed;* should he urine on him, his penis; should he break wind against him, his anus. If he seize by the locks, or by the feet, or *by the beard*, or by the throat, or by the scrotum, let the king without hesitation cause incisions to be made in his hands. If any man scratch the skin of his equal, or fetch blood from him, he shall be fined a hundred panos; if he wound a muscle, six nishcas; but, if he break a bone, let him be instantly banished.' [*The italics are mine.*] It is not for me to dictate to the authorities the kind of punishment they ought to adopt or put into effect, to prevent the perpetration or repetition of murders in this Colony by our Coolie immigrants, but I would respectfully suggest the adoption, if possible, of the *cat-o'-nine-tails.* Above any other kind of punishment inflicted on the body, the Indian Coolie detests with perfect hatred and with indescribable horror the *public catting* in the presence of all his countrymen. He would sooner prefer death by strangulation, hanging, or decapitation, to his bare back being torn by the 'CAT-O'-NINE-TAILS.' *So intolerable is the disgrace, so intense the shame.* When a Coolie murder is again committed on any of the estates, let the murderer be forthwith taken before the Chief Justice, and be tried, and if found guilty of the murder, let the culprit be put in irons and kept in solitary confinement. Once or twice in the year, as the case may be, let the murderer be taken to the estate or place where the said murder was committed, and there in the presence of all his countrymen let him be well catted. A trial of this kind in a few instances, I am sure, will teach our immigrant population a bitter lesson, which hanging has not hitherto done. Murder and murderers will soon become scarce.

"It is a well-known fact that a great majority of our Coolies believe that whenever a man dies on the gallows in a strange land, he goes back to his native land immediately after death: consequently hanging is no punishment whatever. Hence, if the system of public catting be considered a cruel or brutal act, may not penal servitude for life in fetters weighing about fifty pounds be calculated to do considerably more good in the way of punishment and also strike terror into the minds of Creoles, Chinese, Portuguese, Coolies, and others, and thus be, if not a prevention, at any rate a check to that frequent wilful murder of the opposite sex among the Indian Coolie Immigrants? Whether the murderer be a Black man, European, Indian or Portuguese, or Chinese Coolie, let the same kind of punishment be awarded to him without any difference whatever. I am, I must tell you, no advocate whatever of the system of hanging in existence in the Colony.

"And if the 'cat-o'-nine-tails,' or being put in fetters for life and kept in penal servitude, does not have the desired effect we wish to see, then I would recommend public decapitation, a punishment to which the Chinese are not strangers, that being considered by them one of the superior class of punishments in China. The partial dismemberment of the bodies of the murderers after they are hanged, recommended by some, will not remove from the minds of the Coolies the notion that death by hanging on the gallows is but a safe and sure passage to their native land. A man must have a head on his shoulders when he goes to India: he can't find himself there minus the head. Therefore instead of bodily mutilation after the hanging, I would strongly recommend beheading or decapitation of the murderer in the presence of all the spectators. It is evident something must be done to put a stop to murders in the Colony."

"Marriage, which is the foundation of domestic society, is contracted among the Hindus at an early age, and as an obligation of religion. It is usually solemnized in the house of the bride's father, where she continues to reside till of age to join her husband. The latter then proceeds to her father's house, attended by his friend, and conducts her home in a procession, usually by night, with torches and great rejoicings, with beating of *tom-toms* or drums. On both occasions considerable expenditure is incurred in feasting. The religion of the Indian Coolies is one of pomp and show, and their marriages in like manner are attended with pomp and show. Except such marriages are solemnized *in a proper fashion*, to use one of their own expressions, by their priests, petty priests, or parsons as they have been generally called in our *Daily* and *Tri-weekly* newspapers, the Coolies don't consider that they are legally or properly married. They attach very little or no importance to marriages performed by the officers of the Immigration department or Magistrates, simply because they are laymen and not Ministers of the Gospel or Gurus. I think that inasmuch as men and women (who in scores of instances leave their married wives and husbands behind when they leave India for this Colony, and form attachments during their journey to the depot in Calcutta from the various zillahs, pergunahs, &c., and sometimes in the depot itself, and sometimes during the voyage) on their arrival in the Colony are registered or recorded as *husband and wife*, and sent to the sugar estate to work, and these alliances are recognized by the Government as valid and good in point of law, so marriages celebrated among the Coolies themselves (though not by any ordained Minister of the Gospel or other agents duly appointed by the Government), in the Colony on the different estates, should be recognized by the Government as valid marriages. The Hindu Coolie does not take a woman in the *Creole fashion* and live with her at once, but he performs certain ceremonies according to his country's custom with the aid of a priest of his own religion, and after certain rites he takes the woman home to be his wife—his better half. Such marriages, I contend, should be recognized by the law of the land. If we admit the legality of the one, we must equally admit the legality of the other.

"*Adultery* among the Hindus *is punished with death*, and hence I believe the reason why murders are committed in this Colony by the Coolies. I extract the following from the *Laws or Institutes of Manu*, a great authority among the Hindus, on this portion of my letter:—'Men, who commit overt acts of adulterous inclinations for the wives of others, let the King banish from his realm, having punished them with such bodily marks as excite aversion; since adultery causes, to the general ruin, a mixture of classes among men: thence arises violation of duties, and thence is the root of felicity quite destroyed. . . . To touch a married woman on her breasts, or any other place which ought not to be touched, or, being touched unbecomingly by her, to bear it complacently, are adulterous acts with mutual assent. A man who commits adultery with the wife of a priest, ought to suffer death: the wives, indeed, of all the four classes [castes] must ever be more especially guarded. . . . A woman, polluting a damsel, *shall have her head instantly shaved*, and two of her fingers chopped off; and shall ride, mounted on an ass, through the public street. Should a wife, proud of her family and the great qualities of her kinsmen, actually violate the duty which she owes to her lord, let the King condemn her to be devoured by dogs in a place much frequented; and let him place the adulterer in an iron bed well heated, under which the executioners shall throw logs continually, till the sinful wretch be there burned to death.' I think it was this Hindu law that the Commissioners had in mind, when they recommended in their Report (*see* 877) that power should be given to flog men convicted of adultery, and to shave the heads of women under certain circumstances. From the *Indian Year Book* for 1861 I extract the following:—'*The Punjab Court*—The decrease of adultery cases was marked, there being only 600 to 873 in the previous year. This crime in the male offender has been punished . . . . with stripes; and the result proves the efficacy of the punishment. It is very important to check this crime; for a large proportion of the murders which annually take place are committed in revenge for adultery.' I observe, therefore, that a mere removal of the Indian Coolie in this Colony, guilty of this crime, from one estate to another estate, will not meet the case, will not satisfy the offended and injured husband, but a public flogging is that which is necessary.

"I am already too long, and I must therefore stop here. I feel greatly interested in the well-being of the Immigrants, and therefore state these facts with a view to benefit them, and if possible to induce you, Mr. Editor, and others to recommend what is good to the Government, so that an end may be put to existing evils among the Coolies."

7. In the neighbouring Colony of Dutch Guyana (Surinam), we have a small number of Coolie Immigrants. There, too, are murders committed by these Coolies, but as death by hanging was totally abolished in Holland many years ago (and although not openly in the Colonies of that country, yet slowly and by degrees it is likely to be abolished altogether), they are not, as a rule, sentenced to death on the gallows. A correspondent from Surinam, writing in the *Argosy*, of January 28, 1882, says:—

"The following well-known incident, which occurred about five years ago, will suffice to explain the matter. A Chinaman was found guilty of wilful murder in Surinam, and condemned to be executed. On the day named for his execution, a great crowd of his countrymen flocked to witness the scene, being previously invited to do so. He was conveyed to the spot selected for his execution, which was at the station *Frederiksdorp*, Commewyne River, by a sloop of war. The hour for execution having arrived, the rope was fixed, but a so-called accident happened by the bursting of the rope twice, and the sentence was commuted for penal servitude. I shall leave it to the option of the reader to form his own estimate of the strength of the rope.

"According to my view of the matter, does this not plainly show that the execution of the man was never intended, beyond to frighten himself and others?"

Another correspondent from the same place, writing in the *Argosy* of January 21, 1882, says:—

"A rather remarkable incident has happened at the Penal Settlement 'Fort New Amsterdam.' A Coolie was tried some time ago on the charge of wilful murder, and, confessing his guilt, was convicted only to penal servitude for twenty years, to work during that time in iron fetters, weighing above fifty pounds. The prisoner objected to his sentence, telling the Judges that as he had committed the crime, he should be hung, but, if the Judges considered the guilt of murder not proven, they should acquit him, for he could not undergo twenty years' penal service in irons, and would rather commit suicide. The Judges adhered to their sentence. On the 24th ultimo, whilst he was working with other convicts at the river-side, he threw himself into the stream and was drowned. His corpse has not been found.

"Almost every year there are some brutal murder cases brought before our Courts of Justice, in which, for the greater part, the offenders are Coolie Immigrants, but they are, as a rule, never sentenced to be hung, getting from ten to twenty years' penal servitude. The last case in which a murderer was hung, I recollect, occurred some six years ago. The criminal was an English Creole, a black man, who was tried for murdering a bread-seller, and convicted, almost solely on circumstantial evidence, there being no eye-witness save his stepson, a boy aged twelve years. Since then, murder cases are continually occurring. About five months ago, a Coolie immigrant of Plantation *Catharina Sophia* was indicted for murder, and was sentenced to (if I am not mistaken) ten years' penal servitude; and I am informed that there is a charge brought last week before the Court, of the same nature, against another Coolie on the same estate. Recently at Plantation *Resolutie*, a Coolie man chopped off his wife's arms, and otherwise wounded her most brutally, with intent to kill her. The woman is now in the Colonial Hospital in a critical position. It is alleged the man was prompted to the act by jealousy, the woman having cohabited with another Coolie man. She, however, asserts that her husband sent her to live with that man as he (her husband) was indebted to the said man, and the debt was to be wiped off in this manner.

"It is indeed very strange there is no example made of these Coolie murderers, by hanging them. Involuntarily, the question arises, 'Is it that the authorities are afraid of a stoppage of the immigration of Coolies from British India?' Any one would be led to suppose so, especially when there is the record that a man has been hung, as related above, upon the evidence of a mere boy."

8. Paucity of Oriental women, and infidelity on their part, are the principal causes of murder among the Coolies in the Colony. The rascals who try to lead astray or draw the wives away from their husbands should be severely punished. The poor Indian Coolie husbands are deeply injured not only by their countrymen, but by others (not natives of the East) who should discountenance all such improper steps and set a better example before these strangers in this strange land. What will my reader say to the following communication which appeared in the columns of the *Demerara Daily Chronicle*, of May 16, 1882? and suppose the individual, the injured husband, had done what was in his mind to do, then what would have been the consequences?—

"Sir,—I have heard it stated that a good deal has been written and said about the colonization of the Coolies, and I have been told that the equalization of the sexes of that race has been a fruitful source for the attainment of such an end. But what of that? The Coolie woman is always prone to be enticed away from her husband when superior intelligence and vain promises are brought to bear. As a proof of this, I will mention an instance in which I myself have had my wife enticed from me, and that, too, not by a Coolie like myself, but a coloured man, and a so-called Christian. I am a free man, and have been married to my wife, according to the rites of my country, about twelve months. In order to assist me in providing for our wants, she sought and obtained employment at the Sea Wall in the making up of the new dam. There she formed the acquaintance of one * * * a coloured man. One thing led to another, and the result was that my wife was enticed from me about five weeks ago, and has gone to live with this man, as the enclosed letter will show. Now, sir, the Coolie, like every other human being, will be glad to live anywhere, providing there is contentment in the bargain; but how can he be expected to rest contented with the continual dread of having his wife taken away from him, with jewels which he has gone to considerable expense in adorning her with, besides? If this is not enough to drive a man mad, I don't know what else can, and had I lived in a less civilized community than Georgetown one can hardly imagine what would happen. Please publish this, and the enclosed, so that the authorities may see what the already down-trodden Coolie has still to suffer at the hands of his more enlightened brethren, and oblige,

"Your Obedient Servant,

"RAMALING JOE his X mark.

"Georgetown, May 9, 1882.

"Witness to mark J. D. TUCKER."

"LETTER.

"18th March, 1882.

"My dear Minama,—I will not believe that you are determined to leave me. If you love me as you say, you would not make both yourself and me so miserable as to leave me. I have given orders to get everything ready for you, and I have engaged a place for you, for I believe you will not be so cruel as to stop away from me. No one can do you anything and I can make you a dozen times more happy than you would be with any Coolie man, for he will be sure to ill-treat you before a month has passed. If you did not trust that girl Lucy we would be together now. Let me hear from you or let me see you to-morrow at twelve o'clock punctually. Do not be unkind to me, but remember how happy we have been for the short time we have been together. Tear this letter up, and believe me,

Always yours,

EDWARD."

9. In British Guyana, the Coolies, Portuguese, and blacks always somehow get themselves into troubles and difficulties, and daily find themselves in the Magistrates' Courts in the city and country districts. The lawyers and Magistrates are constantly at work from morning till afternoon, from January to December, Sundays and holidays excepted. The lawyers and doctors make a fine living in the Colony by their professional labours. Very often persons who have complaints to make, or take out summonses, have to apply to the Magistrates' clerks, or to the Corporal in the Police Station. Here is a copy of an old "complaint" addressed to Stipendiary Magistrate Fleming in 1861, which goes to prove

that twenty years ago the villagers' skill in writing complaints was as wonderful as it is in the present day :—

"The Complaint of Elizabeth Gemima MacKie, againce Patience Harris of La Jellowsue fronth, showeth that the said did on Friday afternoon the 1st Novr. Between the hours of 3 & 4 Oclock unlawfully abused your Complnt without Cause or Provication Now therefore your Complnt begs your Worship to look into the Case and have the said Summoned and your Complnt are in Duty Bound will Ever Pray."

My reader, however, must not suppose from this that the clerks employed in a Magistrates' Court are not men of education.

By the by, talking of Magistrates, I may state here that a few years ago we had a Mr. W. Seon, S.J.P. in the City of Georgetown, who was a most eccentric character. In a case tried before him in September, 1871 :—

"The defendant, a young woman, who was charged with using insulting language, on being asked for her defence, made the following statement :—

"'On being told that the complainant had spoken disrespectfully of her and had also threatened to injure her, she became alarmed, and said that a Judas had betrayed the Saviour.'

"Magistrate (interrupting)—'Oh! G—d. No, no, stop it there.'

"Defendant (continued)—'As Judas had betrayed the Saviour, it could be imagined the complainant would likewise betray her. She recommended him to read the *Pilgrim's Progress.*'

"Magistrate (glancing at the defendant over his spectacles)—'Lor! The Pilgrims carried their burdens on their backs, but you (the defendant) carry yours elsewhere.'

"The case was dismissed. The defendant is *enceinte.*"

"In another case in which a man was charged with an infringement of the breach of trust ordinance, by neglecting to do work for which he had contracted, the Magistrate, addressing the defendant, said, 'Well, Weeks, what have you to say to this?'

"The defendant begged to put off the case, as the matter was very complicated.

"Magistrate: 'Complicated—the devil!'

"Defendant: 'Yes, sir.'

"Magistrate: 'The thing is very plain. If you take any money from the man, pay him, for God's sake.'

"Defendant: 'No, sir. I have a witness.'

"Magistrate: 'All right. Bring your witness here to-morrow. You are a bit of a lawyer, you know. If you have any money for the man you had better pay him outside, for I'll send you to jail as sure as there is a God in heaven.'"

"Another man was brought up and charged with a similar offence. The Magistrate, addressing him, said he had better give the old man (alluding to the complainant) his money back.

"Defendant: 'He meant to do so. He did not intend to rob the man.'

"Magistrate: 'The defendant did intend to rob the man.'

"Defendant: 'He said he did not intend any such thing.'

"Magistrate (in an excited manner): 'You do, sir. By G—d, don't I know all you people?'

"In reply to the Magistrate, the complainant said he gave the defendant, who is a tailor, seven shillings and a bitt to make a coat.

"Defendant: 'No; it was only five shillings.'

"Magistrate: 'He ain't a-going to take that. Pay the man. Among you you rob these poor beggars right and left.'

"Defendant: 'He only owed five shillings.'

"Complainant: 'Please, your Worship, it is seven shillings.'

"Magistrate (to defendant): 'The man gave you a coat to make, ever since the death of his brother—a respectable man—which took place since June; it is four months already. Why, the Queen wears mourning for only six weeks. You had better pay the man.'

"Defendant: 'He meant to do so; he had brought five shillings to pay him.'

"Magistrate: 'It is seven shillings.'

"Defendant: 'He recollected owing only five' (the defendant here counted the money).

"Magistrate: 'Have you another shilling? Split the difference.'

"Defendant consented and gave the other shilling, and the matter ended."

"Before Mr. Wm. Seon, S.J.P.

"Friday, August 22, 1879.

"Dubious Compliment.—A Barbadian woman was charged with abusing her landlord, a Mr. West. The complainant having learnt that his property was endangered by fire by the defendant, took her to task about it. The defendant then applied epithets to him which, to his thinking, were by no means complimentary. The witnesses for the complainant, however, testified that they only heard the defendant call him a 'd——d black nigger,' whereupon the Magistrate observed that since that was the head and front of her offending, the complainant might have saved himself the trouble of bringing her to court. One of the witnesses remarked that notwithstanding the complainant was a nigger, he was a 'gentleman.' The Magistrate, glancing at the man above his spectacles, said he did not wish a dissertation on gentility from him, because he believed he was incapable of the task, and furthermore there were very few gentlemen in this community, for most persons who professed to be gentlemen were not. His worship then said he would discharge the defendant, but before doing so he must advise her not to interfere with the complainant, because he was not only her landlord, but he also seemed quite a 'superior person.' He further advised her to quit his place. For her own sake she ought to leave the place, because she did not know what might be looming in the distance for her, but before doing so she must pay the rent, and the sooner she did so the better."

"A Wolf in Sheep's Clothing.—A decently clad Barbadian woman of fair complexion and blonde hair was charged with using a base expression to a fellow countryman. The offence was clearly brought home to her, but she protested her innocence, and roused the indignation of the Magistrate, who said the evidence did not admit of the slightest doubt as to her guilt, and yet she thought he was such a tyro on the magisterial bench as to be led away by her protestations. By appearance as well as by nature she was a perfect 'wolf in sheep's clothing.' He knew well what vile Barbadian women were capable of doing. He had had some experience of them in their own country; besides, he had had an opportunity of studying their characters here for the last nineteen years, and the least he could say of them was that they had a vocabulary of vile expressions which could not be equalled in any other part of the world. Defendant must go to gaol for ten days with hard labour, and he trusted that her hands would be kept as busy in doing good there as her tongue was kept busy in doing harm outside. The sentence seemed to have had very little effect on the defendant, for she clapped her hands, curtsied, thanked the magistrate, and bounced out of the dock."

And only very recently a small boy summoned an old lady for boxing his ears. He had had a fight over some stolen mangoes with her daughter, a damsel of about eight years, who told him to shut his d——d (distended?) *mouth*, and he retorted, "Why, you don't know your own simple compound long division." This reflection on the girl's character upset the old dame, her mother, so she fell upon the boy. The Magistrate thought these *were* extenuating circumstances, and delivered judgment to suit the case.

10. To a person ignorant of the nature of housebreakers in the Colony, it may appear that householders are too prone to resort to the most deadly weapons in defence, at once; but experience has shown that the only safety for the attacked lies in disabling his enemy the quickest way possible. The housebreaker never enters on his unlawful work unprepared for murder, which he will commit rather than be caught and handed over to the police. Weapons of the most deadly kind have been found on men caught stealing; and the records of the police can prove that where resistance has been offered the thief's arm was quick to drive the blow that brought with it either death or an approach to it. A more complete disregard of human life it would be impossible to conceive than there is amongst the Chinese and other thieves in the Colony; and the likely victim of their plundering habits is forced in pure self-defence, knowing that one life is pretty certain to be sacrificed in a hand-to-hand encounter, to let the thief's be the risk, and to attack him to the best advantage. This practice, justifiable enough in all conscience, does not, however, prevent the person who is forced to adopt it from being placed in the painful position of a criminal charged with murder, in case the thief should die; and there is scarcely a session of the Supreme Criminal Court that does not see some unfortunate man placed

in the dock on the charge. In most cases of the kind the jury, satisfied that the Coolie watchman on an estate had acted in a purely defensive spirit, and that the Chinaman brought about his own death, brought in a verdict of not guilty. It is much to be deplored that there are so many cases of violent deaths occurring in the manner we have described, but it would be hypocritical to express sympathy with the thieves. As long as there is the same callous indifference to human life shown by these wretches, householders must be prepared to meet them on at least an equal footing, and be armed with weapons for their defence not less deadly than those brought to attack them if the thief thinks it necessary or expedient to do so.

11. I have a faint recollection of having either read or heard a strange way in which a Chinese housebreaker was punished. It was a Friday afternoon, when the estate messenger returned from town with a heavy canister of money, so that the labourers the following day might all be paid. A certain "Celestial" about the manager's or overseer's quarters saw the canister of money carried upstairs and lodged in the bedroom. The manager or overseer was in the habit of leaving one of the bedroom windows open at night, and the Chinaman knew that well enough. Just under that window sill there was a large nest of marabuntas, which the thief did not know, and the sting of these marabuntas causes intense pain, swelling, and fever. During the night, however, while every one was sound asleep, and the Indian watchman was elsewhere engaged, John Chinaman set a high ladder against the open window and climbed up, and then in order to get into the room he had to lay hold of the sill of the window, when by some accident he disturbed the marabuntas, which gave him a severe stinging on both his hands and face, and the poor wretch jumped down as fast as possible from the high window, and scampered off to his room in great agony. The estate money that night was saved from this housebreaker in this accidental manner.

12. The Colonial Police Force is composed of all nationalities—English, Irish, Scotch, Portuguese, Barbadians, Indian and Chinese Coolies. A Christian Indian Coolie, belonging to the force, has named it "THE JACKASS FORCE." There is,

however, one thing to be deplored, and that is, that the policemen in this Colony know everything but their duty. They are invested with a certain amount of authority, and that makes them hold very high opinions of themselves. The Police force, it seems to me, has gentlemen in this Colony who, because they receive a large salary, sit down at home and sleep all day, never caring to look into the characters of those that they have under them, commonly called "dog drivers." The dog drivers are in no respect whatsoever better than their friends the citizens. I know of a case that happened here some time ago of a thief being set to catch a thief. In the force here they have thieves, scamps, and villains, and these, I say without any hesitation whatsoever, are the men that are put to keep the peace and preserve order, but are the very ones who do nothing else but cause disturbances and riots.

13. Our jails (gaols) in the different parts of the Colony are principally occupied by the Coolies. In India, in addition to the preparation of prison clothing and the manufacture of goods for sale, the prisoners execute all repairs of buildings, perform all menial services, and cultivate jail gardens, which are almost all in a very flourishing condition. These gardens are of no ordinary value; they insure a regular supply of fresh vegetables, the advantage of which cannot be over estimated in a sanitary point of view; they are economical, in that the prisoners supply themselves with this most essential part of their own diet, and they afford light, healthy occupation for aged and weakly prisoners, by whom they are for the most part cultivated. Prison schools also are in existence, and many of the prisoners have been taught to read and write before leaving the jails. The chained gang, or prisoners who are chained to one another, are constantly employed to sweep and keep the streets of the cities, &c., clean. And why should not such a system be adopted in this Colony? Would it not lessen the expenses of the Government? The Coolies who find their way to the gaol are principally for neglect of estate labour, during the six working days, and for absconding from the estate.

CHAPTER XX.

THE BRITISH GUYANA CHRISTIAN MISSIONS.

1. The Colony of British Guyana is ecclesiastically divided into seventeen parishes—viz., the Trinity, St. John's, St. James's, St. Peter's, and part of St. Luke's, in the County of Essequibo; part of St. Luke's, St. Swithin's, St. Mark's, St. Matthew's, St. George's, also called St. Andrew's, St. Paul's, and St. Mary's, in the County of Demerara; and St. Michael's, St. Catherine's, St. Clement's, All Saints', St. Patrick's, and St. Saviour's, in the County of Berbice. And Methodistically it is divided into eight circuits or principal stations—viz., Demerara (Georgetown) First, Demerara (Kingston) Second, Demerara (Mahaica), Demerara (Golden Grove and Victoria), Demerara (Goed-Fortuin), Essequibo, Berbice, and Coolie Mission. The following are the denominations of Christians whe occupy this great field of missions:—The Episcopal Church of England, the Presbyterian Church of Scotland, the Wesleyan Methodists, London Missionaries, Independents or Congregationalists, Plymouth Brethren, African Methodist Episcopal Church, and the Church of Rome. And to this list we may add some denominations who are not Christians: Jews, who have no synagogue erected here, Mohammedans, Pagans or heathens, including the Buddhists and others, and the fire-worshippers, and the disciples of Foh and Confucius—the Chinese.

2. The Dutch Reformed Church, which was the oldest and most important clerical establishment in the Colony, is now no longer in existence. The Rev. G. Drost, an intelligent and well-educated man, was the last Minister of that Church, and he officiated for some time twice a month in Georgetown, at the Scotch Kirk, and twice a month in Fort Island, at a

chapel erected there. The Dutch Lutheran Church, as it is called, in Berbice, which was formerly in the service of the London Missionary Society, and afterwards occupied by the Wesleyan Methodists, was for a very long time without a Minister. Now the Rev. J. Mittleholzer (an ex-London Missionary Society Minister) is discharging the duties as a Lutheran Minister among the few in Berbice, who profess to belong to that section of the Church, though not very long ago they were all connected with the Wesleyan Church as members of the congregation, and as communicants. From an exceedingly rare and very curious work, entitled, *A New Voyage to the Isles of America*, and written by a French Missionary, who sailed for the West Indies in 1693, we learn that missions had already been established in the French Colonies by the Jesuits, the Capuchins, the Carmelites, and other religious orders, as well as several convents of sisterhoods, Ursulines and others, and that it was contemplated to establish missions in "Caribane," now known as British Guyana. It was some two years after this, in 1695, that a request was sent home to Holland by the Commandeur of Essequibo to send out a "Predikant," or "Priester," to teach people religion.

3. Strictly speaking, the Moravians were the first European Missionaries that visited this Colony. In 1735 steps were taken to establish Missions here, but no Missionary made his appearance till 1738. At the request of the owner of an estate in Berbice County, two Moravian brethren were sent to the Rio Berbice, and these two were the first preachers of the Gospel to the Negroes. This good-meaning planter, who requested that Missionaries should come and labour among his people, and others of his profession or calling, soon discovered that Negroes were not a people who should be taught religion. They as a body either considered that the slaves had no souls, and that they were no better than the irrational creatures around them, or that they were beyond the pale of salvation, and rose in arms against these messengers of peace, truth, mercy, and salvation, and drove them away. Thus one who professed himself a friend of the Missionaries

proved an enemy. The two brethren, despairing of any good results from their labours among the Negroes, betook themselves to a position higher up the Berbice. This newly-formed station—about sixty-five miles in a direct line from the present town of New Amsterdam, but 200 miles by the winding of the river—they called *Pilgerhut*, *i.e.*, Pilgrim's Rest. From this station they traversed the dense forests, or paddled along the broad streams, in search of the native Indians, or Aborigines, to teach them the grand doctrines of Christianity, and win them over to Jesus Christ, their rightful Sovereign. They carried neither purse, nor scrip, nor shoes. They went about doing good, both to the souls and bodies of the Indians, and preached to them "the Gospel of the kingdom for a witness." They were the magistrates, teachers, doctors, and artizans of the Indians. Several other Missionaries from Europe belonging to the *Unitas Fratrum* joined them at different times. Though they had been settled at Pilgerhut since 1738, the first native baptism by them did not take place till 1748. After this scarcely a week passed in which the rite was not administered to one or more, and by the end of June the converts amounted to thirty-nine. Whilst they were thus labouring on comfortably and peacefully, a slave insurrection broke out in the year 1763, which proved to be the death-blow to the Pilgerhut mission. Some of the brethren returned to Europe, some sought safety in Surinam (Dutch Guyana), and two of them, by name Cleman and Vester, remained in Demerara, only to lay their bones in peace in the land where they had borne such grievous crosses for the Gospel's sake. These two brethren never remained idle; they held private meetings for those who had a desire to save their immortal souls. In the neighbourhood of Kingston and the Georgetown Railway Station, these two brethren regularly preached the Word of Life, and commemorated the dying love of the Saviour in the house in which they lodged. For further and fuller accounts of this truly interesting mission, we would refer the reader to the "Historical Sketches of the Missions of the United Brethren for Propagating the Gospel," by the Rev. John Holmes, compiled from histories of missions by the Rev. Messrs. Crantz, Joskiel, Latrobe, and Rister. After a lapse of many years I am thankful to record here that by the kindness and encouragement of Quintin Hogg, Esq., proprietor of several sugar estates in the Colony, the Moravian Church re-established or recommenced its missions on Plantation *Industry* on the East Coast, Demerara, and on Plantation *Reliance*, in Essequibo, in the year 1878. On both Stations the Revd. Messrs. Henry Moore and Alexander Pilgrim have met with great encouragement, and a good work among the Barbadian immigrants and Creoles and Coolies is being done by these two brethren. Several have joined the Church, and the ministers speak well of them.

4. After this mission was thus broken up, the Colony was without a minister of Christ for a considerable time, though there were a few godly laymen doing the work of the Lord in a private and quiet manner, as we shall see in the next paper. In the year 1808 the London Missionary Society sent out the Rev. John Wray, whose praise is in all the Churches, at the request of a certain God-fearing and philanthropic man—Mr. Post, a Dutchman. Mr. Wray at once commenced a mission among the Negroes at Plantation Le Resouvenir, on the east coast, about six miles from Georgetown. The Lord was with him, and blessed his labours. On his removal to Berbice in 1817, Mr. Wray was succeeded by the Rev. John Smith, who died a martyr in the cause of truth, after labouring for some time with a cheering measure of success. A beautiful Christian sanctuary on the Brick-Dam, in the city, and belonging to the London Missionary Society, called "Smith Church," is dedicated to his memory. The London Missionary agents have at different periods realized a large ingathering of precious souls into the fold of Christ. Of late years, however, their cause has suffered, in common with that of other kindred institutions, from the effects of the agricultural and commercial depression which has overtaken the West India Colonies. The number of their Missionaries also has been considerably reduced. The chapel in New Amsterdam, Berbice, is the largest they have in the Colony. Their congregations are good, and very attentive.

5. The Presbyterian Church of Scotland is one of the oldest in the Colony. It comprises nine parishes, in which are to be found good churches, schools, and respectable Ministers. A second place of worship, called St. Thomas's Church, has been erected in the city of Georgetown, and has a resident minister, who is much liked by the people. A third place, St. Stephen's Church, in Charles Town District, has also been built, and is in charge of a Catechist who is paid by the St. Andrew's congregation. Somehow, the Presbyterians are not gaining much ground in this great field of Missions. One of their own Ministers, the Rev. Gordon Lillie, M.A., at the Annual Missionary Meeting of the Presbyterian Missionary Society held in St. Andrew's, Georgetown, 1871, observed :—

"There was no use concealing the fact that Presbyterianism had not been a great success in this Colony. Some people blamed one thing and other people another ; but he believed that the chief cause was because the whole of the Presbyterian service was to a considerable extent very intellectual. It demanded on the part of every one that would worship in the Church an amount of attention, and intelligence, and thought, that really the people—the Creole population—had not, and were not to be blamed for not having. He had always felt that that alone was an essential drawback. It was a serious disadvantage under which Presbyterian Ministers suffered. Another reason was the utter impossibility of ministers in country places getting white elders to support them in their duties. God forbid that he should say one word disrespectful of a man on account of his colour, or complexion, or country ; but he did feel this acutely, that Ministers of the Church of Scotland would have occupied a very different position now in this Colony, if the managers and planters had come forward and rallied round the blue banner of the Covenant as they should have done, one and all. It might be urged that the Scotchmen led such an immoral life here that they were ashamed to become elders of the Church. He would say that was again a scandal and a lie. He knew that in his own parish there were persons qualified by their character and education to demand eldership. Since he had taken over St. Mary's he had been chilled, and depressed, and deadened by the backwardness, by the absolute, not only unwillingness, but determination of those men to leave unsupported the

Ministers whom God had sent to labour amongst them, when they might have given them very warm and cheerful countenance and support by taking their places at the Kirk Session. All this had weighed down the Church of Scotland in this Colony, and prevented it from occupying that position which it ought to."—Extracted from the *Royal Gazette* of Demerara, March 2, 1871.

The Rev. Thomas Slater, a hardworking and painstaking Minister of St. Andrew's Church, a man much beloved and respected by all in the city and Colony, has, humanly speaking, been the sole prop of the Presbyterian Church in British Guyana. The Rev. J. R. Dickson and the Rev. T. H. Trotman, owing to the unjust interference and the harshness which they experienced whilst they were connected with the Wesleyan Methodist body, to prevent any disruption in the Church where they had been brought up, quietly resigned, and found a spiritual home in the Presbyterian Church.

6. The Independents or Congregationalists are a small body in this Colony. They are principally confined to Demerara. Congregationalism may do well in England and Australia, but not in British Guyana. The late Rev. Joseph Ketley, the Pastor of New Providence Chapel, formerly a London Missionary, was very highly esteemed by all classes of people here. His son, the Rev. Joseph Ketley, junr., who succeeded him after his death, has a large church and congregation, and is well supported. The others have small chapels and congregations. The Plymouth or Christian Brethren, as they call themselves, are not numerous here. They are divided into two or three sects—the Newtonians, the Darbyites, and the Ferrierites. They have no dealings with each other, on account of some doctrinal differences.

7. The Episcopal Church of England is the established Church of this Colony. There are some fifty-eight places of worship, some very large, and some small, belonging to this body. The old St. George's Cathedral in the city is no longer in existence. On the same old spot a new iron building will soon be erected. The Bishop of the Diocese (the Right Reverend W. P. Austin, D.D.) is the oldest Colonial Bishop alive now. This Church has

had for many years a promising station among the aboriginal Boks or Indians on the river Essequibo. The Coolie mission, well organized and supplied with four ordained Missionaries and a large number of Catechists, is in a prosperous condition. The Rev. Ebenezer Bhalanoth Bhose, an educated native gentleman, of India, was the first or pioneer Missionary appointed by the Government and Church to labour among the Coolies. He has, however, retired from the mission field. Nearly all the Protestant Institutions in the Colony, such as the Colleges, the Orphan Asylum, the Saffon Educational Institution, are connected with the Church. Bishop Austin is looked upon as the supreme ecclesiastical ruler of the Colony.

8. The Wesleyan Methodist Missionary Society has also been doing much good to the people of this Colony. An influence for good has ever been exerted by the agents and members of this Society or Church. The people have great cause to be thankful to God for Methodist agency and influence. If no other Churches in this Colony can, the Methodist clergy are always sure to command large, crowded, and attentive congregations at all their meetings. The people here are friendly disposed towards Methodism.

9. In connection with the Methodist Body I must not omit mentioning the small section which styles itself "The British Methodist Episcopal Church," or "The African Methodist Episcopal Church." Many years ago there were two Ministers of this branch, one in Essequibo who was looked upon as the Bishop, the Rev. M. Henderson, and the other the Rev. John George Urling who had charge of a station at Buxton Village, on the East Coast, Demerara. After the death of Bishop Henderson, there was no one to take charge of Essequibo. Mr. Urling occasionally went down and preached to the congregation, and tried his utmost to keep the few members together. A few years before Mr. Urling retired from that section of the Church (for he has gone over to the Anglican Episcopal Church), a Rev. Willis Nazrey, a bishop of the Methodist Episcopal Church in the United States, paid a visit to this Colony by the request of a few, with the intention of establishing a cause, and very foolishly and injudiciously under-

took to ordain or set apart two or three men who were quite unfit for the office they were supposed to hold, and thus did a great deal of harm instead of good. Mr. A. L. Pratt, who was for several years connected with the Wesleyan Church as class leader and local preacher, having seceded in 1872, rendered that body great help, but I am thankful to say that he has had cause to regret taking the step he then did, and has come back to the parent church, and is now connected with Bedford Society, in Camp Street. Two men who were sent out by Bishop Nazrey from Canada had soon to retire from the Colony, for they could not get on here. The others belonging to the Colony supposed to be ordained by him are dragging out a miserable existence. A young man, however, who styles himself "the Rev. N. B. Stewart, Acting General Superintendent of the British Methodist Episcopal Church of Canada," is a hard-working young man, but after all he is like the rest of his compeers in that branch in the Colony to which he belongs. The following extracts from the local papers will show the capabilities of "Brother Stewart" (as he is universally called in the Colony) for and in the work he is doing:—

"BROTHER STEWART'S EPISTLE.

"TO THE EDITOR OF THE COLONIST.

"Sir,—Please insert the following lines in your columns concerning the Spiritual progress of the Lepers in the Lazaretto in our City under my supervision the past year to the present time. I having been permitted by those who take part in the supervision of these parties above mentioned their spiritual and temporal welfare. These granted me permission to preach the words of God, in said Asylum to its inmates. I remember, Mr. Editor, having taken a few of these parties over during the past year as communicants in our Society, and since that time the number has increased so that I am able to inform you that I have at present eighteen communicants and a few more candidates and baptized three adults (Females), one Chinese, one African, and one Native of this Colony, and two infants. My chief reason of intimating the fact is that there are many sympathizing Christians in our land who are not aware of the location of those dear ones. The people will be thankful Mr. Editor for your kindness in publishing these few lines so that Christians those of the benevolent Public may assist my weak efforts in a mutual manner; by granting me some aid as to enable me in purchasing small religious books thereby enabling me to meet the requirements of those my dear dear sisters in that institution.

"I am yours,

"N. B. STEWART,

"Acting Superintendent of the British Guyana British Methodist Episcopal Society, Waterloo Street, Lot 185.

"18th May, 1881."

"BROTHER STEWART.

"We have," observes the Editor, "lately received a series of communications from the gentleman styling himself the 'Rev. N. B. Stewart,' descriptive of his 'evangelical tour' on the Arabian Coast, and publicity has been given by us to some portions of these out of pure good feeling towards the gentleman referred to. He states that he has held a number of open-air meetings, and we doubt not his audiences have been entertained, if they may not have been edified. We publish the appended communication from Mr. Stewart, *verbatim et literatim*, and only regret that we cannot lay before our readers a *facsimile* of the manuscript:—

"TO THE EDITOR: 'DAILY CHRONICLE.'

"Sir,—The report of one of your contemporary (Argosy), issue Saturday 11th instant about those poor humble minded Christians Golden Grove as being pugilistic is erroneous. Having been informed with satisfactory account from Brother Sealy (preacher in charge) that the report of correspondent of the aforesaid paper was formed in a Counterfeiting manner so as to cast a burlesque on those so called (visionists) by scoffers of religion. I trust that the report shall not be entertained by those who have noticed such remarks of the past publication Thanking you for the space afforded in your Column.

"Revd. N. B. Stewart Superintendent of the British Methodist Episcopal Church.

"March 19th, 1882."

"BROTHER STEWART'S 'WORK.'

"TO THE EDITOR OF THE COLONIST.

"Sir,—The past Sabbath an anniversary was held on Pln. Leonora, for the Sabbath School. The gathering of children was about 200; also some of the Anna Catharina children were entertained by aforesaid children, tickets were given as reward for their improvement in replying to questions asked from third chapter St. Matthew's Gospel. Cakes, &c., were also handed and the meeting was dispersed. The anniversary was presided over by the Rev. N. B. Stewart, Superintendent of the British Methodist Episcopal Church.

"N. B. STEWART.

"1st May, 1882."

Brother Stewart is indeed a great open air preacher in Bourda District, and has a small hired house in Upper Robb Street which is called "St. Nicholas's Church."

10. In 1874 the Rev. J. C. Brewer, Superintendent of the Golden Grove Wesleyan Mission Circuit, felt it his duty, after a fair trial before a full Leaders' meeting, to expel from church membership some four or five persons who introduced some strange doctrines and ideas. These in time started a place of worship in the village, and called themselves "The Visionists." The following particulars, gleaned from public papers, will give some idea of this sect:—

"On Friday, March 3rd, 1882, one of the so-called parsons, Mr. Trim, entered the building for the purpose of preaching, when 'Bishop' Kit ordered him out as a trespasser. He refused to leave, assigning as a reason, that he was as much master of the chapel as the other. A tussle ensued, when Trim was unceremoniously dragged out by 'Bishop' Kit. The latter then locked the door, and took out the key. Trim, determined to enter, unhasped the padlock. It might not be out of place to state that the 'Mr. Trim' spoken of is the same person that Mr. Hawtayne sent to prison for seven days, for trespassing in St. Augustine's Church some time ago. On that occasion he told the Magistrate that the Lord had sent him there."

The circumstances referred to here are as follows :—

"For some time past a so-called religious sect has sprung up at 'Golden Grove' Village, East Coast, naming themselves the 'Visionists.' This sect is composed of four men, including the defendant, and they have erected a splendid edifice at Golden Grove Village, in which they generally hold service. They are known by the name of 'Visionists' in consequence of one of them having seen (as he alleged) our Saviour in the form of a ram-goat, whilst working in the cane-fields at Enmore; since then they have thrown aside their working implements and assumed a clerical garb as parsons, in consequence of having seen a vision. The defendant in this case, on being asked by the Magistrate his reasons for going into the schoolroom, replied that the Spirit of the Lord Jesus Christ sent him there. The Magistrate addressing him said, —some time ago he was brought before him on a similar charge, and the Rev. Mr. Moulder having expressed a desire to withdraw the charge, he warned him, and he did not see why he should go there again. The defendant then replied again that he was sent by the Spirit of the Lord and could not resist it, therefore he was bound to go. The Magistrate said he was bound to go by the law, and sentenced him to seven days' imprisonment. The defendant was unceremoniously divested of his coat and bib by the police."

This sèct of the "Visionists" has found in "Bro. Stewart" a warm advocate and bold defender of that party, as is evident from the letter I have quoted above.

11. In No. 2 of this chapter I stated that in the year 1693 the French Romish Missionaries contemplated establishing a Mission in British Guyana. In due time Jesuit fathers or priests were sent here, and they have by their untiring labours and perseverance established their churches in almost every part of the Colony. Their present Bishop, Dr. A. Butler, is, like his immediate predecessor, an Englishman. Their Cathedral on the Brick Dam, a strong and magnificent building, which has already cost some thousands of pounds sterling, is yet unfinished. The Roman Catholics are receiving on account of the Portuguese immigrants and others nominally at all events connected with that body, about $12,000, or something like two thirds of the unconditional grant, and there is not, so

far as I am aware, a single Portuguese priest in the Colony. If you speak to the Portuguese about religion, they will tell you that they are Roman Catholics, but that their religion is almost something nominal. They do not understand the language of the priests here, they hate the Jesuits, and long for priests of their own from Madeira. We can understand the position of these foreigners. What I have said is not a reflection on the Jesuit faith, which may, for all that I know, be quite as good as any other form of Roman Catholicism; but any careful observer may see that the Portuguese attend the ministrations of their priests very irregularly, and that no amount of Government aid will induce them to accept heartily the species of Roman Catholicism supplied here.

Several years ago I happened to get hold of a Roman Catholic book, entitled:—*Christian Missions: Their Agents, their Method, and their Results*, by T. W. M. Marshall, Vol. III., published by Burns and Lambert, 17, Portman Street, Portman Square, London. This book is now to be found in the Roman Catholic Convent. Speaking of Methodist Missions and Missionaries in British Guyana, the writer of this book says: "The Negro appears to have profited as little by the presence of the English emissaries. His teachers have been aided during many years by the power and wealth of England, but with so little fruit, as an English writer notices in 1860, that though he considers the Guyana Protestant Negro somewhat superior to his brother in Jamaica, he thus describes the final influence of the teaching which he has received: 'It seems to me that he never connects his religion with his life, never reflects that his religion should bear upon his conduct.' Mr. Trollope adds, that his information was mainly derived from Clergymen of the Church of England, whose candour is perhaps due to the fact *that most of these singular converts had rejected their more tranquil ceremonies for the exciting harangues of the Baptist or Wesleyan preachers, whose sects have, as usual, accompanied the Church of England to Guyana. They sing, and holloa, and scream, and have revivals. They talk of their 'dear brothers' and 'dear sisters,' and in their ecstatic howlings get some fun for their money. And this is all the English*

[Wesleyan Missionaries] *have done in Guyana.* On the other hand . . . . the Catholic Missionaries in British Guyana, who do not receive much aid from patrons of any sort, *and least of all from the Government,*" [and yet the Romish Church in this Colony has for several years past, and long before the book above referred to was published, been drawing from the Colonial chest twelve thousand dollars ($12,000)—*being the* "*least*" *aid* "*of all from the Government*"—per annum] "all are respected for their piety and zeal. The number of Roman Catholics in the Colony is about 10,000." [The italics are mine.] See Chap. IX. pp. 69, 70. The author of this book asserts as an established fact that the WHOLE OF SOUTH AMERICA IS CONVERTED (to the Romish faith), and the people everywhere are living in the fear of God and enjoyment of religion. In reply to this wholesale lying statement I would state that, "Our missions present a noble territory, won from the sea of heathenism, occupied by large and living Churches, which are bringing forth the fruits of righteousness, and peace, and joy. Not that we have not sometimes to insist upon the discipline of the Church, and to mourn over those who are unfaithful and who leave us; nevertheless, West Indian piety is no fiction—it is a glorious reality. Our people love the doctrines of the Gospel; Christ crucified, the Saviour risen, an Intercessor before the mercy-seat, a loving and an ever-present Saviour, are to them themes in which they continually delight." (Rev. D. Barley's speech at Exeter Hall.) The perusal of the annual reports and other works on West Indian Missions will fully convince their readers that Missionary labours in British Guyana have not been a failure, but have proved an incalculable blessing to thousands of the inhabitants. We can point to the erection of the different places of worship, some of which rival for neatness and accommodation those of other bodies, and to the formation of Christian congregations or worshippers in various parts of the Colony.

Though much has been done by the agents of the different Protestant Societies to raise the people to a higher and nobler standard, yet the ugly fact remains to be told, that *all* have not as yet embraced the Gospel and become morally and spiritually good. There are still many other dark places which are full of the habitations of cruelty and wretchedness. The people, especially the labouring Creole population in different parts of the Colony, and more especially on plantations, are still bad, and are faithfully serving the god of this world. In slavery times the people were very fond of dancing and music, using a kind of guitar called a "banjo," and several varieties of drums and tambourines. They accompanied their dancing with strange songs or chants adapted to the style of the dance—sometimes low and monotonous, at others loud and boisterous. The modern Creoles still follow most of these bad practices.

This was the closing shot of an interesting dialogue heard a short time ago, between two black gentlemen, in a local restaurant: "You! you! you hope to get to heaven? No, bo. Niggah has no more business in heaven than a hog in the Governor's garden."

12. The four principal Churches in the Colony which are endowed or State-aided, are the Episcopal Church of England, which gets $50,080; the Kirk of Scotland, $24,500; the Wesleyan Methodist Church, $7,000; and the Romish Church, $12,000. From the Blue Book it would appear:—

"1. That while the Episcopal Church provides only 6,203 sittings more than the Wesleyan Church, it receives $43,080 per annum more.

"2. That the Church of Scotland provides 4,335 sittings less, and receives $17,500 per annum more than the Wesleyan Church.

"3. That the Roman Catholic Church provides 6,524 sittings less, and receives per annum $5,000 more than the Wesleyan Church.

"4. That while the Wesleyan Church employs nearly one-fifth of the Ministers who receive public money, and provides more than one-fourth of the sittings in the State-aided Churches of the Colony, it receives less than one-thirteenth of the amount distributed among the Churches from the Colonial Fund."

The English and Scotch Churches, however, receive public money for the performance of specified duties; the Roman

Catholics and Wesleyans get less of this money, but they can do very much as they please. The money is paid in lump sums to their Bishop or the General Superintendent, and they spend it at their discretion, without any limitations as to time, place, or person, in the matter of services. There are a $1,000 of the unconditional grant for religious purposes given to the Independent Congregational Dissenters.

13. In a published sermon, preached by the Rev. J. Ketley, of Georgetown Providence Congregational Chapel, on Sunday, June 11, 1882, referring to the State Churches, he observes :—

"The Emperor Constantine has been the great curse of the Christian Church. He saw the true worth of the Christian. In all her persecutions he saw what she could do—what she could dare—what she could suffer and endure. Constantine, who was a wise man in his way, resolved to use the Christian for the purposes of the State. If the Christian could suffer and defy death with a heroism far beyond the best of heathen soldiers, why should he be persecuted? Why should those fine qualities not be turned to use for the good of the empire?

"Here began the ruin of the Christian Church. Constantine resolved to utilize Christianity for the benefit of the State. He resolved to strike a blow at heathenism, and to substitute the religion of Jesus Christ in its place. He did so. He took Christianity under his patronage, and he made it the religion of the State, and from that moment Christianity began to lose her power, and to decline. Heathen temples were shut up and destroyed, Christian churches were substituted in their stead, the idols were dethroned, the images of the crucified Christ and Apostles and martyrs took their place. Here is a truly wonderful and instructive branch of ecclesiastical history which I am compelled to pass by, but so it was; persecuted Christianity became patronized Christianity, and from that moment its whole character and nature was changed. Persecuted Christianity was strong, patronized Christianity became diluted, and grew weak. The Church of Christ has gained nothing by the patronage of the world. In fact, it has been her curse. I am purposing to give a series of lectures to prove this; I now pass it by and simply assert on historic truth, that the greatest injury ever done to the Church of Christ was the touch of the State by the finger of Constantine. It was as when Uzziel touched the sacred ark of Israel,—would that he had been smitten in like manner!

"For what has been the result of this interference? What has grown out of it? what good has been done? I will briefly tell you. Three State Churches are now contending, the one against the other. There is the Greek Church, the Latin Church, and the Church of England. These are represented by the Patriarch of Russia,* the Pope of Rome, and the Sovereigns of England. Here are three Christian Churches with three headships, and which of them is the true Church? Each of them has persecuted the true followers of Jesus Christ; each of them is antagonistic to the others. To which of these shall I join myself? Well, I can give you my answer. I can see where the mistake arose; it arose when the human hand touched the Divine Ark. All our discords and divisions have come from that interference, when the power of man intercepted the work of the Church. Had the State left the Church untouched, she would have carried on her work with her united forces, and blessed the whole world."

The State Churchism, whether in the Colony or elsewhere, has led to many sacerdotal pretensions, and the unwarrantable claims of the priesthood. Their pretensions and their claims are unfortunately recognized and admitted by considerable numbers; but who are they? Generally silly women, and still sillier men, pleased with shows and spectacles, and dresses, and attitudes, and meaningless ceremonies. But will any rational or reasonable man say that true religion can consist in any of those things? Will the priests who concoct and devise those shows and spectacles and ceremonies, tell us what dresses Peter and the Apostles wore? Were they clothed in purple, and gold, and fine linen? Were their heads adorned with a mitre? Did the Apostles aspire to kingly and lordly powers and titles? Surely not; they were among the humblest of the humble, and if they stand out prominently as historical characters, it is to be attributed very much to that very humility combined with the important truths they taught. But we search in vain in the Scriptures for anything to warrant the assumption that they had recourse to dresses and attitudes and ceremonies to drive home to their hearers the simple truths they announced.

* Until the reign of Peter the Great.

What we require in the Colony is total disendowment and disestablishment of the State and State-aided Churches. Till this is done, there will be constant vexations and unchristian feelings stirred up between different denominations.

14. As a brief account of the early history of British Guyana Wesleyan Methodism, and its progress in the Colony, may not be uninteresting to my reader, I shall now devote my attention to it. Six years before the arrival of the first London Missionary, the Rev. John Wray, this Colony was visited by Messrs. William Augustus Claxton (whose son, William Claxton, is still alive, active and useful as a Local Preacher and Class Leader, connected with Bedford Church) and William Powell, two members of the Methodist Church from Nevis, one of the Leeward Islands. These two respectable and intelligent men were converted under Dr. Thomas Coke's preaching in the year 1787, when he went over from St. Kitt's to Nevis. Claxton and Powell, on their arrival here, felt it their duty to teach the way of salvation to their fellow-creatures. They went from house to house, holding religious services, and often read and expounded the Holy Scriptures. They were not men who had enriched their minds with knowledge drawn from the instruction of the learned or the schools of science. Their preaching was simple and artless, not adorned by the flowers of eloquence, or the artificial powers of persuasion. And this kind of plain, simple preaching attracted the attention of several slaves and respectable free coloured people. Camp Street (where we now have a handsome chapel called Bedford) was the head-quarters. Here lived Claxton, Powell, Ann Rogers, Nancy (wife of William) Powell, Ann Blake, Titus, Ren Austin, Ashby Plass, Fortuin Crossman, Bakey Crossman, and several other good Christian men and women who proved themselves faithful and true to their profession. They feared not the threats and the persecutions of the wicked. They put their trust in the Lord, and laboured on diligently and successfully. Many a prayer was offered up by them that God would give them that very place where they lived, in order to have a place of worship erected there. Though this prayer was not

answered in their time, yet their prayer was not in vain. God has now answered it by giving us the very place, the very spot where the chapel (Bedford) is erected. The private meetings held by Claxton attracted public notice, and a petition was presented against Claxton and his party. The Rev. Leonard Strong (who afterwards became the leader of a sect called the Strongites or Plymouth Brethren), a Church of England Minister, was deputed by the Governor to inquire into these alleged irregularities. Mr. Claxton having ingenuously explained his proceedings and motives, and shown a copy of the Rules of our Society, he was discharged for the time being.

If the early Methodist Christians in this city had been silent through fear of persecution or loss of life, the very stones would have cried out against their unfaithfulness and want of love to God, and immortal souls perishing for lack of spiritual knowledge. They ceased not, night or day, in proclaiming the love of God, and in holding prayer-meetings and class-meetings, for Mr. Claxton had formed a class consisting of several members, a few of whose names we have mentioned above. Again, another charge was brought against Claxton for holding seditious meetings contrary to the law of the land, and he had to appear before Fiscal Williams, and though nothing could be proved against him, yet he was silenced this time, as it was considered an unpardonable crime for a *black man* to hold public meetings for worship, and to be a "setter forth of strange doctrines." He was threatened with expatriation if he persisted; but this unrighteous, ungodly act of the then "would-be powers of the (British Guyana) world" did not any way silence Claxton and his party. Midnight and early morn were selected as the best times for religious devotions; and as the members, who were continually increasing, were scattered here and there, each house had the benefit of these meetings. Though the Government officials kept a strict watch to apprehend some, if not all of them, they never could succeed. The work went on; and, amid persecution, the nucleus of a Wesleyan Church was formed, amounting to seventy members, besides regular hearers, who were twice as many again as the members, who considered themselves Methodists. And one day, to Mr. Claxton's dread, he was sent for by the then Fiscal, and, to his agreeable disappointment, was told that the Executive had authorized him to give Mr. Claxton permission to resume his religious meetings. Joy now filled every heart, and praises and thanksgiving were sent up to God for His miraculous interposition. Persecution sifted, tried, and purified the early Methodist Church in the city; and God made the wrath of man to praise Him. When the seed sown by these godly men had taken deep root and produced abundant fruit, Mr. Claxton was compelled to write to the Superintendent of the Wesleyan Missions in the West Indian Islands for ministerial help, and the Rev. Thomas Talboys was sent to this country from one of the islands, and arrived here on February 20th, 1814.

But, before the arrival of Mr. Talboys, the Wesleyan Conference appointed the Rev. John Hawkshaw as the first Missionary of this Colony in 1804, but he did not arrive till the following year; and when he did come, he was not allowed to remain here by the governor, and so he had to return to Barbadoes.

The following letter, addressed to the Rev. Dr. Thomas Coke, by Mr. Hawkshaw, will give our readers full information about his visit to this Colony and its results:—

"Barbadoes, Oct. 18, 1805.

"Rev. and dear Sir,—I now take the liberty to acquaint you with the issue of my visit to Demerara. On Sept. 23, being much better in health, I took my departure on board the mail boat, and on the 30th arrived safely in Demerara River, about the town of Stabrock. [This was the first capital of Demerara, and now it is Georgetown.] The day after I went on shore and found several friends, for whom I had letters of recommendation, particularly Mrs. J. Clifton, with whom you had an interview during her visit to Europe.

"She treated me with great respect, and was extremely sorry when she found that the Governor would not suffer me to stay. Several others, for whom I had letters, as soon as they knew my errand to Demerara, were exceeding glad, and hastened to see me and to express their joy on my arrival.

But, alas! I am sorry to say that their joy on that occasion was of short duration. Their highly elated hopes of hearing the Gospel preached by a Methodist Missionary were suddenly cast down. Many of those well-disposed persons had come from the West India Islands, and knew something of the Methodist doctrine. They showed me great kindness, and would have befriended me much, had I been suffered to remain among them.

"On October 2, being the second day after my arrival, I waited on his Excellency Governor Boujon (who is, I believe, a native of Curasson), to give in my name as passenger in the mail boat, conformably to a law of that place. After a short conversation, which consisted chiefly of interrogations, I told him that I was a Missionary in the Methodist Connexion, and that my design was to preach the Gospel, and to instruct the Negroes in the principles of Christianity. Here he interrupted me, and said, 'If that be what you are come to do, you must go back. I cannot let you stay here, and therefore you had best return in the mail boat.'

"I then showed him my credentials, lest he should doubt my right to preach as a Missionary. When he had read the oaths of allegiance, he asked me where I was born. I answered that I was born in England, about twenty miles from the city of York. 'But,' said he, 'you are not ordained.' To this I replied, 'May it please your Excellency, I am ordained as a Protestant Dissenter.' I then showed him the deed of ordination, which he read, and then gave it to me, saying, 'You cannot stay here. You must go back in the mail boat.' I then observed to him that the Methodist Missionaries were tolerated to preach in all the West Indian Colonies equally as in England, and that we had very respectable congregations at Antigua, Nevis, St. Kitts, Tortola, &c., &c., &c., to which he answered, 'Yes; but it cannot be so here.' Thinking that he would deliberate a little on the business, I said, 'May it please your Excellency, may I call upon you in future?' To which he answered, 'No; there will be no occasion, as you cannot stay. I suppose you will return by the mail boat.' I then took my leave of him, and came away with my mind not a little grieved at his conduct. I hope God will forget the many tears that he caused me to shed on that occasion, in a strange land; and that the Lord will soon open a way for the Gospel in that country, where there are many who would be glad to hear it. It seems to me that the Dutch have a very great objection against their slaves being instructed. The mail boat, after this, was detained three days, during which time I frequently prayed and exhorted among the friends with whom I was. On the 8th inst. I sailed from Demerara, and on the 12th I arrived safely at Barbadoes among my old friends, who received me with their usual kindness."

A few days after Mr. Hawkshaw arrived in Barbadoes, "having no appointment, and being unwilling to be idle, he went to Dominica to assist Brother Dumbleton. He arrived at Rosseau December 8, where he stayed five days, and preached twice. He then proceeded to Prince Rupert's Bay, about thirty miles from Rosseau, where a pretty large chapel had been erected, and where there was a congregation of 1,000 people, and a society of 500 or 600 members. After preaching there with great success and comfort for about a month, he was seized, in a very severe manner, with the same fever [evidently the writer means the yellow fever, which was very prevalent at that season of the year] which had before taken off Messrs. McCormick and Richardson, and from which Messrs. Shipley and Dumbleton had with difficulty escaped." He fell asleep without a groan or struggle, and was interred in the ground belonging to the chapel at Rosseau.—*Vide Wesleyan Methodist Magazine* for 1806, Vol. XXIX., pp. 141, 142, and 333.

The sudden departure, or rather return, of Mr. Hawkshaw by the same mail boat was a sad blow to the infant Methodist Society in the city of Stabrock, or Georgetown. It was quite unexpected; and sorrow now filled their hearts. They were like sheep without a shepherd to guide, direct, and watch over them—like children bereft of their parents. Claxton did his best to comfort them and to help them on in the way of truth, righteousness, and peace. The members then were all praying men and women, and they followed the Lord fully. Claxton was their guide, instructor, and spiritual father—yea, their bishop for the time being. The people confided in him. And leader and people all "continued steadfastly in the Apostles' doctrine and fellowship . . . and in prayers;" and "they were of one heart and of one soul; and great grace was upon them all." They "were sorrowful" for a season, "but their sorrow" was now "turned into joy." We have been told by some of the oldest people, still alive, that the meetings of these early Methodists used to be delightful and very refreshing seasons. They had God with them, and that made them happy. The son of old Claxton, the early Methodist local preacher and class leader, is still alive, and is connected with Bedford Society in Camp Street. Like his honoured father, he, too, is a local preacher and class leader. One by one all the Methodists of the former generation are being removed from this to the better land. It is very interesting to hear the old people talk of past times, days of slavery; the attachment of the people to Methodism amid persecution and opposition; and the active piety of their lives and zeal for the salvation of souls.

In the year 1814 the Rev. John Mortier was appointed to labour in this Colony. This was the second Conference appointment. But instead of Mr. Mortier, the Rev. Thomas Talboys came from Trinidad, or from one of the Leeward Islands. Shortly after his landing here, he called upon the Governor to get permission to commence his ministry. After some hesitation on the Governor's part, the necessary permission or licence to preach was granted him. Mr. Talboys then, at once, commenced his ministry in the small preaching-house situated in the corner of Camp Street and Red Brick Dam, which corner is now occupied by the Plymouth Brethren of the Darbyite party. This house was hired by Mr. Claxton himself, when permission was given him to resume his religious meetings. Mr. Talboys preached in this house for nearly nine months. The old Dutch Church (now the Scotch Kirk) in Stabrock was then without a minister, and was offered for sale, which Mr. Talboys engaged to purchase, and turn it into a Methodist chapel. But the proprietors, instead of selling it to him, to be used as a Methodist chapel, sold it to the Minister and members of the Presbyterian Church of Scotland. Report says that Mr. Talboys was greatly disappointed at not being able to get possession of this church, and that on the Sabbath following he preached a sermon in

Camp Street "Preaching-house" from the words, "All men are liars" (Psalm cxvi. 11), in which some reference was made to this circumstance. A few days after this, Mr. Talboys turned his attention to a large coffee logie in Werk-en-Rust, belonging to a French merchant, Phillipark by name. This coffee logie was a den of infamy. People from all parts of the country, the estates particularly, used to assemble there on Sundays, and spend their time in drinking, gambling, cock-fighting, &c. The premises and the logie were bought, and Mr. Talboys spent a small sum in converting the logie into a place of worship. Henceforward the religious services, including preaching, prayer-meeting, and class-meeting, were regularly conducted here. The society from Camp Street was transferred to this new and first chapel, called Trinity. In a very short time the number 70 was increased to 360 Church members.

The Rev. Thomas Talboys, the first Wesleyan-Methodist Missionary permitted by the Government of this Colony to labour here as a Missionary, and to instruct the Negroes and others in the principles of Christianity, met with a cheering measure of success. Numbers who had been a disgrace to society, as ignorant as they were profligate, were awakened to a serious concern for their future welfare, and, abandoning their sins, sought and found the salvation of that Gospel which they heard and believed. But this state of things was not to continue long, as the following account will show. A few months after his arrival here, "Captain Marryat, Member of Parliament and Agent for the West Indies, published a pamphlet containing defamatory charges against the Wesleyan Missionaries in general, and Mr. Talboys in particular, which, reaching Demerara, excited prejudice against the Missionary. . . . About one o'clock on a certain morning they assailed the mission premises, broke open the chapel door, threw the benches into the streets, and broke them to pieces; they even essayed to enter the house in which the Missionary and his wife were domiciled; but William Claxton, heading the band of devoted adherents to the mission cause, magnanimously led them on to withstand the unrighteous attempts of unreasonable and wicked men." The latter charged the servant of God with teaching the slaves and others to steal fowls and eggs, &c., for his maintenance—acts totally beneath his character. But what may not be expected when men become infuriated? Writing at this juncture, the persecuted missionary states: "The chapel and chapel-house were stoned at all hours of the night for nearly three months, while I durst not move out at night, for fear of being assassinated. They would meet me in the open day, look up in my face, and, with the bitterest malignity imaginable, cry out, 'You rascal!' In what place is not my name familiar, branded with the marks of fanaticism, baseness, and disloyalty, an enemy to God and man? marks which have poisoned the public mind against me. What outcries have not been raised against me in Demerara? What endeavours have not been made in the community to get me banished from the Colony? What an encouragement has not been given to foment a spirit of virulence and malevolence, and to draw forth daring threats against my person?" But, although the missionary was "cast down," he was "not destroyed;" "perplexed," he was "not in despair;" "persecuted," he was "not forsaken." The injury which this man of God and the members of the Methodist Church in this Colony had suffered, and the insults they had endured, not only from the mob, but from men officially engaged to protect and defend them, are a disgrace to our national character; and if the half was told, it would startle the humanity and raise the resentment of those whose principles are averse from persecution.

A change for the better, however, soon took place among the inhabitants of this country. The storm had passed away, and the calm ensued. All the past was forgotten; a glorious future awaited Methodism. Since Mr. Talboys' time this country has been regularly supplied with ministerial help from the Wesleyan Missionary Society in England. In 1815 the Conference appointments for this district were Thomas Talboys and William Lill; in 1816, Thomas Talboys and John Mortier; in 1817, John Mortier and Matthew Thackrey, &c., &c.

The Rev. John Mortier,* who succeeded Mr. Talboys, won the esteem of all ranks and classes, and spent the strength of his years in this Colony, which he greatly loved, and in which he resided, with a few intervals, till the year 1844. The barn, or logie, which was used as a chapel by Mr. Talboys, was pulled down, and a new building was put up in its place, by Mr. Mortier in 1821, at a cost of £1,645 sterling. He also built a second chapel at the northern end of Georgetown, called Kingston, which has become an important station in the city, and the head of the Second Georgetown Circuit. In 1843, the Old Trinity Chapel became far too small for the rapidly increasing congregation; the Rev. W. Hudson (who was then superintendent of the Georgetown Circuit) was therefore compelled to raise a certain sum of money, and purchased the premises adjoining the old chapel. The foundation-stone of this new sanctuary was laid in the presence of assembled thousands, on the commemoration of the memorable anniversary of Freedom or Emancipation in 1845, by M. J. Retemeyer, Esq., her Majesty's Colonial Receiver-General, and was opened for divine worship by Mr. Mortier in December, 1846. This [then] new chapel or church (Trinity), "the noble monument of the piety, zeal, and benevolence of our people, as well as of the indefatigable exertions of the late Rev. W. Hudson," was erected at a cost of £4,000 sterling. This chapel, which is now getting old again, requires thorough renovation, and efforts are now being made by the Rev. John Greathead to raise funds towards it. When the Rev. Henry Bleby was chairman of this district and superintendent of Georgetown Circuit, he proposed to the members and congregation of Trinity Church the introduction of an organ, and

* When on August 19, 1823, at break of day, the Militia was summoned to arms, and MARTIAL LAW formally proclaimed in the City of Georgetown, "the Rev. John Mortier, in the excessive exuberance of his loyalty, went to the Government House, and offered to assume the soldier's red coat, and do duty as a militia man. His services were however declined, the Governor politely hinting that he might do more good in his own line of things than by handling a musket." *See Mortier's Letter in the Colonist, January* 7, 1824, and referred to in "*The Demerara Martyr*," by E. A. Wallbridge.

also raised funds towards this object. And Mr. Greathead, who succeeded Mr. Bleby, fully carried out the proposed scheme, and now we have in use one of the best-toned instruments in the Colony. The old chapel, the erection of which in its day was a grand achievement, accomplished by the untiring efforts of the late Rev. John Mortier, has been converted into a spacious school-room, in which a large and efficient day-school is conducted by a talented teacher, who resides in the rooms above, formerly occupied by the superintendent minister. This school-house being found too small and uncomfortable, on account of the continual increase of day-scholars, and also because it was getting old, it became necessary to enlarge and renovate it in the year 1867. Mr. Hudson also purchased for a mission-house a desirable property belonging to one Mr. Vanwell, on the lot next to the old chapel, which is now our school-house. The lot or land on which the John Wesley College is built was also purchased by him for the mission. The old mission-house which had stood for so many years is no longer in existence. The present new and commodious mission-house, which is a substantial building, will remain for several years to come, as the noble monument of the indefatigable exertions of the Rev. John Greathead, and the benevolence of Mrs. Perkins. The college, which was once in use as a training institution, has been abandoned. The work of God has been steadily going on ever since the appointment of Missionaries to this great field of usefulness.

The visit of the Rev. William Taylor, of the California Conference, the great revivalist of the day, to this Colony in the early part of the year 1867, was made a great blessing to the inhabitants. This eminently useful Minister of the Lord Jesus Christ, after labouring with great success for some weeks in the island of Barbadoes, landed in Georgetown on the 9th of February, just at our Annual District Meeting time, and commenced a series of special religious services and midday prayer-meetings, first at Trinity and then at Kingston. He also visited the out-stations and held similar meetings. Large audiences listened with pleasure, deep attention, and profit to his sermons, which were characterized by a beautiful simplicity and earnestness, and were attended by the power of the Holy Spirit. Mr. Taylor's visit to this circuit (Georgetown) was not exactly to start or commence a revival—for before his arrival here, without the use of any exciting means, and without any other preparation than the diffusion of a spirit of prayer and of patient waiting on the Lord, a great and glorious revival had commenced in Trinity, and Mr. Greathead and others who were his helpers were but agents employed by the Holy Spirit—but to strengthen it, and to put more life into the public meetings, and energy into the people. A very large number of people was taken into Church membership; but we deeply regret to say that several of them have gone back into the world. One young man, who had been a member of Society for several months, but who had not experienced the pardoning grace of our atoning Saviour, whilst sitting under Mr. Taylor's ministry, experienced the inward change, and was savingly converted. This young man, the Rev. John R. F. Tull, now labours in St. Vincent, and is a useful and laborious Missionary.

It was in connection with these revival services that the necessity arose for having a third place of worship in Georgetown, in order to meet to some extent the religious wants of a growing population. The two large chapels in Werk-en-Rust and Kingston were invariably filled, and on Sunday evenings generally crowded. With these facts before the brethren, an old house in Camp Street was hired, which was opened for divine worship by us on May 31, 1868, and shortly afterwards a temporary house of prayer (or chapel) was erected, that is, a new piece thirty feet long and fifteen wide was added to the old house. The success attending the labours of both ministers and lay preachers had exceeded the expectations of the most sanguine, there being one hundred and forty persons enrolled as church members, and an average attendance of one hundred and sixty scholars in the day-school. At the commencement of the year 1869, it was resolved to make strenuous efforts to erect a suitable chapel in Camp Street. The old house was pulled down, and the new piece attached to it removed to the Lodge, where we now have a neat little chapel. The foundation-stone of this new chapel (Bedford) was laid by his honour the late Chief Justice, Sir William Snag, on Monday forenoon, August 2, 1869, and was opened for public worship by the Rev. Henry Hurd, chairman of St. Vincent District, on Monday, Sept. 27, of the same year. He preached both morning and evening from the following texts, Matt. xxvi. 13, and Matt. iii. 11. This new chapel is situated in the rear of the Water-works, obliquely opposite the Roman Catholic convent, and almost on the very spot where Methodism first had its birth in this Colony. The congregation is getting larger, and soon we shall be required to build another and larger sanctuary in this neighbourhood. At Bourda, a short distance from Bedford, we have a preaching place in which a day-school is held. Several Indian and Creole Christians worship there, and are connected with our Church as members.

GEORGETOWN, Trinity, has three resident Ministers, who are fully employed. Attached to this we have Bedford. Wesley is in the immediate neighbourhood of Her Majesty's gaol, and at the back of the London Missionary Church. This is only a small dwelling-house, or range, with a low roof, converted into a temporary chapel or preaching-house. Here we have several members and hearers, and a large day-school, which has not in any way affected our other day-schools in the city. Rome and Mocha are country places about four and eleven miles from town. Both the chapels in these villages were built of the same materials, belonging to a large logie, bought by one of the ministers for the purpose. The chapel at Rome or Agricola Village is called St. Peter's. The chapel at Mocha is of recent date. At plantation Henrietta, a little distance from Mocha, a Christian family from town went and resided, and thus Methodism was introduced. The late Mr. Savory, one of our oldest local preachers, used to visit this place on Sundays and week evenings, and hold services. His labours here, as in other places (Ann's Grove Village, Stanley Ville, where he was the means of introducing Methodism), were abundantly blessed by the Great Head of the Church. In time a neat chapel was erected at Mocha; and the old place where service used to be held was given over to the schoolteacher as a residence. Great Diamond, about ten miles from town, is a large sugar estate. In 1862, when I used to go up to this plantation to preach to the Coolies, I generally stopped at the village and conducted divine service in a house which was kindly lent me for the occasion, and formed a class consisting of twelve or fifteen Creole or African members. After a little time I was compelled to give up this extra work; but in the year 1869 it was taken up by the superintendent of the Georgetown Circuit, where we now have a small society and day-school. Mr. Edmund Field, the manager and attorney of this estate, has very kindly given us a small building (which was used as an hospital), in which divine service is conducted. And *Lodge* is a small village about two miles from town. This place was opened up in Mr. Barley's time by his colleague, Mr. Greathead. For a long time service used to be held in a house, but in the year 1869 a small chapel was erected. In the wet season this station is difficult to be worked.

GEORGETOWN, Kingston, is where the second Minister resides at present, and where we have a nice Mission House. Attached to this are Friendship, Mount Pleasant, and Beulah Chapels. One Mrs. Barnard, a very aged member of our Church, still alive, was the one to introduce Methodism in the villages of Friendship and Buxton, a short distance from town on the east coast. This was in the year 1843. Finding that there was a good opening for Methodism in these two villages, the Rev. W. Hudson (then resident Missionary at Victoria, and superintendent Minister of the Mahaica and Victoria Circuit) laid the foundation stone of a Wesleyan chapel on August 1, 1855. This chapel has since been thoroughly repaired and painted by the resident Minister. Mount Pleasant, at Plaisance (a populous village), and Beulah, at Kitty (a small village, two miles from Kingston), were also built by Mr. Irvine.

MAHAICA is about twenty-five miles from the city. This is the fruit of the late venerable Mr. Mortier's labours. Mr. Savory, who was then residing at Mahaica, rendered valuable help to Mr. Mortier, and laboured hard night and day, after his regular duties, in extending Methodism up and down the East Coast. Mahaica is now a most populous village; and is generally known in this Colony as the Wesleyan Methodist parish. The resident Wesleyan Missionary has the whole parish to himself. It is a Scotch Kirk parish, but the Minister's face is seldom seen by the people. The work is very hard on account of the long journeys performed from one chapel to another. In this extensive circuit are contained the out-stations of Mahaicony, Catherine, Stanley Ville, Virginia, and Supply. Hitherto there has been only one minister stationed here for several years. The Rev. John Allan Campbell has worked hard, and deserves great praise for what he has done. A new chapel, at a cost of about 900 dollars, has been built by him at Catherine Ville, a station about twenty-five miles distant from Mahaica, the head of the circuit. Another one at Virginia (or Cane Grove) was attempted, and nearly completed, when by some accident it was reduced to ashes by fire. Great indeed were the disappointments of the people and the minister. Another new chapel however, was in due course erected. The Rev. Alex. Mansie, who was for the time appointed by the Conference to Mahaica, in 1836, and who was therefore a perfect stranger, carried off the Government prize for an essay "On the Apprenticeship system and the duties of the Apprenticed Labourers," of Colonial interest, in the same year.

GOLDEN GROVE AND VICTORIA.—These two are important villages about thirteen and fifteen miles from town. There is only one resident minister here, who has charge of three chapels. Originally these two villages were purchased by the united efforts of the people as a joint stock company. Methodist influence from town was exerted over the people; and in time a cause was established. A church named "Wilberforce," large enough to accommodate seven hundred people, was built by the people, shortly after the emancipation. The minister of this church, the Rev. C. W. Cleeve, B.A., finding that he could not be happy, and disliking Tractarianism, forsook the ranks of the Anglican Church, and sought and found for himself and his people an asylum within the pale of the

Wesleyan Church. The church belonging to Mr. Cleeve was used by the Methodist and Congregational Societies for several years; but in consequence of frequent unpleasantnesses and misunderstandings between the two parties, the Rev. John Greathead, who was then the superintendent of the circuit, after consulting his brethren and obtaining the sanction of the district meeting, erected a new chapel called "Beaumont," in Victoria Village, and another one at Ann's Grove Village. The Golden Grove Chapel was built by the Rev. William Fidler, but finding it was getting very old and unsafe for the people to worship in, the present chairman of the district, the Rev. James Banfield, had it thoroughly repaired and made it almost new. The Mission House at Golden Grove, which originally belonged to Mr. Cleeve, requires thorough renovation. In fact a new house is much wanted.

GOED FORTUIN.—Methodism was first of all introduced here by Mrs. Barnard (above mentioned) in conjunction with Mrs. Yearwood (wife of a planter). Preachers from town went over regularly and held service, till God in His own good time gave us a firm footing, and a place in which to worship Him. The chapel at Goed Fortuin was erected by the Rev. D. Barley; next to the chapel was a small house, the top part of which was occupied by the minister, and the bottom by the Portuguese who kept a shop. In time this property was purchased and converted into a mission-house. There are four other chapels belonging to this circuit, two on the eastern bank of the Demerary, and two on the western bank. Nismes, about five miles from Goed Fortuin, is the mother church, where we still have a large society and congregation. Three miles further up from Nismes we have another place called Sisters, where we have thirty-four members. On the eastern bank of the river are Soesdyke and Supply Villages, where we have small chapels. This is a most discouraging circuit; and yet the services are well attended, and the congregations attentive.

ESSEQUIBO.—Formerly it was known as Abram's Zuill Circuit. This mission was commenced by the Rev. Richard Hornabrook in the year 1836. Wesley at Abram's Zuill was the first chapel built on the west coast of the river Essequibo, and is still the head of the circuit. From here the cause was extended to Zorg, Queenstown, Anna Regina, and Danielstown at first, and when Mr. Irvine took charge of the circuit it was extended to Waakenaan, an island in the Essequibo, and to Aurora, about fifteen or seventeen miles from Abram's Zuill. For several years a Minister resided on Plantation Anna Regina, as the proprieter of that estate had given the Wesleyan Connexion a large building which served as a dwelling-house, and the bottom part of it as a chapel. Mr. Irvine built a new and substantial chapel called Ebenezer, at Burt's Lot, about a quarter of a mile from Anna Regina. Instead of Anna Regina, as formerly, it is now Ebenezer Bush Lot. He also built another chapel called Providence, at Waakenaan, with rooms above for the teacher, and one for the Minister when he visits that station.

BERBICE.—I have already stated that the Lutheran Church was for a considerable period of time placed at our service by the administrators of the Lutheran property. There was a loud call for Wesleyan-Methodist ministry, and under favourable circumstances therefore the mission was commenced in 1847, and more fully organized in 1853; the Rev. John Wood, jun., being the first resident missionary. The work has gone on slowly and surely. The outstations connected with this circuit are Smithtown, Stanleytown, and Cumberland. We now have in New Amsterdam a fine new chapel, erected about two years ago.

The Coolie Mission in British Guyana is for the special benefit of the many thousands of Coolies who have been imported from India to supply the lack of labour which was alleged to exist in the Colony. By this arrangement these heathen strangers have the privilege of hearing the Gospel in their own tongue.

In conclusion, it is a pleasing fact indeed to observe that, notwithstanding all persecutions, oppositions, and difficulties, Methodism has prospered and is still prospering in this Colony. Under the zealous labours of the Rev. Messrs. Talboys, Mortier, Cheesewright, Edmondson, Rayner, Vigis, Hornabrook, Bickford, Banfield, Padgham, Hurd, Bleby, and others of their successors down to the present time, Greathead, Campbell, Wright, Adams, Jones, Grimshaw, &c., &c., hundreds and thousands have been gathered into the fold of Christ, who will no doubt be their joy and the crown of their rejoicing in the day of the Lord Jesus. God forbid that Methodism should ever prove false or unfaithful to her God, and to the Gospel which is committed to her trust.

Wesleyan Methodism in this Colony has exerted a wonderful influence over all other existing Protestant Churches. Methodism has a glorious future before her. As in other countries, so here: she has "set up her institutions; has established a barometer by which to determine the progress of her disciples in religious knowledge and Christian experience. At its weekly class-meetings incipient conviction is detected, and continues to be deepened and strengthened until it terminates in faith in Christ. . . . It carries into the organization of the Church a principle universally recognized in all our schools of science and arts. Even the men of commerce mark the development of their schemes; and the husbandman himself is not indifferent to the progress of vegetation, and the ripening of his crops." Class-meeting is the life, spirit, and soul of Methodism. It would be a sorry case if Methodism dispensed with it either partially or totally. God forbid that it should. But whilst we quite uphold class-meeting as a test of Church membership, we should very much wish to see some change made in the mode of receiving members into our Church, especially in the West Indies. People here like to see strange things, and hence when a confirmation service and the like are held in the Anglican Church, people of all churches run to see. No doubt there is a solemnity, an impressiveness, connected with such a service. Now, we think that, if the American Methodist Episcopal Church way of receiving members could be adopted into our churches in this Colony, and other parts of the West Indies, it would greatly benefit them. In America, individuals are received on trial, and then their names are enrolled in a book—a class-book—by one of the stewards, and they are appointed to classes—each receiving a printed form signed by the Minister, in which is written the name of the leader, and the time and place of meeting. Six months (not, as we have it here, three months) is the period of trial or probation, after which they are publicly, at a special religious service, received into full Church membership. The service itself is solemn and impressive, and calculated to do much good both to the older members and to those to be received. The candidates or probationers come forward to the front of the communion, when the following questions are proposed by the superintendent:—

"'1. Do you here, in the presence of God and of this congregation, renew the solemn promise contained in the baptismal covenant, ratifying and confirming the same, and acknowledging yourselves bound faithfully to observe and keep this covenant? 2. Have you saving faith in the Lord Jesus Christ? 3. Do you believe in the doctrines of Holy Scripture as set forth in the articles of religion of the Methodist Episcopal Church? 4. Will you cheerfully be governed by the rules of the Methodist Episcopal Church, hold sacred the ordinances of God, and endeavour, as much as in you lies, to promote the welfare of your brethren and the advancement of the Redeemer's kingdom? 5. Will you contribute of your earthly substance, according to your ability, to the support of the Gospel and the various benevolent enterprises of the Church?' These questions being answered in the affirmative, the minister addresses the congregation, and inquires if there be any reason why these persons should not be received into the Church. If no objection is alleged, he shakes hands with each, addressing them thus: 'We welcome you to the communion of the Church of God, and in testimony of our Christian affection, and the cordiality with which we receive you, I hereby extend to you the right hand of fellowship; and may God grant that you may be a faithful and useful member of the Church militant till you are called to the fellowship of the Church triumphant, which is without fault, before the throne of God!'"

A service of this kind I am quite sure will not only be imposing, but solemn, interesting, instructive, and impressive to the members and ministers of our own West Indian churches. I believe that when Wesley wrote the 756th Hymn (490), he fully intended that the members should be publicly received and recognised in the manner just described.

This Colony was for a long time a separate district from the islands, under the general superintendency of the Rev. John Mortier; but in 1844 it was joined to St. Vincent and the islands and made into a united district, under the chairmanship of the Rev. John Cullingford and his successors, and remained so till the Conference of 1863, when it was once more separated. And now once more the St. Vincent and the British Guyana Districts are reunited and formed into one large district, of which the Rev. George Sykes is the chairman and general superintendent, and the Rev. David Wright, Deputy Chairman in Georgetown, Demerara.

The ordained agents, Missionaries or Ministers in the Wesleyan Church, both in British Guyana and in all the West Indian Islands, are generally Englishmen or respectable Creoles, whose local experience makes them valuable. The late Rev. Henry Hurd (well known throughout the West Indies and in British Guyana), speaking of the West Indian Churches and native Ministers, at the Exeter Hall Missionary Meeting in 1878, observed:—

"Now, we do not exactly understand each other when upon this platform and when at our Missionary Meetings we speak about a native Missionary—the thing is totally dissimilar to anything you have in any other missionary field. In the West Indies we have no separate congregations—no congregations purely for natives, and no congregations purely for colonists; but they all meet together in the same place of worship, and all are members of the same Church, and all join together in the Sacrament of the Lord's Supper. Consequently, our native Ministers are not of the class that you usually think of as native Ministers. For instance, if it had been announced upon the placard that a native Minister from the West Indies would stand upon the platform to-day, most of you would have come expecting to see a black man. But it is not so. Our Ministers in the West Indies, socially, intellectually, and morally, stand side by side with the Missionaries that you send out from England. We have in the St. Vincent District—or we shall have at the Conference—thirteen circuits, and eight of the native ministers are superintendents of those circuits; and all the offices, with the exception of the Chairman, all the offices of our District Committee are filled by natives. Our Chancellor of the Exchequer is upon the platform to-day; and though you were to use the strongest magnifying glass you have in your possession you would not be able to distinguish him from any one of yourselves, great man as he is—great physically, and mentally, and morally. He is here to-day, and you will have an opportunity of listening to him. Our Secretary is a native of Jamaica, and, indeed, all the offices in that district are filled by natives. They are men of intelligence, and men capable of managing the affairs of the most important circuits in that district."

Perhaps in the Colony and in the islands also there may be one or two educationally and socially inferior to the European and native Ministers (and what church on earth has not such men in its ranks?), but as a rule the native Ministers are not inferiors in any sense of the term to the general run of men sent from England. In general, the Wesleyan Missionaries or Ministers, whether Englishmen or natives, are greatly respected by all classes, Episcopalians, Presbyterians, and others. The mission of the Wesleyan Ministers is principally to the poor, though a great many well-to-do, intelligent, and respectable people form their congregation or flock in various parts of the West Indies. When Christ was in the world, He always preached the Gospel to the poor (though many respectable people too heard Him and received good), and was emphatically the Friend of the poor. It is no disgrace to the Wesleyan Missionaries for their ministry to be confined to the poor in particular; and they preach a pure and unadulterated Gospel, and God, the great Head of the Church, owns their labours and blesses them abundantly. The two following extracts will give my reader an idea of what a preacher is to be, and what a sermon preached by the minister should be :—

"The Highlander's idea of a preacher was given to a gentleman not long ago, who said to him, 'I have heard that your present minister is a superior man to your old crony, Mr. L——. I am told he is both a better scholar, a deeper divine, a more ornate preacher—in fact a person much superior in every respect but one—he does not roar so loudly.' 'Roar, sir; that's a' the difference in the world, sir. It may do weel eneuch wi' you and ither college-bred folk to hear fine-spun sermons, and listen to polished flichts of what ye ca' classic eloquence; but this will not do wi' a real Highlander, sir. Na, na, sir; we maun hae something mair than this, sir; we maun hae a man that can speak out, sir—a man that can fecht in the poopit, sir—a man that can flyte, sir—a man that can shake his neive at ye, sir—a man, sir, that can ca' ye names—in fact, sir, a man that can fricht ye!'"

What a sermon should be, may be gathered from the following:—

"It should be brief; if lengthy, it will steep
Our hearts in apathy, our eyes in sleep;
The dull will yawn, the chapel-lounger doze,
Attention flag, and memory's portals close.

"It should be warm, a living altar-coal,
To melt the icy heart and charm the soul;
A sapless, dull harangue, however read,
Will never rouse the soul or raise the head.

"It should be simple, practical, and clear;
No fine-sprung theory to please the ear;
No curious lay to tickle letter'd pride,
And leave the poor and plain unedified.

"It should be tender and affectionate,
As his warm theme who wept lost Salem's fate;
The fiery laws, with words of love allay'd,
Will sweetly warm and awfully persuade.

"It should be manly, just, and rational,
Wisely conceived, and well expressed withal;
Not stuff'd with silly notions, apt to stain
A sacred desk, and show a muddy brain.

"It should be mix'd with many an ardent prayer,
To reach the heart, and fix and fasten there;
When God and man are mutually address'd,
God grants a blessing, man is truly bless'd.

"It should be closely, well applied at last,
To make the moral nail securely fast:
Thou art the man, and thou alone, will make
A Felix tremble, and a David quake!"

The duty of a clergyman is not merely to confine himself to the bare and cold performance of the routine duties of his office, such as marrying and baptizing, and on Sundays preaching a sermon which occupies about a quarter of an hour. There are other important duties to be discharged. Before finding fault with the Ministers of the Gospel of other Christian denominations, the Clergymen should set about setting their own houses in order. Are they all zealous and devoted men? Do they attend as they ought to do to the duties imposed upon them by their sacred office, not only from a high sense of their moral and religious obligations, but also because they are amply paid and remunerated for their services? Were our clergymen more alive to the importance of the duties imposed upon them, and more zealous in the discharge of their duties, I have little doubt they would soon make an impression on our labouring population.

The study of the rise and progress of Wesleyan Methodism in the Colony of British Guyana leads us to a view of the truth in its beautiful simplicity, and engages us to love it, and renders us zealous in its defence. Persecution, bitter and severe, was connected with its spread. Every attempt was made by the hostile planters and others to impede its progress; but these men have been removed one by one to give to God, the Judge of the whole earth, an account of their actions, and persecuted and despised Methodism still lives and grows. Like the Indian banyan tree, it has taken deep root, and now stretches out its branches far and wide over the whole Colony. Whilst Methodism seeks only the honour and glory of God, and the salvation of precious, immortal souls, it shall never die—

> "Now it wins its widening way;
> More and more it spreads and grows,
> Ever mighty to prevail;
> Sin's strongholds it now o'erthrows,
> Shakes the trembling gates of hell."

Notwithstanding all the good which has been done by the Methodist Church in the world, and in British Guyana and the West Indies particularly, there is a tendency on the part of some of its foes as well as its so-called friends to depreciate it, to say all manner of things against it and its Clergy, which is to be deeply regretted. But no amount of abuse heaped upon it, or its Clergy, can in any way injure it or them. People, generally speaking, judge others by their own actions, and so, I am afraid, the various writers have done. The Methodist Church and the Clergy have been saddled with *deception—hypocrisy*. Perhaps the friends (and friends they are nevertheless) who have used this uncharitable and unkind expression in the heat of letter-writing passion, are now sorry for it. The Methodist Church is too well and too strongly established in this Colony and elsewhere to be uprooted by any of its foes. Reference has been made to the large decrease sustained by the Methodist Connexion during the year 1880. This is a great mistake made by those persons who are not acquainted with the Methodist discipline and usage. The persons referred to have not *altogether left* the Methodist Connexion, but *only ceased to meet in class*. They, with the others, still continue to enjoy all the privileges which the Church can afford. Instead of losing so large a number, as stated by one of the writers, I am happy to say that the Methodist Church has had a large increase in membership throughout the world during the year referred to in the letter. Isaac Taylor, "the most suggestive of writers," declared that "if Methodism had been a little more liberal in her requirements" [I suppose he meant a little more loose in her discipline], "she would have absorbed every Protestant denomination;" that "such was her spiritual power they could not have stood before her." I have no hesitation in saying that Methodism is already the second largest denomination in England, and by far the first in America, and is doubtless now the most numerous and powerful body of Evangelical Protestant Christians in the world, numbering millions in her communion, and multiplied millions of adherents to her faith. The official statistics of Methodism in all her branches in the United States, for the year 1876 for instance, show 3,246,112 actual communicants, and it is estimated that at least sixteen millions [Bishop Doggett], or more than one third of the whole population, are of the Methodist faith; while throughout the world Methodism holds 4,269,561 members, or between four and five millions of communicants, and from twenty to twenty-five millions of adherents to her faith. One sad fact, however, to be deeply deplored, so far as Methodism in this Colony is concerned, is that many persons who had Methodist training, &c., and were *bonâ fide* members of the Methodist Church in their native lands, when they come to this Colony, by certain influences brought to bear upon them, leave the Church of their parents and join other bodies of Christians.

I would strongly recommend my reader to peruse the *Proceedings of the Œcumenical Conference of the Methodists*, held in London in the month of September, 1881.

CHAPTER XXI.

THE INDIAN COOLIE MISSIONS IN BRITISH GUYANA.

1. In the year 1852 the Wesleyan Missionary Society in England, in accordance with the wishes of the Ministers then labouring in the Colony, sent out the Rev. John E. S. Williams (who had laboured for some time in the Island of Ceylon) as Missionary to the Hindu Coolies in Demerara. On the 17th of August, 1853, he travelled to Berbice, and preached at New Amsterdam a sermon of surpassing unction. The next day he was seized with that fatal illness—the yellow fever; and on the 27th of the same month he entered into the joy of his Lord, in the 32nd year of his age. From that time up to the latter end of 1860, no steps were taken to establish any Christian missions among the Coolies of the Colony. In the fall of the year, December, 1860, at the earnest request of the Honourable William Walker, the then Government Secretary of the Colony, the Wesleyan Missionary Committee selected a man in England and sent him out to labour among the Asiatic immigrants. About the middle or latter end of 1861, the Episcopal Church of England sent out a man from India—the Rev. Ebenezer Bhalanault Bhose, who, however, after some years retired from the mission field. The U.P.C. also soon afterwards established a mission on Mr. Crum Ewing's estates on the East Coast. The Rev. Arthur Taylor was the first man, but he soon left it for a more lucrative appointment as Sub-Immigration Agent in the Colonial Government service. Rev. W. Y. Turner, M.D., a Medical Missionary, is now the Pastor of Better Hope Church, Veyheid's Lust. Whilst now the Wesleyan Missionary Society has but one solitary individual in this department of the work, but whose salary is entirely paid by the Local Government, the Episcopal Church of England has some four Missionaries, and several Catechists

attached to each. They, having the ways and means in their hands and at their disposal, are doing a great deal of good among the Coolies. The Wesleyan Missionary Committee in England take very little or no interest whatever in this work. They afford no assistance or aid whatever in furthering the work among the Coolies, and yet I attach no blame to them for this apparent neglect and refusal to aid the Mission in this Colony.

2. The special work of a Christian Missionary is

> "To save poor souls out of the fire,
> To snatch them from the verge of hell,
> And turn them to a pardoning God,
> And quench the brands in Jesus' blood."

A true Missionary feels as the great Apostle of the Gentiles felt, "Woe unto me if I preach not the Gospel." A man, who had once put his hand to a declaration, to strike for the freedom of his country, said to a companion, "You and I may rue it; we may die slaves—die on a scaffold; be it so, be it so; but if it be the pleasure of Heaven, that my country shall require the poor offering of my life, the victim shall be ready at the appointed hour of sacrifice, come when that hour may. This resolution will stand. It may cost treasure—it may cost blood, but it will stand. My whole heart is in it. All that I have, and all that I am, and all that I hope, in this life, I am ready, here, to stake on it; live or die, survive or perish, I am for the declaration." And may not a Missionary of the Cross apply this to himself? Is not his whole heart in it, in spreading his Saviour's name everywhere? Does he not live or die, survive or perish, for Christ?

3. The Missionary must work and pray, and pray and work, both night and day. It is his duty: the results are God's. The Missionary toils hard, and success may not be immediate, but it is sure and certain. Success is the natural reward of honest toil. Of the orchard we plant we hope to enjoy the fruit. In the house we are building, we hope to dwell. Of the seed we sow, we hope to reap the golden harvest. "I believe," beautifully writes the Rev. C. G. Finney, "that the connection between the right use of means to save sinners, and

the accomplishment of that important end, is as philosophically sure as between the right use of means to raise grain and a crop of wheat. I believe, in fact, it is more certain, and that there are fewer instances of failure. The effect is more certain to follow. Probably the law concerning cause and effect is more undeviating in spiritual than in natural things, and so there are fewer exceptions, as I have before said. The paramount importance of spiritual things makes it reasonable that it should be so. Take the Bible, the nature of the case, and the history of the Church, all together, and you will find fewer failures in the use of means for the revival and extension of religion, than in farming, or any worldly business. In worldly business there are sometimes cases, where counteracting causes annihilate all a man can do. In raising grain, for instance, there are cases which are beyond the control of man; such as a drought, hard winter, worms, and so on. So in labouring to promote a revival, there are many things which occur to counteract it: something or other turning up to divert the public attention from religion, which may baffle every effort; but I believe there are fewer such cases in the moral than in the natural world. I have seldom seen an individual fail, when he used the means for promoting a revival, or the conversion of sinners, in earnest in the manner pointed out in the Word of God. I believe a man may enter on the work of promoting salvation of souls, with as reasonable expectation of success, as he can enter upon any other work with an expectation of success, with the same expectation as the farmer has of a crop when he sows his grain. I have sometimes seen this tried, and succeed under circumstances the most forbidding that can be conceived."—*Lectures on Revivals of Religion.*

4. The conversion of Hindu Coolies in the Colony I find to to be twofold: one from Heathenism to Christianity, as a system, and a second from sin to God. Both these are of the greatest importance. Without the first there is no hope of the second. We seldom witness anything like penitence in a heathen. Generally, it is not until they have professed Christianity for some time, that they sincerely seek the Lord.

This, I think, is the great difference between the spread of Christianity in our day, and its spread in the days of the Apostles.

5. Alluding to the subject of the evangelization of the heathen Indian Coolies in connection with the Episcopal Church of England, a certain well known gentleman who was a M.C.P. a few years ago observed :—

"I say it with regret, hitherto we have literally done nothing. It is true we have brought one gentleman from the East Indies who is capable of communicating religious truths to them in their own language; but beyond this they have scarcely had anything done for them; and I say advisedly, that I look upon their present condition as a reflection upon us as Englishmen, and a disgrace to us as professing Christians. There are churches situate in the midst of the principal spheres of labour of these people, and one would naturally have thought that some at least of the Clergy would have some account to give us of the progress made in the conversion of these poor people; but I fear the Clergy are powerless, because they are unable to address them in their native tongue. The simple fact of their being our fellow creatures, whose lot had been cast by Divine Providence in the same land, would alone constitute a claim upon us; but we brought them here for a specific purpose, and, humanly speaking, they have been the salvation of the Colony, for by the continuous stream of labour that they have afforded, she has risen Phœnix-like from the prostration and ruin into which she had sunk, to be the most prosperous place in the West Indies. I fully admit the enormous difficulties of the work. Perhaps no part of the world has cost so much in evangelization, and nowhere has the work been conducted with so much difficulty as in India. But what, may I ask, that is worth doing do we ever undertake, which does not require some exertion to accomplish? There are those among us who can remember the early struggles of this very system of immigration itself, when we had battles with the Anti-Slavery Society, the Colonial Office, and the East Indian Government; until it is now placed upon a sound and satisfactory footing in every particular but this one, which of all others is the most important."

Another gentleman, also a M.C.P., at the same meeting of the Diocesan Synod held in Georgetown in 1871, remarked :—

"Although the work has been most devoted from the beginning to the end, still, as far as we can judge, there has been very little practical result. Now, we must ask ourselves what is the reason of this. The grand cause of the difference between the results attained in the case of the Chinese and of the Indians to my mind is this—the Indian is a man of a totally different habit from the Chinese; he has been brought up with different views; his ideas are of a totally different character; he has more pride of race; he has a keener intellect; and has that feeling of pride of country and of race which prevents him from becoming a convert to any of the new doctrines presented to him. This, and in many instances the great difficulty of *caste*, is the great reason why we have not been so successful amongst the Indians, as amongst the Chinese. In fact the adult Indian immigrant is like the granite stone, which by great skill and much artistic labour may be wrought into a handsome block or figure; while, if we turn to the other hand, and consider the large number of children, we see there the plastic clay, which in the hands of an artificer not so skilful may still be moulded into a form of beauty. Means that would not make any impression upon the obdurate granite, may be sufficient to mould the yielding plastic clay into a form of grace and beauty. Therefore I would respectfully suggest that *in future our efforts should be mainly devoted to try and instruct the children, rather than waste our time and our means in well-nigh futile efforts for the conversion of the adults.* [The italics are mine]. This is the view I take with regard to the question, Whom shall we go to? The next question is, How shall we go to them? If we determine to devote our efforts to the children, I would respectfully suggest that means should be adopted to carry out the school system among Indian children on a much more extended basis than heretofore. Many schools for the education of Indian children have been started on estates. In many instances they have failed altogether; in some they are very successful. The reason is, that in most cases a manager has so many duties devolving upon him, that he does not pay that degree of attention to the school, which is necessary to insure its success. There is a provision for the salary of a Missionary to the Indian immigrants; but it would be folly to expect one man to give his attention, or to direct his efforts, with any effect, over the whole Colony. It is an attempt in which he must fail. If a planter with limited means attempt to cultivate a very large estate, we know that he must fail; whereas if the same amount of money, the same energy and skill, were brought to bear upon a small estate, he would succeed. And so it is with missionary effort. I consider that this Missionary, instead of extending his efforts over a very large tract of country, and wasting his energies to no purpose, should concentrate them upon some one spot of limited extent. If he can establish his principles there, then he may move to another; and so by degrees the Christian leaven which he has put into the heavy lump of heathenism, will leaven the whole Colony."

The Rev. E. B. Bhose, who was then in the Mission field, to whom reference is made in the above extracts, in answer to the remarks on the slow work of evangelization among the Coolies, replied :—

"As one that has been engaged for some years in Missionary work, I may say a few words in reply to what has fallen from previous speakers. Mr. Oliver and some others have mentioned reasons why Christianity has not made more rapid progress amongst the Hindus. I may mention one principal cause why we have not met with the success which was expected. It is that the Coolies will not embrace Christianity, because they say that if they do, they must remain in this country. They are always in the expectation of going home. They came here to work for a number of years, but they expect to go back again. As a matter of fact, most of them stop in this country; but they all think that at the end of a certain period they will have amassed sufficient money to return to their native country, and to live there in affluence and comfort. That is one of the principal reasons why the Coolies do not embrace Christianity. There are other reasons, such as dread of loss of caste; but caste does not exercise the same influence here as in India; and they can always regain their caste by performing certain ceremonies on their return to India. Then there is the migratory character of the people: that also interferes very much with our efforts. As regards the adult population, and the argument for not doing anything for them on the ground of want of success, I think the previous speakers are all mistaken as to the results of our work among the adult population. What is the work we have done? All the previous speakers have gone upon the supposition, that after all our efforts, at the end of ten, fifteen, or twenty years, we have made no progress. Is that the fact? No! I have been one Missionary among forty thousand people; I have been one day upon one estate, another day upon another, perhaps fifty miles off. Work upon such a plan can produce no substantial, permanent result. But little has been done, I admit; but still I think quite enough to justify me in saying, that if in future we work more systematically, we shall meet with more success."

The Episcopal Church of England has, since 1871, increased the number of Coolie Missionaries and Catechists, and other agents, and hence, judging from their published quarterly or annual reports, a good work is being done among the Coolies. Several have thrown aside idolatry, and the garb of heathenism, and are now connected with that body in different parts of the Colony.

6. Whatever may be the opinions of the wise men of our day in this Colony in regard to the conversion to Christianity of the Coolie population, experience has taught me that it is almost impossible to make any impression for good on the minds of the adult Coolies. All the efforts hitherto put forth, both by the Wesleyan, U. P. C., and the Episcopal Church of England Missionaries, for their conversion to Christianity, seem to have been labour lost. The Coolies, as a whole, look upon the Christian Missionaries with suspicion, and merely as paid agents by the Government, for the purpose of making converts of them, and manifest no desire or inclination whatever to accept the truth. Too often the question is put, "How much does the Government pay you for making Christians of us, and how many Christians have you made? Your religion will do for you and for our children born in the Colony, that is, if they do not come to go with us to India when we are ready to start, but that religion won't do for us. We can't forsake the religion of our ancestors for a new one. We have a religion as well as you." The indifference of the Coolies, arising from their belief in fate, their worldliness, and their strong objection to anything like earnest thought and energetic action, is most disheartening. Morally and spiritually they seem as hard as stones, and as cold as icicles. You can get large numbers to listen to the Gospel; and if you

will allow or tolerate a discussion, the crowd will manifest the greatest interest and eagerness in a strife of words; but to come to any practical application of the truth—O, that is an entirely different thing, and not to be thought of. An able Missionary, a good and earnest worker among the teeming population of India, once observed, "I feel that I am nothing more than a witness for Christ," and this, too, when so much has been done to enlighten the millions of Hindus by the agents of the different Missionary Societies. Our friends and well-wishers, however, in this Colony expect the Missionaries to work wonders among the Coolies. It is quite true that the Missionaries cannot display a long baptismal roll to satisfy the cries of these friends. Baptisms are few and far between. And yet I am thankful to say that the Missionaries (notwithstanding many discouragements and oppositions) have not laboured in vain.

7. Hinduism in the Colony is very different from the system contained in the Vedas: for its professors are not allowed to do the things to which they are most inclined. In this country we do not see the streets and estates crowded with temples of all descriptions; we do not see parties of Brahmans and others in procession, with drums and music celebrating some particular holiday; we do not meet with troops of *Yogees*, or penitents, and religious mendicants on the roads journeying to some sacred river to wash away their sins by bathing in it. We do not see in this Colony the Hindu going to *Gaya* to perform the obsequies of his ancestors; to *Juganath*, to prove his faith by self-immolation; to *Cassi* or *Benares*, to wait patiently on the sacred ground, between the Varuna and the Asi, the stroke of death: nor the Hindu female marching to *Tiruputti*, the abode of the husband of the Goddess of Prosperity, also called *Vengaden*—the remover of defects—to wipe away the reproach of barrenness. Although we do not witness these things, yet their religion exercises a prodigious influence over the people. Blind adherence is paid to this cursed system. The Coolies deem it as perilous to forsake their religion as for a locomotive to quit the line. Whatever may be thought by others of the absurdity of the thing, they nevertheless sincerely

believe in the divinity of a dumb idol. The evidence of their senses goes for nothing in the face of time-honoured and hoary tradition. "How came it to spring out of the ground if it were not God? Would their forefathers have worshipped it if it were a mere stone? a mere picture? Does it not avert danger, succour in trouble, remove diseases, send rain and fruitful seasons? And how could it do these things if it were not God? It appears like any other stone or *patthar*, any other picture—*padan*. But it is only in appearance; it is truly God." They believe in the omni-pervasion of God; and conclude that as we cannot see Him, Who is the Creator and Preserver of all things, we must worship something in which He is. No matter what that something be, worship paid to it reaches and is accepted by Him. They are firm fatalists. Every man's destiny is written in his forehead, and not even the gods can alter or efface that writing. They believe in the transmigration of souls; that men are rewarded or punished in the present life for the deeds of a prior existence; that their enjoyments or sufferings respect past births only. Although such is the prevailing belief, there are yet some among the immigrants who are convinced of the falsehood of their religion, and only a lack of moral courage keeps them from openly abjuring it. They are in a state of transition. From the grossest idolatry there has been a reaction towards infidelity. It is no uncommon thing to meet with people who, having cast off the trammels of the false system under which they have been brought up, are at heart infidels. Some, I am afraid, are drifting fast to atheism, or one of the many materialistic or pantheistic theories current at the present time. It would indeed be a difficult task to give a tabulated form of the amount of good done, and the results of Missionary labours in this Colony among the Coolies.

8. The Venerable Archdeacon F. J. Wyatt once observed at a public meeting, "Although we owe much to the children, we owe still more to the adults. My own opinion is, that the two works ought to go on side by side, one with the other. To train up children in a religion which their parents have not accepted, is a matter of impossibility; inasmuch as, to do

that effectually, we must separate them from their parents. I believe we should try to evangelize both together—the parents through the children, the children through the parents."

9. The British Guyana adult Coolies may appear to be a class of people not to be easily won over to Christianity. Humanly speaking, it is a difficult or impossible work to be accomplished by any Missionary, however learned, useful, and pious he may be. What with man is impossible is quite possible with God. Conversion, as already observed, is solely the work of God. He alone is the Author of it. What but the powerful influence of almighty grace can enlighten the understanding; "break the power of cancelled sin, and set the prisoner free;" raise a man above the influence of sensual and worldly things? The husbandman will cast his last handful of grain into the earth, because he knows that the laws of nature are settled and fixed. The mariner will venture on the fretful ocean, beeause he knows that it is governed by immutable laws. The peasant, as he sees the sun setting behind the western mountains, reckons, with unbounded confidence, on the sun's rising on the morrow morning. And God is just as immutable in grace as in nature. God has fixed the laws of grace, which never can be altered. The world will be converted. The decree has gone forth:—"All the ends of the world shall remember and turn unto the Lord: and all the kindreds of the nations shall worship before Thee." "Thou art My Son; this day have I begotten Thee. Ask of Me, and I shall give Thee the heathen for Thine inheritance, and the uttermost parts of the earth for Thy possession."

The history of the past is a pledge of the future triumph of the Gospel. Open the page of sacred history, and we find on the very spot of its apparent defeat Christianity set up its standard; within ten days after our Lord's ascension, three thousand were added to His Church; shortly after the number was raised to five thousand. Then we hear of great multitudes, both of men and women, joining themselves to the Lord; and within thirty years of the death of Christ, it had extended itself to the principal cities of Asia Minor and Greece—to the very heart of the Roman Empire—and set up its banners by the palace of the Cæsars. Rome fell prostrate before Christianity: Goth and Vandal could not stay her progress; Nero could not raise fires hot enough to burn up her energies; the wild beasts of the Colosseum could not daunt the Christian heart; philosophers could not undermine her deep foundations. She has outlived ten bloody persecutions. Other assailants, more subtle than Hume, Voltaire, and Gibbon, may rise and spend their energies, but she will outlive all her enemies, and, like a zone of light, girdle the earth. These past achievements of Christianity prove that it will yet triumph over the nations of the earth. We are fully acquainted with the wonderful success that has attended the preaching of the Gospel, in the conversion of the natives of Fiji, New Zealand, Madagascar, &c. What was the condition of the inhabitants of these regions of the earth a few years ago? They were all sunk in deepest degradation. In the language of St. Paul, they were "filled with all unrighteousness, fornication, wickedness, covetousness, uncleanness, maliciousness; full of envy, murder, debate, deceit, malignity; whisperers, backbiters, haters of God, despiteful, proud, boasters, inventors of evil things; disobedient to parents, without understanding, covenant-breakers, without natural affection, implacable, unmerciful!" And what is the present condition of these once savages? They are clothed and are in their right mind. "Amongst them prayers and thanksgivings are offered to the Father and Creator of the universe by the name of the crucified Jesus." In like manner the work of conversion among our Coolie immigrants may seem somewhat distant, difficult, and almost impossible; but it will come to pass. "The walls of Jerusalem, compactly built together," (observes some one,) "did not fall at once under the battering-rams of the Romans. Blow succeeded blow, before any important impression was made. But at length the huge stones were loosed and shaken, and, in spite of the desperate courage and skill of the defenders, the inner wall was reached; it toppled to its foundation, and a breach was opened into the heart of the city." So with Hinduism; it is being besieged by the Missionaries of the Cross, and an undermining process is going on in the Colony, in the opinions or sentiments of the Coolies in regard to their religions, and ere long we shall witness a general turning unto the Lord.

[The reader will find reference made to this subject in my *Guyanian Indians*, Sections VII. and VIII., which he will do well to read.]

10. Considering all the discouragements, difficulties, and, very frequently, provoking disappointments connected with the work, and though I cannot show such large results as the Missionaries of the Episcopal Church in the Colony, with all the required appliances at their command, can, yet isolated as I am in the peculiarly arduous and uphill work, I am thankful to say, that by God's blessing I have not laboured in vain, nor spent my strength for nought. The efforts put forth for the conversion of the adult Coolies have not as yet proved "a waste of time and of means." I shall now place before my reader a few extracts from the Wesleyan Methodist Missionary Annual Reports, and the Minutes of the British Methodist Conference for the years 1861 to 1870, showing what has been done among the heathen immigrants.

"In the year 1861, just a few months after my arrival in the Colony, there were three Coolies baptized. In 1862 there were four adult baptisms . . One death.—In 1863 four more baptisms. In 1864 there were seven Coolie baptisms. Fourteen full and accredited Church members meeting in class. Contributed by same the sum of nineteen shillings and eightpence in their weekly class meeting towards the support of the Gospel. In 1865 the Coolie class consisted of sixteen full Church members, with four on trial for membership. . . . In the course of the year one member was removed by death, and another had to be expelled for immorality. . . . The amount contributed by Coolie members during the year was £4 13s. 4d. The number of baptisms: six adults. In 1866 eight adult Coolies were received into Church by holy baptism after a lengthened period of probation. In class twenty-seven full Church members, with one on trial. Amount contributed in class, £5 11s. 10d. Deaths two. . . . In 1867 there were five adults and one infant baptized. Five very worthy and praying members of society left the Colony by the *Ganges* for India, with letters of introduction to the Missionaries there. During the year two were expelled from Society . . . and one passed away from the Church on earth to the Church in heaven. Church members thirty-five, with ten on trial. Amount contributed in class towards the support of the Gospel, £6 3s. 8d. In 1868 there were twenty-four Coolies baptized. . . . In class forty-two members, with six on trial . . . Amount contributed £8 19s. 6d. Expulsions from society, two. . . . In 1869 there were three adult baptisms. A decrease in the number of Church members on account of seventeen persons having left the Colony for India. Expulsions, four. Death, one. Number of Church members, thirty. . . . In 1870 one adult baptism. Number of Church members, thirty-seven."

"As I have already in the previous chapter mentioned, it must be remembered that among the Wesleyan Methodist people class meeting is a most essential thing. No man is looked upon or reckoned as a member till he actually attends this necessary means of grace. Wherever Methodism 'sets up her institutions, it establishes a barometer by which to determine the progress of its disciples in religious knowledge and Christian experience. At its weekly class meetings, incipient conviction is detected, and continues to be deepened and strengthened until it terminates in faith in Christ. . . . It carries into the organization of the Church a principle universally recognised in all our schools of science and arts. Even the men of commerce mark the development of their schemes; and the husbandman himself is not indifferent to the progress of vegetation, and the ripening of his crops.' Accordingly all the adult Coolies, as above stated, received into the Church by baptism, had to meet in class, so that they might enjoy all the Christian ordinances and privileges. The want of such a criterion—class meeting—I believe is a great defect in the teaching of the lay and clerical agents of other Christian Churches.

Though much narrowmindedness and bigotry might be manifested by certain Christian Churches in the Colony, so as to ignore altogether the labours of the agents of other Protestant Missionary Societies, yet I always feel glad when I hear of success attending the labours of God's servants, whether they belong to the Episcopal Church or any other Protestant Church.

11. I shall now place before my reader some extracts from my Annual Reports read at the district meetings, and forwarded to the Missionary Committee in London, England, which

will give him some idea of the amount of success in the work of conversion of Coolies to Christianity :—

Report for 1876.—"Our brief, but unavoidable, absence from the mission field last year has somewhat retarded the progress of the work among the Hindu Coolies, and since our return from Europe, as far as our health and strength would allow, preaching and visiting, &c., have been carried on steadily, in various parts of the City of Georgetown, and neighbouring estates, and multitudes of the heathen have heard the Gospel message of a full and free salvation, without pilgrimage to distant shrines, or without exchanging the sweets of home or the love of kindred for the austerities and mortifications of ascetism. The good seed has been sown; the results must be left to Him Who has given us the assurance, 'That at the name of Jesus every knee shall bow, of things in heaven, and things in earth, and things under the earth; and that every tongue shall confess that Jesus Christ is Lord, to the glory of God the Father.' We have the sorrow to observe that during the past year several Christians, Coolies who were living in and about Georgetown, have removed to distant districts in the Colony, and a few have returned to their home—India. . . . We have had two adult baptisms during the latter part of the year. We have connected with us as church members forty-eight persons, with seven on trial for church membership."

Report for 1877.—"The following facts weigh down my spirit: (1) The small number of our members of Society; (2) But a small part of even these afford assurance that they are living members of Christ; (3) Few exert any good influence; (4) Our heathen congregations in both town and villages or estates manifest utter indifference to the truth. In most places the theme and object of our preaching are well known. But it is rare to find any who even thinks himself concerned in them; (5) In most instances we find steadfast antipathy to the Gospel—whilst preaching it we are assailed with the most awful blasphemies against Christ; (6) The abominations of idolatry are shamefully practised before our eyes. Conviction of their wickedness and folly is not succeeded by any diminution of them; (7) We are frequently stunned by language so obscene and polluting, that we should be mobbed were we to repeat it in England or in the Colony; (8) We feel ourselves distressingly below the standard as even instruments of carrying on our work. Our ministrations seem without power. We seem to get no effectual hold of the people. . . . There has also been much to grieve and dishearten us in our work during the past year. The Christians connected with our Church, but scattered here and there on the different estates, and on wood-cutting establishments, had become careless and indifferent. Sins, which ought not to have been named amongst professing Christians, had crept in. Party feeling had sprung up. Drunkenness, with all its attendant vices, was prevalent. Preaching and means of grace had been neglected. And yet, as we look back upon the year, we are assured that God has been with us, and has not forsaken us, and we have also been cheered by proofs of spiritual life amongst individuals. Two adult Christians have been taken from us by death during the year. . . . Seven persons connected with our Church have also left the Colony for India during the year. We have had five baptisms, including an infant, and two Christian marriages. We now have forty-seven members, with two on trial for membership."

Report for 1879.—"Our work among the Coolies is hard and difficult, and this is principally owing to the want of suitble agents. Many of the Coolies who have been hearers of the Word of God have left the Colony after their term of service and residence, and returned to their homes in different parts of India. About eighteen Christian Coolies connected with our Church have returned to their native land during the year, and hence we have to report a large decrease in Church membership. Of those who are now connected with us as Church members we have to say that it is very seldom we get an opportunity to see them, on account of their being widely scattered, and living at a considerable distance from each other, and also on account of their roving or migratory habits, which is one of the difficulties we experience in the formation of settled congregations. . . . Other Churches in the Colony take a great interest in the education and evangelization of the Creole Indians, but we simply do nothing for the want of funds. . . . We now have connected with our Church thirty-eight members, with three on trial."

Report for 1880.—"At Golden Grove (East Coast) we have a large number of Christian Coolies connected with us as members. Beside a few that Brother J. A. Campbell baptized during our unavoidable absence from the station, we baptized about eighteen persons, young and old, belonging to Plantations *Enmore* and *Ruinveldt*, and all of them are giving us great satisfaction in their profession and general behaviour. Several

Christian Coolies also once connected with our Church have recently returned to India. It is to be hoped that they will be preserved in their native land from making shipwreck of faith and of a good conscience, and be enabled to walk worthy of the vocation wherewith they are called. Of the Christian Coolies who are members of our Church we regret to say that on account of their being so widely scattered in the Colony &c., we seldom see them so as to exert Christian and ministerial influence over them. This also cannot be avoided. . . . We have had five deaths during the year. Connected with our Church at present we have forty-three full Church members, with twelve on trial who are under religious instruction and training."

Report for 1881.—"The word preached during the past year has not altogether been in vain. Here and there it has found a lodging place in the hearts of the hearers. During the year eight persons, adults and children, were received into Church by baptism, and now we have connected with our society as Church members forty-five persons, but who are unfortunately scattered in various parts of the Colony, so that we seldom get an opportunity of seeing them, for they are always on the move, going from place to place. . . . A few of the members, however, we are happy to say, are striving hard to do what is well pleasing in the sight of God. John Ganess, a Christian Brahman, with his wife, Thomas, Lazarus, &c., returned to India last year: total persons who left the Colony for India during the year with their certificates of Church membership and letters of introduction to Christian Missionaries are fifteen. We also had four deaths during the year. We have a fine field in the Colony, but we need help, without which much good result cannot reasonably be expected. The Christian Coolies, and other hearers, are not at all satisfied with the way in which our Mission work is done. The Missionary cannot always be on the spot and at home when they feel disposed to come to town to see him. They mostly attend our public services in town and country chapels, and if the Missionary were put in charge of some country or town station or congregation connected with the general or regular work, where his constant presence and attendance could be depended on, a better work might be done among the immigrants; several of them might be drawn to the house of God."

At Banda Chapel School, at present, we have several Christian Coolies, who have attached themselves to the Church as members, and a few of them have bought a bell for the use of the chapel, to be used on Sunday mornings.

12. The following particulars I extract from the *B. G. C. M.* Report of the Episcopal Church of England for the year 1881:—

"The Rev. F. P. L. Josa, of *Nonpareil Mission*, says that on his return from England he found that during his [short] absence no less than 70 of his converts had either died, left the district, or returned to India; and 27 more were removed from his list from the same causes during the last six months of 1881. In the second paragraph of the Report Mr. Josa writes, 'If you wish for a proof that Christianity is growing, I can only say, Look around. At Pln. *Mon Repos*, in 1878, there was only one Christian, now we have 16. We can boast of a small range of Christians. At *Enmore*, in 1878, we had 20 Chinese Christians and no Coolie Christians; now we have 69 Chinese and 20 Coolie Christians (I am including *Parachni*), or in all 89 souls. At *Nonpareil*, that same year, we had actually no Christians at all: now we have 26 (I am including *Strathspey* and *Bladen Hall*). I think that very soon we shall have a great increase.' The Rev. R. H. Moor, of *Belair Mission*, speaks of some 'who have been baptized and afterwards gone back to idolatry. Others are living in sin, and are ashamed to face the *padre sahib*.' 'Some of my Coolie Christians,' he says, 'have left the Belair Estate, and have settled in Georgetown, to get—as they say—"Colony work."' At *Belair*, in 1881, there were 30 Coolie baptisms; at *Nonpareil*, 30; at *Le Resouvenir* there are 33 Coolies attached to the Mission; and at *Legua*, 108 Christian Coolies. According to the Report, the whole number of Christian Coolies in the Colony probably does not much exceed 1,000. Notwithstanding all the drawbacks and difficulties (the Missionaries write) that have tended to retard operations, the position of affairs is decidedly in advance of what it was last year (1880). The cords of the Gospel tent have been extended and its stakes strengthened; and we may look forward to more successful results in the immediate future, if we go forward in faith, remembering that the work is His, Who has promised that His word shall not return to Him void, but shall prosper in that whereto He sends it."

13. Although the number of conversions (whether in the

Episcopal Church of England, or the Wesleyan Methodist Church, the Moravian Church, or the U. P. Church) is not very large, but small, yet it is a pledge, an earnest of future large ingatherings into the garner of God. At the annual meeting of the Presbyterian Missionary Society, held in St. Andrew's Kirk, on August 9th, 1882, (Wednesday), presided over by Dr. Finlayson, it was stated that the Council had in consideration a scheme for the employment of two ordained Ministers to labour among the Coolies in the Colony. The Rev. T. Slater in his report stated :—

"In the Coolie Mission department, there has been no change in respect either of measures or men since the date of last report. Lala, under the superintendence of Dr. Turner, continues his labours on Plantations Chateau Margot, La Bonne Intention, Success, and the estates of the Messrs. Ewing, while Mr. Kennedy works as before in the very large field presented by the estates in St. Luke's parish. The efforts of both are directed mainly to the holding of conversational meetings with the inmates of the hospital, with such audiences as can be collected at non-working hours from the roughs and yards, and to the instruction of the children. These appear to be the only modes through which direct attempts at evangelization can be put forth at present. Both catechists are indefatigable in the performance of their duties; Mr. Kennedy's visits to eleven of the estates averaging sixty in a month. On three of the estates, he holds a Sabbath School for Coolie children, the attendance at each of which varies from fifteen to thirty. Five adults and two children have received baptism in his district during the year; and in Lala's, the rite has been administered to seven adults."

14. Borrowing the words of one of my reports sent to the Missionary Committee in London, I may truly say, "We feel this Mission among the tribes of India to be as necessary as it is important, and, while much gratified and encouraged by past success, we are impressed with the greatness of our responsibility, and contemplate with feelings of peculiar tenderness and sympathy the absolutely degraded heathenism of the many thousands of them in this Colony, amongst whom murders,—of their wives chiefly—are very frequent, com-

mitted under the wildest hallucinations originated in their own land; for hardly does a Quarterly Criminal Session occur without several, or at least one, of them being hanged for homicide of the most atrocious character, which only tends to awaken more pathetically our concern for their eternal interests, and leads us to redouble if possible the means already vigorously used for their enlightenment and salvation."

15. There is one other particular in the Indian Coolie Mission, which must always occupy a prominent place in all Missionary operations, and that is—schools for heathen children. The Episcopal Church of England has the largest number of Coolie schools. The Wesleyans and others also pay some attention to the heathen children. Speaking of the education of the Coolie children, Bishop Austin, in his *Charge delivered to the Clergy* in the year 1864, says:—

"It is most important that the children of the heathen should early be made familiar with our language (*i.e.* the English). I see no other way of evangelizing the great multitudes which are dispersed over the globe under British rule and protection. Through these children, as they grow up, we cannot doubt will be laid open to the minds of their parents, not only the treasures of our religion and knowledge, but, as the first of our Indian prelates so well expressed it, our habits of thought and feeling; and this sympathy will form a bond of union between the peasantry and their rulers, far stronger than any which can otherwise exist. The first teachers of Christianity, as the same learned divine proceeded to remark, had a great advantage in the prevailing use of the Greek tongue; and we ought, as he argued, to disseminate our own language as much as possible, with a view to the possession of similar facilities." With respect to the character of the teachers employed to impart instruction to the immigrant children, his Lordship observes, "With thankfulness do I notice the care bestowed upon their people by certain resident proprietors, and by the representatives of absentees who have charge of some of our principal estates, upon which are located considerable numbers of heathen immigrants from India, China, and Africa. Female teachers are generally to be found over such schools; and from my own experience, and from the testimony of the clergy, I am led unhesitatingly to recommend the employment of mistresses. It is not only that the remuneration required is generally considerably less, but because I have observed that heathen parents cannot at once understand the discipline and restraint, and let me add, the correction, which are requisite in large schools; and there is an aptitude in female teachers, which enables them to dispense with too severe a rule, owing to the greater patience which they ordinarily exercise. I cannot too strongly urge you to do all that is in your power, to impress upon our proprietary body generally the desirableness of multiplying such schools."

16. It has now become a law that all the sugar plantations should have schools for the Coolie children, and on many of the estates there are suitable female teachers employed to instruct the young. I cannot, however, say that all the schools are well attended by children. Though the estate schools are kept open, not one-fourth of the Coolie children on the respective plantations attend. On a great plantation in one of the counties of the Colony, and on which, as a matter of course, are located a large number of Coolies, the ordinary attendance at the school had been between thirty and forty. One of the Government Educational Officers paid a couple of visits to that estate, and the effect was magical; the attendance bolted up suddenly to the figure of 120. The great want in this Colony is the compulsory and undenominational system of education. A native gentleman writes to the *Friend of India* from Behar:—"I asked an opulent Zemindar the other day, 'Why don't you educate your son, instead of loading him with ornaments as a temptation to some ruffian to murder him?' With a grave face he told me that his nephew had learned to read and write, and was looked upon as a learned young man in the village; but he died of small-pox, and the same coincidence having occurred in his uncle's family, it is now settled once for all that 'learning in our family is inauspicious, and brings adversity and death.' It is the fact that nothing will induce any member in this family to learn. 'Do we not see hundreds of educated men,' added he, 'absolutely starving, while ignorant men are enjoying ease and comfort? Besides, learning unfits a man of our clan to follow his walk of life, and in ninety-nine cases out

of a hundred learning makes a man good for nothing.'" I very much fear that a similar indifference, apathy, in regard to education, is manifested by the black Creole and Indian Coolie population in the Colony. Though there are some who are strongly opposed to compulsory education, so far as the East Indian Coolie children—and, indeed, all the Creole children—are concerned, yet I think, and maintain, the balance of all sound arguments on the subject will be in favour of extending every enactment in the matter of education as well to Coolies as to others. Is not the Coolie a British subject, standing before the sacred majesty of the law as a possessor of natural and civil rights, equally with the estate-attorney and the black Creole labourer? If it is the duty of the State to provide for the education of its subjects—to compel that its subjects receive a modicum of elementary instruction; then the Coolie falls, equally with others, within the comprehension of these duties. It should be the earnest aim of Government to have all the Coolie children taught to read, write, and cipher, as well as the children of every other race beneath the British sceptre. If the Coolie is a blessing to this Colony—a fact which will not be denied; and if education is a blessing to the possessor—a fact which cannot be doubted; then is it not a matter of simple gratitude on the part of the Colony to endeavour to supply the Coolie's child with the blessing of an useful education? Happily, the laws of the Colony do provide for the supply of that blessing; and the estate proprietors, who are, for the most part, Christians and philanthropic gentlemen, are anxious that these heathen children should be elevated by means of education and religious instruction; and if the Government should commission officers to go even on the sugar plantations and see to it, that these children do, even in spite of the ignorant prejudices of their heathen parents, avail themselves of the educational advantages provided for them, what right should managers and attorneys have to complain that the Coolies are tampered with by the educational officers? It will be said that most of the Coolies are still heathen, and cannot be brought fully to appreciate the value to their offspring of an English education; but I do not see that we should argue from all this to the necessity for being lax towards the Coolie children in the duty of communicating to them the blessing of elementary instruction. I do not believe that it is practicable to compel all parents in the Colony to send their children to school. The compulsory enactments can be effectively carried out only in Georgetown, New Amsterdam, and some of the villages; but cannot yet, without much extra expenditure, be applied to labourers resident on all the plantations. It is not because we should deal with the Coolie children in the matter of education differently from the Creole children; but simply because of the impracticability of effectively applying the compulsory enactments to the peasantry resident on all the estates, that we would deem it unadvisable that the educational officers should go on some particular estates to compel the attendance at school of the Coolie children on such estates, when the same proceeding cannot be practically carried out all over the Colony of British Guyana. Were it possible to form a plan by which to compel all the labourers on all the estates in the three Counties to send their children to school, then there is no reason why the Coolies should be excluded from the operation of that scheme. I believe that official visits paid to the estates by faithful and impartial educational officers would be very helpful to the whole cause of education.

17. Since the arrival of the East Indians, the Colony of British Guyana has made excellent progress through the means of their labour; but the members of the Court of Policy seem to be very hard upon the young generation of the East Indian Immigrants in introducing elementary education amongst them. I go further, and say that education always civilizes nations, and makes them industrious, patient, and able to conquer all criminal temptations. Moreover, I am happy to say that English Colonial Governments have established some educational system to educate the poor and rich, and several of the Colony's specially voted sums are on account of the East Indian young generation. I refer to the practical speeches of other Colonial Legislators. This is the only Colony that shows such a distinction, and tries to keep the

poorest classes in fetters, and not to enjoy English freedom. I am of opinion that plantation authorities—estates owners, attorneys, and managers, should, in every possible manner, uphold the inspectors of schools, and other district educational officers, in compelling the immigrant children to attend schools, and not discourage and oppose them, and the Government should also offer extra encouragement to the teachers of Coolie schools in their very difficult task of teaching their scholars to read and write. The utterances of our legislators on the whole subject of the education of the children of the labouring classes are distressing in the extreme; and the logic of those utterances cannot but be characterized as false and fallacious, and not very creditable to gentlemen to whom are, to a very large extent, entrusted the sacred destinies of the community.

18. In the three Presidencies of India, Madras, Calcutta, and Bombay, in addition to Missionary and other private schools, which are all more or less superintended by the Director of Public Instruction, there is a large number of Government or State aided schools which have been a boon to the children of all classes. Agricultural and industrial schools are everywhere in existence, and the children of the lower classes or orders are taught useful trades, so that when they leave school they do not feel at a loss for something to do. We need in this Colony similar Government schools where the children of our labouring population might be taught useful arts or trades in addition to reading and writing. In the present system of education a group of young and promising labourers have been forced away from their fields to spend long and weary years of study for schoolmasterships and other positions in life, which nature had never intended them for, and when forced from their original calling to seek such as were by no means suited to them, they fail and are left with a puffed-up pride of heart, ashamed to go back to what was really their proper calling, and so a criminal influence enters their minds, and instead of giving satisfaction to a generous public, they darken the whole of their future prosperity and bow their heads to the ground. In order, therefore, to make educa-

tion the success it ought to be in British Guyana, there are three indispensable conditions which must be fulfilled. Its scope must be restricted, only really competent teachers must be authorized to train the young, and discretion to wield the rod with energy, in case of necessity, must be vested in them. The half time system is also as necessary in Demerara as in England. It is the hardest lesson in juvenile life to make a sustained effort for daily bread, and the experience of each succeeding day demonstrates that it is all the harder in a tropical climate. If the young agricultural labourer does not take to the hoe and shovel kindly in early life, his aversion is likely to grow with his years. It is infinitely easier to reconcile the juvenile mind to the labour of half a day than of a whole one; and by dividing the youthful energies between field work and the study of the school-room, a double object would be served. And if we have well trained and competent schoolmasters throughout the Colony (such as Messrs. H. J. Cockett, E. H. Smith, D. Mitchell, K. Joseph, J. McFarlane, W. Osborne, and others), I do not see why Algebra, Book-keeping, and if possible Latin and Greek, should not be taught to some promising pupil-teacher, who is already beginning to prepare himself for some future schoolmasters' examination, in which he may wish to pass creditably. No harm can possibly result to the cause of education from this course. But no such subjects as these are taught in any of our common schools which are aided by the Government. There is no attempt made by any of the teachers to introduce in their schools such subjects. Hence for any member of the Honourable Court of Policy, or any one else, to make an assertion of the following kind—that "Algebra and book-keeping, and such rubbish," are taught in our common schools, shows an amount of ignorance which is astonishing, and which would be condemned in lower orders of society, if such a statement is made publicly.

19. We need throughout the Colony the compulsory and undenominational system of education. This is the only system which I believe is calculated to benefit all parties and improve the state of the Colony. But who would benefit by this change? Most certainly THE MINISTERS OF RELIGION:

because the "Caves of Adullam," which now exist only by what they get in the shape of school-grants, would be closed. THE TEACHERS: with larger schools there would be better salaries, and with superintending committees instead of patrons, there would be more independence; the advancement of young teachers would depend on their merit, not on their toadying the patron or playing the harmonium. THE SCHOLARS: under a comprehensive system there would be more emulation; scholarships and prizes are strong inducements to industry. THE PARENTS would benefit in getting a good education at little or no cost. THE PLANTERS AND RESIDENT GENTRY would lend all their help to a National School; now the school is the patron's "peculium." THE COMMUNITY generally would be more satisfied when they got for less money a larger return. POSTERITY would bless us for starting the *right thing*, and for leaving them a race of good masters such as only can be trained under a large and liberal system.

[The reader will find some further remarks on the education of the Coolie and Creole children in the *Guyanian Indians*.]

20. In conclusion, I observe that there are some people in the Colony, as well as in England, who call themselves Christians, but who look with jealousy on Christian Missions. They take the annual reports of the different Missionary Societies, and calculate the amount of success from numerical *data*. They perhaps may not be aware of it, but their principles are identical with those of Simon Magus, who determined the value of the gift of God, and the worth of the soul, by a money standard. With regard to the general conduct of the baptized Coolies, I would say that, with a few exceptions, they are walking in the faith and fear of God; but with regard to the catechumens, I fear there are numbers who have come forward with motives not strictly pure, and with mistaken views of Christianity. This we must expect, and not be surprised if we find tares mixed with the wheat. To have a Church unspotted, free from all vices, is next to impossibility. If in the days of Apostles wicked men crept into the Church (witness the state of the Corinthian Church, and individuals whom we find made

mention of in the Acts of the Apostles, and in the Epistles of St. Paul), how much more now, when we possess not the like gifts they did? So that the ill walk of some of the members of our Christian community should not dishearten or discourage us in our work, but we should go on "making the crooked ways straight, and the rough paths smooth," with entire dependence on the Almighty, praying that He would bring them under the sanctifying influence of the Holy Ghost, and cause them to act in conformity with the religion they have embraced, and "that they might walk worthy of the Lord unto all well-pleasing, being fruitful in every good work, and increasing in the knowledge of God." The following recorded "Actual Conversation on Missions between a Chaplain and a Missionary," published in the columns of *The Ceylon Observer*, of March 27th, 1880, will give my readers some idea of the character of the Christian work among the Coolies of British Guyana, and of the profession of Christianity on the part of those who have been baptized :—

"MISSIONS:—AN ACTUAL CONVERSATION.

"Chaplain: 'Well, Mr. P., how is your work getting on? Are there many of the Hindoos or Mahomedans becoming Christians?'

"Missionary: 'Yes, every month we have more or less accessions, and the number of the Native Christians is steadily increasing.'

"Chaplain: 'If you only made them *good* Christians, I could take more satisfaction in it, but they are such a miserable set.'

"Missionary: 'Miserable set! I would put my Church against yours any day, and not be at all afraid of the comparison.'

"Chaplain: 'Why, whatever can you mean? I do not understand you.'

"Missionary: 'I mean that my Church, which you are pleased to call a "miserable set," is better than yours.'

"Chaplain: 'Better than mine? In what way, pray?'

"Missionary: 'They come nearer to the standard of Christian living as it is laid down in the New Testament, they follow the commands of Christ more closely, and are more thorough in their religion every way than those who belong to your Church.'

"Chaplain: 'O, you refer, I suppose, to the soldiers who are so apt to get drunk occasionally.'

"Missionary: 'No, I refer to your whole Church, from the judge down to the soldiers, and affirm that they will not stand comparison with mine.'

"Chaplain: "O,—well, you see, they have been away from England a long time, out here in this country where are fewer restraints, and many of them have got careless, I admit.'

"Missionary: 'Yes, there it is, you can find excuses for these men in high position, men of education, men of Christian ancestry and training, who have had such abundant opportunities for knowing and doing the right, yet show such a bad example; while for the poor native Christians, right out of the slough of heathenism, ignorant and rude, with generations of heathen fathers back of them, and heathen vice all about them, for these you make no allowance, and you call them a miserable set!'"

The above is a substantially accurate report of an actual conversation which took place a short time ago in one of the smaller stations of North India. There is a lesson in it for those who are so fond of vilifying the character of the Native Church of India. Those who know least about it, are the ones most forward and ready with words of strong depreciation. The hard-working, frugal, thrifty, native Christian farmers, and shoemakers, and shopkeepers, and clerks, and artisans, and labourers of various kinds, who are doing their duty quietly and steadily day by day, these eager critics do not see, or know anything of, or care to inquire concerning. They see a few untrustworthy or unskilful servants, a few lazy tramps, or a few who have acquired, from too much mingling with Europeans, the bad habit of drinking intoxicating liquors, and then straightway they remark with much satisfaction and assumption of wisdom, as one editor did the other day, "There can be no question that native converts, as a whole, are rendered worse men in every respect under the so-called converting process than they were before being operated upon." It is worthy of note, though not at all other than might be expected, that these most unjust and sweeping depreciations of the character of the native Christians come, as a rule, from those whose own characters will not bear the closest inspection, and who might well ponder the stern words of Jesus Christ, expressly made to be quoted under just such circumstances: "Thou hypocrite, first cast out the beam out of thine own eye, and then shalt thou see clearly to cast out the mote out of thy brother's eye."

If these Indian editors were better men, and knew themselves a little better, they would be far less harsh in their criticisms upon native converts. And the same result would follow if they had some farther acquaintance with the facts in the case. The Missionaries, who do know the facts, tell a totally different story. Testimony on this very head, respecting the moral life of the native Church, was carefully gathered a month or two ago by a Missionary in Rohilcund from many most trustworthy sources. One said, "I esteem it encouragingly above that of the Hindus among whom they live." Another, "The moral tone of the community is so high that it frowns on such as are guilty, and in no way winks at wickedness or looseness in morals; we find honour and truth among our members." One man of large observation and sober judgment reported, "The moral life of the most of our native Church is much in advance of the European community about us, and it is manifestly improving every year."

We need not say more. These attacks on Missions and the fruits of Missions are no new thing, nor is it at all difficult to comprehend why they are made. The ungodly of Christ's generation could see no beauty in Him that they should desire Him, "no form nor comeliness." He was "despised and rejected of men." Nevertheless He triumphed. And so shall it be with His despised followers, spoken against and cast out now, but sure to conquer in the end.

HOLBORN PRINTING WORKS, FULLWOODS RENTS, HIGH HOLBORN.

PRICE THREE SHILLINGS AND SIXPENCE.

Our Sea-girt Isle: English Scenes and Scenery Delineated. By the Rev. J. MARRAT. Imperial 16mo. Map and 153 Illustrations.

'An unusually readable and attractive book.'—*Christian World.*
'A very pleasant companion.'—*Daily Telegraph.*
'A very pleasant companion for spare half-hours.'—*Leeds Mercury.*

Rambles in Bible Lands. By the Rev. RICHARD NEWTON, D.D. Imperial 16mo. Seventy Illustrations.

'From the juvenile stand-point, we can speak in hearty commendation of it.'—*Literary World.*

'Land of the Mountain and the Flood': Scottish Scenes and Scenery Delineated. By the Rev. JABEZ MARRAT. Imperial 16mo. Map and Seventy-six Illustrations.

'Described with taste, judgment, and general accuracy of detail.'—*Scotsman.*

Popery and Patronage. Biographical Illustrations of Scotch Church History. By the Rev. J. MARRAT. Imperial 16mo. Ten Illustrations.

'Most instructive biographical narratives.'—*Derbyshire Courier.*

Wycliffe to Wesley: Heroes and Martyrs of the Church in Britain. Imperial 16mo. Twenty-four Portraits and Forty other Illustrations.

'We give a hearty welcome to this handsomely got up and interesting volume.'—*Literary World.*

John Lyon; or, From the Depths. By RUTH ELLIOTT. Crown 8vo. Five Full-page Illustrations.

'Earnest and eloquent, dramatic in treatment, and thoroughly healthy in spirit.'—*Birmingham Daily Gazette.*

Chronicles of Capstan Cabin; or, the Children's Hour. By J. JACKSON WRAY. Imperial 16mo. Twenty-eight Illustrations.

'A perfect store of instructive and entertaining reading.'—*The Christian.*

The Thorough Business Man: Memoir of Walter Powell, Merchant. By Rev. B. GREGORY. Seventh Edtn. Crown 8vo, with Portrait.

The Life of Gideon Ouseley. By the Rev. WILLIAM ARTHUR, M.A. Eighth Thousand. Crown 8vo, with Portrait.

'We hope that this memorial of the "Apostle of Ireland," as Ouseley has been called, will be read far beyond the precincts of Methodism.'—*Dickinson's Theological Quarterly.*

Missionary Stories, Narratives, Scenes, and Incidents. By the Rev. W. MOISTER. Crown 8vo. Eight Page Illustrations.

'Intensely interesting.'—*Methodist New Connexion Magazine.*

Sunshine in the Kitchen; or, Chapters for Maid Servants. Fourth Thousand. Crown 8vo. Numerous Illustrations. By Rev. B. SMITH.

Way-Marks: Placed by Royal Authority on the King's Highway. Being One Hundred Scripture Proverbs, Enforced and Illustrated. Crown 8vo. Eight Page Engravings. By Rev. B. SMITH.

'The pages are concisely written, anecdote is freely used, and the book is most suitable for gift purposes, being capitally got up.'—*Methodist Recorder.*

Scenes and Adventures in Great Namaqualand. By the Rev. B. RIDSDALE. Crown 8vo, with Portrait.

Gems Reset; or, the Wesleyan Catechisms Illustrated by Imagery and Narrative. Crown 8vo. By Rev. B. Smith.

Vice-Royalty; or, a Royal Domain held for the King, and enriched by the King. Crown 8vo. Twelve page Illustns. By Rev. B. Smith.

The Great Army of London Poor. Sketches of Life and Character in a Thames-side District. By the River-side Visiter. Third Edition. Crown 8vo. 540 pp. Eight Illustrations.

'Admirably told. The author has clearly lived and mingled with the people he writes about.'—*Guardian.*

PRICE TWO SHILLINGS AND SIXPENCE.

Little Abe; or, the Bishop of Berry Brow. Being the Life of Abraham Lockwood, a quaint and popular Local Preacher in the Methodist New Connexion. By F. Jewell. Crown 8vo. Cloth, gilt edges. With Portrait.

'The racy, earnest, vernacular speech of *Little Abe*, and his quaint illustrations and home-thrusts, are humorous indeed. . . . Cannot fail to be a favourite.'—*Christian Age.*

Cecily: a Tale of the English Reformation. By Emma Leslie. Crown 8vo. Five full-page Illustrations.

'This is an interesting and attractive little book. . . . It is lively and healthy in tone.'—*Literary World.*

Glimpses of India and Mission Life. By Mrs. Hutcheon. Crown 8vo. Eight Page Illustrations.

'A well-written account of Indian life in its social aspects, by the wife of an Indian missionary.'—*British Quarterly.*

The Beloved Prince: a Memoir of His Royal Highness, the Prince Consort. By William Nichols. Crown 8vo. With Portrait and Nineteen Illustrations. Cloth, gilt edges.

'An admirable condensation of a noble life.'—*Derbyshire Courier.*

Glenwood: a Story of School Life. By Julia K. Bloom-field. Crown 8vo. Seven Illustrations.

'A useful book for school-girls who think more of beauty and dress than of brains and grace.'—*Sword and Trowel.*

Undeceived: Roman or Anglican? A Story of English Ritualism. By Ruth Elliott. Crown 8vo.

'In the creation and description of character the work belongs to the highest class of imaginative art.'—*Free Church of England Magazine.*

Self-Culture and Self-Reliance, under God the Means of Self-Elevation. By the Rev. W. Unsworth. Crown 8vo.

'An earnest, thoughtful, eloquent book on an important subject.'—*Folkestone News.*

A Pledge that Redeemed Itself. By Sarson, Author of 'Blind Olive,' etc. Crown 8vo. Numerous Illustrations. Cloth, gilt edges.

'We are informed in the preface that it is "an etching from life," and we can well believe it, for it bears all the marks of a genuine study of living men and women.'—*Literary World.*

Pleasant Talks about Jesus. By John Colwell. Crown 8vo.

The King's Messenger: a Story of Canadian Life. By the Rev. W. H. WITHROW, M.A. Crown 8vo.

'A capital story. . . . We have seldom read a work of this kind with more interest, or one that we could recommend with greater confidence.'—*Bible Christian Magazine.*

Old Daniel; or, Memoirs of a Converted Hindu. By the Rev. T. HODSON. Crown 8vo, gilt edges.

The Story of a Peninsular Veteran: Sergeant in the 43rd Light Infantry during the Peninsular War. Crown 8vo. 13 Illustrations.

'Full of adventure, told in a religious spirit. We recommend this narrative to boys and young men.'—*Hastings and St. Leonard's News.*

Rays from the Sun of Righteousness. By the Rev. RICHARD NEWTON, D.D. Crown 8vo. Eleven Illustrations. Cloth, gilt edges.

'The sermons are ten in number, and, while enforcing evangelical truth, are full of illustrative anecdotes, which are so useful in engaging the attention of children.'—*Liverpool Daily Courier.*

In the Tropics; or, Scenes and Incidents of West Indian Life. By the Rev. JABEZ MARRAT. Crown 8vo, with Illustrations, etc.

'A vivid description of scenes and incidents, . . . with an interesting record of the progress of mission work.'—*Sheffield Post.*

Climbing: a Manual for the Young who Desire to Rise in Both Worlds. By the Rev. BENJAMIN SMITH. Crown 8vo. Sixth Edition.

Our Visit to Rome, with Notes by the Way. By the Rev. JOHN RHODES. Royal 16mo. Forty-five Illustrations.

The Lancasters and their Friends. A Tale of Methodist Life. By S. J. F. Crown 8vo.

'A Methodist story, written with a purpose and with a heart.'—*Methodist Recorder.*

Those Boys. By FAYE HUNTINGTON. Crown 8vo. Illustrated.

MARK GUY PEARSE'S WORKS.

Seven Volumes, Crown 8vo, Cloth, Gilt Edges. Price 2s. 6d. each.

1.—**Daniel Quorm, and his Religious Notions.** FIRST SERIES. 66,000.

2.—**Daniel Quorm, and his Religious Notions.** SECOND SERIES. 18,000.

3.—**Sermons for Children.** 15,000.

4.—**Mister Horn and his Friends; or, Givers and Giving.** 17,000.

5.—**Short Stories, and other Papers.** 5000.

6.—**'Good Will': a Collection of Christmas Stories.** 6000.

7.—**Simon Jasper.** (A New Story.) 6000.

Homely Talks. 5000.

'Scarcely any living writer can construct a parable better, more quaintly, simply, and congruously. His stories are equally clever and telling. . . . One secret of their spell is that they are brimful of heart. . . . His books should be in every school library.'—*British Quarterly Review.*

Leaves from my Log of Twenty-five years' Christian Work in the Port of London. Crown 8vo. Eight Illustrations. 2s. 6d.

'We have in this pretty volume a large number of anecdotes of the right sort, . . . a valuable treasury of instructive and touching facts.'—*Hastings and St. Leonard's News.*

PRICE TWO SHILLINGS.

Sir Walter Raleigh: Pioneer of Anglo-American Colonisation. By CHARLES K. TRUE, D.D. Foolscap 8vo. 16 Illustrations.

'We have here a book which we strongly recommend to our young readers. It will do boys good to read it.'—*The Methodist.*

The Great Apostle; or, Pictures from the Life of St. Paul. By the Rev. JABEZ MARRAT. Foolscap 8vo. 28 Illustrations and Map.

'A charming little book. . . . Written in a style that must commend itself to young people.'—*Sunday-School Times.*

Martin Luther, the Prophet of Germany. By the Rev. J. SHAW BANKS. Foolscap 8vo. 13 Illustrations.

'Mr. Banks has succeeded in packing a great deal of matter into a small space, and yet has told his story in a very attractive style.'—*London Quarterly Review.*

Homes and Home Life in Bible Lands. By J. R. S. CLIFFORD. Foolscap 8vo. Eighty Illustrations.

'A useful little volume respecting the manners and customs of Eastern nations. It brings together, in a small compass, much that will be of service to the young student of the Bible.'—*Watchman.*

Hid Treasures, and the Search for Them: Lectures to Bible Classes. By the Rev. J. HARTLEY. Foolscap 8vo. With Frontispiece.

Youthful Obligations. Illustrated by a large number of Appropriate Facts and Anecdotes. Foolscap 8vo. With Illustrations.

Equally Yoked: and other Stories. By S. J. FITZGERALD. Frontispiece.

Master and Man. By S. J. FITZGERALD. Frontispiece.

Eminent Christian Philanthropists: Brief Biographical Sketches, designed especially as Studies for the Young. By the Rev. GEORGE MAUNDER. Fcap. 8vo. Nine Illustrations.

The Tower, the Temple, and the Minster: Historical and Biographical Associations of the Tower of London, St. Paul's Cathedral, and Westminster Abbey. By the Rev. J. W. THOMAS. Second Edition. Foolscap 8vo. 14 Illustrations.

The Stolen Children. Foolscap 8vo. Six Illustrations.

Peter Pengelly; or, 'True as the Clock.' By J. J. WRAY. Crown 8vo. Forty Illustrations.

'A famous book for boys.'—*The Christian.*

My Coloured Schoolmaster: and other Stories. By the Rev. H. BLEBY. Foolscap 8vo. Five Illustrations.

'The narratives are given in a lively, pleasant manner that is well suited to gain and keep alive the attentionof juvenile readers.'—*The Friend.*

The Prisoner's Friend: The Life of Mr. James Bundy, of Bristol. By his Grandson, the Rev. W. R. Williams. Foolscap 8vo.

Female Heroism and Tales of the Western World. By the Rev. H. Bleby. Foolscap 8vo. Four Illustrations.

'Useful and valuable lessons are drawn from the incidents described.'—*Derbyshire Courier*.

Capture of the Pirates: with other Stories of the Western Seas. By the Rev. Henry Bleby. Foolscap 8vo. Four Illustrations.

'The stories are graphically told, and will inform on some phases of western life.'—*Warrington Guardian*.

Adelaide's Treasure, and How the Thief came Unawares. By Sarson, Author of 'A Pledge that Redeemed Itself,' etc. Four Illustrations.

'This graphic story forms an episode in the history of Wesleyan Missions in Newfoundland.'—*Christian Age*.

Coals and Colliers; or, How we Get the Fuel for our Fires. By S. J. Fitzgerald. Crown 8vo. Illustrations.

'An interesting description of how we get the fuel for our fires, illustrated by tales of miners' families. There are capital pictures of mines and mining apparatus.'—*Christian World*.

James Daryll; or, From Honest Doubt to Christian Faith. By Ruth Elliott. Crown 8vo.

'We have seldom read a more beautiful story than this.'—*The Echo*.

The 'Good Luck' of the Maitlands: a Family Chronicle. By Mrs. Robert A. Watson, Author of *Crabtree Fold*, etc. Five Illustrations. Crown 8vo.

PRICE EIGHTEENPENCE.

'Little Ray' Series. Royal 16mo.

Little Ray and her Friends. By Ruth Elliott. Five Illustrations.

'A touching story of the life of a London *gamin*. . . . Written both with tenderness and graphic power.'—*The Nonconformist*.

The Breakfast Half-Hour: Addresses on Religious and Moral Topics. By the Rev. H. R. Burton. Twenty-five Illustrations.

'Practical, earnest, and forcible.'—*Literary World*.

Gleanings in Natural History for Young People. Profusely Illustrated.

Broken Purposes; or, the Good Time Coming. By Lillie Montfort. Five Page Illustrations.

'Perhaps the best thing we can say of this book is, that having begun the story we were anxious to read it through, it proved so pleasant and so suggestive.'—*Warrington Guardian*.

The History of the Tea-Cup: with a Descriptive Account of the Potter's Art. By the Rev. G. R. Wedgwood. Profusely Illustrated.

'It has seldom fallen to our lot to read a book so full of interesting details.'—*Sword and Trowel*.

The Cliftons and their Play-Hours. By Mrs. Cosslett. Seven Page Illustrations.

'Teaches several useful lessons. . . . So woven into the story as to be neither obtrusive nor tedious.'—*Folkestone News*.

The Lilyvale Club and its Doings. By EDWIN A. JOHNSON, D.D. Royal 16mo. Seven Page Illustrations.

'The "doings" of the club decidedly deserve a careful perusal.'—*Literary World.*

The Bears' Den. By E. H. MILLER. Six Page Illustrations.

'A capital story for boys.'—*Christian Age.*

Ned's Motto; or, Little by Little. By the author of 'Faithful and True,' 'Tony Starr's Legacy.' Six Page Illustrations.

'The story of a boy's struggles to do right, and his influence over other boys. The book is well and forcibly written.'—*The Christian.*

A Year at Riverside Farm. By E. H. MILLER. Royal 16mo. Six Page Illustrations.

'A book of more than common interest and power.'—*Christian Age.*

The Royal Road to Riches. By E. H. MILLER. Fifteen Illustrations.

Maude Linden; or, Working for Jesus. By LILLIE MONTFORT. Four Illustrations.

'Intended to enforce the value of personal religion, especially in Christian work. . . . Brightly and thoughtfully written.'—*Liverpool Daily Post.*

Oscar's Boyhood; or, the Sailor's Son. By DANIEL WISE, D.D. Six Illustrations.

'A healthy story for boys, written in a fresh and vigorous style, and plainly teaching many important lessons.'—*Christian Miscellany.*

Summer Days at Kirkwood. By E. H. MILLER. Four Illustrations.

'Capital story; conveying lessons of the highest moral import.'—*Sheffield Post.*

Holy-days and Holidays: or, Memories of the Calendar for Young People. By J. R. S. CLIFFORD. Numerous Illustrations.

'Instruction and amusement are blended in this little volume.'—*The Christian.*

'Meant for young readers, but will prove instructive to many "children of a larger growth." It is prettily illustrated.'—*Hastings and St. Leonard's News.*

Talks with the Bairns about Bairns. By RUTH ELLIOTT. Illustrated.

'Pleasantly written, bright, and in all respects attractive.'—*Leeds Mercury.*

My First Class: and other Stories. By RUTH ELLIOTT. Illustrated.

'The stories are full of interest, well printed, nicely illustrated, and tastefully bound. It is a volume which will be a favourite in any family of children.'—*Derbyshire Courier.*

'Wee Donald' Series. Royal 16mo.

An Old Sailor's Yarn: and other Sketches from Daily Life.

The Stony Road: a Tale of Humble Life.

Stories for Willing Ears. For Boys. By T. S. E.

Stories for Willing Ears. For Girls. By T. S. E.

Thirty Thousand Pounds: and other Sketches from Daily Life.

'Wee Donald': Sequel to 'Stony Road.'

PRICE EIGHTEENPENCE. *Foolscap 8vo Series.*

Two Standard Bearers in the East: Sketches of Dr. Duff and Dr. Wilson. By Rev. J. MARRAT. Eight Illustrations.

Three Indian Heroes: the Missionary; the Soldier; the Statesman. By the Rev. J. SHAW BANKS. Numerous Illustrations.

David Livingstone, Missionary and Discoverer. By the Rev. J. MARRAT. Fifteen Page Illustrations.

'The story is told in a way which is likely to interest young people, and to quicken their sympathy with missionary work.'—*Literary World.*

Columbus; or, the Discovery of America. By George CUBITT. Seventeen Illustrations.

Cortes; or, the Discovery and Conquest of Mexico. By GEORGE CUBITT. Nine Illustrations.

Pizarro; or, the Discovery and Conquest of Peru. By George CUBITT. Nine Illustrations.

Granada; or, the Expulsion of the Moors from Spain. By GEORGE CUBITT. Seven Illustrations.

'Interesting, comprehensive, and compact narratives. . . . These admirable books should find a place in every boy's library.'—*The Christian.*

James Montgomery, Christian Poet and Philanthropist. By the Rev. J. MARRAT. Eleven Illustrations.

'The book is a welcome and tasteful addition to our biographical knowledge.'—*Warrington Guardian.*

The Father of Methodism: the Life and Labours of the Rev. John Wesley, A.M. By Mrs. COSSLETT. Forty-five Illustrations.

'Presents a clear outline of the life of the founder of Methodism, and is calculated to create a desire for larger works upon the subject. The illustrations are numerous and effective,—quite a pictorial history in themselves.

Old Truths in New Lights: Illustrations of Scripture Truth for the Young. By W. H. S. Illustrated.

Chequer Alley: a Story of Successful Christian Work. By the Rev. F. W. BRIGGS, M.A.

The Englishman's Bible: How he Got it, and Why he Keeps it. By the Rev. JOHN BOYES, M.A. Thirteen Illustrations.

'A mass of research ably condensed, and adapted to the needs of the young.'—*Christian Age.*

Home: and the Way to Make Home Happy. By the Rev. DAVID HAY. With Frontispiece.

Helen Leslie; or, Truth and Error. By ADELINE. Frontispiece.

Building her House. By Mrs. R. A. Watson. Five Illustns.

'A charmingly written tale, illustrative of the power of Christian meekness.' —*Christian World.*

Crabtree Fold: a Tale of the Lancashire Moors. By Mrs. R. A. WATSON. Five Illustrations.

Davy's Friend: and other Stories. By Jennie Perrett.

'Excellent, attractive, and instructive.'—*The Christian.*

Arthur Hunter's First Shilling. By Mrs. CROWE.

Hill Side Farm. By ANNA J. BUCKLAND.

The Boy who Wondered; or, Jack and Minnchen. By Mrs. GEORGE GLADSTONE.

PRICE EIGHTEENPENCE. *Crown 8vo Series.*

Those Watchful Eyes; or, Jemmy and his Friends. By EMILIE SEARCHFIELD. Frontispiece.

Auriel, and other Stories. By RUTH ELLIOTT. Frontispiece.

'Pervaded by a tone of simple piety which will be grateful to many readers.' —*Christian World.*

Rays from the Sun of Righteousness. By the Rev. R. NEWTON. Eleven Illustrations.

'It is a simple, sound, sensible, interesting book, calculated to accomplish much good.'—*Lay Preacher.*

A Pledge that Redeemed Itself. By SARSON.

'A clever, sparkling, delightful story.'—*Sheffield Independent.*

In the Tropics; or, Scenes and Incidents of West Indian Life. By the Rev. J. MARRAT. Illustrations and Map.

Old Daniel; or, Memoirs of a Converted Hindu. By Rev. T. HODSON. Twelve Illustrations.

CHEAP EDITION OF MARK GUY PEARSE'S BOOKS.

Foolscap 8vo. Price Eighteenpence each.

1. Daniel Quorm, and his Religious Notions. 1ST SERIES.
2. Daniel Quorm, and his Religious Notions. 2ND SERIES.
3. Sermons for Children.
4. Mister Horn and his Friends; or, Givers and Giving.
5. Short Stories: and other Papers.
6. 'Good Will': a Collection of Christmas Stories.

PRICE ONE SHILLING AND FOURPENCE.

Imperial 32mo. Cloth, gilt lettered.

Abbott's Histories for the Young.

Vol. 1. Alexander the Great. Vol. 2. Alfred the Great.
,, 3. Julius Cæsar.

PRICE ONE SHILLING. *Royal 16mo. Cloth, gilt lettered.*

Ancient Egypt: Its Monuments, Worship, and People. By the Rev. EDWARD LIGHTWOOD. Twenty-six Illustrations.

Vignettes from English History. By the Rev. JAMES YEAMES. From the Norman Conqueror to Henry IV. Twenty-three Illustrations.

Margery's Christmas Box. By RUTH ELLIOTT. Seven Illusts.

No Gains without Pains: a True Life for the Boys. By H. C. KNIGHT. Six Illustrations.

Peeps into the Far North: Chapters on Iceland, Lapland, and Greenland. By S. E. SCHOLES. Twenty-four Illustrations.

Lessons from Noble Lives, and other Stories. 31 Illustrations.

Stories of Love and Duty. For Boys and Girls. 31 Illusts.

The Railway Pioneers; or, the Story of the Stephensons, Father and Son. By H.C. KNIGHT. Fifteen Illustrations.

The Royal Disciple: Louisa, Queen of Prussia. By C.R. HURST. Six Illustrations.

Tiny Tim: a Story of London Life. Founded on Fact. By F. HORNER. Twenty-two Illustrations.

John Tregenoweth. His Mark. By MARK GUY PEARSE. Twenty-five Illustrations.

'I'll Try'; or, How the Farmer's Son became a Captain. Ten Illustrations.

The Giants, and How to Fight Them. By Dr. RICHARD NEWTON. Fifteen Illustrations.

The Meadow Daisy. By LILLIE MONTFORT. Numerous Illustrations.

Robert Dawson; or, the Brave Spirit. Four Page Illustrations.

The Tarnside Evangel. By M. A. H. Eight Illustrations.

Rob Rat; a Story of Barge Life. By MARK GUY PEARSE. Numerous Illustrations.

The Unwelcome Baby, with other Stories of Noble Lives early Consecrated. By S. ELLEN GREGORY. Nine Illustrations.

Jane Hudson, the American Girl. Four Page Illustrations.

The Babes in the Basket; or, Daph and her Charge. Four Page Illustrations.

Insect Lights and Sounds. By J. R. S. CLIFFORD. Illustrated.

'A valuable little book for children, pleasantly illustrated.'—*The Friend.*

Leaves from a Mission House in India. By Mrs. HUTCHEON.

The Jew and his Tenants. By A. D. WALKER. Illustrated.

'A pleasant little story of the results of genuine Christian influence.'—*Christian Age.*

The History of Joseph: for the Young. By the Rev. T. CHAMPNESS. Twelve Illustrations.

'Good, interesting, and profitable.'—*Wesleyan Methodist Magazine.*

The Old Miller and his Mill. By MARK GUY PEARSE. Twelve Illustrations.

'This little book is in Mr. Pearse's choicest style; bright, wise, quaint, and touching. Mr. Tresidder's pictures are very good.'—*Christian Miscellany.*

The First Year of my Life: a True Story for Young People. By ROSE CATHAY FRIEND.

'It is a most fascinating story.'—*Sunday School Times.*

Fiji and the Friendly Isles: Sketches of their Scenery and People. By S. E. SCHOLES. Fifteen Illustrations.

'We warmly recommend this little volume to readers of every sort.'—*Hastings and St. Leonard's News.*

The Story of a Pillow. Told for Children. Four Illustrations.

NEW SHILLING SERIES. *Foolscap 8vo. 128 pp. Cloth.*

Gilbert Guestling; or, the Story of a Hymn Book. By JAMES YEAMES. Illustrated.

'It is a charmingly told story.'—*Nottingham and Midland Counties Daily Express.*

Uncle Dick's Legacy. By E. H. MILLER, Author of 'Royal Road to Riches,' etc., etc. Illustrated.

'A first-rate story . . . full of fun and adventure, but thoroughly good and healthy.'—*Christian Miscellany.*

Beatrice and Brian. By HELEN BRISTON. Three Illustrns.

'A very prettily told story about a wayward little lady and a large mastiff dog, specially adapted for girls.'—*Derbyshire Advertiser.*

Tom Fletcher's Fortunes. By Mrs. H. B. PAULL. Three Illustrations.

'A capital book for boys.'—*Sheffield and Rotherham Independent.*

Guy Sylvester's Golden Year. By JAMES YEAMES. Three Illustrations.

'A very pleasantly written story.'—*Derbyshire Courier.*

Becky and Reubie; or, the Little Street Singers. By MINA E. GOULDING. Three Illustrations.

'A clever, pleasing, and upon the whole a well-written story.'—*Leeds Mercury.*

The Young Bankrupt, and other Stories. By Rev. JOHN COLWELL. Three Illustrations.

Left to Take Care of Themselves. By A. RYLANDS. Three Illustrations.

Mischievous Foxes; or, the Little Sins that mar the Christian Character. By JOHN COLWELL. Price 1s.

'An amazing amount of sensible talk and sound advice.'—*The Christian.*

Polished Stones from a Rough Quarry. By Mrs. HUTCHEON. Price 1s.

'A Scotch story of touching and pathetic interest. It illustrates the power of Christian sympathy. . . . Sunday school teachers seal this little volume and learn the results of such labour.'—*Irish Evangelist.*

Recollections of Methodist Worthies. Foolscap 8vo.

PRICE NINEPENCE. *Imperial 32mo. Cloth, Illuminated.*

1. **The Wonderful Lamp**: and other Stories. By RUTH ELLIOTT. Five Illustrations.
2. **Dick's Troubles**: and How He Met Them. By RUTH ELLIOTT. Six Illustrations.
3. **The Chat in the Meadow**: and other Stories. By LILLIE MONTFORT. Six Illustrations.
4. **John's Teachers**: and other Stories. By LILLIE MONTFORT. Six Illustrations.
5. **Nora Grayson's Dream**: and other Stories. By LILLIE MONTFORT. Seven Illustrations.
6. **Rosa's Christmas Invitations**: and other Stories. By LILLIE MONTFORT. Six Illustrations.
7. **Ragged Jim's Last Song**: and other Ballads. By EDWARD BAILEY. Eight Illustrations.

8. Pictures from Memory. By ADELINE. Nine Illustrations.
9. The Story of the Wreck of the 'Maria' Mail Boat: with a Memoir of Mrs. Hincksman, the only Survivor. Illustrated.
10. Passages from the Life of Heinrich Stilling. Five Page Illustrations.
11. Little and Wise: The Ants, The Conies, The Locusts, and the Spiders. Twelve Illustrations.
12. Spoiling the Vines, and Fortune Telling. Eight Illustrations.
13. The Kingly Breakers, Concerning Play, and Sowing the Seed.
14. The Fatherly Guide, Rhoda, and Fire in the Soul.
15. Short Sermons for Little People. By the Rev. T. CHAMPNESS.
16. Sketches from my Schoolroom. Four Illustrations.
17. Mary Ashton: a True Story of Eighty Years Ago. Four Illustrations.
18. The Little Prisoner: or, the Story of the Dauphin of France. Five Illustrations.
19. The Story of an Apprenticeship. By the Rev. A. LANGLEY. Frontispiece.
20. Mona Bell: or, Faithful in Little Things. By EDITH M. EDWARDS. Four Illustrations.
21. Minnie Neilson's Summer Holidays, and What Came of Them. By M. CAMBWELL. Four Illustrations.
22. After Many Days; or, The Turning Point in James Power's Life. Three Illustrations.
23. Alfred May. By R. RYLANDS. Two coloured Illustrations.
24. Dots and Gwinnie: a Story of Two Friendships. By R. RYLANDS. Three Illustrations.
25. Little Sally. By MINA E. GOULDING. Six Illustrations.
26. Joe Webster's Mistake. By EMILIE SEARCHFIELD. Three Illustrations.

PRICE EIGHTPENCE. *Imperial 32mo. Cloth, gilt edges.*

The whole of the Ninepenny Series are also sold in Limp Cloth at Eightpence.

Ancass, the Slave Preacher. By the Rev. HENRY BUNTING.

Bernard Palissy, the Huguenot Potter. By ANNIE E. KEELING.

Brief Description of the Principal Places mentioned in Holy Scripture.

Bulmer's History of Joseph.

Bulmer's History of Moses.

Christianity compared with Popery: a Lecture.

Death of the Eldest Son (The). By CÆSAR MALAN.

Dove (Margaret and Anna), Memoirs of. By PETER McOWAN.

Emily's Lessons; or, Chapters in the Life of a Young Christian.

Fragments for Young People.
Freddie Cleminson.
Janie: a Flower from South Africa.
Jesus, History of. For Children. By W. MASON.
Precious Seed and Little Sowers.
Sailor's (A) Struggles for Eternal Life. Memoir of Mr. JAMES BOYDEN.
Saville (Jonathan), Memoirs of. By the Rev. F. A. WEST.
Soon and Safe: a Short Life well Spent.
Sunday Scholar's Guide (The). By the Rev. J. T. BARR.
Will Brown; or, Saved at the Eleventh Hour. By the Rev. H. BUNTING.
The Wreck, Rescue, and Massacre: an Account of the Loss of the *Thomas King*.
Youthful Sufferer Glorified: a Memorial of Sarah Sands Hay.
Youthful Victor Crowned: a Sketch of Mr. C. JONES.

PRICE SIXPENCE. *Crown 16mo. Cloth, Illuminated Side and Coloured Frontispiece.*

1. **A Kiss for a Blow**: true Stories about Peace and War for Children.
2. **Louis Henry**; or, the Sister's Promise.
3. **The Giants, and How to fight Them.**
4. **Robert Dawson**; or, the Brave Spirit.
5. **Jane Hudson, the American Girl.**
6. **The Jewish Twins.** By Aunt FRIENDLY.
7. **The Book of Beasts.** Thirty-five Illustrations.
8. **The Book of Birds.** Forty Illustrations.
9. **Proud in Spirit.**
10. **Althea Norton.**
11. **Gertrude's Bible Lesson.**
12. **The Rose in the Desert.**
13. **The Little Black Hen.**
14. **Martha's Hymn.**
15. **Nettie Mathieson.**
16. **The Prince in Disguise.**
17. **The Children on the Plains.**
18. **The Babes in the Basket.**
19. **Richard Harvey**; or, Taking a Stand.
20. **Kitty King**: Lessons for Little Girls.
21. **Nettie's Mission.**
22. **Little Margery.**

23. Margery's City Home.
24. The Crossing Sweeper.
25. Rosy Conroy's Lessons.
26. Ned Dolan's Garret.
27. Little Henry and his Bearer.
28. The Little Woodman and his Dog.
29. Johnny: Lessons for Little Boys.
30. Pictures and Stories for the Little Ones.
31. A Story of the Sea and other Incidents.

The whole of the above thirty-one Sixpenny books are also sold at Fourpence, in Enamelled Covers.

PRICE SIXPENCE. 18mo. *Cloth, gilt lettered.*

African Girls; or, Leaves from Journal of a Missionary's Widow.
Bunyan (John). The Story of his Life and Work told to Children. By E. M. C.
Celestine; or, the Blind Woman of the Pastures.
Christ in Passion Week; or, Our Lord's Last Public Visit to Jerusalem.
Crown with Gems (The). A Call to Christian Usefulness.
Fifth of November; or, Romish Plotting for Popish Ascendency.
Flower from Feejee. A Memoir of Mary Calvert.
Good Sea Captain (The). Life of Captain Robert Steward.
Grace the Preparation for Glory: Memoir of A. Hill. By Rev. J. Rattenbury.
Hattie and Nancy; or, the Everlasting Love. Book for Girls.
Held Down; or, Why James did Not Prosper.
Hodgson (Mary Bell). A Memorial.
Impey (Harriet Langford). Memorial of.
John Bunyan. By E. M. C.
Joseph Peters, the Negro Slave.
Matt Stubbs' Dream: a Christmas Story. By M. G. Pearse.
Michael Faraday. A Book for Boys.
Ocean Child (The). Memoir of Mrs. Rooney.
Our Lord's Public Ministry.
Risen Saviour (The). Gilt edges.
St. Paul, Life of.
Seed for Waste Corners. By Rev. B. Smith. Gilt edges.
Sorrow on the Sea; or, the Loss of the *Amazon*. Gilt edges.
Street (A) I've Lived in. A Sabbath Morning Scene. Gilt edges.

Three Naturalists: Stories of Linnæus, Cuvier, and Buffon.
Young Maid-Servants (A Book for). Gilt edges.

PRICE FOURPENCE. *Enamelled Covers.*

Precious Seed, and Little Sowers.
Spoiling the Vines.
Rhoda, and Fire in the Soul.
The Fatherly Guide, and Fortune Telling.
Will Brown; or, Saved at the Eleventh Hour. By the Rev. H. BUNTING.
Ancass, the Slave Preacher. By the Rev. H. BUNTING.
Bernard Palissy, the Huguenot Potter.

PRICE THREEPENCE. *Enamelled Covers.*

'The Ants' and 'The Conies.'
Concerning Play.
'The Kingly Breaker' and 'Sowing the Seed.'
'The Locusts' and 'The Spiders.'
Hattie and Nancy.
Michael Faraday.
Three Naturalists: Stories of Linnæus, Cuvier, and Buffon.
Celestine; or, the Blind Woman of the Pastures.
John Bunyan. By E. M. C.
Held Down; or, Why James didn't Prosper. By Rev. B. SMITH.
The Good Sea Captain.

PRICE TWOPENCE. *Enamelled Covers.*

1. The Sun of Righteousness.
2. The Light of the World.
3. The Bright and Morning Star.
4. Jesus the Saviour.
5. Jesus the Way.
6. Jesus the Truth.
7. Jesus the Life.
8. Jesus the Vine.
9. The Plant of Renown.
10. Jesus the Shield.
11. Being and Doing Good. By the Rev. J. COLWELL.
12. Jessie Allen's Question.
13. Uncle John's Christmas Story.
14. The Pastor and the Schoolmaster.

The above Twopenny Books are also sold in Packets.

Packet No. 1, containing Nos. 1 to 6, Price 1/-
Packet No. 2, containing Nos. 7 to 12, Price 1/-

LONDON:
T. WOOLMER, 2, CASTLE STREET, CITY ROAD, E.C.

.S

Lightning Source UK Ltd.
Milton Keynes UK
UKOW01f0658100914

238278UK00008B/166/P

9 781141 868728